THE OTHER ADAM SMITH

The OTHER ADAM SMITH

Mike Hill and Warren Montag

STANFORD UNIVERSITY PRESS
STANFORD, CALIFORNIA

Stanford University Press
Stanford, California

Library of Congress Cataloging-in-Publication Data

Hill, Mike, author.
  The other Adam Smith / Mike Hill and Warren Montag.
      pages cm
  Includes bibliographical references and index.
  ISBN 978-0-8047-9194-6 (cloth : alk. paper) --
  ISBN 978-0-8047-9294-3 (pbk. : alk. paper)
  1. Smith, Adam, 1723-1790. 2. Philosophy, Modern. I. Montag, Warren, author.
II. Title.
  B1545.Z7H55 2014
  192--dc23
                                    2014025816

ISBN 978-0-8047-9300-1 (electronic)

Typeset by Bruce Lundquist in 10/14 Minion

TABLE OF CONTENTS

ACKNOWLEDGMENTS

The authors would like to thank Emily-Jane Cohen for her steadfast support of this project in its incomplete stages, and her patience throughout the book's development and completion. Among several readers of our early drafts, we would like to single out Eric Schliesser and Michael Shapiro for constructive early readings. Nancy Armstrong's comments on *The Other Adam Smith* in its earliest stages were both formidable and formative. We thank Tania Flores for her assistance with the manuscript, as well as the editorial team at Stanford—Emily Smith and Jennifer Gordon, especially. Any errors that remain are of course entirely our own.

In addition, Mike Hill would like to thank the following colleagues and friends who read and commented on portions of the manuscript at various stages, or were otherwise supportive in its completion: Richard Barney, Kevin Frye, Laura Hill, Melvin Jackson, Tony Jarrells, Devoney Looser, Mort Schoolman, and Clifford Siskin. During the writing of most of this book, Hill was chair of the English Department at the University at Albany, SUNY. He wishes to thank his colleagues there for allowing the necessary distractions from administrative duties to keep the scholarship going. Dean Elga Wulfert of the College of Arts and Sciences at UAlbany also granted him a semester's leave to complete work on the book. Finally, Hill would like to thank the graduate students who offered comments and challenges in several seminars on the Enlightenment over the last several years.

Warren Montag would like to thank Richard Barney, Timothy Campbell, Roberto Esposito, David McInerney, Robert Markley, and Christian Marouby—all of whom contributed ideas and inspiration. He is grateful to Jorge Gonzalez, vice president of academic affairs at Occidental College, for his generous support for this project.

ABBREVIATIONS, ACRONYMS, AND SHORT FORMS

Many of the more commonly cited works in *The Other Adam Smith* are abbreviated or referred to in a shortened form. Often these abbreviations, acronyms, or short forms appear in parentheses with page numbers for the specific reference.

"AL"   "Account of the Life and Writings of Adam Smith"

AT   *An Abstract of . . . A Treatise of Human Nature*

BP   *The Birth of Pandora and the Division of Knowledge*

BR   *Barbarism and Religion: Narratives of Civil Government*

CCP   *Crowds, Culture, and Politics in Georgian Britain*

CEN   *Chance and the Eighteenth-Century Novel: Realism, Probability, Magic*

CL   *The Constitution of Liberty*

Companion   *The Cambridge Companion to Adam Smith*

Correspondence   *Correspondence of Adam Smith*; vol. VI of *The Glasgow Edition of the Works and Correspondence of Adam Smith*

Dialogues   *Dialogues Concerning Natural Religion*

E   *Ethics* [Spinoza; plus part number and specific proposition]

EB   *The Enlightenment and the Book*

EBA   *Essays upon Several Subjects Concerning British Antiquities*

EC   *Elements of Criticism*

ECH   *Enquiry Concerning Human Understanding*

"EDWN"   "'Early Draft' of Part of *The Wealth of Nations*"

EHU   *An Essay Concerning Human Understanding*

EML   *Essays, Moral and Literary*

EMPL   *Essays Moral, Political, Literary*

ENCP   *An Essay on the Nature and Conduct of the Passions and Affections, with Illustrations on the Moral Sense*

EPP   *An Essay on the Principle of Population*

EPS   *Essays on Philosophical Subjects*

"ES"   "Of the External Senses"

"FA"   "False Alarm"

FC   *The Financial Crisis and the Role of Federal Regulators*

"FF"   "The First Formation of Language"

"FH"   "On Fictitious History"

FL   *The Figural and the Literal: Problems of Language in the History of Science and Philosophy, 1630–1800*

HA   *Human Action: A Treatise on Economics*

"HA"   "Principles Which Lead and Direct Philosophical Inquiries; Illustrated by the History of Astronomy"

HCS   *An Essay on the History of a Civil Society*

HE   *The History of England* [Hume; plus volume number]

Hinton   *Hinton v. Donaldson, et al., The Decision of the Court Session, Upon the Question of Literary Property*

Hotbed   *A Hotbed of Genius: The Scottish Enlightenment, 1730–1790*

HS   *The History of Scotland* [Robertson; plus volume number]

"IA"   "Of the Nature of That Imitation Which Takes Place in What Are Called the Imitative Arts"

IDC   *The Idea of a Democratic Community*

IS   *Intending Scotland: Explorations in Scottish Culture Since the Enlightenment*

"LIR"   "An Enquiry into the Causes of the Late Increase of Robbers"

LJ   *Lectures on Jurisprudence* [plus manuscript letter]

LRBL   *Lectures on Rhetoric and Belles Lettres*

MM   *The Machiavellian Moment: Florentine Political Thought and the Atlantic Republican Tradition*

New Voices   *New Voices on Adam Smith*

NHR   *A Dissertation on the Passions; The Natural History of Religion*

OC   *On the Citizen*

"OOC"   "Of the Original Contract"

OU   *Observations Upon Liberal Education, in All Its Branches*

"PS"   "Patrician Society, Plebeian Culture"

RAS   *Reading "Adam Smith"*

RN   *The Reading Nation in the Romantic Period*

"RP"   "Riot and Popular Jacobitism in Early Hanoverian England"

RS   *Rebellion and Savagery: The Jacobite Rising of 1745 and the British Empire*

S   *Socialism: An Economic and Sociological Analysis*

SHM   *Sketches on the History of Man*

SPP   *The Street Porter and the Philosopher: Conversations on Analytical Egalitarianism*

SSP   *Subverting Scotland's Past: Scottish Whig Historians and the Creation of an Anglo-British Identity, 1689–c. 1830*

STS   *Social Theory of the Scottish Enlightenment*

T   *Theodicy*

The History   *The History of England from the Revolution in 1688, to the Death of King George the Second; Designed as a Continuation of Hume* [Smollett]

THN   *A Treatise of Human Nature*

TIE   *This Is Enlightenment*

TMS   *The Theory of Moral Sentiments*

UU   *Union and Unionisms: Political Thought in Scotland, 1500–2000*

WC   *Whigs and Cities: Popular Politics in the Age of Walpole and Pitt*

Wealth   *An Inquiry into the Nature and Causes of the Wealth of Nations*

WW   *The Work of Writing: Literature and Social Change in Britain, 1700–1830*

THE OTHER ADAM SMITH

INTRODUCTION
"A TENDENCY TO ABSENCE"
Which *Other* Adam Smith?

IN OCTOBER OF 2008, in the midst of the most serious economic crisis since the Great Depression, the Committee on Oversight and Government Reform of the U.S. House of Representatives held five hearings to arrive at a preliminary understanding of the global financial collapse.[1] The Committee's fourth hearing, according to Committee Chair Henry Waxman, concerned "the actions—and inaction—of federal regulators," given the "prevailing attitude in Washington . . . that the market . . . knows best" (hereafter *FC* for *Financial Crisis*). To this end, the former chairman of the Federal Reserve Board, Alan Greenspan, was called on Otober 23, 2008, to testify about the role of federal regulation, or lack thereof, in the crisis. Waxman did not mince words in his questioning of Greenspan. Perhaps his most damning question involved reading Greenspan's own words back to him: "I do have an ideology. My judgment is that free, competitive markets are by far the unrivaled way to organize economies. We've tried regulation. None meaningfully worked" (*FC*). Given the obvious fact that the lack of meaningful regulation had led to a global accumulation of toxic assets (most of which originated in the United States), which were sold, repackaged, and resold until the entire financial system began to collapse, Waxman could only ask whether Greenspan had not been a prisoner of his own thinking: Had the former chair of the Fed made decisions on the basis of an ideology that, in the light of a global financial crisis, he would now have to admit was wrong?

In response to such a question, Greenspan admitted not only that he'd had an ideology but also that "everyone has one" (*FC*) and, yes, that his had proven incorrect in certain respects. What respects? Greenspan's answer was evasively technical: It was not the unregulated securitization of sub-prime mortgages, but rather the failure of what he called "counterparty surveillance" (that is, the knowledge necessary to pursue one's self-interest in a competitive environment, on the part of both financial institutions and investors) that engendered the crisis. Thus, self-interest and the knowledge necessary to its pursuit—the surest, natural, and endogenous (as opposed to artificial, external, and exogenous) form of market regulation—had failed. The result was a "once-in-a-century credit tsunami" (*FC*).

The consequences of the financial collapse of 2008 have become mercilessly clear: Rather than questioning an ideology that had so clearly failed, the prevailing economic powers have simply reaffirmed their faith. As we move further into the twenty-first century, the commitment to austerity has perhaps never been so firm: the hollowing out of the welfare state; the dismantling of civic institutions, including public higher education; a relentless privatization not only of formerly state functions but of the very elements, water and air; the increase of inequality both within and between nations.[2]

Today, even Smith's rather limited ability to sympathize with the laboring poor seems like a moralism without any legitimate place in the debates concerning how best and how fast to shrink the already shrunken state. Clearly, the failure of ideology to which Greenspan refers, however technical the language of his confession, was anything but a technical matter. It was the failure of an ideology according to which only originally dissociated individuals, left free to pursue their self-interest in the most rational way possible, could efficiently produce and distribute the world's wealth. The presumption of rational self-interest led to the law of supply and demand that not only explained price fluctuations but also insured the efficient allocation of labor and capital, and thus advanced the ever-increasing development of a society whose crises were nothing more than the corrections necessary to further prosperity.

It is important to note that throughout his testimony to the House Oversight Committee, Greenspan never refers to his theory, but to his "ideology." When he invokes a model, it is clear that this model—the regulation of derivatives markets by the immanent principle of "counterparty surveillance"—is in fact a subsidiary of the ideology itself. An ideology is far more expansive than a theory or a model, and its success paradoxically depends on what it obscures or excludes: It is nothing less than a worldview, which in this case, as in all others, implies not only an economics but also a politics, an ontology, and, finally, a kind of economic theology, if the notion of economy is historically separable from those of theodicy and providence.

The term "ideology," used as an unlikely keyword by Greenspan, sometimes means no more than its etymology implies: a system of ideas. But ideas about what? And which ideas are included, which necessarily excluded, from a given ideology? More often, however, especially in the twentieth century, the term has been used, if at all, pejoratively. One would denounce one's opponent's discourse as ideological rather than objective or scientific. Ideology often bears the taint of outright falsification in the service of some political project or agenda, as we say today; or it is at least often understood as a harmful distortion of agreed-upon facts, something that disturbs and contaminates rational discussion. But here the case is even more serious: The ideology that guided an individual like Greenspan in his commitment to regulation-free markets exceeds the ideologist's awareness and necessitates an act of confession in which the sin becomes intelligible to the sinner only after its commission. Thus, we could say that Greenspan is in the grip of an ideology that he only partly intuits, and that he is forced by the situation to become more critically self-reflective than he otherwise might be.

The idea of the self-regulating market itself rests on a whole set of presuppositions about the nature of the individual, about the relation of the individual to other individuals, and finally about the means by which the social order is promoted or endangered. In this sense, the noun "ideology," as used by Greenspan, might be regarded as the stand-in for a proper name: Adam Smith, whose famous notion of the invisible hand illustrates allegorically the proposition that social harmony is a product of *partially* intelligible (because individual) but *universally* effective (because mutually beneficial) human action, but not of human design. Greenspan—who appropriately enough delivered the Adam Smith Memorial Lecture in Kirkaldy, Scotland, a mere three years before the collapse that had occasioned the House Oversight Committee's hearings—remains bound to a version of Smith that, while not exactly false, can be sustained only by suppressing the enormous complexity and constitutive contradictions of his actual work.[3]

There is perhaps no greater index of the contested meaning of Adam Smith's writing than the fact that at the very moment Alan Greenspan admitted to a flaw in the worldview he derived from reading Smith in one way, the prominent Marxist sociologist Giovanni Arrighi was championing Smith in another. For Arrighi, Smith provides the answer to the very crisis that had, for Greenspan, called the Smithian worldview into question.[4] Of course, Arrighi's Adam Smith is not Greenspan's. Arrighi's Smith is a theorist of commercial society who rejects the idea of a self-regulating market and sees the necessity for state intervention to insure economic growth and protect against crisis. Further, according to Arrighi's Smith, only state intervention can mitigate the necessary but disruptive effects that attend the long march toward national prosperity, a point from which North American and European policymakers are today in full retreat. Arrighi's Smith bemoans the effects of the division of labor necessary for the production of capital and thinks that these effects (for Smith, potentially stupefying) must be offset by state-supported public education.

Like so many recent commentators outside the discipline of economics, but perhaps more audaciously than they, Arrighi argues not only that Smith was never the proponent of laissez-faire capitalism he was reputed to be, but that he had never been a proponent of capitalism at all. Rather, Arrighi's Smith is the unrecognized champion of a *non*-capitalist commercial society or, at least, a very deliberately legislated, state-controlled market society. He refers here not to the European social democratic experiments of the postwar period, but instead to the benignly authoritarian regime of the People's Republic of China, whose highly productive economic system, he insists, is not (or, at least, is not yet) capitalist, despite appearances. In a highly polemical (and selective) reading of Smith's portrayal of China in *The Wealth of Nations* (hereafter *Wealth*), Arrighi sees the revolution of 1949 less as a bold new social experiment than as a restoration of an integrated state/economic system that had endured for nearly two thousand years, interrupted only for a relatively brief time by the intrusion of European and Japanese imperialist powers that the Chinese revolution succeeded in repelling. The Chinese economy weathered the global financial meltdown, according to this argument, because the regime had understood and held fast to principles that Arrighi's Adam Smith had so comprehensively demonstrated, principles that Smith's self-proclaimed Western disciples had overlooked or half-consciously ignored.

The juxtaposition of these particular, and particularly wide-ranging, readings of Smith, both of them responding to capitalism's latest great crisis, is revealing in a number of ways. While the loss of faith in capitalism's ability to correct itself led, as Greenspan noted, to a generalized turn to Marxism during the Great Depression, today it appears impossible to abandon the terrain constituted by Smith's texts. It is no longer a question of whether one is for or against Adam Smith. Rather, the problem seems to be *which* Adam Smith one prefers, or perhaps which Adam Smith must be ignored.[5] Ironically, today the architect of the unrestricted market, who seeks to coordinate individuated self-interest with national wealth and universal social harmony, implausibly coexists with the radically inverted figure of Adam Smith, the unwitting social democrat whose work demonstrated the impossibility of market rationality.[6] It is worth remarking, however, that the division of Smith into incompatible versions of himself is in no way peculiar to the beginning of the twenty-first century.[7]

In fact, radical differences in the evaluation of his work have troubled Smith scholarship from its earliest incarnations. The idea of a bifurcated Adam Smith—an early moral philosopher and thinker of what would come to be called intersubjectivity, in opposition to the later theoretician of the market who focused on individual self-interest—was articulated by the German scholar August Oncken in 1897 as "Das Adam Smith Problem."[8] The *locus classicus* for this perception of a bifurcated Smith in the United States is the work of Jacob Viner, who found it impossible to reconcile the Smith of the earlier *Theory of Moral Sentiments* (hereafter *TMS*) and the mature writer of *Wealth*.[9] Viner's view of a divided Smith—a Smith split between individualized capitalist self-interest on the one hand and virtuous social harmony on the other—was revised by the consensus of later critics who sought to balance *Wealth* and the *TMS*. Marking the 150th anniversary of *Wealth* in 1926–27, the University of Chicago group heard influential lectures from such writers as Glenn Morrow and Viner.[10] These lectures remain one of the most important sources of the longstanding interest in having an integrated, and more or less unified, Adam Smith.

But one could remark that this integration of competing versions of Smith—call it a twentieth-century "Adam Smith Solution"—was itself predicated on the unwitting ignorance of his so-called minor works.[11] Moreover, the positing of a simple dualism within Adam Smith's published material of an economic and an ethical Smith forgoes the problem of (authorial) individuality and (textual) collectivity. The architectonics of Smith's bibliography as a whole (or what passes from one moment to the next as a whole) is worth highlighting here because, as we shall see throughout *The Other Adam Smith*, it is precisely the problem of particularity and unity—of individuals and collectivity—that governs the Scottish Enlightenment's preoccupation with division and categorical completeness at each and every level of concern. It was Smith's contemporary Adam Ferguson, the early historian of civil society and chaplain of the Highland's Black Watch (about whom more in Chapter 3), who proclaimed a new approach to "thinking itself in this age of separation."[12]

Whether in the realm of epistemology, ethics, nationalism, or political economy, the *other* Adam Smith problem, and the one we will argue has not been fully addressed in recent scholarship on Smith's more complete oeuvre, begins with the question of how to achieve universality in any meaningful sense of the term given modernity's theoretical and political prioritization of individual interest over universal need. The same problem of parts rendered whole, of how to settle the specific into the general, the individual into the universal, particularity into unity—there are many ways to put this *other* Adam Smith problem—is evident even at the bibliographical level in terms of the availability of Smith's own texts (or more precisely, those texts that most scholars have agreed to attribute to him). Indeed, about half a century after Oncken postulated an Adam Smith who occupied two opposing positions in the late 1890s, more than double the amount of words published in the two more famous works of *Wealth* and the *TMS* have found their way into the remainder of the *corpus* most scholars currently attribute to him.[13]

Thus, part of Smith's history seems to have doubled in size over time. The response to this problem of scale by the majority of recent commentators has an almost reflexive and, as we shall see in the four chapters that follow, very Smithian desire both to sort and divide Smith's new work, while making it consistent with the earlier material. Late discoveries of student notes on Smith's rhetorical and belletristic lectures, his philosophical writings (also thought lost), and two different juridical texts, these too in note form, in the decades after Oncken bring yet another Adam Smith problem into relief: This new problem does not compel or even allow us to choose one or the *other* Adam Smith, nor does it require that we begin with the premise that the more recently discovered texts fit unambiguously into the framework of the old based on an assumption of authorial unity.

The fact that two long manuscripts remain missing should also be noted: One seems to have contained a treatise on the "History of Law and Government" and another, a study of "the different branches of literature." This clearly marks a major gap in Smith's oeuvre. Thus, in addition to the (changing) problem of scale in determining which Adam Smith to identify, we must also consider the implicit problem of absence: Which themes, conclusions, references, and writing go missing in Smith, even as we widen the bibliographical frame?[14] What we have in mind is a reading of Smith in relation to other significant eighteenth-century thinkers that focuses on those places in his work where the desire for organizational wholeness does not, or does not easily, supersede the persistence of multiplicity. At four different levels—the epistemic, the subjective, the national, and the economic—our interest in an *other* Smith is to reanimate the question of parts and wholes, immanent in our very object of study, Smith himself, where multiplicity is least resolved and most intense.

The belated arrival of the vast quantity of additional material attributed to Smith, his so-called minor work, paradoxically raises a new set of Adam Smith problems directly related to the presuppositions of the ideological blindness that Greenspan was forced to address. The oscillations of meaning within the discursive network constituted by and around Smith's known texts are determined in the first instance by the arrival of newly discovered writing unknown to Oncken and his kin. In this sense, and we think the admission (this time, our own) is crucial, the question of *which* Adam Smith is available to put on offer is subject to historical fortune. Ours is both a historical and a contemporary Adam Smith: The expanded object of study that includes Smith's late recovered texts contains ambivalently within it emergent forms of division and collectivity that are to this day struggling to be known.

As early as 1967, a year auspicious for popular contention in the United States and Europe, Ronald Meek aptly noted that the first problem one encounters in writing on Adam Smith is the sheer volume and diversity of extant interpretations.[15] Since there are good summaries of recent Smith scholarship, and a recently established periodical review that bears his name, we do not need to rehearse that body of scholarship here. Let us instead simply underscore by way of introduction that this question of volume and divergence in the reception of Smith makes him both a popular figure in the most crucial sense of that term and nothing if not contentious in the same way. Historian H. T. Buckle remarked, with the enthusiasm characteristic of his nineteenth-century capitalist good faith, that Smith's *Wealth of Nations* "is probably the most important book that has ever been written."[16] This may not be as hyperbolic as it sounds. While the *TMS* had already made Smith famous, the later book, his last, sold out within six months of its publication and went through ten editions very soon after. In addition to an American edition (1789), *Wealth* appeared immediately in German (1776), in Danish soon after (1779–80), and in French (1779–80), Italian (1780), Spanish (1794)—and even Gaelic—by the end of the eighteenth century.[17]

In these introductory remarks, what concerns us about the fact that Smith is a popular figure is how the problem of popularity itself operates within the materiality of his writing—that is, not only at the level of Smith's reception but also, almost uncannily, in ways that match Smith's own thematic preoccupations. The problem of the popular, the problem of calculating the multiple and the multitudinous, is at the core of Smith's work and surrounds it. Indeed, Smith repeatedly reaches certain impasses as he pursues the question of what it means to be an individual—as well as to *individuate*—while being part of a collective arrangement that exists, provisionally and often perilously, by what it excludes from itself. Whether that precarious collective arrangement is achieved through the proper divisions and categories of a universal knowledge system, or through the modulated distinction between oneself and another, say, between Briton and Scot, or the desired harmony between the few capitalist owners and the majority of laboring men and women, it is the problem of mediating between individuation and unity and of confronting this process of mediation as anything but complete or guaranteed.[18] The various kinds of impasses over philosophical, ethical, national, and economic unity that emerge as much around as *within* Adam Smith—the impasses to which Greenspan, for one, bears apologetic witness—are certain to arise again. History proceeds to change, time moves, categories mutate, and anomalies amass within and against peaceable collective arrangements; and these things happen in ways neither Smith (nor his readers) could (or can) know in advance.

Thus, the broad spectrum of views on Smith continues to increase in complexity and scope, and perhaps also in volatility, as we find ourselves in the present age faced with competing claims for and against the legacies of the Enlightenment. There still exists a paradox of multiply regnant *Smiths*—from Greenspan to Arrighi, and beyond and between—that somehow settles under his name. Such a paradox is surely one of the more widely applicable lessons about history, reading, and, not least, the often-surprising encounter with interpretive difference over time that Greenspan's testimony before the congressional committee so perfectly captures.[19]

The Other Adam Smith does not assume that we are limited to a choice between Greenspan's or Arrighi's Smiths—or something in between—preferring instead to focus on individuality and collectivity as an eminently Smithian problem that remains to be explicated. We might simply call this the problem of popular contention, a problem that extends from the popular status of Adam Smith and his tumultuous readership to the preoccupations with collectivity and conflict that he pursued through the realms of epistemology, ethics, governmentality, and, not least, wealth. We are not content to produce either a flat-footed indictment or celebration of Smith's political economy, and certainly not at the expense of the vast and varied kinds of work now available as Smith's own. Rather, *The Other Adam Smith* sets out to read him as the conflicted interlocutor and sometimes the initiator of a far-reaching set of discourses concerning the production of knowledge, affect, freedom, and markets, as well as social and economic justice, and to consider certain facets of his legacy in a way that is focused on a wider set of texts than is typical in more conventional studies.

The time has come to read Smith as a broadly systematic thinker, one who cannot be understood on the basis of a few well-known passages from the two more famous books, *Wealth* and the *TMS*. Our book will offer something more complex and variegated, and yet, to stay within the register of an entirely Smithian problem, also something more widely connected than what has been associated with him in the past: We call this something an *other* Adam Smith. But our use of the term "other" is designed not to reconvene a discussion of him as *either* commercially *or* morally oriented; nor do we feel compelled to reconcile these tendencies in a unified whole. We use the term "other" before the proper name Adam Smith in the same way we refer to popular contention: a kind of conceptual shorthand for the ways in which difference and plurality remain irreducible and lead to revealing points of impasse that disrupt accepted forms of coherence as history (his as much as ours) continues to change. To articulate this point about popular contention in a different register, we could say that the opposite of individual subjectivity is not the "other." Rather, this subjectivity is historically conceived as a counterpoint to the problem of masses.

Given the availability—without authorial consent—in the 1970s of Smith's *Lectures on Rhetoric and Belles Lettres* (hereafter *LRBL*), the two versions of student notes comprising the *Lectures on Jurisprudence* (*LJ*, plus A or B indicating which manuscript) in the 1950s, the 1980 Oxford University Press reprinting of his *Essays on Philosophical Subjects* (*EPS*), and the collected correspondence and his early literary-critical writing, István Hont and Michael Ignatieff were right to call for a "renaissance" in the studies of Adam Smith.[20] They were right to insist that such work include a reconsideration of Western modernity that, it turns out, emanates in large part from the unlikely location of the United Kingdom's periphery, North of the Tweed.[21] They were right, especially because the vast catalogue of Smith scholarship up until the final decades of the twentieth century remained ignorant, willfully or not, of Smith's *corpus* beyond the two most famous works—the *TMS* and *Wealth*—that bookend his long career. Thus, in 1992, in a volume honoring the bicentennial of Smith's death, John Dwyer, among ten Nobel laureates collected in the volume, reiterated the call for a "renaissance" in Smith scholarship.[22] But the unfortunate history of Smith studies up to the late 1990s, with exceptions we are willing to grant, is primarily oriented toward a rather partial aspect of a thinker bent vehemently on promoting impartiality, as the famous term "impartial spectator" (about which more in Chapter 2) suggests.

Two points can be made, for example, about work on Adam Smith from about the bicentennial of *Wealth* (1976) forward. First, of the two collections that emerged in direct response to this event, none of the forty-four essays deal in any sustained way with the problem of the poor. A four-volume collection of 150 "critical" assessments of Smith by leading economists has one essay on poverty and one on the policy of social welfare.[23] Smith's repeated characterization of the laboring poor as the "majority of men" makes these omissions particularly stark.[24] Second, the necessity of reading Adam Smith today, or indeed, of reading in general as a socially relevant act, should not be a foregone conclusion. Reading itself only became important as a form of social agency during Smith's time and for reasons he and his cohort were much committed to promoting.[25]

It is true, and hopefully a sign of things to come, that in the first decades of the twenty-first century significant attempts have been made to reconsider Smith's more familiar works in relation to concerns in the lesser known essays and lectures.[26] The 2006 appearance of *The Cambridge Companion to Adam Smith* (hereafter cited as *Companion*) served as a corrective to the dominant trend of too narrow a focus, as "an up-to-date examination of all aspects of Smith's thought."[27] The first two chapters of this influential volume are on the imagination and belletrism in Smith, respectively; the third chapter, on language. But there is a certain problem with the *Companion* that perhaps no volume (no companion?) can escape and that is the Smithian problem of particularity that the word "all" as in "all aspects of Smith's thought" would seem to override. While agreeing with Knud Haakonssen (*Companion*'s editor) and Donald Winch that Smith wanted to "counteract the avariciousness of the rich, so it [government] can remedy the corruption of the poor," in his review of the *Companion* Eric Schliesser points out an "anti-philosophical *bias*," which is expressed in the exclusion of certain topics and in the "intellectual orientation of the contributors," but also "in the editors' treatment of the legacy of Smith."[28] In particular, Haakonssen and Winch distinguish "between legitimate and illegitimate legatees" (*Companion* 367). The latter category consists of readers who do not treat Smith's oeuvre as a unified whole, whose parts cannot be understood independently of the totality that determines the meaning of each particular text, even as the editors themselves admit that Smith's *corpus* is incomplete (certain of his lectures are still missing, and Smith left unfulfilled a promise to complete a grand synthesis of his work, connecting topics in the various essays and other books).

Once Smith's "intellectual enterprise is taken as a whole" (*Companion* 367), we have satisfied the desire for unity that Smith unsuccessfully demanded of himself.[29] Further, Smith's philosophical wealth has attracted "a crowd of enthusiastic claimants," among whom it is necessary to distinguish those whose claims are legitimate from those whose claims are baseless if not fraudulent. It is significant that a word like "crowd" (let alone "enthusiasm," as we will see with Hume in Chapter 3), a word so important to eighteenth-century political thought, is used without historical reflection, even as the editors repeat the Smithian gesture of sorting particularity into proper categories and governable collectives. In this sense, the word "coherence" (but who could argue against "coherence"?) enables and in fact compels twenty-first century readers of Adam Smith to ignore those passages in his work that seem to conflict with or diverge from the legitimate meaning of his thought. These silences, or gaps, cluster around the points at which he arrives at the problem of popular contention, signaling certain limits in Smith's arguments and explanations and obscuring what might lie beyond them.[30]

Eric Schliesser and Leonidas Montes's collection, *New Voices on Adam Smith* (*New Voices*, like the *Companion*, was published in 2006) seeks less to establish what is legitimate than what is genuinely new in the study of Adam Smith.[31] Haakonssen's foreword to this volume marks what is by now the commonplace problem for newcomers to Smith of "a sense of bewilderment at the sheer variety of angles of approach and topics of discussion offered by commentators" (*New Voices* xvi). Even as he resorts again to the language of inheritance, legacy, and thus to the problem of the transfer of property across generations, noting the "multiplicity of academic disciplines which can lay 'claim' to Smith" (*New Voices* xvi), he nevertheless praises the *New Voices* volume insofar as it "should help to further the diversification that is necessary when dealing with Adam Smith" (*New Voices* xviii). This diversification is made necessary above all by the variety of Smith's recovered *corpus*, but also by our knowledge that it was originally even more diverse. Haakonssen, for example, draws our attention to lectures by Smith, specifically on natural theology, of which we have no written record but whose absence has certainly shaped the reception of Smith.

The problem of diversification within unity, or better, the difference that prevents texts and even parts of texts from cohering into a whole, is not only something one encounters in rereading Smith's enlarged *corpus* but also something that appears in his work across what we only *retroactively* call the modern disciplines. Indeed, in Chapter 1, we explore precisely the problem of modern disciplinary partitioning, of fitting parts into categories in the name of unification, which generates the unique and enigmatic forms of epistemic impasse we are drawn to in Smith. *New Voices* is a book organized by subsections on Smith's sources, moral theory, and economic theories. But perhaps most significantly for getting at the word "new" (which in this case also means scholars relatively early in their careers who wrote dissertations on Smith between 2000 and 2004), the final section, "Adam Smith and Knowledge," marks the point at which *The Other Adam Smith* begins.

In *The Enlightenment and the Book* (hereafter *EB*), Richard Sher draws our attention to William Guthrie's widely read 1770 publication, *A New Geographical, Historical, and Commercial Grammar; and Present State of the Several Kingdoms of the World*, to show that "eighteenth-century Britain [and *uniquely* Britain] was leading the way not only in the 'rapid progress' of learning . . . but also in its 'general diffusion of knowledge.'"[32] Few scholars of the Enlightenment would deny that the newly United Kingdom was the capital of the European book trade and that conditions of freedom, especially in Scottish universities, allowed for decisive changes in the dissemination and organization of knowledge. In Guthrie's terms, Smith was in the vanguard of the general diffusion of what he would have called, interchangeably, philosophy or science, as a stand-in for knowledge in general.

With his mentor Henry Home, Lord Kames (pronounced "Hume," as in the name of his relation, Smith's close friend David Hume), Smith's influence played a part in the legal abandonment of perpetual copyright that allowed for a massive increase in the circulation of books after 1774.[33] But perhaps more importantly, Smith and his cohort struggled to contain and categorize the eighteenth-century explosion of new writing into a set of more and less generalizable forms, responding to Pope's famous protest in *The Dunciad* against the "swelling" of prose into verse with new disciplines, canons, and genres.[34] We will therefore begin *The Other Adam Smith* in Chapter 1 by showing how Smith played a decisive role in the making of the modern disciplinary divisions to which his work remains subject. According to Smith's own epistemology, a certain categorical imperative became the means by which the world's bewildering array of objects and mixed objects *might* be organized (the process is always contingent in Smith). But this project was troubled and conflicted. For Smith and his cohort, the will to categorize brought about both the contraction and displacement of philosophy, by which they meant knowledge in general, by narrowing human understanding into increased forms of specialization, and at the same time an increased dissemination of printed material. Further, as Smith makes clear in his work on knowledge, division—not only the division of knowledge but also the division between mental and manual labor—allows us to differentiate subspecialties within both. There is a dramatic struggle in Smith over the corporealization and *de*-corporealization of labor that is part of the question of how to divide the different specializations of work within itself. He and his contemporaries—Kames, Hume, Ferguson, and others—struggled to determine to what effect we should adhere to both kinds of division, and they did so with a wary eye on popular contention.

We begin *The Other Adam Smith* with a chapter focused on Smith's interpretive system and its relation to the specialties and subspecialties of labor. We do so because we want to examine a set of knowledge problems that should be combined with his more familiar theories, both economic and otherwise; this combination allows a more critical and more careful examination than has been the case in the relatively short period of sustained scholarly focus on the lesser read works. Thus, at least one of the *others* in *The Other Adam Smith* is a philosophically, aesthetically, and from there, a socially minded Adam Smith who exists in a vexed—let's avoid Oncken's path by too simply saying *oppositional*—relationship to an Adam Smith designated as the world's most famous booster of an untroubled free-market system.

Among the recent wave of Smith scholarship we have already noted, Michael Shapiro's *Reading "Adam Smith": Desire, History, and Value* (hereafter *RAS*) moves in a uniquely critical direction.[35] Rather than seeing a homology between Smith's theories about the development of language toward complexity and transparency over time during the rise of commercial society, Shapiro argues that, for Smith, "*value* emerges precisely at the point at which flows [of meaning] are inhibited . . . [during] the process of linguistic exchange" (*RAS* 46). He continues, provocatively, that Smith's "sensationalist [by which he simply means, affectively based] epistemology," rather than securing peaceable reciprocity through consensus-oriented communication between equal subjects (real, or more likely imagined), instead reveals a "fear of the disruptive forces of desire and therefore of the singularities of subjects" (*RAS* xix). Shapiro makes a useful point here for our purposes of introduction. Yet, as is characteristic of an emergent set of new scholars who have looked in a developed way at Smith's interest in language, Shapiro's approach is perhaps too strictly focused on the literary-philosophical instead of the political-economic, missing the ways in which these discourses remain entangled throughout Smith's other work.[36]

Within economics proper, while some scholars have begun to consider the importance of subjective, nonrational factors in the decision making of actors,[37] few indeed have examined the complex history of the set of assumptions underlying notions like "the economy" or "the market" in which certain behaviors are deemed rational or irrational. And while specialist treatments of Adam Smith that remain within the discrete domains of natural law, moral philosophy, or, less commonly, literary studies do exist, we have not yet seen a sustained argument about how the division between, for example, economy and what is today too simply called "culture" is itself a core problem that plays out across the epistemic, ethical, and juridical interests that remain antagonistically proximate to one another in the work of Smith at large.[38] Accordingly, we want to resist the premise that the affective and material charges of Smith's efforts are self-evidently correspondent. Whatever alternate readings might emerge as scholars proceed to take seriously Smith's work as a whole (which it can never be), we need first to question the disciplinary divisions that have been retroactively and anachronistically assumed to exist there.[39] What we might call the generalist's dilemma only becomes a dilemma in an age still too resolutely attached to the need for division and specialization. This attachment emerged—and as we will argue, did so problematically—as Smith himself was writing it into existence.

A popular social commentator who eschewed the modern pressures of disciplinary specialization—apposite for us at least by way of introduction precisely because of his renown—is Irving Kristol. By combining Smith's *Theory of Moral Sentiments* with *Wealth of Nations*, Kristol becomes an unwitting figurehead for a chorus of twentieth-century scholars whose interest in the history of capitalist institutions is limited by their commitment to moralizing its destructive exigencies—and indeed, the history of popular resistance to them—away.[40] Instead of merely rejecting Kristol's interpretation as a misreading, we want to investigate the possibility that the moral sentiment of sympathy might provide support for Kristol's fear of the masses.[41] Smith's interest, stated in the *TMS* for the first time in 1759 as an affective—before an economic—moment in Jupiter's great invisible plan, both posited and problematized a notion of intersubjectivity that cannot be summed up as an order of procedural liberalism, communicative reason, or consensus untainted by affect.[42]

Indeed, against a figure like Habermas, Smith admits a central if also highly conditional relation of affect, one he eventually links to the tradition of Stoicism. This does not mean that Smith was "a Stoic" or that he simply appropriated wholesale a worldview from the Stoics. While Smith certainly sought to defend certain key elements from the Stoic tradition against the attack on that "sect" by his teacher, the intuitional father of Scottish moral philosophy Francis Hutcheson, he appropriated these elements for his own purposes in a very different context from that in which they emerged. In *An Essay on the Nature and Conduct of the Passions and Affections, with Illustrations on the Moral Sense* (hereafter *ENCP*), his work on the conduct of human passions and affections (1728), Hutcheson is one of the few Scottish Enlightenment figures to use the common word "multitude" affirmatively, as in "making the multitudes happy."[43] And he refers to "the Stoick sect" as "a sublimely selfish discipline" (*ENCP* 83).

Our reading of Smith's use of Stoic philosophy contrasts sharply with those who see nothing in the *TMS* but the unequivocal benevolence of an "analytically egalitarian" or, as Smith would say, "natural" ethical system. Our reading of Smith is a critical account of morally restrained intersubjectivity, or procedural virtue too weak to protect the poor in a free market system, though this notion, which has also been called "the Christian virtue of benevolence," is celebrated in the dominant liberal line of Smith's twenty-first century supporters against those who might instead explore alternatives to a market economy.[44] As we establish further in Chapter 2, Smith's celebrated impartial spectator can arise only from the absence of affective imitation or communication that is endogenized within the social conflicts that Smith himself puzzled over.

Smith's characteristic worry that partiality might stand in the way of an entirely idealized vision of social harmony has special relevance for managing the spectacle of poverty. This is true especially regarding the relative privileges of British middle-class sociability, which itself waxed and waned in the face of continued poverty and exploitation at considerable moral and material cost. Of course, middle-class sociability was neither a given nor a stable prospect for the majority of Britons, let alone the *Britons* who were at the same time *Scots*, during the period within which Smith was composing his texts. Smith's work in the *TMS* is structured in opposition to the notion of a transindividual subject as developed by Spinoza, in which the ethical individual is a composite singularity that retains an uneasy relationship to Smith's idealized commercial *socius*. As such, the singular subject eludes the homeopathic opposition between subjectivity and popular contention.

The eighteenth century, in Scotland particularly, was a time of fierce debate over modernity's basic concepts of cognition and affective experience. The term "Scottish Enlightenment," as Neil Davidson reminds us, was first used by William Robert Scot's biography of Francis Hutcheson in 1900 to signal the central relation between cultural production and societal improvement more generally.[45] As is well known, Scotland's financial innovations—the Royal Bank of Scotland invented the cash credit system in 1728—were decisive in the formation of modern commerce.[46] And its relatively progressive social institutions were well ahead of those of the London city center, as well as, for a time, the rest of Europe.[47] As early as 1696, ironically the same year that religious blasphemer Thomas Aikenhead was indicted (and executed a month later), an Act for Setting Schools was established by the Scottish parliament, putting a school in every parish not already equipped with one. To the establishment of early modern education we should also add the Society in Scotland for the Promotion of Christian Knowledge (SSPCK), whose overt goal was to find schools "where religion and virtue might be taught" (there were 5 SSPCK schools in 1711, and 189, with 13,000 pupils, by 1808). SSPCK's purpose was of course not a disinterested one, especially in the agitated Highlands. By the 1740s its itinerant Anglican teachers set out with the express task of preparing a mindset for Scotland's northernmost peoples that would counter Roman Catholic influences and Jacobite tendencies, as well as be amenable to wage labor and commercial husbandry in the new economy.[48]

In the 1720s, Allan Ramsay set up the first English circulating library from his Edinburgh bookstore, which allowed weekly borrowing for a small subscription fee. Robert Foulis, like Smith a student of Hutcheson, established the first School for the Art of Design in Glasgow in 1753. The ideals of polite conversation and enlightened taste—proffered for public consumption by Joseph Addison in *The Spectator* and embodied in such literary societies as the Tuesday Club, the Poker Club, the Oyster Club, the Mirror Club, and the Select Society—flourished for those who had access and helped establish the rise of sociability over political partisanship and against the divine right of kings.[49] In contrast with the torpor of tradition-bound scholasticism in the English universities, by the time Smith matriculated at Glasgow in 1737, and throughout the period of his later lectures there, Scottish centers had advanced the premises of civic humanism, public virtue, and disciplinary innovation in a way that was decisive to the origins of modernity.[50] In a phrase David Daiches appropriated from the literature of the period, the Scottish Enlightenment was a hotbed of genius.[51]

Eighteenth-century Scotland also signifies a moment in which the deliberations over the geographical unity called Great Britain—deliberations that throughout the period moved back and forth between the streets, the public house, and the halls of the soon-to-be abolished Scottish parliament—generated their own amount of political heat. If Scotland was the site of modernity's commercial and intellectual revolutions, it was also a place of grave anxiety about political violence emanating from the North, designated after the Act of Union in 1707 as Britain's savage periphery—bordered below by a civilized world that originated in England and the Lowlands, some would argue, when the Romans turned away in disgust from the Picts.[52] One writer in 1745, characteristically for the time, positioned the Highlands as passed over by the stadial (sequential, or stage-based) progress from hunter-gatherer to commercial society. Another contemporaneous commentator eschews standard forms of developmental history altogether and proclaims, "from being a savage, man rose to be a Scotchman."[53] Highlanders were consigned to "those early ages before mankind had begun to form themselves into large societies,"[54] that is, as off the proper historical course, as remarked upon by Geoffrey Plank in *Rebellion and Savagery* (hereafter *RS*). Defoe compared contemporary understanding of Highland life as being as occulted to the anthropologist (a term not introduced until Kant) as "the inner parts of Africa" (*RS* 12).

The idea of union was unpopular in Scotland as early as Cromwell's invasion in search of the eventually beheaded Charles I, who ruled from 1625–48. The exile, four decades later, to France of his son, King James VII of Scotland and II of England (1685–89), on account of his openly stated purpose of making the realm Catholic, marked the beginning of the Jacobite cause, which was triangulated through foreign affairs given the interests of Louis XIV in addition to the Vatican. Immediately upon the news of James's flight to France, Scottish parties assembled in London to protect the power of the Presbyters in spite of a formidable Jacobite party. This protection was realized by the offer of the Crown, heavily influenced by Scotland's unique internal politics, to William and Mary in the so-called Bloodless Revolution of 1688.[55] The thirty-eight Mac-Donalds, who were murdered in 1692 for being slow in declaring allegiance to the new king while hosting his forces as guests, and the women and children, who died of starvation after being burned out, hardly experienced the celebrated arrival of the Prince of Orange as bloodless.[56]

Ostensibly, the invitation to William, who was raised a Calvinist, was proposed to solve the problem of the right to resistance and to settle the issue of the previous civil war under Cromwell: that of replacing the sovereign's *jure divino* appointment to rule with a notion, inscribed in England's new Bill of Rights in 1689, of having a king *jure humano*. But as Tobias Smollett points out in his *History of England* post-1688 (hereafter *The History*), "their [the people's] deliverer seems to have overshot their attachment to their own liberty and privileges."[57] William could still dissolve Parliament at will, and "remained the master of all the instruments and engines of corruption and violence" (*The History* 16).

Smollett, a Scot, traditionally better known as one of the literary front-four in the canon of mid-eighteenth-century English novels (with Richardson, Fielding, and Sterne), is useful if for no other reason than his divergence from the period's dominant Whig historians. He wrote for the Tory prime minister, also a Scot, John Stuart, the Earl Bute, in the short-lived periodical *The Briton*, which inspired the ire of John Wilkes in the publication of *The North Briton*, famously attached to the Wilkes Riots of the same period. Beyond providing an alternative to the Whig party's perspective, insofar as his history runs from 1688 to the death of King George II in 1760, Smollett, who died eleven years later, was also writing a history of the present and very near past. Throughout *The History* he shows a keen eye for what can only be construed as the myth of national coherency in the period, especially in Scotland, which was cross-cut with political allegiances and codes of custom too numerous to reduce to the simple opposition of being England's inverted—and therefore subsumable—other. As regards the unity of England itself, no sooner had William been appointed king by a coalition of parties, Smollett eagerly remarked, than "this tie was broken . . . [and] William soon found himself the head of a faction" (*The History* 16).

Queen Anne's noncontroversial coronation in 1702 upheld the line of royal succession, and as Smollett writes, "even the Jacobites seemed pleased with her elevation" (*The History* 179). But she was not permitted to recognize the faith of her papist half-brother, the Old Pretender, James III and VIII, according to an Act of Settlement that sealed her already strong Protestant commitment to the Church of England (there was no mention of Scotland in the act). To do so would have meant abdicating the throne. This is what Smollett refers to, with an appropriate eye on the power of chance at the highest political levels, as the "strange vicissitudes of fortune in the consequence of the father's [James II's] expulsion" (*The History* 179).

Ironically, the decisive influence of Scottish politicians in establishing Anne's succession (she was Mary's sister, in addition to having a direct genealogical connection to the exiled Stuart line) enabled anti-Scottish legislation. One particularly telling example, a harbinger of the controversial Act of Union under Anne, is the Alien Act (1705). According to this law (passed by the English parliament just two years before the question of union was at least legally resolved), unless the Scots accepted the Hanoverian succession by Christmas of that year, they would be treated as aliens, and their commercial interests would be radically curtailed. The more famous Jacobite uprisings in 1715 and 1745 (there were others), the massacre at Culloden by British forces in 1746 (which included the execution of noncombatants, deportation to the American and other colonies, deliberate starvation, and rape), the Disarming Act (1747), the Dress Act (1746–82) forbidding tartans (excepting the Black Watch), and the subsequent Highland Clearances provide important points of reference for reading Smith and his cohort. Plank's comment is surely accurate: "Britain's soldiers in 1745 were fighting in the presence of philosophers" (*RS* 106). We suggest the inverse is equally true: The principal thinkers of the Scottish Enlightenment were doing their thinking while the nation was at war with itself.[58]

The relatively recent title "professor of humanity," whose lineage is traceable directly to Smith's teaching at Glasgow, was used first by his successor, Thomas Reid, who was chair of moral philosophy there. Reid wanted to distinguish the kind of public lectures, like Smith's courses on the imitative arts, from those, also given by Smith, of "Professors of Logic . . . [,] Moral . . . [,] and Natural Philosophy."[59] The goal here, as we have already intimated, was a disciplinary one. And as such, the new ways of diffusing knowledge and of collectivizing experience had fundamental applications to imagining a more unified sense of the public *qua* British national coherence.[60] In Chapter 3 of *The Other Adam Smith*, which will also consider Smollett's relation to the unprecedented amassing of a new genre called the English novel, we read the phrase "British national coherence" as a historically enigmatic one, localizable to grave tensions surrounding the dissolution of the Scottish parliament and Scotland's contentious integration into a greater Britain. The problem of individuality and collectivity that we take up as an issue related to the organization of knowledge in Chapter 1, and of affective relations in Chapter 2, is played out here in expressly geopolitical terms.

The significance of popular contention over the Act of Union, which lasted until about the middle of the eighteenth century, reveals the same problem of particularity and unity that we have introduced regarding Smith's epistemo-logical and ethical interests. Even when Scottish ministers responded positively to pressures from Anne and her administration on behalf of union, they did so while having to deal gingerly with the clamor of Jacobite crowds on both sides of the Tweed. Unionist members of the Scottish parliament leading up to its abolition were never sure they could escape the commentary of the streets, "rude, ignorant, and desperate fellows, mad women and boys," who congre-gated for Scottish independence right outside the door.[61] Smollett reports Lord Bacon as saying the union was

> contrary to the sense of the Scottish nation: that the murmurs of the people had
> been so loud as to fill the whole kingdom: and so bold as to reach even the doors
> of parliament. . . . The aver[sion] to an incorporating Union is one of the most
> dangerous experiments to both nations. (*The History* 244)

Lord Haversham "supposed the Union made up of so many mismatched pieces, of such jarring, incongruous ingredients" as to require a standing army to keep it from bursting asunder (*The History* 243). Smollett's paraphrase of Bacon continues:

> [A] unity pieced up by direct admission of contrarieties in the fundamental
> points of it, is like the toes of Nebuchadnezzar's image, which were made of
> iron and clay; they may cleave together, but would never incorporate. (*The His-
> tory* 243)

The archaic reference to Nebuchadnezzar, the Babylonian king widely known for conquering Jerusalem and sending the Jews into exile (see the Book of Daniel), is significant on a number of levels and goes directly to the point of the complex, highly contentious *intra*-national political situation between England and Scotland at the time. The first part of his name may be translated as "pro-tect the border"; the second part, Bakhat Nasar, means "winner of the fate," or literally "fate winner."

Bacon's evocation of Nebuchadnezzar (or if you like, Smollett's evocation of Bacon) signals a fear about the proximity of national difference *within* what were only relatively lately construed as separate nations, as well as divisions within the sense of greater British nationhood then being proposed. Indeed, the entire string of citations from Smollett's rehearsing of *English* parliamen-tary debates on the union are commonly preoccupied with the problem of uni-fying particulars, not only Scottish particularity into a Greater British unity but also the problem of achieving union given the nonunified conditions of the two parts that politicians supposed might be put together. There is further anxiety expressed in the Bacon citation about the course of history insofar as sovereignty may (still, even after William) be subject to the twist and turns of a temporal process no party may control in advance. We will have a good deal more to say about the function of aleatory events in history, specifically as related to plebian Jacobitism, in Chapter 3, which is focused on an array of Scottish conjectural historians.[62] For now we note that the reference to the Jewish exodus by Bacon does not, as one might expect, lend itself to a politics of the simple oppositional nationalism of the Scottish versus the English state. Rather, the prevailing theme is one of *statelessness*, of belonging to God knows what geopolitical entity, or better, of being unevenly attached to an entity that simply does not exist in advance of one's arrival.

The risky part of Bacon's "dangerous experiment" thus brings us squarely back to the way in which we introduced the term "other" in referencing the other Adam Smith. There, our proposition was that Smith's *corpus* at large could not be reduced to being either a theory of the immanent rationality of the market or the expression of an original intersubjectivity grounded in sympathy, or even an ingenious amalgamation of the two. On the contrary, Smith's works more often than not produce the very contradictions on which they founder: The market performs its miracles (above all in the corn trade) only at the expense of the life it is supposed to support, just as sympathy arises precisely from the impossibility of a communication of sentiments between individuals.

The impulse to demonstrate the existence of the whole necessarily engenders gaps, the trace of what has been excluded, in order to fabricate the whole, just as every unity is threatened by plurality, by a "multitudinousness" that cannot be constrained but constantly arises (the noun "insurrection" is derived from the Latin verb "insurgo"—"to rise or rise up"). Thus, we do not seek to legislate an act of union on that composite object called Adam Smith. Above all, the impasses and gaps in his work appear particularly around the notion, from which he never strays very far, of popular contention or the power of the multitude, which we will spend the rest of *The Other Adam Smith* presenting in detail. At the same time, Adam Smith in his own historical moment was (and to the present remains) fully infused with the complicated stuff of popularity itself, in every sense of the term: We want to read his work not only to see what was said about the multitude but also to note how the historical traces of eighteenth-century popular contention both discompose and disorder this work. Finally, we hope to outline the causes that determine what his work can (and cannot) say in the first decades of the twenty-first century.

According to Dugald Stewart, in his "Account of the Life and Writings of Adam Smith" (hereafter "AL"), the 1793 biography prepared shortly after Smith's death for the Royal Society of Edinburgh, the great man always had a "tendency to absence."[63] "I hate biography," Stewart remarked in a letter of 1797, a few years after preserving for the world a genius in the story of Smith's life that he wrote despite hating the genre.[64] Stewart's biography registers apposite tension originating with the very first critical assessments of Adam Smith. He begins with a narrative, too delicious not to be true, of an "accident . . . when [Smith] was about three [where] he was stolen by a party of vagrants" ("AL" 269).[65] This original mishap, as if making more fragile so valuable a life, is further compounded by Smith's social eccentricities, as well as the great difficulty Smith had in getting to his own writing, as he later confessed ("AL" 372). He was in his mid-thirties when he published his first book in 1759, but matriculated at Glasgow in 1737 at the then-not-uncommon age of fourteen. According to Stewart, Smith's social habits ranged from "speaking to himself when alone," to showing what the biographer calls, once again, "*absence* in company" (emphasis Stewart's, "AL" 270). Alexander Carlyle called him "the most absent man in Company that I ever saw, moving his Lips and talking to himself, and Smiling, in the midst of large Company's."[66]

Smith's many particularities rendered him, Stewart says, "certainly not fitted for the general commerce of the world, [or] for the business of active life" ("AL" 329). "Not perhaps uncommon among *absent* men," he continues, Smith's "comprehensive speculations . . . rendered him inattentive to familiar objects and to common occurrences" (emphasis ours, "AL" 330). His "recluse habits," his "embarrassment . . . in the company of strangers . . . [,] and still more, his consciousness of this," complete Stewart's proto-Romantic portrayal of a singular thinker not completely in or of this world. His particular way of putting this is, simply, "*my* Smith" (emphasis ours, "AL" 315). In a letter to Smith from 1759, which Stewart includes in the biography, David Hume attempts to console his friend and ally, who is anxious about the public reception of his first book, the *TMS*: "Compose yourself in tranquility," he advises. "Think on the emptiness . . . and futility of the common judgments of men. . . . Philosophical subjects . . . exceed the comprehension of the vulgar" ("AL" 297); and therefore, "nothing indeed can be a stronger presumption of falsehood than the approbation of the multitude" ("AL" 298).

Significant in this string of citations is that Stewart establishes Smith as subject to disappearance and chance—a singular but pluralized Adam Smith. He then moves, *avant la lettre*, to an almost Byronesque portrayal of a brilliant, solitary Smith, a sort of *economiste maudite*. In this fashion, Smith's tendency to absence works as yet another way of confronting the paradox of particularity, incalculable numbers, Hume's "multitudes," parts destined *not* to fit into this or that unity, problems we have grouped under the general heading of popular contention. Hume's point is that the vulgar must be kept at proper distance from philosophy so as to be properly objectified by it. Consistent with the mandates of Smith's own manner of conjectural history (the term belongs to Stewart, "AL" 293), Stewart takes Smith back from the vagrants, fashioning a historical figure that is all the more valued for having almost (always?) been lost.

Stewart's Smith is both specialized and specializing, in that the biography begins a hundred-year plus tradition that extends through the nineteenth century to read Smith as the master economist. And there he stayed until a more recent time when, reoriented by the chance finding of absent texts among the vulgar (Smith's 1748 *Lectures on Rhetoric and Belles Lettres* were made public in the early 1960s after having been discovered in an Aberdeen junkshop), we could start reading Smith differently, and once again. But before that chance discovery, Adam Smith was portrayed by Stewart as a biographical object whose genius is narrowed by—or better, who gains genius by narrowing in on—what Stewart highlights as his most important legacy in shaping "the commercial policy of Europe" ("AL" 270). According to the logic that Smith and his cohort struggled to invent, his was a unique and particular life, sometimes given over to bad fortune but finally rescued by a disciplinary homecoming for the economic mind. The sleight of hand that allows the production of value— here the value of Smith's varied scholarly identity—works in a very Smithian way by moving between the particular and general, and doing so in a manner that narrowly escapes the literal loss of the scholar himself in any number of ways (the vagrants, his character, his texts).

Instead of conjecturing our way into a conflict-free Adam Smith, *The Other Adam Smith* embraces the occasions within his work where Smith divides and in so doing becomes himself divided, especially when he approaches the problem of popular contention and insurrection. We do this because the very problem of divisibility as Smith constructs it both affirms and denies the force of alternative collective orders, precisely those rendered inconceivable in existing accounts of his work. Smith's work in the broadest sense is anything but a closed order of coherent propositions: It is in fact forced open by the sheer weight of its gaps and absences, open to futures that remain to be seen.

The following chapters focus, respectively, on Smith's models of knowledge, affect, nation, and economy.

Chapter 1, "'The Pleasing Wonder of Ignorance': Adam Smith's Divisions of Knowledge," focuses on the centrality of *genus* within Adam Smith's epistemology, predominately in his posthumously published essays on method and philosophical progress, and his posthumously published work on the "fine arts" in *Lectures on Rhetoric and Belles Lettres*. We argue, first, that Smith's theory of moral sentiment rests upon an analytic that promises to ensure a peaceable *socius* through increased disciplinary specialization. Second, we show how the attention he pays to ignorance in his interpretive system—what he simply refers to as "gaps"—stand in as epistemic analogues to the risks of mass agency and popular reading. Turning to Kames, Hume, Reverend Knox, and George Turnbull, we explain how a new disciplinary specialty called literature, taking imagination as its own special province, displaced the more general applications of philosophy. As leisurely intellectual work increasingly came to occupy a category apart from physical labor, so too the imagination was to be cordoned off within a cul-de-sac of literary criticism and good taste.

Chapter 2, "'Tumultuous Combinations': The Transindividual from Adam Smith to Spinoza," takes sympathy as the logical starting point of Smith's discussion of morality. It can fulfill this function, however, only to the extent that Smith empties the affective relations that necessarily constitute sympathy of any content or significance that would exceed the boundary of the individual. Where Smith is generally considered the proponent of ethical restraint based on recognition of the other (the impartial spectator), we see him pursue a strategy (first described by Shaftesbury) that resists the transindividual dimension of human interaction, and does so by means of the very vocabulary of transindividuality. Thus, the objective of the *TMS* is not so much to refute or disprove the idea of a transindividual dimension as it is to render it unimaginable.

Neither Hume's hesitating and inconclusive remarks, nor Malebranche's more substantial but finally ungrounded comments on sympathy, pose enough of a threat to prompt Smith to readjust his idea of what he terms "conditional sympathy." For Smith, those who suffer from poverty excite little compassion. Smith calls on the Stoic doctrine that a wise man never whines (Smith's word) about his fate to place the laboring poor as an anomaly outside the social work of moral sympathy. In order to clarify Smith's stoically oriented acts of self-restraint and separation, we draw on Spinoza's idea of the imitation of affect, which offers a corporeal reorientation of affective connection independent of the will. We see Smith's objection to what he calls "tumultuous combinations" as the accidental eruption of passion, or the contagion of affects, as his attempt to avoid the Spinozist implications of popular contention.

Chapter 3, "'Numbers, Noise, and Power': Insurrection as a Problem of Historical Method," begins with an account of popular Jacobitism. We realize of course that organized military rebellion on behalf of the Stuart cause should not be flatly equated with popular contention writ large. But they crossed over in important ways that for eighteenth-century thinkers were subsumed under the protean heading of the "multitude." In our account of unrest around the Stuart cause, we want to show how descriptions of Jacobite and other "mobs" as being antithetical to stadial historical progress bear comparison with Hume's rejection of *a priori* notions of cause and effect.

From here, we move from popular Jacobitism and kindred activities to an account of eighteenth-century historiography proper: How was the social and political concern with insurrection—for Hume, Robertson, and others, reaching back to the precarious union of crowns under James VI and I in 1603—addressed by epistemic debates over so-called conjectural thought?

Our next move delves in a more focused way into the relationship between multiplicity, novels, and history. At issue in this section is how the unprecedented amassing of novels themselves presented a problem of "numbers" in the form of literary overproduction akin to the one that designates the fear of insurrection in eighteenth-century historical writing.

Finally, we develop the ambivalent value that Scottish historians gave to what they called "martial virtue," a way of canalizing insurgency on behalf of the state monopoly of violence, that was also supposed to stem the deleterious effects of capitalist luxury. Here popular contention presents a permanent problem—sometimes governable, sometimes leading to riot, insurrection, and war. As such, what Hume called "the fury of the multitude" signals the dangers of popular resistance to historical progress and complicates the ability to produce effective historical narrative written in stadial terms.

Chapter 4, "'Immunity, the Necessary Complement of Liberty': The Birth of Necro-Economics" argues that in *Wealth* Smith posits the rational form of self-improvement through financial gain as a quasi-universal impulse proper to humankind as such. In his work more generally, however, this impulse tends to be shadowed by perverted or improvident forms of self-seeking that sacrifice future improvement to an intensity of present pleasure. Here, we refer to the criminals who populate the pages of the *TMS*: the pickpockets, house-breakers, and horse thieves (Fielding's famous archnemeses) who can hardly be restrained even by the near certainty of capital punishment.

The pursuit of one's betterment is the outcome of an internal struggle against the temptations of bodily pleasure—not only the pleasures of the flesh but also those of mere comfort and ease, those of the palate and eye, or more commonly those of avoiding the exigencies of a life of hard labor. As Smith says in the *TMS*, the design of modern society is itself part of a universal design, a political economy that is part of a greater "oeconomy of nature," that is, a continuation in the human world of the providence that governs all things. Thus, if societies, by virtue of the oeconomy of nature, are to promote and guarantee the unhampered market (above all, the market in food, espe-cially grains), then the state must allow (*laisser*) individuals to be exposed to death, if to make food available to them means violating the natural laws of free commerce. While Smith does not directly address these questions, so central to French political economy, his notion of the market constitutes a response to them not only by avoiding the legal and political issues involved but by inscribing this avoidance in his theory itself.

In conclusion, we turn to the thought of those usually considered Smith's direct intellectual descendants—from Malthus to Ludwig von Mises and Friedrich Hayek. We show that while often critical of Smith, these successors incorporated his concept of life itself and more precisely the exposing of life to death.

1 "THE PLEASING WONDER OF IGNORANCE"
Adam Smith's Divisions of Knowledge

The pleasing wonder of ignorance is accompanied with the still more
pleasing satisfaction of science. We wonder and are amazed at the effect;
and we are pleased ourselves, and happy to find that we can comprehend,
in some measure, how that wonderful effect is produced.

Adam Smith, "Of the Imitative Arts"[1]

THE WORD "IGNORANCE" designates a two-part sequence in the epigram above, which we have lifted from an incomplete, posthumously published, and—to scholars of Adam Smith the political economist—a somewhat minor text. The collection, *Essays on Philosophical Subjects* (*EPS*), within which this piece on the imitative arts appears, was first published in 1795 but connects back several decades to Smith's earliest scholarly preoccupations. The imitative arts essay is important for us because it establishes Smith as what might be called—with 200-plus years of specialization between his time and ours—an interdisciplinary scholar, before disciplines as such. The full volume of the *EPS* ranges in scope from astronomy and physics, to music and dance, to metaphysics and vision, and to the comparative study of verse, at times mixing one topic into the other.

The *EPS* thus takes its place among so much other would-be ephemera—in particular, the *Lectures on Rhetoric and Belles Lettres* (*LRBL*) from 1748. In the imitative arts essay (hereafter "IA") and in the earlier lectures, Smith examines what his 1790s biographer Dugald Stewart loosely called the "fine arts" in his biography ("AL").[2] As we've noted in the Introduction, it is curious that the material regarded by most scholars of Smith as his minor writings—work that is marginal to his magnum opus, *The Wealth of Nations* (*Wealth*), or the earlier *Theory of Moral Sentiments* (*TMS*)—in fact comprises the majority of what is now available as Smith's *corpus* at large (student notes, lectures, fragments, letters, as well as the different versions of the major books).[3] This curiosity contains within it a historical puzzle about the distinctions of value that we now want to trace between this or that *genus* of eighteenth-century knowledge and, implicitly, about how such distinctions of value emerge within and between Smith's so-called minor and major texts. Stewart remarked about Smith's breadth of interest that he "tended to generalize a little too much" ("AL" 306). Whether this is true or not, insofar as Smith the generalist may be claimed as a key figure—perhaps *the* key figure—of the Anglo-Scottish Enlightenment, then we might also say that the problem of generalizing itself—the problem of particularity and universality, of division and wholeness, of specialization and comprehensiveness—is precisely what continues to comprise modernity's core philosophical problem. This at least is the point of our beginning with the epigram from Smith on the fine arts.

In this epigram on the pleasures of knowledge, the first part of the surprise-wonder-admiration sequence is related to the affective connotation of ignorance, a sort of angst-producing epistemic tripwire that eventuates if processed correctly in the initial pleasure-producing effect Smith registers as wonder. Secondarily, and with that much more satisfaction, ignorance is supposed to be recollected by a different knowledge mode. The pleasing wonder of ignorance is provisionally circumscribed, we could say, reworked within what Stewart—not altogether positively—called Smith's "love of system" ("AL" 306). In this way, the distress of interruption called surprise is contained or properly canalized, slowed down by contemplative wonder, and rendered pleasingly objectified in a temporary moment of stasis called admiration.

This three-part movement between ignorance and understanding gives the "various powers of the human mind" ("AL" 274) a greater pleasure-producing capacity than static contemplation can provide; or better, in keeping with the paradoxical nature of disciplinary division, we see here a certain regularity that is achieved while change is simultaneously encouraged. Moreover, Smith makes a distinctly Enlightenment move by positing a notional "we" at the beginning and end of the epistemic production line. In this way, his apparent displacement of individual by socialized forms of pleasure would seem to occur by a more rationally oriented commitment to what he would call, in the broadest possible sense, the achievement of "science." But what is enigmatic is that the move from ignorance to science, from wonder to pleasure, and finally, from still more pleasure to that sociable state that Smith calls "ourselves," is that a fully realized overcoming of ignorance is neither desirable nor really ever possible ("IA" 185).

In tracing Newtonian (and, contrastingly, Humean) influences on Smith's epistemology, Eric Schliesser does well to insist on the essentially "open-ended enterprise of [Smith's] successive approximations."[4] For Schliesser, Smith's reliance on approximation is consistent with his distinction between natural price and localized price, which would be achieved if the obstructions (luxury, monopoly, and what today we would call unions) that prevent the free movement of capital, labor, and goods were removed.[5] But commensurate with the market realities of Smith's day (and our own), freedom of movement—call it, in the epistemological sense, open-endedness—is less an issue of debate than the specific directions, channels, and boundaries that delimit the circulation, commonly, of ideas, people, and things. The opening through which surprise eventuates in admiration is directed, as we will show in this chapter, by an emerging sense of disciplinary division. And this disciplinary order, to extend Schliesser, is what replaces simple obstructionism once the majority of mankind (as Smith would put it) is sufficiently conditioned to work.

Smith's epistemology is no less idealized—a term Schliesser uses in a different essay—than is his desire for an obstruction-free capitalist market.[6] This in part is what distinguishes Smith's relative optimism from Hume's mitigation of Pyrrhonian doubts.[7] For Hume in *Enquiry Concerning Human Understanding* (hereafter *ECH*), the philosopher's ability to be "be sensible of our ignorance" burdened the progress of knowledge perhaps more than it augmented it.[8] Smith is somewhat less burdened. Still, Smith's epistemology is saturated with anxiety and discomfort when "new or singular" events occur. Smith is generically weary of "tumult,"[9] and this is where imagination can offer a palliative effect.

Thus, at closer look, let's begin with two points: First, *pace* those who would argue that Smith is a radical egalitarian, his collective "we" is achieved in the form of a particular, rather than the imagined and idealized general sense of collective-*cum*-intellectual becoming. Comprehension occurs only "in some measure," just as obstructions within an idealized capitalist market—and "tumult" is precisely the right term here—are liable to pop up without warning. And, as we shall see, those tumultuous obstructions do arise, especially when the paradox of seeking generality through division is applied.

Second, the anxieties and *dis*-pleasure attendant on surprise must be kept in mind. Smith's interest in knowledge production places science within a certain volatile zone (the surprise experience) that is subsequently stopped by wonder, then reasoned through according to the norms of admiration: Again, we can only ever comprehend wonder "in some measure"; pleasure overcomes anxiety in the encounter with wonder and the partial (read "select," "normative," "socially or epistemologically appropriate") recollection of it. The logic then, if we follow the move from wonder to achieving a "we," is that whatever human collectivity exists under the provisional heading of "ourselves" must also be based on a certain tension where the aleatory charges of ignorance continue to disrupt science rather than being rebuffed by it.

The question, which must remain a question—a moment of ignorance, an unknown, absence, all variously manifest in Smith's work, as the threat of a "tumult"—is how effectively that disruption is managed. Through what openings, in the face of what obstructions that must either be ignored or eliminated, are the orders of knowledge and the organization of commercial society ideally supposed to emerge?

We should emphasize again that in Smith's historical moment aesthetic pleasure was not yet cordoned off from social life. Smith holds no truck with the Romantic-individualist discourse that came after him, where the enjoyment of wonder needs vast empty spaces dotted here and there by the Highland lass, the hermit, or the leech gatherer, and where pleasure accrues—Wordsworth's pitch for common language aside—in inverse proportion to its public accountability.[10] Smith denounces "the gloomy horror of the cavern"—and mentions the hermit, specifically—as leading to "prophetical inspirations and revelations" (*LRBL* 71). By contrast, for Smith aesthetic pleasure is processed across what only later appear to be more discrete disciplines, and it does so in a collectively oriented and successive (that is, nonprophetical) way; but note too, that it is in this movement toward collectivity that ignorance retains an ambivalent location within science. Ignorance remains, or can remain, a crucial counterpoint to the so-called open-endedness of simply pushing knowledge through the doors and windows of our disciplinary homes in a smooth, or as Smith would have it, *contra* Hume, a more or less successive way.[11] The caveat about science being possible only "in some measure" gestures toward a theory of understanding that is a decidedly collective achievement but also—and this is essential—an achievement that remains unsettled, because while potentially massive, it is irritatingly incomplete.

This lacuna in Smith, which troubles the manifestation of surprise on its way toward the more settled achievement of admiration, would escape the appreciation of William Wordsworth for reasons beyond having too much to do with the world. This time, the problem is disciplinary. In his 1815 "Essay Supplementary to Preface," Wordsworth refers to Smith as "the worse critic . . . that Scotland, a soil to which this sort of weed seems natural, has produced." It is relevant to our discussion of what Wordsworth called the "obliquities of admiration" that he is here taking issue with Smith on the belated high reputation of *Paradise Lost.* Wordsworth valued Milton's epic precisely because its lasting significance, while missed in its day, became a canonical text of English literature given "the slow process of time." Wordsworth impugns Smith in note 3 of the "Essay" for presuming that literary value is rather a more mutable affair than good poetry ought to be and that pleasurable thought is available even when the nonliterary specialist (never mind, the Scotsman) is at work.[12] By the early nineteenth century, the notion that an economist could have literary sensibility, or that anyone should care, would have been a displeasing breach of the newly codified laws of disciplinary specialization. However, in Smith's interpretive system, the frisson by which knowledge is produced can be read as having a certain historically specific permissiveness, evidenced through the problem of disciplinary change. Criticism, *contra* Wordsworth, was not yet fully subdivided from science when Smith was lecturing and writing, nor science from philosophy, nor, for that matter, philosophy from knowledge production in general.[13]

The issue of disciplinary change is largely missed by the more recent wave of scholarship on Smith, even though this work has taken us in the productive direction of recognizing the value of Smith's so-called minor texts. Such work has at least admitted the appropriateness of reading the work on the history of language, rhetoric and *belles lettres,* epistemology, and so on. For example, Neil De Marchi traces a consistency across Smith's work regarding the function of imitation, which is described by Smith in an essay dedicated to the imitative arts. De Marchi sees in Smith that "pleasure stems from ingenuity," which overcomes "a disparity in kinds by linking them in appearance."[14] What is useful here is that De Marchi is attempting, as we are, to address the problem (still a problem when his essay appeared in *The Cambridge Companion to Adam Smith* in 2006) that "Smith's essay on the arts has attracted insufficient modern commentary, and that small amount [of such work comes] mostly from scholars who view the essay as a contribution to aesthetics."[15]

De Marchi's attention to discipline is useful, even if it occurs mostly in passing. But what is missed in his reference to Smith's supposed transcendence of the problem of epistemological division is the serious difficulty that attended the way different kinds of knowledge emerged in the eighteenth century, how they proceeded over time to divide. Of paramount concern to Smith and his circle was the question of how to properly demarcate one kind of knowledge from another, if one must proceed in dividing knowledge at all. What remains insufficiently unexplored, not only by De Marchi but also by most scholars who are beginning to engage what we will highlight as a conflicted exchange between aesthetics and philosophy—especially in eighteenth-century Scotland—is the historicity of disciplinary change. What we are offering below is an account of the very Smithian—and, to repeat, paradoxical—commitment to seeking unity through division: specifically, the modern orders of institutionalized imaginative work.[16] This history is especially intriguing regarding the imagination, which became, at least ideally—with the stark exception of that anxiety-inducing pop-cultural genre called the novel, which we'll explore in Chapter 3—cordoned off from social life by the end of the eighteenth century within the more proper, perhaps ultimately less "tumultuous," category of literary study.[17]

In Smith's early work on the fine arts, as we have stated, the disorienting capacity of wonder was not securely segregated from the public applications of knowledge, where sociability and thinking are both defined according to their resistance to completion in any full measure. There is thus an occulted, one is tempted to say after Wordsworth, an "oblique" restlessness in Smith's epistemology, which in some ways defies his alleged love of system and which cannot be fully articulated within the disciplinary orders of thought he helped initiate and that determined his later institutional fate. For Smith, the unreconstructed generalist, ignorance retains a paradoxical vitality in that "we" attempt to overcome it but also accept that we cannot. This obstacle marks a historically specific set of social and epistemic relations, which as we will see in what follows, underwrites Smith's aesthetic- *qua* moral-philosophical project.

In Smith's early preoccupation with the fine arts, at a time when the strict division between this and other forms of intellectual focus was only beginning to become institutionalized, pleasure continues to reach across an experience versus reason divide. Only later, after Adam Smith and the process of confining Smith to his *economic* disciplinary home, does pleasure become codified as a specific kind of knowledge called *literary*. Let us simply settle on this point then, by way of introduction, that ignorance remains a crucial feature, and pleasure a highly complicated aspect, of how Smith constructed his interpretive system.

But in what follows we do not simply want to say that Adam Smith the critic should achieve a literary apotheosis and finally rise above the dismal sciences of politics and economic study. We do not want to construct a mid-eighteenth century *literary* Adam Smith against a more sober-minded nineteenth-century political-*economic* figure. The point of this chapter, commensurate with the larger goals of *The Other Adam Smith*, is to provide a historical argument and a new reading of Smith's more neglected texts that together interrogate the divisions between different forms of eighteenth-century knowledge. Ultimately—that is, beyond accounting for these epistemic divisions—we want to challenge a more general division that Smith, often ambivalently, initiated in order for Wordsworth to complete: a supra-division between the physical hardships of the working majority and those few literary men who had the privileges of abstract (read here, in Smith's technical parlance, "imaginative") thought. Not yet a time when new knowledge could be separated within the confines of intellectual genius, all ranges of the scriptural professions up until Smith were simultaneously active: advocates, lawyers, all the *petite noblesse*; and all would have been simply designated "writers." But Smith is on the cusp of a dramatic historical change.

Richard Terry and several others before him have called the invention of English literature in the eighteenth century a truism, and one he means to question and refine.[18] Terry's piece is worth highlighting because in his fine-tuning he mentions both the technological and sociological aspects of eighteenth-century disciplinary division.[19] First, in pointing to certain lexical evidence before the eighteenth century, Terry is able to show how the term "literature" was used to designate imaginative writing, but not exclusively. Indeed, the term "*belles lettres,*" which Smith used in his own lectures, was a cultural buzzword for eighteenth-century writers, apparently as coined by the French critic René Rapin who used the term in the title of his 1686 collected works. Think too of Cardinal Richelieu who, in founding the Académie Française in 1634, promised the encouragement specifically of *belles lettres*.

For Terry, what changes more remarkably than the gradual semantic restriction of literature to imaginative written work—like romances, novels, poetry, and drama—is the new factor of print. Written imaginative work is disseminated throughout the period on an unprecedented scale in the form of purchasable (or rentable) books, magazines, newspapers, and so on. Terry calls this focus on media a more modest claim than the larger one that there was no literature per se before the Enlightenment.[20] But is it modest, in fact? Not if we are keeping in mind that one of the key challenges of disciplinary division was to manage the problem of scale, of sorting vast multitudes of data, printed material, and new sense impressions gathered far and wide, not to mention the potentially "tumultuous" agency of increased numbers of people brought into the literary as well as the modern labor market.

It might well be asked then at what point literary study and all that it entails (leisure, abstraction, distinction from quotidian words) came to presume a fundamental opposition from physical work as such. To cite Terry once more, he calls this the point when *belles lettres* "straddled . . . division," which had "a tendency to conflate creative and critical discourses."[21] As we shall see, Smith's ability to negotiate this conflation became more difficult as the century moved on, and ironically, became more difficult based on the principles of division he helped to create. For Smith, to square a peaceable *socius* with a commercial market divided by specialization and wage labor meant that the conflicts surrounding physical work were defanged, and to the extent that sociability was properly operating, could not become antagonistic to society at large.[22] Sociability in the sense of preempting labor antagonism entailed the professionalization of letters and the disciplinary entrenchment of imaginative thought in ways Smith invented but may not have liked. That we can today even speak of a division—again, only beginning to emerge in the Anglo-Scottish Enlightenment of the mid-eighteenth century—between a knowledge-experience that Smith solved by processing ignorance quasi-aesthetically on the one hand and a meta-cognitive mode of comprehending the cause of ignorance if only "in some measure" on the other belies a crucial struggle within Smith's *corpus* that we must properly call a disciplinary one.

Stewart says in his biography ("AL") that criticism was a favorite topic of Smith's ("AL" 306). And Nicholas Phillipson cites in his intellectual biography a letter related to Smith's first university post that singles out an uncommon proficiency for "protecting ye letters and Industry of His Country, which are the two most genuine marks of patriotism."[23] But keeping with Terry's fine-tuning of the rise of literature argument, Smith himself used such words as "criticism" and its correlate "taste" without distinguishing between literature and moral philosophy more generally. Smith writes about "the science which is properly called ethics," which, "like criticism . . . does not admit of the most accurate precision, [but] is, however, both highly useful and agreeable" (*TMS* 329). At other times, without much worry over the terminological slippage, he used "criticism," like his Romantic successors, to refer to literary studies specifically.

For Smith, the ability to sort a variety of objects according to the cultivation of taste was itself an activity mixed among the disciplines that very

shortly came in his wake. In the course of working out a division of disciplinary order that he was never able to complete, we see a move in Smith's time
increasingly, but with hesitations and certain key lacunae, toward the kind
of knowledge specialization that would comprise the model of liberal learning he would help invent. Thus in what follows we will examine the gradual
move from science (or philosophy) as at one time subsuming imaginative
thinking, to an initial division between this and another, specifically, literary
kind of knowledge. Eventually, this category of knowledge emerged as more
or less exclusively equipped to handle the matters of imaginative pleasure.
The concurrent preparative arrival of a criticism, as part of an explosion of
what Clifford Siskin calls "commenting culture," also emerged at this time as
a discourse focused on the *literary* canalization of pleasure and the normative
values of taste.[24]

Another effect of this process of specialization, we want to add, is to demarcate imaginative thinking from precisely what Smith called "industry"—that
is, from bodily work. (We will cover patriotism more completely in Chapter 3.)
The keyword, which was used to settle the controversy over *British* copyright
law in the *Scottish* courts in Smith's day, was "de-corporealization": a jump from
oral to written texts in a way that legally retained what his mentor, Lord Kames,
and other court figures elaborated on as the nonmateriality of an idea.

By 1742, George Turnbull, teacher of Thomas Reid, himself the founder
of the Scottish School of Common Sense and Smith's eventual replacement
at Glasgow, could refer to taste both as a way of cultivating "affection in the
human breast" by teaching English and achieving the sociable integration of
what he called "the many hands of labor."[25] Turnbull's stance on liberal education (cited in *Observations Upon Liberal Education,* hereafter abbreviated *OU*)
was to "give them [here, children] a taste of our best poets, and make them
read aloud gracefully" (*OU* 31). Thus, the "inward work of regulating fancy" as
a print-based practice was coequal with "rectifying opinion . . . , [achieving]
order and good discipline" (*OU* 137). While Pope's notes on Homer signified for
Turnbull a true model for criticism, the ends and rules of criticism were fundamentally connected "with natural or moral philosophy" (*OU* 397).

For Hugh Blair, who effectively inherited the more refined institutional
mantle of literary critic that Smith was only beginning to develop, true criticism was a matter of the speculative application of taste, which meant valu-
ing artistic production insofar as it could be said to ascend "from particular
instances . . . to general principles."[26] Similarly, in the *Discourses on Art,*

Sir Joshua Reynolds resisted the insipid matter of gothic antinomies, here in terms of painting, in order to evoke the virtues of "the general and invariable ideas of nature."[27]

For Smith, the problems of division versus wholeness, of particularity versus universality, or indeed, of the bodily drudgery of labor (*OU* 120) versus the humanist arbitration of taste, never fully or coherently square. In the generation of Scottish intellectuals before Reynolds and Blair, that is, before mid-century, Smith makes a remarkable—and initially, more institutionally vexed—contribution to the taste debates by asserting that this middle ground of the general, in social relationships as well as certain of the fine arts, never really exists: Generality as such can only be accessed vis-à-vis the imagination; and the imagination is used with only *partial* success as we have said to fill in for ignoring that which threatens to subvert sociable ideals. By the latter decades of the eighteenth century, imagination becomes bracketed, on the one side, by the rarified but paradoxically no less universal pleasures of literary studies, enjoyed by those fit few with the good fortune to have access to it. On the other side, the hardships of the laboring majority are kept in a carefully managed relationship to an imagined collective ideal by the tasks of reading as such.[28] The most vital energies of English, in this sense, come home for us today, some 300 years after Smith. On the verge of another revolution in media technology, where the boundaries of intellectual and material work are changing once again, and arguably, where unanticipated collectivities are also asserting their presence, we are obliged to think anew about the opposition between thinking and work.

To begin this process of rethinking, the remainder of this chapter proceeds in two sections: The first section, called "Knowledge Divides," focuses on the centrality of *genus* within Adam Smith's epistemology. While in Chapter 2 we will directly examine the relation between imitation and affect in the *TMS*, this first chapter will at least introduce an account of moral sentiment that is motivated specifically by Smith's interest in the production of knowledge, philosophical and otherwise. Here then, to begin with, we are concerned with morality as an analytic. Smith's divisions of knowledge founded a new subject form, constituting a sociable but in its way also anatomized—commercially ready but highly abstracted—individual *qua* human being. J. G. A. Pocock has usefully developed this event in marking an eighteenth-century transition from civic duty to civic humanism, which moves the science of man into the domain of sociability and politesse.[29]

In our first section, we will address that transition within the more and the lesser-examined work of Smith. But beyond sociability and humanistic knowledge, we will emphasize how the pleasing wonder of ignorance proceeds through the divisions of knowledge to produce philosophical objects by trying to overcome what Smith refers to time and again as epistemological gaps. We want to show how Smith's preoccupation with the absences within knowledge production—and we read these absences as the ignorance precisely of the many hands of labor—belies an equally enigmatic problem of social incompleteness. If, as Smith remarks in an early draft of *Wealth of Nations* (hereafter "EDWN"), philosophy—as distinguished from physical work—"produces nothing," then to what effect does this "nothing" operate in Smith's theory of interpretation?[30]

For Smith, philosophy provides reconciliation between anxiety of surprise and the pleasure of wonder, arriving at a provisional point of admiration and finitude according to Jupiter's invisible hand (about which more in Chapter 4). But how should we understand this invisible force insofar as it is intrinsic to the divided, and dividing, capacities of the well-trained imagination? How to trace the eternal return of ignorance within science, the persistence of gaps across divisions that demarcate discrete knowledge processes, and the "nothing" that philosophy produces in the Enlightenment process of gaining categorical precision, while losing disciplinary privilege? Is it possible to read Smith from the position of his gaps in order to come to terms with the ways in which social and epistemological ignorance underwrites his turn to the imagination in order to overcome the anxiety produced by surprise?[31]

The second part of this chapter reloads the question of Adam Smith's divisions of knowledge by examining the unprecedented increase of printed material in the early modern period.[32] The turn here is directly toward Smith's belletristic interests, and to the revolutionary changes both in Scottish liberal education, as well as in a key decision already mentioned on British copyright law by the Scottish courts in 1774. Both are of central importance to the way print-based forms of knowledge were categorized following the union of British and Scots parliaments after 1707. The proliferation of writing at this moment is managed through aesthetic education as a matter of increasing rather than suppressing knowledge through a process of continued division. In different terms, we will have already explained the paradox of disciplinary thinking in the first section of the chapter, for example, as a project of universalizing through narrowing, controlling through growth, and expanding general education in properly homeopathic doses to the laboring masses.[33]

But, here again, the paradox of divided wholeness is especially pronounced in eighteenth-century applications of the standards of taste.[34] While the word "taste" as an indicator of politeness and civility was in use as early as the 1720s, it becomes more *narrowly* applied depending on disciplinary specialty, but also more *widely* cultivated by those invested in the emerging discipline of literary studies.[35] By 1762, Voltaire would begrudgingly concede, "today it is from Scotland that we get rules of taste in all the arts, from epic poetry to gardening."[36] Indeed, in Smith's *Lectures on Rhetoric and Belles* Lettres (*LRBL*), in Lord Kames's newly specialized work *Elements of Criticism* (hereafter *EC*), and in others—like Hume, Oxford's Reverend Knox, and George Turnbull in his *Observations Upon Liberal Education*—we see the divisions of knowledge play out commonly as a problem of disciplinary specialization, that is, a problem of dividing the manifold in the interest of achieving imaginary wholeness.[37]

Without ignoring the differences between these philosophers, we can say that Smith, Kames, Hume, Knox, Turnbull, and others we will not list are significant for their proximity to a decidedly Scottish revolution in liberal learning and the circulation of writing from about the mid-eighteenth century on. As such, they faced a modern problem of categorizing multiplicity, of variously skirting the problem of (not least, Scottish) particularity at both the social and the epistemic levels. This skirting, we argue, occurred through emergent disciplinary practices that mobilized aesthetic appreciation for the many and by the few.

At this historical moment, the vulgar, or common (read "the laboring") subject—the mass of people, whose vacant hours of leisure might be troubled or not by the pleasant task of imaginative reading—enters the scene of writing for the first time in history as a force for the moderate literati to reckon with North of the Tweed.[38] The lowest ranks encountered imaginative knowledge in a way that was tantamount, at least potentially, to overturning the whole philosophico-social arrangement. This arrangement was itself based on ranking the manifold, specifically along the lines of thinking and work. Thus, as we will show, there are several levels of abstraction at work here: First, there is the abstraction of the object-anomaly that turns surprise through wonder into admiration; second, there is the abstraction of thinking from labor; and finally, there is the abstraction that moves imaginative thought into the eventually socially transcendent discipline of literature.

One provocative history of English literature is that it made its institutional debut in Great Britain only after the British (and the Scottish landed classes) made inroads in India following the renewal of the East India Company's charter in 1813.[39] Such an argument is provocative because it provides a disciplinary history that locates literature's origins at the margins of empire, reversing the traditional placement of metropolitan national identity over colonial other. But this later geopolitical division is already worked out in the context of a colonial process previously staged by the colonized themselves within a newly unified Great Britain.[40] Englishness emerged as a fringe concept both in its epistemic and national dimensions, almost a hundred years before the apex of the UK's colonial conquests. And literary study, the penultimate new disciplinary specialty with universal purpose, finds entry from a point that was neither totally within nor totally outside Great Britain proper.

Again, we will discuss the geopolitical implications of Englishness as such in Chapter 3. For now it must simply be noted that English, in the sense of a literary discipline, makes its historical debut by trying to achieve a reconciliation between margin and center, between particularity and generality, or if you like, between individuality and society. In this sense, the twin paradoxes of divided wholeness—one epistemic and the other national—rallies in the work of Smith and his cohort around the notion of imaginative writing now delimited within a literary field.[41]

Criticism brings to the fore the question of writing as a socially embedded and distinctively imaginative medium that is doubly located, at once more generalized and made more particular: The masses, vulgar, common, lower ranks, great mob of mankind, multitudes, the majority of men, and so on must themselves be treated according to disciplinary techniques that also sort knowledge in general into an arrangement of specific disciplinary categories. The standards of taste worked sometimes successfully and sometimes not to produce a more peaceable collective subject—in some instances, working to ward off what the Oxford Fellow Knox in his *Essays, Moral and Literary* (hereafter *EML*) simply called "sedition . . . [and] civil war."[42] Thus we will end this chapter by discussing the way in which writing becomes a techno-economic node for bringing individuality, imagination, and sociability together such that popular contention is immunized against the volatile paradox of divided wholeness. To what effect does the so-called great mob of mankind come to letters insofar as letters also present the problem of sorting its own *greatness* in the double sense of achieving collectivity and assigning good taste? How does ignorance require the cultivation of philosophy; or better, how does philosophy, as it divides into greater forms of imaginative specialization, remain divided by the gaps it has historically concealed?

Knowledge Divides

To all such mighty conquerors [as Caesar or Alexander] the great mob of
mankind are naturally disposed to look up with a wondering, though, no doubt,
with a very weak and foolish admiration. By this admiration, however, they
are taught to acquiesce with less reluctance under that government which an
irresistible force imposes upon them.

Adam Smith (*TMS* 253)

In this digression within Smith's *TMS*, which moves from the technical operations of moral sympathy to the governability of the "great mob of mankind,"
the word "admiration" is striking. For it is here, within a theory of sociability
predicated on what Smith crucially refers to as impartiality and self-command
(*TMS* 15, 34) that a link emerges between Smith's social and his epistemic concerns. The entire system hinges on a transformation of the mob into the unitary *philosopheme* of man. This transformation is at once transcendental and
marked by appropriate divisions through Smith's insistence on intersubjective
dimensions of moral sympathy that somehow also maintains the difference
between subjects.

As the passage suggests, Smith is by no means partial to the conqueror's
tyrannical threat of irresistible force. The stadial theory of historical development that is laid out in Smith's *Lectures on Jurisprudence* (*LJ*) reinforces the endorsement of humanist virtue, as intimated here. That said, the word "however"
before the phrase "acquiesce with less reluctance" is pivotal. It reveals Smith's interest in a closer proximity between the mob and government that changes the
matter of resistance from one strictly of might into a fully interiorized zone of
conflict resolution where the words "wonder" and "admiration" now apply. The
mob wonders *upward* in its earlier historical rendition, we could say, underscoring a passing hierarchical relation that disallows the form of morally based
individuality that would be apposite to Smith's endorsement of the free market.
But what Smith is getting at by negative example is a way for the mob to better
wonder *inward*. This arrangement is horizontal, associational, divided, and fully
individuated, but in its way universal as well. And while "foolish[ness]" would
appear a necessary step in the development of ancient into modern society, the
movement from wonder to admiration belies a connection to acquiescence that
Smith will retain and develop toward further efficiency.

The word "admiration" provides a good sense of how that development is
detailed. It signals a manner of imaginative cognition that allows Smith to offer
reciprocity and individuation so as to cover the core paradox of achieving uni-

versality through division. Consider moral sentiment at the level of object relations in the *TMS*:

> [W]hen they [the sentiments of our companion] not only coincide with our own, but lead and direct our own; when in forming them he appears to have attended to many things which we overlooked, and to have adjusted them to all the various circumstances of their objects; we not only approve of them, but wonder and are surprised at their uncommon and unexpected acuteness and comprehensiveness, and he appears to deserve a very high degree of admiration and applause. (*TMS* 20)

It is precisely that which is overlooked that triggers the sorting of variation into the sense of a universally representable object. This object is representable insofar as it elicits the unified collective response of admiration. The movement through wonder to a form of comprehensiveness adjoins the knowing companion to an ignorant friend.

And here the coincidence of their admiration remains uncommon while—to the extent that the friend's knowledge is of what we overlook—providing a basis for Smith's imagined sense of communal reciprocity. What we overlook is not known, or not exactly, by the ignorant companion, but sentiment mediates an affective transfer at the level of what many people can applaud. Indeed, the potentially anarchic nature of the senses, the inherent slipperiness of an object's status according to the mob's fleeting comprehension of the multiple circumstances of meaning, renders the modern *socius* dependent not only upon the justness of taste but also, more troublingly, upon "fortune's . . . influence over the moral sentiments of mankind" (*TMS* 252). If the interpretive system is working effectively, change is directed by a coincidental attachment to previous categories of objects. These objects remain praiseworthy, or ought to, even if certain adjustments are needed. But "as she [fortune] is either favorable or adverse, [she] can render the same character the object either of general love and admiration, or of universal hatred and contempt" (*TMS* 252–253).

And again, from a letter of 1759 (hereafter *Correspondence*), while "universal approbation is altogether *unattainable*" (emphasis ours), we can in the face of this unattainable universality seek what Smith calls certain functional indifference: "a man in general, and impartial spectator [can] consider our conduct with the same indifference with which we regard that of other people." Admiration is predicated on a way of working through that which cannot be known and letting it remain so, unless chance dictates otherwise: If an object cannot be generalized, it must either be rendered unto ignorance or disciplines must change. For Smith this will toward categorization is primary, and, as we shall see, so are the gaps that it leaves.

The indifference that Smith refers to above does not of course mean ignoring your neighbor. It means attending to her in a careful and particular way. Indifference here has both a technical sense (as in sameness: the care not to retain any parts) and a practical sense (as in ignorance: the letting go of bad fortune, even when it is grossly unfair). In an essay from *Essays on Philosophical Subjects* on the external senses, written roughly at the same time as the first edition of the *TMS* in 1759, Smith offers the term "ascribe" to elaborate on the stakes of imagining mankind as both divided and whole.[43] In speaking of how small a chair may look at a distance as opposed to being close, he writes in "Of the External Senses" (hereafter "ES"): "We know that the tangible object which they [the chairs] represent remains always the same, [so] we ascribe them to a sameness which belongs altogether to it."[44] The "it" in question is the general category of the chair, which we must begin with before sight, and which prohibits rather than promotes the object's ascription to sameness. Here Smith adjusts Dr. Berkeley's *New Theory of Vision* to remark, "objects of sight . . . constitute a sort of language" ("ES" 156). And he proceeds along a path of Saussurian semiotics more than two centuries *avant la lettre* by noting: "As is common in language, the words or sounds bear no resemblance to the things which they denote, so in this other language [of sight] the visible objects bear no resemblance to the tangible object they represent" ("ES" 156); and, "the characters themselves [of the alphabet] are altogether arbitrary" ("ES" 157).

We shall discuss Smith's extended foray into sociolinguistics further below. For now, simply note that Smith gives an additional set of terms within his system of philosophical investigation that adjoins the analytics of sameness not to tangibility, which would inhibit the categorical imperative, but to an internal act of abstraction that (a) begins from the general; (b) sorts particulars into an imaginary form of representation within a given generality; and (c) disregards the rest as singular, infinite variety, arbitrariness, or what we could simply call, after Smith himself, an inassimilable and conflicted condition of the so-called real: "Though I am apt to *fancy* that all the chairs and tables . . . appear to my eye always the same . . . their appearance in *reality* is continually varying" (emphasis ours, "ES" 155).

Now it is important to point out that Smith is not proposing a positivist notion of reality within which an object's pure evidentiary status can simply be recited and recalled without change.[45] Fortune, as we have seen, as much as historical specificity, is always in effect and thus prohibits immutable value and limits whatever guarantee of epistemic and social equilibrium we might hope to imagine. The "mob," recall, is Smith's dangerous social analogue for the changeability of form at the epistemic level. Smith's reality, as he uses the term here and in other places we shall mark, is entirely perspectival, even while that perspective is necessarily rendered intangible.

Note that fancy goes to work, and ignorance becomes active, when perspective retains a form of particularity such that all chairs are perceived as essentially different, indeed singular, depending "not only on variation and distance . . . but according to the insensible variation in the attitude of my body. . . . Perspective varies according to all, even the smallest of . . . variations" ("ES" 155); and finally, "no corporeal substance is ever exactly the same, either in whole or in any assignable part, during two successive moments, but by perpetual addition of new parts, as well as loss of old ones, is in continual flux and succession" ("ES" 121). To reduce this citation to its essentials, the corporeal is surprise, which is ignorance, which is the great body of working women and men. Smith's reality, or better put, his reference to corporeality, means addressing change as akin to the painful feeling of interruption: the relation between the subject and the movement of an un-representable all-ness, call it singularity but also a problem of incalculable scale, that Smith repeatedly connects to the word "real."

To continue from the essay: "The things out of which all particular objects seem to be comprised are the stuff of matter, and the form of specific Essence, which determines them to be this or that class of things" ("ES" 125–126). We see an allusion to totality approachable as essence. But again, we see totality here not as unattainable universality this time but as mass of matter wherein every conceivable particularity exists in the wonderfully imprecise (because a-categorical) mass of what Smith simply calls "stuff." Reality must be ascribed to the sameness that it does not have. And this happens according to a special "aptitude for signifying" ("ES" 158).

Fanciful ascription on this order works not (or not yet, anyway) according to a simple real versus fanciful division but by encouraging alternative relations that are socially agreeable if not also imagined. We could say then that a corporeal perspective is precisely that which my mind shall not know. More precisely, a cultivated *in*-sensibility to the reality of whatever alternative bodily orders might exist is licensed by Smith according to the generalities of form that sensibility projects without thinking.

It is here that Smith connects the affective charge of ignorance, of admiration against the surprise of whatever composite singularity (again, read here "the so-called real"), to the matter of public security that Smith mentions in other contexts. Again recalling fortune, Smith writes, "this great disorder in our moral sentiments is by no means . . . without its utility" (*TMS* 253). "By this admiration of success we are taught to submit more easily to those superiors, whom the course of human affairs may assign to us" (*TMS* 253). In the sentence preceding this one, the word "may" is connected to the phrase "necessary for establishing the distinction of ranks" (*TMS* 253). The conditional word "may" takes the problem of rank out of any assessable logic and renders to chance the unknowable arrangements of individuation, the phantasmatic (or arbitrary) value of an object, and the invisible processes of connectedness-through-division upon which a peaceable society depends.

Note especially in this cluster of quotes the essential disorder subtending the divisions of rank. There is slippage here between surprise and admiration that provides the soft utility for disorder in *order* to get around the paradox of divided universality. Order stays together invisibly, and concealed connectedness is available to affective registers that ought eventually be reduced to applause: surprise, rectified by admiration. Comprehension is available as displaced reality as real objects of value are overcome by fortune and detached from whatever references lay beyond the friendly brotherhood of man. Smith is not prone to the fixity of cultural value, as we have said, which gives his system of division its apparent flexibility and strength: "discordant opinions . . . prevail in different ages and nations [according to] custom and fashion" (*TMS* 194). And the acceptability of discord on this order is entirely consistent with Smith's notion of object adequation. As he offers in a repetition of a standard formula of both Locke and Hume: "When two objects have frequently been seen together, the imagination acquires a habit of passing easily from the one to the other" (*TMS* 194).

This is to say that disorder between superiors and inferiors is relegated to—and *regulated* by—a sentimental response that is necessarily placed beyond real understanding per se. We ought to take careful note when deciding—or of having the good or bad luck—to disrupt habitualized modes of thought because to do so can produce academic as well as social tumults. The popular reputation Hume had as a nonbeliever, which brought an anxious James Boswell to Hume's deathbed "like a man in sudden danger seeking his defensive arms" in 1776, serves as a case in point.[46] (Samuel Johnson thought Hume was lying about facing death with such good cheer without God.) The careful acknowledgement of our habits of belief, which variously irritated Hume and shored him up, stood in for the "stuff" of social coherence. In Smith's hands, habit appears in the polite codes of impartial spectatorship as an organic indication that we have a sense of self sufficiently restrained to make the social contract to begin with. "Under the boisterous and stormy sky of war and faction," Smith writes in an appropriately martial register, "[under] public tumult and confusion, a sturdy severity of self-command prospers the most, and can be the most successfully cultivated" (*TMS* 153).

In Chapter 2 we will mine the *TMS* and other sources for Smith's connection to Stoic self-command as it relates to the suffering of the unfortunate masses. For now, let us continue with a different though related question: How is self-command on the order Smith requires successfully cultivated, and to what end does the practice of restrained subjectivity work in the context of his philosophy of knowledge?

"Against public tumult," Smith remarks earlier in the *TMS*,

> The patriot, who lays down his life for the safety . . . of this society, appears to act with the most exact propriety. He appears to view himself in the light in which the impartial spectator naturally and necessarily views him, as but one of the multitude . . . bound at all times to sacrifice and devote himself to the safety . . . of the greater number. . . . His conduct, therefore, excites . . . our highest wonder and admiration. (*TMS* 228)

The patriot is wonderful because while he is *not* like us, paradoxically, he engages in a process of self-sacrifice, and even death, as model behavior in the interest of public security. On the grounds of admiration, Smith sorts the problem of multiplicity once again—the volatility of the greater number—by having the mob command itself. Smith flips the agency of the many—"we are but one of the multitude"—by modeling heroic self-effacement in the name of the patriot who dies on behalf of the formal arrangement he calls human affairs. Under the transcendental heading of the human, the greater part of men may find themselves under the submission of rank. Thus the effect of patriotic self-detachment is to remove the possibility for imagining collectivity anywhere outside the ranks as they exist between us and a set of superiors for whom the multitude might rightly die. (We should allude here to our fourth and final chapter on what we call Smith's *necro-economics*, which greatly expands the centrality of death in reference to Smith's system of wealth distribution.)

Smith grants a wonderful uniqueness to the patriot that is so severe in its self-command that the patriot literally self-effaces. Moreover, it is only in the no-man's land of the afterlife that real (in Smith's sense of real, that is, as impossible) equality can be imagined. As we have seen before:

> Our happiness in this life is . . . dependent upon the humble hope and expectation of a life to come: . . . That there is a world to come [marks a place] where exact justice will be done to every man, where every man will be ranked with those who, in the moral and intellectual qualities, are really his equals. (*TMS* 132)

The patriot is self-regulated to the point of literal removal (by dying) so as to secure society against the sorts of public tumult that might mobilize collectivity according to the exact justice and real equality (again, Smith's phrases) that identity must disregard.

In an early draft of *Wealth* ("EDWN"), Smith is clear:

> [W]ith regard to the produce of the larger numbers of a great society there is never any such thing as a fair and equal division. . . . [In a] society of an hundred thousand families, there will perhaps be one hundred who do not labour at all . . . [,] who . . . either by violence or by the more orderly oppression of law, employ a greater part of the labour of society than any other ten thousand in it. ("EDWN" 565)

While Smith believed in the principle of high wages, as far as real equality is concerned, he also observes, "those who labour most get the least" ("EDWN" 564). Indeed, impartiality—the achievement of defining oneself and plotting one's action according to an abstract and imaginatively transcendent notion of generality—means that the orderly suppression of law is at work, we could say, at the level of thinking itself. Un-equal division, or better, the acceptance of un-real equalities, is the problem that impartiality is designed to dissolve in a realm outside knowledge (because, like God and death, unknown to living morals). Indeed, Smith's phrase "generality of mankind" is nothing if not ambivalently placed within a category of universal equality, never really supposed to be there.[47]

The real in question next to equality is phantasmatic in Smith: Impartiality is proposed "notwithstanding . . . great inequalities of property" ("EDWN" 564, 566). By shorthand, and according to his terms, we may say that reality is a matter of what goes missing in a commercialized ethical system, at least insofar as equality is ruled out of existence in the name of public peace. The patriot, who must be modeled in his singularity, views himself under the universalizing eyes of an (also nonexistent) impartial spectator. We in turn wonder inward according to the same spectatorial logic. This multi-leveled abstraction of self-surveillance underscores the paradox of human generality that is, in point of fact, divided by rank, un-equal and un-real, but in its imaginary state pretending toward a harmony of commercial and, equally, affective exchange.

Thus the nature of reciprocity as outlined in the *TMS* is based on a dynamic of mutual watching in a highly individuated—but nontransparent—zone of affective transference. The inequities implicit to Smith's investment in submission emerges through the wonder of ignorance, bridged by wonder, and finally overcome by an imagined cord of mutuality writ as admiration. "For every rich man, there must be at least five hundred poor, and the affluence of the few supposes the indigence of the many" (*Wealth* 177) Smith would write almost two decades after the *TMS*. But the inherent divisions between rich and poor are for Smith always already resolved through socially responsible self-identification. Such conflict is short-circuited within an arena of civil society where—according to Smith's Lockean rule[48]—one also finds "the security of property . . . [and] the defense of the rich against the poor" (*Wealth* 181).

The boundaries of morality for Smith are contained within a form of capitalist sociability maintained by a certain way of mediating whatever form of multiplicity (be it social or epistemological) meets the impartial and therefore peaceable eye. As is evident in Book II, Chapter 3 of *Wealth* (167ff.), which echoes his blueprint of moral sentiment in the earlier treatise of 1759, partial behavior on either side of class division is reduced to the supra-materialist realm of character, conduct, and so-called general admiration (*TMS* 250). It is also worth noting, and we will make more of this later on, that use of the word "class" to signal a system of divided yet generalized individuals gains historical traction—*against* the multitude of indigence—at precisely this time.

To step away from Smith momentarily for the sake of lexical clarity, in 1705 Defoe remarks, "the dearness of wages forms our people into more Classes than the nations could show."[49] But in offering a sevenfold set of divisions and highlighting the excess of this division beyond national coherence, this notion of class conflict could hardly be reduced to the bifurcated version of class that Malthus would offer in 1798 as "society divided in to a class of proprietors and a class of laborers."[50] Fielding's Jonathan Wild remarks in 1743, "mankind are . . . properly to be considered under two grand divisions, those that use their own hands, and those who employ the hands of others."[51] The key phrase here is "to be."

Though free trade policies were put in place by William Pitt the Younger—a self-proclaimed Smith disciple—between 1784 and 1794, the industrial revolution in Scotland is typically dated as coming to fruition in the first third of the nineteenth century.[52] Commercial society was not fully anticipated by Smith as a bifurcated transformation along class lines in the 1760s and 70s, nor was it in the earlier decades of the *TMS* and *Lectures on Jurisprudence*.[53] Between Malthus and Defoe, that is, around the middle part of the eighteenth century, the reconciliation of self-evident class struggle was less a matter of dualistically conceivable social opposition, which comes later, than of classificatory speculation against the faction, sedition, or (better) multiplicity, which comes before.[54]

The very conception of class begins as a matter of how to make knowledge before it subsumes labor production. And this twin development happens at a time when certain key divisions between labor and thought, as much as divisions within thinking, were beginning to achieve their modern forms.[55] The term "class" was as likely to refer to the Methodist's system for studying the Bible, or the class system of the classroom, than it was more exclusively later to denote the greater part of laboring women and men.[56] This relation between the *greatness* of the "greater part of mankind" and the desire for classification in its own right is precisely where we must locate Adam Smith. In a society necessarily un-equal and un-real, the capitalist spectator finds experiential correspondence within civil society as fellow feeling (*TMS* 10). Individuals are thus able to correspond by way of self-interest, as much as self-command, within and—crucially—across the distinction of ranks. Social organization depends in this sense upon the individual's capacity for virtue and propriety, which in turn makes social divisions peaceable.[57] The enigmatic point is that this capacity for reconciling division occurs *non*-repressively through increasing not diminishing further forms of distinction. For Smith, social concord is dependent upon sorting the manifold rather than repressing self-evident forms of oppositional disequilibrium, which could only become apparent once the sorting had already been done.[58]

We have gone far enough in exploring the way in which moral sympathy is immanent to the arrangement of social organization as both divided and general in Smithian terms. But before leaving off this issue, to be picked up again in Chapter 2, we should note one other feature of the *TMS* that is important to our concern with Smith's divisions of knowledge. We should emphasize once more the centrality within Smith's epistemology of imagination. The imagination, as we have been suggesting, is Smith's technical term for the means by which surprise is tempered by admiration. It is furthermore a socially embedded enterprise connected as much to the peaceable divisions of social rank as to division of knowable objects in the face of the incalculably massive array of objects and mixed-objects that Smith aptly termed "stuff." And as we have also argued, both threads of his discourse—the social and the epistemic—emanate from the suitably *de*-corporealized register of ignorance.

Let us concede then that Adam Smith's theory of moral sympathy is more complex than it appears on first encounter. "We suppose ourselves the spectators of our own behavior," he writes, "and endeavor to imagine what effect it would, in this light, produce upon us. This is the only looking-glass by which we can, in some measure, with the eyes of other people, scrutinize the propriety of our own conduct" (*TMS* 16). The primary feature of the moral looking glass is not simply that it proposes to be circular but that: (a) it requires supposition— we imagine an invisible third person, an impartial judge (*TMS* 135) so as to render ourselves "the proper objects of . . . approbation" (*TMS* 308); and (b) we can neither really commune with the other, nor need we dwell on our own station in relation to the greater (i.e., laboring) part of mankind. Recall, "they [our senses] never can carry us beyond our own person, and it is by the imagination only that we can form any conception of what are his sensations" (*TMS* 9).

The keyword, of course, remains imagination: "the creation of an imaginative self-projection into an outsider whose standards and responses we reconstruct by sympathy" (*LRBL* 10). In Smith's humanist formula, the expression of outward sympathetic feeling is only the initial step in an infinite spectatorial chain. The sympathizing subject not only measures and corresponds his own experience with the object of his gaze, but also internalizes this correspondence such that the first subject/object relation is reproduced as the secondary propriety of voluntary self-restraint. "A prison is certainly more useful to society than a palace" (*TMS* 30), Smith would remark in anticipation of Bentham's panopticon. But the disciplinary procedures spelled out by Foucault are in Smith's earlier example rather more efficient, softer in appearance but no less material in effect, than the bricks and mortar of early modern punishment.[59]

For Smith, the propriety implicit in his circular moral gaze is at work by epistemological necessity, as we shall see, and indeed, at the level of language itself. Beyond the spectators of his teacher Francis Hutcheson, or Smith's friend David Hume, both of whom gave prominence in their ethical theories to sympathetic experience, Smith's morality emphasizes the normative (because reasoned) but also implicitly unsettled (because affective) nature of communicative exchange. The key move in the *TMS* links the imagined reconciliation of so-called real nonequivalence (the basis for self-command within rank) with good taste (the basis for propriety of conversation within polite or learned society). The sympathetic feelings of an impartial spectator depend upon being well informed if not also forewarned (*TMS* 49).

A communicative ethic such as the one Smith prescribes, which emerges concurrent to the market at its normative core, operates somewhat differently than Jürgen Habermas's otherwise similar and well-known formulation of the Enlightenment public sphere.[60] Like Habermas, Smith's spectator may be traced to the polite conversation of imaginatively presumed equals characteristic of the early eighteenth-century coffeehouse. Indeed, Smith's moral spectator can be traced directly to Joseph Addison's journal by that very name.[61] And the coffeehouse culture of his intellectual circles, like the Select Society and his own Poker Club, each with more than eighty members, were unusually vibrant in Smith's Glasgow and Edinburgh.[62]

But in the place of Habermas's disinterested rational critical debate, Smith offers room for the more affective, and in a Humean sense, conflict-ridden dimensions of feeling put to rest, *pace* Hume, by the ideals of admiration. The term "admiration" allows for a redoubled correspondence implicit in the adherence to this or that disciplinary norm. Indeed, we must imagine ourselves precisely out of whatever local and specific context of difference we may naturally find ourselves in:

> We can never survey our own sentiments and motives . . . unless we remove ourselves . . . from our own natural station, and endeavor to view them as at a certain distance from us. But we can do this in no other way than by endeavoring to view them with the eyes of other people, or as other people are likely to view them. (*TMS* 110)

Thus runs Smith's internalized spectatorial doublet: First, correspondence is imaginatively calibrated to take place between the spectator and his object; and second, such correspondence is to take place in the objectification of the looking-subject as, in turn, appropriate in the eyes of an impartial (though nonexistent) third-party witness. This denotes a certain self-imposed pacification of whatever local reality exists. "By finding a vast variety of instances that one tenor of conduct constantly displeases the mind . . . we form general rules of morality" (*TMS* 320). "Generality" is the template by which too much vastness and variety is relegated to a zone of ignorance also called the real. General rules mark the individual's membership within the faux totality of mankind—ironically, a vantage point from which mass suffering finds an appropriately impartial distance from whatever collective response might upset a market-based social ideal.

The imagination then is an inexact practice in Smith, and it is this inexactness that allows us not only sufficient distance between subject and object but also the dream of sustaining—at least until chance awakens us—a peaceable yet unequal *socius* of individuals. "By the imagination we place ourselves in his [the sufferer's] situation; we conceive ourselves enduring all the same torments . . . and become in some measure the same person with him" (*TMS* 9). Conception, as imaginative abstraction, exists, as we have noted before, only in some measure. And it is a necessarily approximate relation, one that we must learn to make a habit (a Humean term) and one that keeps the (laboring) majority and (wealthy) minority from becoming too close. Indeed, the sufferer is repeatedly counseled in Smith, another feature of his ethics that we take up in Chapter 2, against excessive grief. Through the abstraction of impartiality, the sufferer must keep an internal warden in mind and learn to "bring down his emotions to complete harmony and concord with those of the spectator" (*TMS* 45). The sufferer must flatten excessive complaint; reduce it to harmony, Smith cautions. Our sympathies are thus never really in unison.

But unison is precisely *not* the point, rather a certain individuated correspondence through division is. We must be masters of ourselves and "bring down our passion to [a] pitch of [socially responsible] tranquility" (*TMS* 23). A properly individuated subject, sufficiently sturdied against misfortune (others' and our own) by impartial self-command, works to create an imagined social whole. Generality of this sort is predicated less on a unity with the suffering masses than with the concord and harmony of society, which is divided but nonetheless harmonious in its way (*TMS* 22). That for Smith real unity is impossible in an admittedly unequal *socius* belies the ultimate vacuity of the key terms "mankind" and "human affairs." This empty—and because empty, secure—generality of being circumscribes the "painful industry" of the inferior ranks of people when individuality is writ as impartial self-command (*TMS* 201). In an important sense, mankind is founded on never actually becoming anything at all beyond imagination. Totality rests on what it disallows, that is, on what the individual must flatten, reduce, bring down, conceal, or simply smother (all Smith's terms), in the interest of infinite deferral. Mankind is predicated on an idealized distance to suffering, as individuality insures humane intra-division and, at best, a moderately measured expression of sympathetic response.

Here mankind is barred from the reality of suffering beyond a certain measure; or better, mankind establishes an empty universal category whose purpose is to keep inequity on sufficiently individuated grounds. The ideals of the impartial spectator—Smith's ethical commitment, on the one hand, to expansiveness and increase, and, on the other, to individuation and division—allows us to expand on the essential role that *genus* plays in Smith's epistemology. In the *TMS*, mankind, for which Smith here substitutes human society, necessarily emerges in a philosophical light. Indeed, philosophy's propensity toward dividing objects into *kind* is the epistemological analogue to man, just as mankind is essentially partitioned by the peaceable amalgamation of so many self-monitored and individuated subjects:

> Human society, when we contemplate it in a certain abstract and philosophical light, appears like a great, an immense machine, whose regular and harmonious movements produce a thousand agreeable effects. As in any other beautiful and noble machine that was the production of human art, whatever tended to render its movements more smooth and easy, would derive a beauty from this effect, and, on the contrary, whatever tended to obstruct them would displease upon that account: so virtue . . . [,] the fine polish to the wheels of society, necessarily pleases; while vice, like the vile rust, which makes them jar and grate upon one another, is as necessarily offensive. (*TMS* 316)

There is a great deal to lift from this passage. Note first that human society is itself the effect and not the origin of philosophical abstraction. Therefore, the purpose of thought as a "noble" art is to produce regular and yet increasingly diffuse knowledge-effects, all toward consensus where the tendency is otherwise. When we keep in mind that this manner of increase, regularized by an attendance to beauty and pleasure (recall: admiration), we see that competing modes of collectivity (as, alternatively, "tumult") can also emerge. It is wrong to suggest that Smith simply represses the greater part of men from excessively exhibiting their suffering. His system is more efficient than that. The production of agreement vis-à-vis pleasure and the imagination operates in the first instance as a modality of thought that has its own logic of increase. In that sense, harmony occurs—artificially, as through a human-made "machine"—which has its own way of canalizing growth. We could say that Smith's philosophical light emanates from a kind of perverse generosity to include even the most marginal of sufferers (about this perversity there is more below).

It is essential to point out that, in Smith's own terms, while the human

makes the machine, the manufacturing of the human is itself a rather more occulted process. This is because a manufacturing of this order is designed to render to ignorance whatever irregular tendencies or particularities of labor might
remain in the making. The keyword "virtue" is mentioned here precisely as an
effect of rendering to ignorance the paradoxically specific nature of universal
design.[63] Virtue assures sociability on the grounds that its function is to keep
the wheels of humanity operating without obstruction. But vice always threatens to jar or rupture harmony, which is a cursed (i.e., "vile") if also necessary
event as inescapable as rust on steel. Thus we should not understate Smith's
point: that there is a constant need to secure ourselves against the jarring and
grating that is immanent to the activity of thinking. To activate philosophy is
to polish and be polished, which, as we shall see, gains for the philosopher the
dignity of good taste instead of the hardship of labor.

Thus we might say that philosophy, as Smith develops it in the *TMS*, is the art
of *not* knowing well, and by *not* knowing well, we mean knowing what there is *not*
to know, what remains inaccessible to knowledge. This *not* knowing, because it
begins and ends with being agreeable, ensures a certain social regularity between
the ranks, a proper rhythm between obstructing and smoothing out, that reduces
socio-epistemic irregularity into a properly measured new *genus* or species. Indeed, "the reasonings of philosophy . . . can never break down the necessary connection [of] Nature" (*TMS* 283). The best we have are the knowledge machines,
technologies for manufacturing smoothness, in spite of rust—techniques that are
always turned on and whose real outcomes are in the end rendered to chance:
"whatever fortune can befall me . . . [,] [r]iches or poverty, pleasure or pain, health
or sickness, all is alike" (*TMS* 276). It is the propensity of philosophy to make likenesses where there are none and to polish the inequivalences of division away.
"Whether we are to be drowned," Smith writes, "or come to a harbor, is the business of Jupiter, not mine. I leave it entirely to his determination . . . [I] receive
whatever comes with equal indifference and security" (*TMS* 277).

In a further example of philosophical abstraction, marking here another
link between wisdom and the un-real, he continues:

> The wise man . . . enters . . . into the sentiments of . . . divine Being, and considers
> himself as an atom, a particle, of an immense and infinite system, which must and
> ought to be disposed of, according to the conveniency of the whole. (*TMS* 276)

What we want to emphasize here is what this convenience of the whole leaves
out philosophical understanding. The problems that Smith returns to time and

again of infinity, opposition, variety, variation, vastness, disorderly assemblage, unconnected objects, invisibility, rust, the monstrous, and, we should not hesitate to add, the painful spectacle of poverty—in short, the obstruction of the manifold and particular—are sorted by philosophical abstraction into proper categorical division. We could say following Smith then that the very notion of wholeness contains within itself not just the transcendence of particularity but also its pacification.

Smith writes affirmatively of a

> reverential submission to . . . that benevolent wisdom [read "Jupiter," "invisibility," "God," "providence"] which directs all the events of human life, and which . . . would never have suffered . . . misfortunes to happen, had they not been indispensably necessary for the good of the whole. (*TMS* 292)

In his usual preoccupation with the limits of human understanding, Smith willingly concedes, "it is impossible . . . to express all the variations which each sentiment either does or ought to undergo, according to every possible variation of circumstances. They are endless, and language wants names to mark them by" (*TMS* 328).

We will detail the connection between "sentiment" and Spinozist themes of infinity in the next chapter. For now, note that in raising the stakes of object adequation, Smith writes in an essay on ancient physics, "objects . . . by the variety of their species . . . are apt to embarrass and perplex the mind."[64] As we have seen above, Smith encourages the expansiveness of expression at least insofar as it allows maximal social assimilation. This passage is another example of the need to produce a technique of self-expression that is automatic—both habitual and subject to carefully circumscribed forms of change—rather than prescriptive in its application to social harmony.

Smith's analytics of embarrassment, where sociophilosophical anomaly always wants a name, commands the imperative to divide variation into more and less proper affective occasions:

> [W]hatever variations any particular emotion may undergo, it still preserves the general features which distinguish it to be an emotion of such a kind, and these general features are always more striking and remarkable than any variation which it may undergo in particular cases. (*TMS* 324)

It is not the emotion itself that is agreeable in its particularity, be it anger, which is the example Smith uses, or the spectacle of suffering, or "the painful industry" of "the inferior ranks," but the proper measurement of emotion and its placement, its de-*particularization*, into generalizable and connected variations of kind.

Philosophy functions like a divining rod in Smith to select features among the infinite grains of meaning in and around a given object, which is itself only given vis-à-vis the categorical imperative with which one begins. And these objective features are to an extent preprogrammed to suit an imaginary sense of wholeness, which suits above all the historical myth that the market economy is at least tacitly acceptable while generating untold (if not untellable) violence and despair. "In each species of creatures," Smith writes, "what is most beautiful bears the strongest characters of the general fabric of the species, and has the strongest resemblance to the greater part of the individuals with which it is classed. Monsters . . . are always most singular and odd" (*TMS* 198). We see here what are by now familiar features of Smith's interpretive system: his reliance on beauty to inspire admiration as elemental to moral sympathy's philosophical task. And we can now underscore the paradoxical centrality of division, between and within species, as a way to imagine generality, connected despite inequality, in a way that shows social propriety while keeping the reality of suffering more or less at bay. We need now to better surmise the necessity in Smith of treating connectedness less as an object of philosophical understanding and more as an unknowable arrangement that we make smooth through abstract categorical reception.

We said above that *genus* functions like a divining rod in Smith's system of knowledge, and this was not meant at all lightly (see ahead to Chapter 4 on Smith's indebtedness to the agency of providence in *Wealth*). From the 1759 letter we quoted above, Smith writes, "the loudest acclamations of mankind appear but as the noise of ignorance and folly. . . . [But] the inmate of the breast [the impartial spectator], this abstract man, is the representative of mankind and substitute of the Deity" (*Correspondence* 56). We see a similar pattern here from before: From the ignorance of particularity we draw lines of division that are then bridged by abstraction so as to belong to the vacuous generality of mankind. And we should remark in accordance with the rule of invisibility that mankind is dubbed here a matter not for contemplation but, like the deity, for conflict resolution through heightened affective connection given what amounts to faith. For Smith, Jupiter's famous invisible hand ultimately "direct[s] . . . the spectacle of human life" (*TMS* 59). If there is an act of representation involved, surely this is an act that should be indifferent to what cannot be represented, even though this technique of ignorance may in some way show traces of what Smith will call "gaps."

Smith's definition of exchange value in *Wealth* is a later development based on this earlier example of the social necessity of nonintelligence: The individual "neither intend[s] to promote the public interest, nor knows how much he is promoting it . . . as in many other cases, [he is] lead by an invisible hand to promote an end which was no part of his intention" (*Wealth* 456). We shall *not* know Jupiter's plan; nor shall we attach consequences of intention to our own security and self-interest. And *not* knowing is how the wise man masters adversity, alone—or better, alone with a lot of other people:

> He [the wise man] enters . . . into the sentiments of that Divine Being, and considers himself as an atom, a particle, of an immense and infinite system . . . disposed of, according to the conveniency of the whole. . . . [W]hatever lot befalls him, he accepts it with joy, satisfied . . . [as] if he had known all the connexions and dependencies of the different parts of the universe. (*TMS* 59)

In this passage, which was a late addition to the final (sixth) edition of the *TMS* at the end of Smith's life, the categorical imperative gives way—and joyfully—to the essential inability, indeed the needlessness, of knowing our earthly "connexions," especially when those connections prove to adversely obstruct the machine.

Smith's appreciation for the noble Stoics (*TMS* 60) is something we take up at length in the next chapter. For our purposes here and to simply foreshadow this later discussion, what is remarkable for tracing the wonders of ignorance is how Smith surrenders so-called impartiality, now warded off as infinity against social convenience—to the fictional register of an almost suicidal, or at least indifferent—"as if." The wise man suffers best by knowing least, and any form of attraction that would draw wisdom too close to another's adversity risks "artificial commiseration . . . [which is] not only absurd, but seems altogether unattainable . . . impertinently dismal and disagreeable. . . . [And] perfectly useless" (*TMS* 140). As Smith notes, and as we will emphasize in Chapter 2, "mere poverty . . . excites little compassion. . . . We despise a beggar; . . . he is scarce ever the object of any serious commiseration" (*TMS* 144).

The central point is twofold. First, Adam Smith's ethical system operates on the order of how we view the beggar—that is, according to what philosophy designates as a private affair, rendered necessarily un-*real* and invisible to thought. Second, the way we make peace with Jupiter's invisible hand (*TMS*

185) is artificially and technically (according to that rusty, man-*made* and man-*making* machine) through a form of impartial self-command that divides us from others for a peaceable sense of the whole.

We can now more effectively consider Smith's definition of philosophy as a science of connection, and beyond that, his use of *genus* to make connections that are either not really there or must be manufactured to do the work of manufacturing. To review, at the level of his ethical system, we have located the paradox of mankind as an empty, because thoroughly partitioned historical arrangement, unique to the historical advance of commerce. From there, at an epistemic level, we have begun to see the way in which philosophy is predicated on designating the other-than-real—that is, on working the imagination—so as to smooth over whatever obstruction of particularity slows the general production of our individuated selves. Having accomplished this much, we need to do some additional work on the question of how particularities are subsumed by *genus* in Smith; and we need to do this as a lead-in to showing how philosophy is modulated by division in yet another way—that is, as being cordoned off from the burden of bodily work. Because it is divided from labor as such, knowledge is given a nontechnological status, claiming an imaginative approximation of unknowable reality, and a commitment not to *know* Jupiter's invisible hand, but instead to *feel* it for a little bit and for a little while, if also by chance. We have cited above numerous examples in the *TMS* of the imagination's role in securing impartiality. And we have proposed that this is an example of idealist abstraction, akin to Jupiter's ghostly unintelligibility.

Let us now turn more directly to the *Essays on Philosophical Subjects*. Let us tighten the frame and detail the way in which *genus* not only presumes imagined likenesses within and between the wondrously inassimilable masses of objects but also how Smith's categorical imperative retains the traces of epistemic absence that become the philosopher's task to bridge. Once we have remarked on the generative nature of absence that continues to haunt Smith's attention to matters of kind, and once we have further connected generative absence to the philosopher's unique responsibility to—as Smith insists—produce "nothing," we will have completed section one on how knowledge divides. We can then close this section and turn to the final move in this chapter on how knowledge is divided. We can turn to the way in which philosophy, as a practice of knowledge geared for arbitrating division, comes itself to be divided not only from labor but—because noncorporeal—divided also from a later specialty of knowledge called English literature, per se.

In his 1746 essay, "Principles Which Lead and Direct Philosophical Inquiries; Illustrated by the History of Astronomy" (hereafter "HA"), which was deliberately set aside by its author to be spared from the burning of his other papers, Smith sums up the advance of knowledge in terms that originate in Plato's association of philosophy and wonder:

> Wonder, Surprise, and Admiration, are words which, though often confounded, denote in our language, sentiments that are indeed allied. . . . What is new and singular, excites that sentiment which, in strict propriety, is called Wonder; what is unexpected, Surprise; and what is great or beautiful, Admiration.[65]

We return here to what by now should be a familiar theme: The singular object "stands alone in [the spectator's] imagination as if it were detached from all the other species of that genus to which it belongs" ("HA" 40). To "get rid of that Wonder," Smith continues, requires the "connecting principles" of philosophy as an "art, which addresses itself to the imagination" ("HA" 46).

Smith's definition of philosophy, which is as yet insufficiently distinctive in its dynamics from the imitative arts associated with *belles lettres*, is essentially a narratological foray into the sequencing of phenomena within their proper species and *genera* ("HA" 40). In moving from surprise to admiration, the goal of knowledge is to seek in the classification of things the same continuity of object division that is fundamental to moral sympathy and the impartial spectator ("HA" 39). From the momentary loss of reason experienced when an object is dissimilar, unexpected, strange, disjointed, or for that matter, new, agitation is anesthetized within a natural order of succession. Echoes of Locke and Hume's emphasis on succession are again evident here. By putting extraordinary and uncommon objects into proper classes and assortments, philosophy redresses the imagination such that it "may fill up the gap, [and] like a bridge, may . . . unite those seemingly distant objects, [so] as to render the passage of thought betwixt them smooth" ("HA" 42).

John Barrell makes a point regarding eighteenth-century landscape that is equally applicable here. "Political authority," he writes, "is rightly exercised by those capable of thinking in general terms; . . . those capable of producing abstract ideas—de-complex ideas—out of the raw data of experience."[66] For Smith, de-complexification is tantamount to methodized arrangement. The mind takes pleasure "in observing the resemblances that are discoverable between different objects" of thought ("HA" 36). What Barrell rightly attributes to "taste" (about which more below), Smith leaves well enough alone as pleasure. However, we should keep in mind George Drummond's 1740 definition of taste in "The Rules of Conversation" as "the art of making [oneself] agreeable."[67] According to pleasure, which is produced in the move from wonder to admiration, Smith's ethics merge with his epistemology. Both are founded on a proper distance between subject and object that paradoxically ascends to particularized universality. And both sociability and human understanding in Smith are haunted by the unthinkable thoughts that are rendered unthinkable by the mind's propensity to *feel* rather than *think* its way through division in the least dis-"agreeable" way.

The key problem here is that of bridging gaps by using the imagination in the service of category, and doing so in a way that presumes that categories themselves do not retain division. Philosophy is not only tasked with bridging moments of ethical and epistemic absence—what we have cited above by a variety of Smithian terms, like invisibility, infinity, singularity, and, not least, bodily labor—but with doing so vis-à-vis the imagination. And by achieving its task imaginatively, philosophy "abridge[s] labour" by rising above corporeal work. When Smith speaks of methodizing the ideas of as yet un-assorted objects, he evokes knowledge as having a *generic* rather than a *productive* function. And this tends to obscure the productive capacities of classification itself. However, as divisions in kind are prone to retain a critical caesura, category retains a difference that threatens to upset the balance between reason and experience:

> [W]e need to pause upon this interval [between categories] to find out something which may fill up the gap, which like a bridge, may so far at least unite those seemingly distant objects, as to render the passage of the thought betwixt them smooth, and natural, and easy. ("HA" 41–42)

The "something" referenced above remains entirely unnamed by Smith, or takes on, as we have seen, the metaphoric beckoning of rust on the "machine" that Jupiter would otherwise smoothly assemble, and which philosophers should simply believe. This "something" is, at least as far as philosophy goes according to Smith, precisely "nothing" insofar as it is the imaginary bridge across which the epistemic gap is in the end pleasingly traversed. But this "nothing" is also *everything*: a supremely nonproductive activity that unites distant objects among the mass of "stuff" and projects a commerce-oriented social imaginary onto the perversely inclusive (because, totally hypothetical) category Smith calls "mankind."

This something that is both nothing and everything is finally the proper preoccupation of philosophy. Philosophy, as Smith defines it in the "Astronomy" essay, "by representing the invisible chains which bind together all these disjointed objects, endeavors to introduce order into this chaos of jarring and discordant appearances" ("HA" 46). We must note, and this is crucial, that connectivity as such remains invisible, even once philosophy pacifies the "discordan[ce]" of the particular and the manifold that may exist at any number of levels: As the "science of the connecting principles of nature . . . which appear solitary and incoherent" ("HA" 45), wonder belongs to the career of the imagination. Indeed, harkening back to Smith's account of imaginative habit, abstract philosophical supposition means that we may "anticipate, before it happens, every event which falls out according to [the] order of things" ("HA" 41). Smith is not saying that all events are previously prescripted, only that the philosophical mind comes equipped with proper sorting tools and should be able to assimilate whatever singularities might appear to disrupt an otherwise stable categorical system.[68]

Smith's critique of Samuel Johnson's *Dictionary*, as reviewed by him in the *Edinburgh Review* of 1755–56, was that the "present . . . very extensive . . . undertaking" was "defec[tive]" for not "digesting . . . different significations . . . into classes."[69] And he would later advance this as a categorical imperative at the linguistic level. In an early essay called "The First Formation of Language" (1762) (hereafter "FF"), which is part of the posthumously published collection on rhetoric and *belles lettres*, Smith refers to the mind's innate generic sensibility as a process of sorting what he calls the "great multitudes of objects." This process is central to the history of language itself (*LRBL*, 205). For Smith it is the presence of multitudes within the association of words that hurries the mind toward object correspondence at the experiential level.[70]

The fellow feeling between sufferers and witnesses across an antagonistic divide is thus first played out in a pre-political (because generically naturalized) horizontal continuity between objects and language in thought. Multiplicity (surprise and wonder) is immanent to meaningful discourse in the commercial *socius* and always threatens to upset its otherwise natural experiential harmonies (rational admiration). But again, interruption within this social system is to be effectively recuperated—before it ever fully speaks—in the production of knowledge itself, and at the semiological level in the correspondence of words to things. Indeed, the more potentially violent the uncommon object, the more satisfying its eventual adequation in imaginary exchange ("HA" 35).

Thus for Smith morality is method; subjectivity, a careful social grammar. The definition of sympathetic moral spectatorship as "emotions . . . just and proper, and suitable to their objects" (*TMS* 16) finds its premise in the fabric of words. The social arrangement of the market is in this way granted through a philosophico-hermeneutic technique that is itself a matter of associational mandate: smoothing out otherwise unexpected, violent, or convulsive objects by the habit of the imagination to arrange each disruption according to its moral propriety ("HA" 41). In Smith's history of language, for example, mutual wants are advanced in the progress of civilization as nouns-substantive (simple designations of a thing, e.g., caves, trees, and so on) develop into nouns-adjective (descriptive divisions that cluster things according to finer-tuned categorical likeness (e.g., green tree, dark cave, and so forth). Smith defines language development as

> mankind['s] natural disposition . . . to nominate a multitude . . . [and] the appellation of an individual to a great multitude of objects, whose resemblance naturally recalls the ideal of that individual . . . that seems originally to have given occasion to the formation of those classes and assortments, which, in the schools, are called genera and species. ("FF" 205)

Linguistic development "distinguishes particulars . . . from others . . . under general appellation," just as the savage moves from "expressing not the coming of a particular object but the coming of a particular kind" ("FF" 217).[71] Note above the phrase "coming of," which works according to Smith's notion of *genus* at a temporal level where kind precedes signification and is, once again, in accord with maintaining a succession of shared epistemological habits.

The problem of particularity this time, expressed at the sociolinguistic level, offers the same ethico-philosophical solution of the division and categorization of a multitude. "What constitutes a species," Smith writes, "is merely a number of objects, bearing a certain degree of resemblance . . . denominated by a single appellation" ("FF" 205). That species only works to properly designate objects to a certain degree belies the more complicated problem of rendering invisible those features of an object that betray the dictates of *genus*. Smith would no doubt prefigure such a betrayal as that about which we have no choice but to be indifferent, as a matter of infinity, singularity, a mass of "stuff." "Imagination is necessary here," Smith continues, "though we will call it by a more proper name: all verbs have become personal, [and] mankind [has] learned by degrees to split and divide every event into a great number of metaphysical parts" ("FF" 217). Division occurs here by way of "metaphysics," a term that designates for Smith the same principle of abstraction he finds in philosophy's address to the imagination. Here, as in both philosophy at large and with regard to language, we have the familiar disturbing prospect of a "tumult" of numbers: "The number of words are almost infinite," Smith notes; thus, "[m]emory found itself quite loaded and oppressed by the multitude of characters" ("FF" 217).

The progress of society in opposition to inassimilable multitudes is a problem central to language, which by continuing to divide its objects more precisely should "still grow more general in its signification" ("FF" 217). From an adjectival operation, which supposes a comparison and works according to accumulation by *genus*, society advances toward "prepositions . . . , words which express relations considered, in the same manner [as adjectives], in concert with the co-relative object" ("FF" 206). Smith continues, "comparison, likewise, supposes some degree of abstraction. The invention . . . even of the simplest nouns adjective must have required more metaphysics than we are apt to be aware of" ("FF" 207). Smith mentions the increase in linguistic abstraction repeatedly in the essay on language, which resolves the founding opposition between language as a multitude against its proper division, rank, and categorization, so as to make language advance toward the general. As in his ethico-philosophical system, Smith's insistence on linguistics as a matter of metaphysical abstraction nudges connectedness in the direction of an impossible infinitude of signification that Smith constantly alludes to as the "real."

We mentioned above one remaining aspect of Smith's divisions of knowledge, not simply philosophy's propensity to divide multitudes into *genus* but here too the moment in Smith where thought becomes divided from physical work. Philosophy is granted a sufficiently abstract, and though pleasing, a reductive—or de-complicating—effect. And now we must show how this process of *de*-complexification also delineates thinking from the activity of labor. Philosophy's penultimate act of division, we should say, begins when thought divides itself from the lower and more physical employments. In this way, Smith's system of interpretation renders itself always other than productive.

This de-linking of work and thought is an essential move in Smith's epistemology, which further links his imaginary political arrangements to the pleasing wonders of ignorance. To cite Barrell again, this time from *The Birth of Pandora and the Division of Knowledge* (hereafter *BP*), "experience that falls in the way of [man in general]—especially if he follows, not a liberal profession, but a mechanical art—will be too narrow to serve as the basis of ideas general enough to be represented as true for all mankind" (*BP* 20). In this manner, Barrell writes, "the structure of employment . . . becomes the guarantee of unity."[72]

To put this in terms apposite to Smith, philosophy's categorical imperative turns in on itself and proceeds down a path of specialization—first, as it designates a specific rank of non-labor, and second, as a break within knowledge that eventually displaces the surprise of philosophical disruption with the sociability of admiration. To foreshadow a later section of this chapter, admiration is writ eventually as abstract aesthetic appreciation (i.e., taste).

The problem, then—and this goes to directly the paradox within Smith's divisions of knowledge—"is that of defining the place from which [a] social coherence [of generality] could be perceived, for the discourse of the division of labour seem to deny the very possibility of the social knowledge it sought to invent" (*BP* 90). The keyword from Barrell here is indeed "denial," for the effect of making absent is what Jupiter's slight of hand achieves. And the invisible hand of Jupiter works beyond even the process of abstraction and de-complication that we have been sussing out of Smith's philosophical ethics. Jupiter ensures philosophy remains centered precisely on that which cannot be thought. "Philosophy becomes less plural," Barrell continues, "and less directly comparable with manual trades . . . a specialist participating in the market economy . . . accredited with an impartiality, and integral subjectivity" (*BP* 91). And from here, "ignorance . . . becomes the property of a particular class, the class which is the object of knowledge, and so the object of discourse" (*BP* 92). One recalls here Locke's attention to the races of animals as being designated "under names . . . [determined by] the similitude it [human understanding] observes amongst them, [in order] to make abstract [into] general ideas." This, Locke says "is the great business of *genera* and *species*" (emphasis in original).[73]

Mary Poovey's work on cartography in 1650s Ireland uses the term "economical thinking" or simply "economy" in a de-disciplinary way to sum up the general business of creating a new national form, the assembly of parts into wholes, through the mapping of boundaries.[74] Uniquely among writers on Smith, Poovey marks the element of *not* knowing—of what we have called the pleasing wonder of ignorance—as fundamental to Smith's understanding of wealth. She moves from the division of labor in *Wealth*, directly to the ownership of ignorance, by way of what she calls the rise of stupid labor: the forms of "objectification and aggregation . . . throughout *Wealth of Nations*." Poovey writes: "Even when [Smith] describes an individual poor man, [he shows] a use of generalizing abstractions [that] render[s] the object of his analysis a type of reified, stupefied labor."[75] The citation from Smith she has in mind pertains to his ambivalent concern with the "ignorant and stupid" multitudes that threaten society with "the most dreadful disorders" (*Wealth* 738, 740). The location of stupidity within a specific division of the working ranks is in turn objectified by a particular occupation of knowledge designed to create epistemic value through dividing.

We have noted many times how "philosophy . . . represents the invisible chains which bind . . . disjointed objects, [and] endeavor[s] to introduce order" ("HA" 46). What we need to address more completely as the closing step of section one of this chapter is how Smith divides thinking from work. From there we can set up the argument for how philosophy conceived as knowledge production in general disappears in the wake of further subdivisions within humanistic knowledge. This disappearing act is one appropriately designated on behalf of the laboring many by the contemplative few.

When Smith concedes that "by nature a philosopher is not, in genius and disposition, half so different from a porter" ("EDWN" 573), he signals equivalence between the two occupations that registers according to the generality of mankind. There is a species affiliation, and as men, the porter and the philosopher are not so different "as a mastiff from a greyhound, or a greyhound from a spaniel, or this last from a sheep dog" ("EDWN" 573). But the philosopher's task is connected with the porter in a species way as the two are individuated from each other by task but also unified as men. Thus our argument about Smith and the distinction between thinking and work runs counter to the idea presented by Sandra Peart and David Levy in *The Street Porter and the Philosopher* (hereafter *SPP*); they argue that Smith's famous reference to the philosopher and the porter reveals his adherence to analytical egalitarianism.[76] For them this term designates "a theoretical system that abstracts from any inherent difference among persons" (*SPP* 1).

But this is only half the story, since that form of theoretical abstraction, to the extent that it renders to ignorance what Smith calls the "real" (i.e., massive, tumultuous, singular, surprising, and so forth) differences between ranks, and indeed between different kinds of work, is not entirely benign. The disagreement is not over Smith's rejection of "inherent differences"; rather, our concern is to point out that the differences that do interest him, some of which, like occupation, wealth, and poverty, can be surprisingly difficult to reduce under the heading of so-called man in general. The phrase "natural equality" for Smith, we are arguing, paradoxically allows for a divided and presumptively generalizable notion of society, if it does so in an imaginary way (*SPP* 2). While it is true, as Peart and Levy note, that for Smith "competition gives all persons potential access to every position" (*SPP* 3), there is no logical way that the few best positions can be accessible to everyone at the same time. That reality is best left to fortune, which is to say, best left within the realm of wonder and ignorance—Jupiter's way of handing out life, or more appropriately, death. Abstract equality is thus the consolation we get in the face of what Smith calls "real" difference, though recall, equality is certain to come in a *postmortem* kind of way.

To make the point of divided unity at the level of distinguishing different kinds of work, we should recall again in Smith that the philosopher gains a unique capacity to do "nothing" and therefore rises above corporeal labor:

> [H]e who first thought of employing a stream of wind for the same purpose [work], was probably no workman of any kind, but a philosopher or mere man of speculation; one of those people whose trade it is not to do anything but to observe every thing, and who are upon that account capable of combining together the powers of the most opposite and distant objects. ("EDWN" 570 and *Wealth* 21)

The workman is defined here precisely as that particularity that must be subsumed within a system that the work itself cannot make clear. The philosopher is no workman of any kind; but he does the kind of work that, more privileged than most, creates and coordinates generic divisions. As a mere man of speculation, the philosopher erases his activity as labor and claims the relative privilege of not doing anything: Philosophy, Smith says, does no "kind of work." Yet its value lies in the ability to divide objects precisely into kind and render that process of generic division itself, after the pleasing wonder of ignorance, an unremarkable if not eventually invisible event.

In the essay on imitative arts from *Essays on Philosophical Subjects*, Smith singles out special praise for the musical passions, because through "harmony"—a keyword for Smith that has social as well as epistemic implications—melody in music "in fact signif[ies] and produces nothing" ("IA" 206). Indeed, Smith again refers notably in *Wealth* to the many activities, public servants, the sovereign, "players, and buffoons," the most "frivolous of professions whose work it is to produce nothing" (*Wealth* 331). "That unprosperous race commonly called men of letters" is included in this motley mix of nonproducers. To signify precisely nothing, to do nothing, while pretending toward connections with incalculable orders of reality is the task of philosophical knowledge in Smith. By doing nothing, Smith continues, "philosophy belongs to those only who have a greater range of thought and more extensive views of things than naturally fall to the share of a mere artist [e.g., artisan or craftsman]" ("EDWN" 570).

Again, in the essay on music, Smith refers to "harmony" as dependent on order and method, a "great system [of succession, as] in any other science" ("IA" 205). But music is distinct from other imitative arts in that it arrives to the listener "complete in itself, [and] require[s] no interpreter to explain it" ("IA" 205). Here the problem of division is addressed at the level of representation, which depends for poetry and philosophy alike on activity of imagination. Smith distinguishes these interpretive arts from music by using familiar terms: Poetry is burdened with producing its effects by "connect[ing] variety of succession ...; but Music frequently produces its effects by repetition of the same" ("IA" 192).

Hume too worried about aesthetics leaking too much into philosophy and interrupting succession, which it perhaps did in triggering Hume's adherence to mitigated skepticism: "The imagination of man," he writes, is "delighted with whatever is remote and extraordinary, and running without control, into the most distant parts of space and time in order to avoid the objects which custom has rendered too familiar too it." In the face of such object avoidance, Hume suggests, "the more sublime topics [ought to be left] to the embellishments of poets and orators" (*ECH* 118).[77] In the posthumously published *Dialogues Concerning Natural Religion* (hereafter *Dialogues*), Hume's Philo expresses to Cleanthes the fragility of object adequation: "Unless the cases be exactly similar, they repose no perfect confidence in applying their past observation to any particular phenomenon" (*Dialogues* 57). In his adamant rejection of the "anthropomorphists" (*Dialogues* 71), which complicates Smith's overreliance on the generality of man, Philo notes, "a change in bulk, situation, arrangement, disposition of the air, or surrounding bodies; any of these particulars may be attended with the most unexpected consequences" (*Dialogues* 57). To these variables, Hume, in the voice of Philo, notes others, such as: "differences of time ..., weather ..., food ..., books; or any of these particulars more minute" (*Dialogues* 72).

Revealingly, Hume insists that "the disposition of the body" is also one of the "curious variables ... [of] the material world" (*Dialogues* 72), which could go on *ad infinitum*. But for Hume, not only is the corporeal condition that which taste must rise above in order to achieve divided wholeness, but the body is also quite literally a multitude:

> [T]he muscles alone [have] above 6,000 several views and intentions ...; the bones ... 284. ... But if we consider the skin, ligaments, vessels, glandules, humours, the several limbs and members of the body; ... descry still, at a distance, farther scenes beyond our reach; in the fine internal structure of the parts, in the oeconomy of the brain, in the fabric of the seminal vessels ... (*Dialogues* 126)

Moreover, and this is consistent with Smith, the problem of inconceivable numbers is the exact condition of physical work over which philosophy struggles to transcend. The closest one can get to the problem of labor writ here as conceptual incalculability—what we have been calling "ignorance"—is to leave such human misery in its overwhelming fullness to "the poets, who speak from sentiment, without a system" (*Dialogues* 104).

Demea, who cites Milton's "pathetic enumeration" of death as man's final hope, presses Philo in the *Dialogues* to account for: "labour and poverty . . . , [as they] are the certain lot of the far greater number" (106). Philo grants that of the four natural evils that attend mankind, which he does not want to treat in a simplistically oppositional way within the Manichaean system (*Dialogues* 121), the "violent necessity [of] labour" is one of them. The other three are: luxury, also a corporeal ill; the ignorance of God's providential plan; and relatedly— *contra* Smith—the preponderance of chance, "the parts perform[ing] not regularly their proper function" (*Dialogues* 116–120).

All of these evils relate to the way ignorance, as a problem of too many, functions in relation to labor. The "greater number," the laboring body in historical aggregate, is a limit beyond which the operations of a well-disciplined imagination may not go—or may go at a very high risk.

> Could a peasant [for Hume in this text, used interchangeably with "the vulgar" and "the laborer"], if the *Aeneid* were read to him, pronounce that poem to be absolutely faultless, or even assign it its proper rank among the productions of human wit; he, who had never seen any other production? (*Dialogues* 77)

According to Philo's (and via Locke, Hume's) reliance on experience for conjecturing reality, certainly a peasant may not have the right taste for the *Aeneid*. But this is only the first order of ignorance we find in "the stupid mechanic." If we look at the arts of the workman, say, if we survey the building of a ship superficially, we might get a sense of his superior ingenuity. But examined in a more philosophical way—that is, as situated within a successive temporal process—we see this merely as having "copied an art, which, through a long succession of ages . . . had been gradually improving." What we do not see in this history, as Philo puts it (with Milton in mind?), is "much labour lost" (*Dialogues* 77).

And it is not at all that conjecture can or should attempt to recover this absence, which is ignorable not least because it exists in the form of excess, that is, of "too much." As Philo continues, "In such subjects, who can determine where the . . . probability . . . lies; amidst a great number of hypothesis, which may be proposed, and a still greater number, which may be imagined" (*Dialogues* 77)? The *imagining* that is referred to here is partly philosophy's work. But at some point, where phenomena, like corporeal labor, reaches beyond our ability to objectify it by either going too far (contemplating the universe), or coming too close (for Philo, the vulgar's small-picture thinking as much as the microscope), philosophy must give over to the nonsystematic stuff of poetry.

This emergent disciplinary logic is consistent in both Smith and Hume. But Hume's natural evil number four, specified above as parts failing to add up to a whole, belies a more pronounced anxiety than in Smith about "revolution" (their term) and the high stakes of unanticipated change. After leaving over to the poets the privilege and the risk of being able to speak from sentiment rather than system, and just before Demea's adjoining of the physical hardship of labor to the far greater number of people, Philo describes a Hobbesian world in which "the stronger prey upon the weaker, and keep them in perpetual terror and anxiety." What at least partially underwrites Hume's concern over the persistence of partiality—a dangerous anomaly immanent to Smith's generality of man—is that "the weaker too, in their turn, often prey upon the stronger, and vex and molest them without relaxation" (*Dialogues* 105). It is not so much that this reversal between the weak and the strong, like Hume's "labour lost," goes missing in time. Rather, a specific experience of time as historical succession serves to cancel out such episodes.

Succession is repeatedly mentioned by Hume's reference as requiring the bridging of gaps (i.e., of conjecture) by imaginary means even while imagination itself brings danger to philosophers but can be dealt with more effectively within the permissions granted to the literary fine arts. The greater number of people, the "vulgar, . . . hurried on by the smallest similitude" (*Dialogues* 57), must be handled with care on both counts. We see in Smith a similarly emergent logic of disciplinary division. What troubles "fine writing" and *not* "mathematics and philosophy" is the burden of "public opinion": The closer knowledge is to admiration writ as "public applause," rather than the acknowledgment of good taste among experts, the more crucial it is to salve the irritating paradox of divided wholeness.[78] The reason writing *for* the public instead of writing *about* it is hard—and this too should be familiar ground by now—is because the public itself is incorrectly apt to divide into "faction and cabals" ("IA" 124). "Poets," Smith continues, "or . . . those who value themselves upon what is called fine writing . . . , are very apt to divide themselves into . . . literary

factions; . . . employing all the mean arts of intrigue and solicitation to preoc-
cupy the public opinion in favour of the works of its own members" ("IA" 125).

Academic and other interpretive experts are presumed to do no such thing.
It could be said that the aspiration of philosophical interpretation, which has
better chances than the fine arts without its own experts to succeed, is to move
beyond the interpretive difficulty immanent to it. To the extent that interpretation is necessary, it must render completeness according to a transcendental
indifference to inescapable gaps that Smith links to speculative thought. Here,
too, the paradox of generality through division is consistent; but this dynamic
works in the case of dividing other arts from music according to a specifically
disciplinary commitment that begins to cordon off the philosopher as uniquely
able to manipulate the scale and range of interpretive difference, while remaining impartial, at the same time ("EDWN" 570). This emergent division between
thought and work will find additional nuance in the specialized imaginative
thinking later singled out as criticism, as we shall see. And it is entirely consistent with Smith's rejection of what he calls the "corporeal" perspective that we
have highlighted already above.

As we have seen throughout this first section, philosophy is the art of har-
moniously dividing a multitude of objects into a metaphysics of kind. We are
adding here two additional turns toward absence where philosophy mounts its
various disappearing act by dividing itself, first, from productive bodily labor;
and second, from other nonproductive subdisciplines (like musicology) within
the emergent fields of humanities knowledge. Thinking is uniquely tasked with
doing "nothing," as we have seen. But a final enactment of disappearance, where
philosophy's imaginary actions are themselves occulted in their origins, is still
harder to detect. What shall not be interpreted are the ways in which interpretation becomes an increasingly *wide* problem (of public reading), accompanied
by an increasingly *narrow* solution (of well-disciplined taste).

Smith's final set of disappearing acts presents a series of issues about where
the imagination goes in the wake of philosophy. We say in the wake of philosophy, because imaginary thinking on this order becomes increasingly narrowed
into yet another division of written discourse—criticism—as writing proliferates as a new media technology. Printed material *itself* becomes a problem of
the multitude: a problem that is immanent to Enlightenment interpretation
and linguistic exchange. But how is it that writing, now the "stuff" of so much
matter in its own right, goes on after mid-century to disavow its corporeal status? We turn now to a final question that arises after knowledge self-effaces,

even as it accumulates: How does Smith's interpretive system both progress and become invisible? Below we will answer these questions by examining how writing accumulates, in the context of Scottish copyright law, according to what we have already traced to an epistemology belonging to Smith: proliferation, abstraction, division. These terms denote a process that displaces, or effectively cancels out, the knowledge called philosophy with new forms of aesthetic appreciation. At the same time writing is judged—literally, according to the Scottish courts—to be something other then "real" property.

Knowledge Divided

Many idiots, with no more than an ordinary education, have been taught to read, write, and account tolerably well. Many persons, never accounted idiots, notwithstanding the most careful education . . . have never been able to acquire . . . any one of those three accomplishments. . . . Some idiots, perhaps the greater part, seem to be so [idiotic] . . . from a certain numbness or torpidity in the faculties of the understanding. But there are others in whom those faculties do not appear more torpid or benumbed than in many other people who are not accounted idiots.

Adam Smith (TMS 260–261)

What can we say about the idiot by way of Adam Smith? Or, better, why is idiocy important in the context we have offered on Smith's divisions of knowledge thus far? Why must we summon the idiot to transition now from philosophy's preoccupation with invisibility and ignorance to the final disappearing act of philosophy's own displacement with yet a further division of knowledge, cordoned off from science in general, that will come to be called English literature per se?

The passage above is not entirely pejorative in the sense one might expect from a writer firmly committed to the wonders of contemplative abstraction. Rather, there is a certain democratization of ignorance that belies the paradox we have been calling, among other terms, "divided wholeness." If inequalities, whether social or epistemic, must be overcome imaginatively by dividing multiplicity into their proper categories of thought, as well as dividing thought from corporal particularity *qua* labor, then it should be no wonder that the idiot is key. Reading the epigram closely, idiocy is a condition upon which abstract equivalency becomes ordinary; but idiocy also recalls terms that are the unique provenance of the philosopher, sensibly attuned to the pleasing wonder of ignorance.

This double association begs a characteristically Smithian question: Can the idiot be both ordinary and unique? Can ignorance signal the individuating capacities of philosophy to go on distinguishing wondrous particularities while imagining social and epistemic completeness? And in that sense, is idiocy simply the most condensed way to speak of living partially and impartially at the same time? There are keywords in the passage that should not require a great deal of unpacking at this point: the words "numbness" and "torpid" are consistent with Smith's affective charge that moral sentiment is also an analytical mode; and the words "account" and "accounted" appear in the epigram as extensions of Smith's trust in the provisionally final—if imagined—reduction of multiplicity into discrete objects, knowable within their proper categories of distinction.

Christopher Berry provides a useful way to think about idiocy in this epistemological sense by focusing on the political problem of imagining the generality of mankind as having to square with individualism, having to square, that is, if the effect of general knowledge is to preserve the transcendence of liberal capitalism.[79] In *The Idea of a Democratic Community* (hereafter *IDC*), Berry's focus on idiocy reveals "how the operation of liberal capitalism militates against the realization of its own goals and values . . . [;] how the inequalities it generates inhibit the efficacy of the freedom it celebrates" (*IDC* xi).

To live comfortably under these conditions, to live and, as we will argue under the heading of *necro-economics* in Chapter 4, to also let die, begs the question of what Berry calls idiotic politics (*IDC* 1). He takes seriously the term "idiotic," tracing it back to its origin in antiquity, which from the Greek shares the root word "idiom," as in "idiosyncrasy" (*IDC* 1). The Greek root *idios* denotes the personal or peculiar, a layman—or, in Smithian parlance, the particular. Berry is interested in examining the assumption that idiot individualism underlies the market economy (*IDC* xi, 1). He suggests, "to lead an idiotic life is to lead a privatized life, or a life of privation, whereby one is deprived of public or communal existence" (*IDC* 19). But this would not be appropriate to Smith, since in his more nuanced account idiocy—or, at the very least, ignorance—is a shared social condition. It may be shared, however, in different quantities and with different effects depending on the distance you may or may not have from physical work.

What we want to transition toward now is how liberal learning and print undergo nothing short of revolutionary transformations in mid-eighteenth century Scotland, which does not mean that idiocy disappears. What does disappear is the kind of disciplinary permissiveness that Smith, with the qualifications we have named, attached to the term "philosophy" in its reliance on imagination. And what appeared in its place was another act of division, as well as displacement, if not also erasure: the displacement of philosophy by the narrower discipline of literary criticism as such.

By way of setting up a final set of moves, which brings this act of displacement together with the technical advances of new media, we need to pause a moment further over the almost heroic agency of the idiot in what is quoted from the *TMS* above. Smith is suggesting here not that the more learned person is guaranteed to achieve the modern trifecta of a modest education (reading, writing, and accounting) but that the idiot may better achieve this standard and, thereby, be more socially accountable than those who were never accounted as idiots. The idiot counts in a number of important ways: First, he is precisely able to *do* accounting. The idiot is able to proficiently divide and accumulate not so much by the strict calculation of numbers as by negotiating the affective twists and turns initiated on a newly massive scale by the printed text; second, because he is proficient in accounting (in the interpretive sense, as an adjunct to reading), the idiot counts within moral economy as part of a greater, more peaceable, and newly calculable *socius*. He may in fact count beyond the significance of the traditionally educated elite, who Smith implies can (and maybe ought to) be counted as idiots too.

Of course, this brand of what we might call ignorance-equality is itself carefully divided as a consequence of Smith's own uniquely unmarked position of spectatorial abstraction. The idiot-hero, because he accounts, is therefore accountable. As such, he is redivided according to the impartial standards of knowledge we have noted before. Even with—or we should say, because of—adequate textual aptitude accompanied by the techniques of division, the idiot-hero must ultimately be, as Smith continues, "agreeable to the impartial spectator. . . . [The idiot] esteems himself as he ought, and no more than he ought, . . . He desires no more than is due to him, and he rests upon it with complete satisfaction" (*TMS* 261).

We must note then that there is a third form of accounting that makes the idiot significant for Smith. This accounting presents a perversely democratic gesture to make the wonders of ignorance more equally accessible, if also subject to more specialized processes of cultivation and control that remain well out of the hands of the many (the ordinary person, the lower ranks, the laboring sort, and so on). Thus, a third way the word "accounting" works in the *TMS* passage is according to an inward calibration that characteristically resolves Smith's vexed preoccupation with the manifold: Accounting encourages the greater part of mankind, who may well remain idiots, to become socially accountable, and no more, given the precise right of existence that Smith offers through the concept of invisibility, the right of *really* not counting at all.

This application of idiocy, which we earlier called perversely democratic, does not ignore the idiot and neither does it exactly repress him. While the many, as always in Smith, remain the repository of nonintelligence—like Jupiter's invisible infinity, the multitude neither knows nor can be known—there is in the epigram a concentrated effort to coax a wider group of idiots out of torpor. Indeed, Smith does so in a way that creates a certain imagined mobility between the ranks. This mobility levels the ordinary against the presumptively educated, as long as the arrangement of abstract equivalency is not upset. Account and be accountable, but no more.

We want to show at this point how Smith's perversely democratic distribution of the wonders of ignorance, corrected as it must be in the end by universal approbation, turns around mid-century to a more refined application of nonintelligence, or what we have heretofore called imaginative knowledge. This is not a political economy of knowledge in Siskin's sense (*The Work of Writing*, hereafter *WW*), but more accurately a political economy of ignorance (*WW* 28). Our adjustment of the phrase goes more directly to the point regarding wonder's new expansiveness among the generality of mankind, something that could not have happened without the newly expansive technologies of eighteenth-century writing.

To follow the thread in Smith's idiot passage, the political oeconomy of ignorance takes place not (or not simply) according to philosophy's habit of dividing objects in order to deliver imagined epistemic and social connections but through a third order of division, such that philosophy itself is displaced by a more specialized—*and* wider-spread—modality of admiration. This more specialized and wider-spread modality of admiration is newly institutionalized in the second half of the eighteenth century as criticism. Here then we must outline a constellation of change unique to Scotland in the latter part of Smith's career—particularly, around print culture, the heavy interpretive pressures wrought by imaginative reading on a mass scale, and the latest divisions of university learning. These historical episodes allowed for *wider* application of philosophical activity that was characteristically based on a moment of simultaneous disciplinary *narrowing*. This narrowing was itself so narrow (and so widespread) that it eventuated in philosophy's final disappearing act—namely, its historical invisibility as a discourse privileged to do imaginary work.

Before we trace this process, and to highlight the stakes of what we mean by an oeconomy of ignorance, consider Smith's attraction to the idiot a little further still. Smith, as we said, gives us a sort of idiot-hero who if not exactly ordinary (he is not the greater part of men) is not exactly extraordinary either. He is of course the impartial ideal thinker, the nonexistent middling sort who lives in a universal no-man's land adjoining nonequivalent ranks. He is modest in his learning and desires, with reading, writing, and accounting well enough in hand. The oeconomy of ignorance—precisely because it suspends whatever real (again, Smith's illusive term) differences exist between those who labor and those who do not—projects an association of imagined equals who come together out of a respect for impartial knowledge rather than according to a conflict of particular position.

Contrast this perverse inclusiveness with less sanguine commentators on the new conditions of eighteenth-century knowledge: Oxford's Reverend Knox, who will be addressed at greater length below and whom Smith would have scorned, writes in *Essays, Moral and Literary* (1792): "He who undertook to prevent the dispersion of books . . . [undertakes a] task as arduous as the destruction of the Hydra" (*EML* 376). Knox complained mightily of "disseminating novel systems [of knowledge] subversive of the dignity and happiness of human nature . . . [, and the] offensive profusion [of books] from the vain, the wicked, and the hungry" (*EML* 376). From the anonymous pamphlet, *The British Tocsin; or, Proofs of National Ruin* (1795), we are warned of "the extravagance of the last thirty years [when] a new mode of thinking has been adopted, and a revolution has taken place in the fashions of the mind." "The British Nation," the text continues, "now invents queries . . . and pries into . . . abuses, with an inquisitorial nicety," which includes such potentially turbulent questions as: "who reaps the produce of his labour?"[80] The wealthy British publisher James Lackington comments in 1774—a key date as we will see—that "all ranks now read," which may be an exaggeration, though the increase in reading certainly contributed to his vast fortune.[81] Hannah Moore wrote derisively against the "vulgar and indecent penny books [that brought] speculative infidelity down to the pockets and capacities of the poor, [and] form[ed] a new era in our history."[82] And, as Soame Jenyns admonished in 1757: "To encourage the poor man to read and think, and thus to become more conscious of his misery, would be to fly in the face of divine intention."[83] We could continue.

Why offer this list of distinctly British responses to the print revolution in the eighteenth century?[84] Better, why recall here the *British* formulation of the problems of "novel systems" of knowledge, the profusion of books, the question of bodily labor, speculative infidelity, and the notion of "our history" (about which more in Chapter 3), in the context of distinctly *Scottish* solutions? Smith continues to enjoy a heap of praise for having commented in *Wealth*, "the labouring poor, that is, the great body of people, must necessarily . . . become . . . stupid and ignorant . . . unless government take some pains to prevent it" (*Wealth* 782). In the biography, Stewart was the first to highlight that, for Smith, the "propagation of light and refinement arising from the influence of the press, seems to be the remedy . . . against the fatal effects which would be otherwise produced by the subdivision of labour" ("AL" 313). What Smith has in mind here, as a correlate to reading, writing, and accounting, is nothing less than public education, a "state imposed . . . necessity of learning" (*Wealth* 796). "Notwithstanding the great abilities of the few," Smith does in fact commit to the education of "the great body of people" (*Wealth* 784).[85]

A little more than a decade before, in his *Lectures on Jurisprudence*, Smith likewise remarks that among the "inconveniences . . . arising from commercial society . . . [,] education is greatly neglected."[86] But there is a particular mode of educating that Smith has in mind: the cultivation of affection and good taste through a mode he calls "comparing and computing" (*OU* 383, 402). While we are not suggesting that by the term "computing" Smith is harkening back to an outmoded notion of political arithmetic, we are saying that the necessity of overcoming of particularity through the operations of category, comparison, and in the end, a wholly ambivalent pitch for the common is what underwrites the concern for education here. The goal for Smith is to seek the reconciliation of difference vis-à-vis impartially, and to do so in order to preserve the public peace. Public education matters for subsuming the "low people, [who at present] are exceedingly stupid" (*LJ* B, 539) into an accessible system of liberal indifference that keeps the inequalities of wealth and ownership well enough intact. "Thro' want of education," Smith continues, "they [working boys] have no other amusement . . . but riot and debauchery" (*LJ* B, 540). This is not simply an argument on behalf of good manners and clean living. "Riot" here has a more dastardly application, and education carries with it the fate of British national security.

Smith is especially cautious with regard to the Jacobite insurgencies that began as soon as the Act of Union and lasted through the genocidal treatment of the Highlanders by the Duke of Cumberland's troops at Culloden in 1745 (*LJ* B, 541). With the blood spilled at Culloden in mind, we must also note the gentler forms of Highland discipline on offer by the Society in Scotland for the Promotion of Christian Knowledge (SSPCK).[87] The overt goal of this organization was to find schools where religion and virtue might be taught (as we mentioned in the Introduction, there were 5 SSPCK schools in 1711, and 189, with 13,000 pupils, by 1808). SSPCK's purpose was of course not a disinterested one, especially in the agitated Highlands. By the 1740s its itinerant Anglican teachers set out with the express task of preparing a mindset for Scotland's northernmost peoples that would counter Roman Catholic influences and Jacobite tendencies and make the Highland populations amenable to wage labor and commercial husbandry in the new economy.[88] Clearly, so-called public education was as problematic as it was promising in Smith's place and time.

The complete passage on worker education from the *Lectures on Jurisprudence* suggests that stupidity among the low people must be reconciled on the order of divided wholeness, a process of *genus* making, which functions according to the enigmatic principle of divided wholeness we have been tracing all along. Smith offers the important caveat that "the common people cannot, in any civilized society, be instructed as people of some rank and fortune." And Stewart highlights this qualification, noting that while we can "make [educational refinement] effectual . . . , wise institutions . . . adapt the education of the individuals to the stations they occupy" ("AL" 313). The so-called common, writ as low individuals indifferent to their stations, belies the way in which Smith sets up the pitch for worker education in the measured form of print-mediated subjective accountability. This was the education provided to the idiot mentioned above in the *TMS*, who learns to read, write, and *account* (emphasis ours, *Wealth* 784).

"Science," Smith continues,

> is the great antidote to the poison of enthusiasm. . . . [T]he gaiety of public diversions . . . [likewise] amuse and divert the people by painting, poetry, music, dancing; all sorts of dramatic representations [which would] dissipate . . . that melancholy and gloomy humor which almost always nurse popular frenzies. (*Wealth* 796)

To the same extent that Smith promotes good roads and communication, he endorses dissipative appreciation as a necessary diversion and regards "education and religious instruction . . . [as] beneficial to the whole of society" (*Wealth* 815). Smith writes in contrast to certain British anxieties (or, more likely, neglect) concerning education that the state should not only support but "impose [reading] on the whole common people" (*Wealth* 784), an "impos[ition]" he modeled on the Scottish parish schools (not to mention the heavier hand of the SSPCK) in the Highlands. "In Scotland," he writes, "such parish schools have taught almost the whole common people to read, and a very great portion of them to write and account" (*Wealth* 785). Unlike many of his English counterparts, Smith would have the great body of people, the laboring poor, be "instructed in the elementary parts of geometry and mechanics," such that the "literary education of this rank of people would be perhaps as complete as it can be" (*Wealth* 785).

It should be clear in this string of citations that Smith is answering the education question according to a solution that is consistent with his divisions of knowledge. It is provocative to argue, after Joseph Cropsey (on his reading of Marx), that Smith's caveat about the emergent stupefaction of mechanical labor merely functioned "to palliate the ill [of creating an industrial mob] with a wide system of almost . . . *gratis* education."[89] Clearly for both Smith and Marx, as the social division of labor becomes more complex, the role of the individual worker becomes simplified. But by noting how Smith puts the ordinary duties and private life of the laborer in a humanizing and inclusive— as well as subordinate—relationship to the mandates of collective intelligence, we can also see how Smith's treatment of the laboring poor is consistent with the imaginary bases of his interpretive system. Smith's model was the parish school system of Scotland, maintained partly at public expense and partly with low private fees. The establishment of such institutions in the eighteenth century, which were more universally accessible than the English charity schools, helped provide the conditions for literacy as a new mass phenomenon.

But it is the troubled relation between the configuration of mass agency and knowledge production that we are trying to unpack in this closer look in Smith's idyllic model of impartial thought. On the one hand, the great many who labor designate a decidedly unknowable partiality in that they do not represent the social ideal. On the other hand, they are always described in the *TMS* and *Wealth* as being the greater number. In the case of applying knowledge to the public, or better, of encouraging knowledge activities such that a public is imagined to exist without substantive internal antagonism, it is the nonproductive few who model the abstract thinking necessary to achieve collective peace of mind.[90] The mechanic's work remains—always paradoxically in Smith—a mass particularity that must be outside knowledge proper as infinity, invisibility, ignorance, and, equally, as faction or rebellion. Society is imagined through the omnipotence of *genus*, and in this way, the divisions between different kinds of phenomena extend to the idealized reconciliation between those who labor and those whose business it is to produce "nothing." This zone of philosophical vacuity is crucial on political—as well as epistemic and affective—grounds, where imaginary notions of transcendent equivalence find an appropriately measured application across the ranks.[91]

A perverse generosity of this order is to be imposed presumably by state support for education. But our use of the word "imposition" must be adjusted to capture the quieter efficiency (and the risk) with which the idiot-hero is idealized. Smith writes, "the first remedy [against the ruin of the common people] is the study of science and philosophy, which the state might render almost universal among all people of middling or more than middling rank and fortune" (*Wealth* 796). The notion of a middling rank is, again, obviously notable here as providing an approximated bridging function between the laboring and the nonlaboring ranks, the latter being those relative few who get to exercise the philosophical task (*Wealth* 796). We have seen how—distinct from stupid labor—philosophy comes to be divided in Smith from corporeal occupations. This is not to say that philosophy fails to deal with the pleasing wonder of ignorance (indeed, the contrary is true). The philosopher is he who accounts for the accounting, the nonproductive thinker who can best gauge and speculate his way out of the so-called reality of physical work. "A teacher of science," Smith writes, "is certainly the natural employment of a mere man of letters" (*Wealth* 812).

Thus again Smith divides off the rare philosophical privilege *of* dividing. But this points out a different application of knowledge—and in Smith, a different application of *not* knowing—than exists in the attitudes of angst and refusal that are available elsewhere in the eighteenth century, particularly in the newly united kingdom of Great Britain. "Though the state," Smith remarks,

> derive[s] no advantage from the instruction of the inferior ranks of people, it would still deserve its attention that they should not be altogether uninstructed. The more they are instructed . . . the more they are disposed to examine . . . the interested complaints of faction and sedition. . . . They are therefore more disposed to respect their superiors. (*Wealth* 788)

The emphasis here is placed not only on the limited skill of accounting done by the lesser (and paradoxically more multiple) ranks but also on keeping those ranks from coming together outside the very specifically individuated-yet-general category of mankind.

The continued existence of the division of ranks within Smith's commercial *socius*, even in the context of his commitment to liberal education, should come as no surprise. Recall, it is the imagined concord of the paradoxically divided and harmonious society that the impartial spectator delivers against the unknowability of the manifold. Jupiter's indivisible operation of social coherence is a given for Smith. Indeed, not knowing the real consequences of self-interest is a moral necessity, then as now. This is one of the points we have been making about Smith's oeconomy of ignorance so far: A perverse equality of individuation regards the greater part of men as capable beyond presumed idiocy to achieve spectatorial neutrality and amend whatever potential for sedition that the knowledge of (and by) multitudes might otherwise produce. Our overall argument up to this point has been that ignorance in Smith's interpretive system is not simply a matter of marking the limit of his commercial state of mind.

More crucially, the pleasing wonder of ignorance is geared toward constituting the social imaginary itself as a peaceable arrangement—invisible to the many, imagined, at least for the record, by the few. By insisting that no individual go *altogether* uninstructed, Smith marks a thoroughly unique challenge within modern civilized society, what he calls "the liberal, or if you like, the loose system" (*Wealth* 794) of bringing the individual *en masse* to a peaceable, positive, if not also pleasurable concord with the imagined organization of equals he calls the state. The question of the state at this historical moment, of course, also contains at its very heart the question of particularity and wholeness, of divided universality, and of so-called English literature in the form of Scotland's still recent attachment to a Greater Britain after 1707.[92] In geopolitical terms, and with the violence of Jacobite rebellion in 1715 and 1745 at the center of debate in Smith's social and scholarly circles (e.g., at the Poker Club, as well as other philosophical fraternities), Scotland becomes that manifestation of the aesthetico-empirical surprise. But like surprise, Scotland is properly reduced—as it would be by Sir Walter Scott—to admiration, and from there to imagined social continuity in proleptic form. Implicit to this process, and as we shall see further, implicit to the distinctly Scottish home of the Enlightenment, is a kind of literary experiment that insures the spontaneous operation of a community of self-interested individuals. Smith endorsed a liberal approach to knowledge in such a way that would be appropriate to each in his rank. And a generous but highly specified dissemination of nonintelligence on this order is the way in which knowledge goes massively public for the first time. It is entirely consistent with the achievement of social concord against the partiality of inassimilable multitudes that, as we will detail in a moment, English literature originates on its territorial periphery well to the north of England proper.

Numerous scholars have documented the proliferation of print in the early modern period, and we will not rehearse that history in detail here.[93] Technological innovations such as moveable typeface, cheap and domestically produced ink, steam-driven presses, mail, circulating libraries, periodicals, and so on produced an unprecedented communicative infrastructure in the decades following the lapse of the (nominally censorious) Licensing Act during the 1694–95 English parliamentary sessions.[94]

And we should point out that the amassing of print in the eighteenth century—*contra* what Smith might have desired—did not occur according to a successive pattern of increase in books, writers, and readers, along the smooth numerical curve. In a particularly well-documented account of what he calls the reading nation (hereafter *RN*), William St. Clair notes that before the late eighteenth century, textual demand was concentrated among the higher income groups (*RN* 62). In the early seventeenth century, the archives show, "printer/ publishers were amongst the main commissioning agents of new titles, investing their own money in publishing almost all of the titles printed for sale" (*RN* 20). St. Clair reveals that only after an early period of contest (surprise), worry (wonder), and enthusiasm over print (admiration) does there gradually emerge a "text based culture of the people of England . . . [,] simultaneously centralised, controlled, and made more uniform, in a regime of regulated printed-book production that was both financially and culturally self-reinforcing" (*RN* 65). In the years immediately following Smith's most active writing period, St. Clair notes that

> a revolution in the production, selling, and in the reading of books in Great Britain had begun. . . .
>
> . . .
>
> After 1774 a huge, previously suppressed, demand for reading was met by a huge surge in the supply of [new] books, . . . [and] old printed texts . . . [in] the public domain. (*RN* 115)

As to the significance of such a precise date for the surge, we will have to wait for a moment. Simply note for now St. Clair's documentation of

> "a fourfold increase in output during the last quarter of the century . . . [and an] increase in acts of reading . . . of about fifty times" (*RN* 118).

St. Clair is careful to point out that, after about mid-century in Scotland, "membership [in reading societies and circulating libraries] was more socially mixed [than in England] and reached further down the income scale" (*RN* 251).[95] Indeed, by the early nineteenth century, many of the large numbers of "mechanics institutes, . . . [of which there was] a disproportionately large number in Scotland," had libraries containing "copies of Smith's *Wealth of Nations*, . . . [giving] many mechanics . . . better access to modern thought than their economic and social superiors" (*RN* 260). In this manner, St. Clair shows a later division within the division of work-related occupations, the organization of a newly educated aristocracy

> of labour, the natural leaders of the emerging urban working classes, and by giving them a share of the national reading from which they had been excluded, they would raise the moral level, as well as the economic efficiency, of the nation. (*RN* 260)

Smith was fully aware of the writing revolution and its special location in the university towns of Scotland. And he worked out the appropriate reception of the new media technology in terms that were consistent with his commitment to approbation and admiration. Without again rehearsing the sequence of the surprise of the new, through the pleasing wonder of ignorance, and ultimately, to admiration, we can instead refer briefly to "Lecture 11" of the *Lectures on Rhetoric and Belles Lettres* (*LRBL*). Here Smith focuses on the rules of criticism and gives a close reading of Shaftesbury's writing style, which he likens to the latter's constitution as being "puny" and "weakly" as well as "fatiguing" (*LRBL* 56). Smith thus cautions, as "writing . . . makes a man agreeable in company, . . . the agreeable man will regulate his natural temper. . . . [He will] lop off all exuberances and bring [his temper] to a pitch agreeable to those about him" (*LRBL* 55–56).

Smith characteristically does not oppose reason with affective response in order to achieve "regulate[d]" social "agreement": "The facts which are most commonly narrated and will be most adapted to the taste of the generality of men will be those that are interesting and important" (*LRBL* 90). We will have more exacting things to say about the keyword "taste" in a moment. For now, to further connect the moral-philosophic implications of the *TMS* with the proliferation of eighteenth-century writing, recall that earlier in this chapter we examined Smith's essay on the first formation of language as a smaller scale version of the impartial spectator's desire for social agreement. Smith's notion of abstract divided wholeness, we have seen, is traceable to the ethico-philosophical system described in the *TMS*. We have also remarked before how Smith bases his history of communication on the categorical imperative: "mankind['s] natural disposition to give to one object the name of any other, which resembles it, and thus to denominate a multitude" ("FF" 205).

We must now consider how "denominat[ing] a multitude" occurs on the more macrocosmic scale of written discourse as a mass event in its own right. Put simply, writing is also a "multitude" in need of "denominat[ion]." Writing initiates a uniquely powerful socio-affective ordering system—and *becomes* one—in that, in writing's newly institutionalized form, as it also goes massively public, interpretative worries intensify over how to circumscribe the generality of men where conflicts of partiality, affective and otherwise, might arise. Accordingly, Smith writes:

> The same sort of progress seems to have been made in the art of speaking as in the art of writing. . . . [T]hough particular words were thus represented by a greater number of characters, the whole language was expressed by a much smaller [number], and about four and twenty letters were found capable of supplying the place of that immense multitude of characters which were requisite before. . . .
>
> . . .
>
> As the numbers of words must, in this case, have become *really* infinite, in consequence of the *really* infinite variety of events, men found themselves partly compelled by necessity, and partly conducted by nature, to *divide* every event into what may be called its metaphysical elements, and to institute words, which should denote not so much the events, as the elements of which they were composed. . . . Expression, . . . became in this manner more intricate and complex, but the whole system of language became more coherent, more connected, more easily retained and comprehended. (emphasis ours, "FF" 218)

We see in Smith the characteristic mention of reality as unknowable and infinite. Reality, once again, is managed such that an incomprehensible scatter of factors that are implicit in a given event are made knowable according to how one divides them into generalizations. This process—echoing the omnipotence of *genus* for Smith—produces connectedness that is by definition somewhere on the other side of that which is "real."

At exactly this point of impasse between the real and the generalizable, we may consider the effects to which Smith adjoins his philosophical program to taste, and from there, the way in which the amassing of eighteenth-century writing raises the stakes of taste as a matter of social redress. The "Rules of criticism and morality," Smith writes, "when traced to their foundation, turn out to be some principles of common sense which everyone assents to. . . . [Both] are equally applicable to conversation and behavior as writing . . . [as both] make a man agreeable company" (*LRBL* 55). The word "common" here is characteristically amorphous, as in "*some* principles of common sense," as long as those principles deliver a more or less stable—if also fictional—arrangement of collective assent. And it is the association between moral philosophy and criticism *qua* writing that gains a certain public expansiveness for achieving divided wholeness. As we shall see in a moment, Smith's overlapping of philosophy and criticism as part of the same epistemic foundation becomes a focus for further division in its own right by other thinkers, as Smith's interpretive system is processed through the narrower standards that monitor aesthetic appreciation in a specifically literary form.

Siskin makes an important point regarding eighteenth-century disciplinary change that relates to what we have been calling philosophy's final disappearing act. We introduced this dynamic just above regarding the union of the English and Scottish parliaments. "Scotland," Siskin reminds us, "was the Enlightenment home of philosophical inquiry" (*WW* 80). The more important point for our purposes is that philosophy's disciplinary value diminishes as eighteenth-century writing proliferates and is further divided into more specialized disciplinary branches. In relation to Smith, a process of infra-divisional specialization *qua* displacement occurs—once again—by the management and further sorting of a multitude. Split off from philosophical prose, this instance of sorting was implicit to the proliferation of distinctly imaginative writing. A worried tension between the particular and general within a new specialty of criticism thus parallels a geopolitical tension between the early modern British nation and its (now internal) Scottish periphery. This geopolitical problem is one we take up in further detail in Chapter 3. Note for now that the disciplinary turn from philosophy broadly conceived toward the more individuated, yet somehow also more universalizing, discipline of literary studies occurs according to a fragile balance between the particular and the general already implicit within Smith's oeconomy of ignorance. This oeconomy, as we have seen many times over, is predicated not just on divisibility but on invisibility too.

Thus Scotland is not only set to become an object of wonder in a the Romantic zone of Highland nonintelligence (before Scott, the case in point here might be Wordsworth's "Highland Lass" in "The Solitary Reaper," who sings a pleasing but, for Wordsworth, incommunicable song of lost times in the formerly outlawed language of Gaelic); nor is Scotland designated as simply a marginal presence against which the British cultural center can be conceived.[96] We should say instead that Scotland became a historically unique geopolitical—as well as epistemological—*multiplier*. It occasioned the amassing, division, and eventual unification of bodies, nations, and books.

The most curious part of (Scottish) philosophy's historical displacement by (English) literary criticism is that it occurs by extending the very philosophical program that was itself about to be erased. The "British discipline," Lord Kames writes in *Elements of Criticism* (*EC*), "is susceptible of great improvements . . . [and would provide] a complete system of education" for the newly unified empire (*EC* 3). Worth noting here is that the strategy of improvement and completion occurs for Lord Kames, as for his younger colleague and mentee, not by way of categorical opposition per se, but less perceptibly, by processing multiplicity through an innovative knowledge system such that new divisions, spurred on by those surprisingly powerful gaps, as well as new unities could appear. In mid-eighteenth century Scotland, the future knowledge specialty called literary criticism emerges, on one hand, by looking forward to a branch of liberal learning designed to manage the proliferation of printed imaginative text precisely through such proliferation. But on the other hand, if philosophical inquiry advanced in this way, it also worked in reverse such that certain philosophical tendencies toward division are ironically sussed out of the advance of liberal learning so as to make the earlier privileges the philosophical imagination itself go away. According to this final act of disciplinary disappearance, the predominance of a general practice of knowledge called philosophy could finally go toward having a historically invisible presence of its own in the rising shadow of the literary arts. Philosophical inquiry was alas cordoned off as sufficiently distinct from criticism and aesthetic appreciation. As it became of secondary value given literature's monopolization of imaginative thought, philosophy's greatest historical achievement in the final part of Smith's career was to dissolve.

That Smith joined taste and morality on behalf of social agreement only seems puzzling if we look backwards through a series of critics—Scottish critics—who would coax ahead his principles of philosophical division further than his own writings do. Which critics, and why Scottish, we may now better surmise. David Hume and Lord Kames are significant additions to Smith, and not just because of their friendship or professional proximity to him. They are important figures for their development of a specifically literary criticism in the period. As such, they pursue the advance of taste in the Smithian terms of particularity and wholeness, of imaginary transcendence over the real infinity of numbers, and of the few tasked with sorting the many. Again we must mark the problem of the manifold here not only as a matter of subjects aligning with objects but also as retaining an almost overwhelming sense of writing's own multiplication.

For the Scottish intelligentsia, the revolution in writing gains special intensity as a problem immanent to dividing multitudes. As early as 1712, Swift famously called not only for "correcting, [and improving] . . . the English tongue" but also, less famously, for ascertaining it as well.[97] Scottish literacy was already at seventy-five percent by mid-century, almost 90 percent by the time of Smith's death, the highest in the Western world. Whereas only two books of English grammar were published in the sixteenth century, and only seventeen for the next hundred years, by the time of the writing revolution in mid-century Scotland, there were thirty-five different grammars available, and five times that number by the eighteenth century's end. In addition, Scotland's population grew five times faster than England's between 1750 and 1800, providing unprecedented growth in the number of readers and students.[98] As Thomas Laqueur notes, by the late eighteenth century reading by the working class was no longer just a leisure activity.[99] But what happened before that? We want to show now how print-based forms of reason were established by attending to the so-called multitude in a way designed to lessen the conflict between ranks while treating the proliferation of writing itself as a mass problem in need of dividing. Thus let us now turn to a Scottish legal case that contributed greatly to the mass commodification of writing in the eighteenth century and advanced the standards of taste along the lines of Smith's pleasing wonders of ignorance.

Several steps above we noted the association between a nonexclusivist approach to the availability of print and the emergence of mass morality, and we should reconnect with that association here. Having set the stakes for the emergence of a reading public, we can now better address the date of 1774, in *Scotland*, as a crucial time and place for a numerical spike in the multiplication of books, especially *English* literary books. At issue here is a defining piece of Scottish jurisprudence that overturned the English law of perpetual copyright established by the 1710 Statute of Anne.[100]

Given the new pressures attached to the increasing book trade after mid-century, the King's Bench in London was forced to review the law, offering a split decision on whether to sustain the statute in 1773. As the case involved both London (the plaintiff) and Edinburgh (the defendant) booksellers, and as significant numbers of the book in question were sold in Scotland (some ten thousand copies), it was appropriate that Scottish law offer an opinion, which overturned the earlier English statute. It is apposite to the changing media culture of the early modern period that, according to the judgment of the Scottish bench overturning the statute, which emanated from a system based not on common law but on Roman law, the publication industry of Great Britain would have been declared a pirate industry for the previous sixty-four years. In the case of *Hinton v. Donaldson*, the Scottish court's challenge to common-law property rights was applied to printed knowledge. This was designed to maximize the public's interest (and the printer's profit) in the publication of new titles.

Significantly for our purposes, a mass of backlisted books and ancient printed texts could now enter the public domain. Indeed, the book in question in the 1774 decision, a Bible with commentary, had been originally published in 1567. The court's near unanimous decision (James Burnett, Lord Monboddo being the single holdout) was decisive in the material establishment of English literature in its micro-institutional form of the anthology. Thus the first widely circulated volumes of English literature enter here: Bell's *The Annotated Edition of the English Poets* (a shilling per volume); Percy's *Reliques of Ancient English Poetry*; Peyton's *History of the English Language, 1771*; and the first monograph on English literature, Thomas Warton's *History of English Poetry*.[101]

Indeed, this early modern media bubble marked the largest case ever to come before the Scottish courts, worth a sum of about 200,000 pounds. *Hinton* proved to be an exponential multiplier for the production and circulation of printed material in England and Scotland: The 1774 judgment not only put more new books into circulation, but by making books less expensive, it also put more readers into contact with a great number of out-of-print books, which in turn needed to be sorted by the standards of taste.[102] The urgency in that kind of sorting is clear: On the one hand, Lord Kames (in *Sketches on the History of Man*, hereafter *SHM*) could complain mightily that the "great revolution in printing, [which provided] the opportunity to furnish multiple copies [of books], has degraded writing."[103] On the other hand, he and his Scottish cohort would rise to the occasion they created in order to introduce a tasteful appreciation of imaginative work in the formal appearance of English literary studies in Edinburgh, Glasgow, and the like.

That Adam Smith was an advisor to the court on the *Hinton* case enhances the significance of a Scottish judgment in determining the reading practices of England. In arguing against the monopoly of trade in *Wealth*, Smith uses the challenge to perpetual copyright for the printers in the emerging book trade as his primary example. To grant a limited monopoly to a "company of merchants [when they] undertake . . . to establish a new trade with some remote and barbarous nation . . . [are the] same principles upon which a like monopoly is granted . . . [for] a new book to its author" (*Wealth* 754). (Smith himself shrewdly negotiated a deal with his Edinburgh bookseller to buy back some of the books he purchased once Smith had read them.) Lord Kames, the author of *Elements of Criticism*—which was cited in *Hinton* during the argument for the defense—offered a formal opinion as a member of the Scottish bench that draws on the vocabulary of Smith's oeconomy of ignorance.

Indeed, the key component of Smith's imagined concord of divided wholeness was firmly in place as a challenge to the Statute of Anne. Kames, for example, is convinced that "lifetime copyright . . . [would limit] the interest in learning in general."[104] He goes on to appeal to the principles of sorting, of maximizing the circulation of writing but minimizing the standards of taste, as a matter "singularly beneficial to the public" (*Hinton* 20). The court documents thus remark on the "*incorporeal* substance of an idea . . . [as a] non-entity" (emphasis ours, *Hinton* 7). And this process of *de*-corporealization of what, for a little while anyway, might have otherwise been counted as "real," is essential, as Kames puts it elsewhere, to the "maturity of civil society."

Up until this moment, which the *Hinton* case was expressly made to bring about, "man is almost all body" (*SHM* I, 333); "dull and stupid" (*SHM* I, 106); prone to "degenerate into oysters" (*SHM* I, 107). The argument here proceeds precisely according to the method of abstraction outlined by Smith, a canceling of material infinity, a process of *de*-corporealization that gives thought, or more specifically writing, a uniquely phantasmatic status at this point: Beyond the realm of physical work and its multitudes, print is encouraged to proliferate (and can be sorted) on the basis of its legally mandated *immateriality*. As Lord Coalston adjudicates in the *Hinton* transcripts: "property . . . should relate to something corporeal and tangible; whereas abstract ideas are not corporeal, but purely spiritual and mental" (emphasis ours, *Hinton* 27). This decisive change of statute on copyright is peculiar. Note that the so-called mystery of authorcraft after 1774 is both specified by and attached to that rare genius thinker—the few learned writers, as Kames remarks (*Hinton* 20).

But note, even more crucially than this, that literary writing also signals a new kind of non-corporeal collective ownership. Written intellectual property builds in its own negation as a spiritual and mental object of appreciation. And this process of *de*-corporealization takes place according to the by now familiar dynamic of dividing the manifold (as labor, body, masses) into socially peaceable categories that are established by the few. "The act of reprinting," Lord Gardenston opines, "is merely mechanical. . . . The stupid mechanic . . . [has] no similarity with the author's art of genius" (*Hinton* 24). We have seen this evocation of "stupid" (because merely corporeal) labor before. The best—because least turbulent—form of social organization is recommended by the (learned) few, and imagined to apply to the (laboring) many. Again, paradoxically, a multitude is worked into appropriate divisions such that the great bulk of mankind exists on an unknowable side of reality, while at the same time it surrenders when good taste is at work to the wonderful fictions ordinary readers might now safely acquire (*Hinton* 19). As Kames argues in the *Hinton* case:

> [A]n author has an interest . . . in the productions of his own brain, by which he is at liberty to publish or conceal them; and to make what conditions he chooses on communicating them, either to intimates or the public. When he has committed them in writing . . . this property, in so far as it exists, is merely a creature of civil society. (*Hinton* 32)

Writing, as we have already detailed with the impartial spectator within civil society, is likewise phantasmatic. More precisely, thoughts, once published, exist in a zone given over in Smith's ethico-philosophical system as well as in the *Hinton* case to the imagination variously conceived. The Scottish ruling did not vacate copyright, exactly, though it limited the book trade in a way that modulated the materiality of writing such that it could also proliferate in unprecedented ways. Writing is here both a particular kind of something, and equally, a privileged way of doing nothing: a nonentity that men of letters make available for general admiration. The laws of real property no longer govern writing. And writing cannot be called production in the sense of belonging to real and corporeal (in Smith's sense of those terms) labor. Rather, it is like Jupiter's invisible hand, a point of invisibility beyond which our knowledge cannot go.

What Kames legally defends—indeed, before it needs defending—is the "interest of literature" (his phrase) as it takes on a newly capacious *and* specialized role in attempting to resolve Smith's paradox of divided wholeness. "There is no foundation for this [perpetual] *copy-right* [for] authors in the common principles of law," Kames continues. "The only ground for it [written property] is this, that, from the love of knowledge, and the admiration of the works of learning and genius, mankind are prone to give to authors . . . the reward that is due to them for their work" (*Hinton* 15). It is better for the writer-genius to be loved than paid. Smith's oeconomy of ignorance thus advances in a next phase according to the de-corporealization of literary property. To quote Kames a final time from the 1774 *Hinton* decision:

> Property, when applied to ideas, or literary and intellectual compositions, is perfectly new and surprising. In a law tract on these species of property, the division of its subjects would be perfectly curious; by far the most comprehensive denomination would be, a property in nonsense. It must also branch out into the property of bawdy, blasphemy, and treason. (*Hinton* 25)

The defense of literature occurs at the very moment literature is conceived, and its defense rests decidedly on Kames's ironic but totally appropriate juxtaposition between property and nonsense.

This juxtaposition marks the nonintelligence implicit within the circulation of written knowledge as an immaterial force, now legally insured. Thus nonsense—for which we can supplement Smith's wonder of ignorance—is equal in the sense that everyone can have it (recall Smith's idiot-hero) but nobody can own it; nobody can trace it to the question of money, the greater part of the majority, or for that matter, "real" work. "Comprehens[ive] denomination," because *un-knowable* as it is now rendered *un-ownable*. This is ultimately what contrasts "nonsense" with "property": The former cannot be specified save by the *de*-corporealization of the book into a sense of common ownership that exists nowhere save in an abstract imagined ideal. It is this fictional sense of common ownership that transcends a society that is really (Smith's term) predicated on the dynamics of unequal ownership, the dynamics that no one—save the blasphemous, riotous, or treasonous—can speak.

The legal de-corporealization of the book is accompanied, as we shall now further detail, by a more specific terminology of criticism. This is the terminology of taste and admiration, divided ever more precisely under the emergent heading of English literature. As we have noted, Smith developed such terms in a less specialized way according to the general interpretive system of moral philosophy. But soon enough, philosophy was divided further: Its purchase on imaginative work found a several hundred-year-old resting place as having at best a secondary purchase on the imagination after literature. In the *Hinton* case, Lord Gardenston goes out of his way to dismiss the "great bulk of books" (*Hinton* 23), which, he remarks, do not deserve Kames's reward of approbation and praise (*Hinton* 18). Gardenston admonishes:

> [He] who steals from common authors, steals trash; but he who steals from a *Spencer*, a *Shakespeare*, or a *Milton*, steals the fire of heaven, and the most precious gifts of nature—So we must have new statutes to regulate those literary felonies. (*Hinton* 26)

A statute that would mandate an English literary canon by Scottish jurisprudence was not to be: Bad taste and idiocy were never made illegal. But that is only because a more efficient—because self-administered—mechanism of affective regulation was developed along the lines of Smith's loose system of liberal education: a sleight of invisible hand that both narrows the selection of heavenly inspired geniuses and widens accessibility to select texts according to their hierarchical rank.

Smith thus confronted a Janus-faced problem: on the one side, an *expansion* of print culture from the Scottish provinces; and on the other, a *narrowing* in on English writing. Working toward greater generalization through new forms of division—the effacement of both national and epistemological difference—is the paradox that the Enlightenment's moderate literati teach us not to examine too closely. "Scotland," Smith writes in his friend Alexander Wedderburn's short-lived *Edinburgh Review* (1755–56), is

> just beginning to attempt figuring in the learned world. [It has] so few works of reputation [that it is] scarce possible [that] a paper which criticizes upon them chiefly should interest the public. . . . Imagination, genius and invention seem to be the talents of the English. (*EPS* 242–243)

While man is "made a social being," the 1774 court documents state, "at the same time he [is] made an imitative being in order to follow what he sees done by others" (*Hinton* 19). Our earlier point about the displacement of philosophy by literature should thus be seen as a Scottish preoccupation with so-called English genius that eventually effaces Scotland's decisive contribution to literary studies (*EPS* 242).

We can now turn to certain Scottish harbingers of English literature—Smith and Hume, and more importantly Kames—that help to sort great literature from the great majority of other books. From here, we can see how Smith's oeconomy of ignorance exists not just at the social and epistemic level but also in a more developed way as a problem of modern disciplinary formation.

Looking to Hume, we may simplify the process cultivating indifference toward the majority in a way akin to Smith's earlier use of the term "indifference" as ignorance toward the multitude.[105] To repeat, by evoking Smith's term "indifference," we are not saying that there was a simple absence of care. It is the generative power of absence (of ignorance, gaps, imagination) and the particular measure of care (about bodies, workers, and books) that we are after by focusing on Enlightenment indifference. Smith was famously aware in *Wealth* and other places of what later comes to be called class conflict, the misery of the poor and the indigent, as we will elaborate on at length in Chapter 4. With our focus on the divisions of knowledge in mind, think here of indifference as a condition inspired by that which cannot be divided because it exceeds categorical circumscription. This is the same condition of so-called reality—like bodily work for the idiot majority—that dare not speak its name in the tight circles where imaginary thinking is professionally done.

In this sense of indifference, there is the familiar notion of abstract universality across the real division ranks—not simply as ranks exist in the form of interpretive objects but also in terms of the kinds of communities those objects create. "The study of the beauties," Hume suggests in *Essays Moral, Political, Literary* (hereafter *EMPL*), "give [true critics] a certain elegance of sentiment to which the rest of mankind are strangers" (*EMPL* 7). And the "delicacy of taste . . . confin[es] our choice to few people, . . . making us indifferent to the company and conversation of the greater part of men" (*EMPL* 7). By "what marks are they [critics] to be known," Hume asks? "How [to] distinguish them from pretenders"—of which, with the new surplus of written texts, there had to be more than ever (*EMPL* 241)? (Let's also note the cagey evocation of the Jacobite threat behind the word "pretender," which we will cover more completely in Chapter 3.) Hume requires a "delicacy of passion, . . . a cultivating of that higher and more refined taste . . . [to] judge the characters of men, of compositions of genius, and of the productions of the nobler . . . liberal arts" (*EMPL* 6). The "knowledge of *both books and mankind* [may be enjoyed] but in the company of a few select companions. . . . All the rest of mankind fall short" (emphasis ours, *EMPL* 7).

It is not so much what Schliesser recalls as the vanity of the philosopher that is of interest for our purposes. He may be correct that Hume was "a passionate elitist," while Smith remained "ambiguous"—or we would say, conflicted—by the relationship between the thinker and the so-called general-ity of mankind.[106] Elsewhere Schliesser admits that Hume's benignly dubbed "community of experts" becomes for Smith "a distinction between the 'bulk of mankind' and 'philosophers' [that] manifests itself in a difference in curiosity." But he also adds, and we agree, that this "difference is largely the effect of the divisions of labor."[107] Schliesser accepts that Smith's philosophy, insofar as it reconciles benevolence with self-interest, might "save society from the narrow interests of the profit-earning class."[108] But he leaves room for more nettlesome possibilities, by remarking that Smith was also quite aware of the Enlighten-ment's limits.

Lauren Brubaker, who highlights the lack of guarantees in Smith's philo-sophical *qua* social system, is one of a handful of essays on "the popular En-lightenment" that introduces what those limits eventually turned out to be.[109] Brubaker's is a far more circumspect Smith, with a wary eye on political fac-tion. Exactly which faction(s), and how close they may be with the working poor, are left unnamed. Smith's Enlightenment is thus recast from the liberal optimism it has for more orthodox Smith scholars to being "a limited and cau-tious Enlightenment."[110] Exactly in what way limited, and with caution related to whom and to what, are questions we want to answer here by detailing how philosophy worked in Smith's time. Imaginative work certainly did not cut ex-clusively in the direction of serving the working poor. Clearly, for both Smith and Hume what can be agreed upon is that the work of the many enabled the thinking of the few,[111] and that such a form of enabling should be explained much further, especially when it comes to the imagination.

The job of the critic in Hume, like Smith who comes after him, is specifically a matter of using imagination to do species work. The critic "marks the distin-guishing species of each quality [of an object], and assigns it suitable praise or blame." In this way, the object is itself less an object as such than a complex amalgamation of elements that criticism sorts in order to accomplish the same sorting at the level of a unified social imaginary: The critic, Hume continues, "discerns that very degree and *kind* of approbation of displeasure, which each part [of an object] is naturally fitted to produce" (emphasis ours, *EMPL* 237). "A man" (read "a non-leisured man") "who has had no opportunity of compar-ing the different kinds of beauty, is indeed totally unqualified to pronounce an opinion with regard to any object presented to him" (*EMPL* 238).

Certain key elements of Smith's oeconomy of ignorance are at work in Hume's literary essays, and they are easy to point out: division, species, rank, indifference, and, finally, appreciation writ as the refinement of taste. In Hume, more decidedly, books and man present a common dynamic of sorting the manifold by those fit few who claim no particular connection to self-interest at all. "The mass [of mankind] cannot be altogether insipid, from which such refined spirits are extracted," Hume writes in a more modest example of Smith's perversely democratic endorsement of liberal learning (*EMPL* 114). The term "mass" clearly indicates Hume's careful attention to composite singularity into a more properly divided sense of wholeness that the leisured few will designate in relation to the laboring majority. "Those who cultivate the sciences in any state, are always few in number: . . . taste and judgment . . . always [exist in the] few in all nations and ages" (*EMPL* 114). As such, the "critic . . . consider[ing] [him]self as a man in general, [must] forget, if possible, [his] individual being and . . . peculiar circumstances" (*EMPL* 239). It is thus a crucial part of creating literary posterity for the critic to entertain equal portions of forgetfulness. Here "forgetfulness" is of his own and everybody else's peculiarity of judgment. And that kind of forgetfulness functions more effectively to produce the myth of universal approbation as enjoyed by learned initiates than it does for the masses of others. Hume insists, only "one accustomed to see[ing] . . . and weigh[ing] the several performances, admired in different ages . . . [can] assign [them their] proper rank." And to be so accustomed, "the elegant part of mankind, who are not immersed in the animal life [of work], but employ themselves in the operations of the mind, . . . require leisure and solitude . . . [over] labour" (*EMPL* 533).

Hume writes further, those who are placed among the lower rank of men "have little opportunity of exerting any other virtue, besides those of patience, resignation, industry, and integrity" (*EMPL* 546). To the erasure of corporeal work by philosophy, to the *de*-corporealization of a printed idea, and to the eventual erasure of philosophy according to the same habits of increased division, we could add a bigger species problem: the "animal." This could be contrasted with Francis Hutcheson's earlier assessment, ignored by Hume, that "the lower rank of Mankind, whose only revenue is their bodily labour, . . . have often more correct imaginations . . . than others can acquire by Philosophy."[112] In the process of evoking taste on behalf of social cohesion and toward the abridgment of philosophical gaps, Hume posits taste and criticism above animals and physical work, creating a yet further refined capacity that divides the leisured from the industrious classes. Hume's call for the latter's resignation (or as Hume insists, their "patience") is where he parts from Smith's more optimistic interest in liberal learning. But in common they share the concern of finding a more or less peaceable way of processing the great bulk of mankind, which for Smith rather than Hume is to be acquired by *their own* proficiencies in "reading, writing, and accounting." Hume writes:

> To say, that any event is derived from chance, cuts short all farther enquiry concerning it, and leaves the writer in the same state of ignorance with the rest of mankind. But . . . he may then display his ingenuity, in assigning these causes; . . . [H]e has thereby an opportunity of swelling his volumes . . . observing what escapes the vulgar and ignorant. (*EMPL* 111)

As we shall see, that zone of ignorance occupied by the vulgar majority is analogously the focus of wonder that the *literary* writer—finally, quite apart from the philosopher is able to do within the new discipline of literary studies. A properly cultivated mass readership joins criticism in providing both for swelling volumes and narrowing taste. As we'll see now, this happened according to a more finely divided form of writing, unique in Scotland, that in turn spawned a new English literary landscape. But here too—like the eventual displacement of philosophy by a more specialized kind of thinking—the divisions between those two nations are supposed to disappear.

Within the eighteenth-century surge of Scottish learning, Lord Kames is clear on the connection between Scotland's unity with England as being predicated on the ignorance, impartiality, invisibility, and indifference that become the unique provenance of literary studies as it nudges philosophy into a more narrow sector of the "liberal arts," disinterested and *de*-corporealized as criticism (and the law) proceeded to make it. Indeed, Kames develops Smith's oeconomy of ignorance by offering us the additional terms: momentary stupefaction, void, vacancy, unreal presence, vacuity in the mind, and, simply, fiction. Kames dedicated *Elements of Criticism* to King George III, uncle to Culloden's Butcher, the Duke of Cumberland, whom we have mentioned in association with the anti-Jacobite massacres there. The fine arts, he assures the sovereign, "by uniting different ranks in the same elegant pleasures . . . promote benevolence . . . [,] love of order . . . [, and] submission to government." In appealing to his majesty for patronage, Kames's *Elements of Criticism* (*EC*) "attempts to form a standard of taste . . . that ought to govern the taste of every individual" (*EC* 3).

We need not over-read this set of citations in order to mark the similarity between Smith's interest in taste as a principle of impartial spectatorship and Kames's rather more explicit endorsement of the kind of elegant pleasures that insure coherence of the state. The philosopher-generalist and the literary critic both offer a way to parse every individual through the division of ranks and finally into the abstraction of national wholeness. Kames employs the term "discipline" in its two senses throughout *Elements of Criticism* to designate both the divisions of knowledge and the "ideal presence" from which "is derived that extensive influence . . . [that] strengthens the bond[s] of society" (*EC* 74). For Kames, the uniformity of taste equals the uniformity of national form, or should ideally. And it is the task of criticism in particular to de-particularize the "bias of the mind" that makes us "wander from truth as well as from justice" (*EC* 74). That it also, as we have seen, works to de-corporealize the text is also important. "Justice," as Kames uses the term, is predicated on an encouragement of pleasurable distinction that reduces injustice to a matter of putting the manifold into an individuated and properly ranked metaphysics of universal abstraction. "The acquisition of knowledge," Kames writes, "results chiefly from discovering resemblances among differing objects, . . . abstracting from the knowledge we acquire, . . . [and] preserving a middle rate between too great uniformity and too great variety" (*EC* 226). In short, "the mind relisheth not a multiplicity of figures" (*EC* 226). The similarity to Smith on moral philosophy, impartiality, indifference to multitudes—and on ignorance—is notable here.

But we should underscore that Kames provides the name "criticism" rather than "philosophy" as that modality of thinking that imaginatively "abridges" (Smith's term) the unforeseen interruptions of epistemic and as sociopolitical gaps that obedient men of good taste teach the rest of us to ignore and forget. This further division within the specialty of literary criticism belies a certain anxiety about the institutionalization of a modern disciplinary category that is worth mapping now. By the word "institution," we mean to introduce our final move in this chapter, which is to remark upon the formation of English as a specialty within Scotland's uniquely liberal university system. For Kames, the incalculable problem of multiplicity is finally addressed. Like Smith, the multitude lies outside the ken of rational thinking; but unlike Smith, or better, advancing Smith's divisions of knowledge one step further than he did, Kames proposes to overcome the manifold with a still finer-tuned version of imaginative writing. Literary study—a more limited *and* more massively available new disciplinary practice—emerges over and beyond the general principles of general philosophical thought.

Indeed, as we have emphasized, the term "philosophy," as the term "science," for Smith simply meant rigorous intellectual exercise. Hume, recall, was not an academic, try though he did. According to criticism's triple move of literary development, philosophical displacement, and institutionalization, Kames introduces the term "fiction." He writes, "the power that fiction hath over the mind affords an endless variety of refined amusements, always at hand to employ a vacant hour." The "endless variety," and the hopes and fears they generated for the masses, especially in the form of reading novels, we will detail in Chapter 3. In contrast to, Kames continues,

> examples confined to *real* events . . . no other sort of discipline [as the improvement from fable] contributes more to make virtue habitual. . . . [The power of fiction] is a fine resource in solitude . . . [and] contribute[s] mightily to social happiness. (emphasis ours, *EC* 77)

Note here that the fictional "endless[ness]" that Kames finds acceptable over reality is not the multiple or infinite, which he finds decidedly dangerous. "In some instances," he writes, "an unexpected object overpowers the mind so as to produce a momentary stupefaction: where the object is dangerous . . . without preparation, [it] is apt totally to unhinge the mind" (*EC* 188).

The reference to stupidity this time is made to trigger special preparation. It exists, as in Smith's oeconomy of ignorance, as if in a moment of dangerous surprise; but the moment is almost immediately short-circuited by an invisible activity of philosophical reflection *qua* epistemic division that is taking place within a new disciplinary boundary. In Kames's case, the activity is already taking place according to the preprogrammed appreciation of literary texts: first, as literary criticism displaces the more general philosophical practice of knowledge, and, second, as literature itself is allowed to safely circulate in an institutionalized form. The value of stupefaction—its pleasure and its ability to inspire political passivity (Hume's "patience")—is realized according to admiration (*EC* 185). In this way "we"—and the collective pronoun is crucial—"are soon reconciled to an object" (*EC* 186).

This process of reconciliation and refinement is notable in Smith but is applied in a more urgent and focused way in Kames. For both, refinement fills a vacancy that is precisely the rejection of a "real" event. For both, the "common nature in every species, paves the way finely for distributing things into *genera* and *species;* to which we are extremely prone." Kames continues, "[The] common nature of man . . . is invariable [and] not less than universal" (*EC* 721). We can extend the critical frisson that pops up between imagination and reality, between philosophical bridging and gaps, and between thought and corporeal production in this set of passages, and trace Smith's oeconomy of ignorance to Kames's fictional representation of the "real." Note that universality is once again achieved by the massification of fineness writ as getting division correct. What Kames is careful to endorse is a specific fineness of the fine arts found through criticism (*EC* 221). If universal distribution is necessarily absent save in a literary form, it is because commonness paradoxically achieves its empty successes through an abridging of properly divided *genera*. As with Smith, we can link Kames's commitment to vacant sociality with "fine"—instead of a "real"—commitment to universal distribution. In this manner, Smith's attention to the "real" as the unintelligible agency of multitudes is equal to Kames's bracketing of the "real event" (his term) as a fleeting moment of stupefaction. The "stupid" and the "real" are the twin opponents of "taste" because neither conform to its disciplinary standards.

Our focus on the *vacancy* of reality in Kames—vacancy writ here counterintuitively as simply containing *too many* objects, bodies, books—takes us back to the issue of stupid labor. As we have noted, the multitude, this problem of too many, is imagined by the few elegant thinkers to be reconciled with morality, for Kames explicitly, as a kind of binding *un*-reason of state. We have addressed the issue of critical nonintelligence in Smith as general philosophical wonder and the disinterested production of what he called "nothing." In Hume, we have remarked on the privilege of criticism's few true practitioners to claim universality over the laboring masses. We have also addressed this issue of sorting the manifold in simpler terms in both Smith and in Kames as what we called *de*-corporealization, yet another level of division that designates the separation between contemplative abstraction and bodily labor, where the former gains its special dominion over the latter given the inevitable inequalities of rank. In Kames, the massification of the fine arts vis-à-vis the physical numerical increase in literary books, combined with the rarefication of the standard of taste, throws the thinking versus labor distinction into even sharper relief. And that sharper relief brings a special set of anxieties about literary admiration, to which we alluded above: Not only does fictional abstraction mark a more specialized achievement of the imaginary task of criticism to displace the more general practice of philosophy, but this division of knowledge also more strictly divides the difference between writing and bodily work.

More so than Smith, Kames appears sanguine about "the separation of men into different classes, by birth, office, or occupation" (*EC* 724). And while all "classes" should have pleasures in common, Kames writes, "we justly condemn every taste that deviates from what is thus ascertained by the common standard" (*EC* 724). It should come as no surprise that for Kames, "those who depend for food on bodily labour, are totally void of taste" (*EC* 726). And in *Sketches on the History of Man*, he is even more explicitly clear on the division between writing and physical work: "young persons who continue there [in charity schools] so long as to read and write fluently, become too delicate for hard labour, and too proud for ordinary labour" (*SHM* II, 535). More than that, "knowledge is a dangerous acquisition to the labouring poor: . . . a shepherd, a ploughman, or any drudge" (*SHM* II, 534).

Smith makes a similar opposition between labor and taste in his lectures on *belles lettres*, with a characteristically enigmatic nod to the all-important "nothing" and "no one" attached: "There are many who are not obliged to labour for their livelihood and have nothing to do, but employ themselves in what most suits their taste." With further acknowledgment of the proliferation of writing, Smith continues, "In this state it is that prose begins to be cultivated. . . . Prose is the style in which all the common affairs of life [and] all business agreements are made" (*LRBL* 137). "No one," Smith has famously remarked, "ever made a bargain in verse" (*LRBL* 137). Thus, commonality is achieved—again consistent with an epistemology of division—both by allowing greater access to the fine arts, and, to refer back to Kames, "the exclusion of classes so many and numerous reduces within a narrow compass those who are qualified to be judges" (*EC* 727).

Against this sort of commonality, the empty space of labor exists as a majority—a commonality of "nothing" and a "no one"—whose effect on thought is evacuated save by the prescriptions of so-called public approbation. In *Observations Upon Liberal Education* (1742), George Turnbull remarks "it is manifestly necessary to the general good, that very many men should . . . be fitter for execution by bodily labour than for invention" (*OU* 119). Again, we do not wish to deny that there are important differences between Turnbull and the Aberdeen group (which included Reid and Ferguson) and Smith's Edinburgh and Glasgow cohort.[113] But citing Turnbull does allow us to see the different directions that a certain Smithian focus on divisions could take. Turnbull continues, "the general good requires that men should be, as it were, divided by nature into the labouring or executing part, and the consultative or directing part . . . though we cannot positively say whether it be in consequence of an original partition of abilities" (*OU* 119).

Criticism, named by Kames as the penultimate achievement of prose, achieves exclusion and cultivation at one and the same time—a partition *and* a general good; and the greater (i.e., laboring) parts of men are increasingly nudged outside the privilege of invention. "In the fine arts," Kames continues, "taste must be improved by education, reflection, and experience . . . [such that we] give welcome to every rational pleasure without indulging any excess" (*EC* 727). The proper exclusion of "excess" via the proliferation of imaginative writing is the special dynamic Kames wants to achieve in these passages. We could say that if the 1774 *Hinton* case against perpetual copyright judges on behalf of the widening availability of literary works, then it is precisely the capacity to judge those works in a tasteful way that authorizes criticism in the opposite direction of narrowing imaginative pleasure.

This oscillation between the widening dissemination of writing and the narrowing of disciplines is worth developing as we close this chapter with some remarks on the Scottish university. Kames, as we have said, develops the divisions of knowledge such that the more specialized discipline of literary criticism displaces the more general philosophical project provided by Smith. In this way, the standards of taste continue to provide a mechanism against which to separate the imagination's task from bodily labor. Turnbull, Hume, and Smith, while they differ in their levels of hope for, or fear of, the corporeal condition, have commonly referred to it as a "multitude." Again counterintuitively, the empty space of corporeal labor outside criticism is coequal with the greater part of men, who themselves must be moved by way of spectatorial abstraction toward public peace.

To refer once more to Oxford's yet more extreme Reverend Knox, what he calls the "Hydra-headed" proliferation of books is itself a problem of numbers; but books are a problem of numbers designed to solve other numbers problems. "Particularly in the present age," Knox writes, "the dispersion of books . . . strike at the root of piety and moral virtue by propagating opinions favorable to the materialist, the skeptic, and the voluptuary" (*EML* 376–377). By narrowing in on taste as a rarified, soon to be academic sensibility—*contra* Knox—Kames narrows the imaginative capacities of moral philosophy into the discrete domain of the "fine arts." It is not as if morality and literature fail to work in common, of course. Rather, at this historical moment in the Scottish educational system, as we shall see, imaginative writing is institutionalized according to the spectatorial indifference of criticism, the moment literature as such comes to exist.

Thus in addition to Kames's appeal to pleasures in common, we must note that he insists upon "distinguishing the moral sense [of right and wrong] from the sense of right and wrong in the fine arts." He continues: "The former, as a rule of conduct, and as a law we ought to obey, must be clear and authoritative. The latter is not entitled to the same privilege, because it contributes to our pleasure and amusement" (*EC* 725). The fine arts without criticism are in this sense inconceivable—*precisely* inconceivable—both as pleasing ignorance and as a problem of sorting the manifold. Kames continues:

> The standard of taste in the fine arts is not yet brought to such perfection [as other branches of knowledge;] . . . the sense of right and wrong in the fine arts is faint and wavering, because its objects are commonly not so clearly distinguishable from each other. (*EC* 725–726)

Thus for Kames, "more circumspection is requisite with respect to the fine arts than with respect to morals [and therefore] a wary choice is necessary" (*EC* 726). We have already reviewed Smith's wariness over poetry (not to mention Romance) as a problem of too much interpretive difference. This is something, recall, with which music does not have to contend and is less a concern with mathematics and natural philosophy. In the episode of increase set up by Kames, the word "more" in the phrase "more circumspection" marks a tendency for literature-without-criticism to resist its later objectification, which is to say, resist becoming literature as such among so much other learned writing.

Kames, by noting a faint and wavering capacity of sense in the newly accessible fine arts, inadvertently puts on the table a troubling—because potentially massive—antiformalist notion of the imagination that erupts in the way surprise did in Smith's general interpretive system. As a not yet realizable branch of the liberal disciplines, literature's original incompletion spells out an ambivalent role for the pleasing wonders of ignorance against what would otherwise be a canonically adequate series of aesthetic texts. In this manner, a different conception of the common is half-consciously introduced. And by extension, the redivision of a formerly illiberal knowledge system is projected for an instant in a state of worried incompletion. Outside the laws of judgment, wealth, and taste, a wavering—if also vacant, imperfect, and potentially nonauthoritative—set of social and epistemic alternatives seem to flash before us here.

This flashpoint is the moment at which the establishment of English literature within the Scottish university finds its conservative cause. When Smith praised the cheapness of a literary education in *Wealth*, which he linked directly to decisive changes in the art of printing, he was referring to the most significant set of events around disciplinary change within modern higher education. Having been at Oxford himself for a period, Smith remarks in a letter to William Cullen that the organization of the university is of great interest to him (*Correspondence* 173). "I have thought a great deal upon this subject," he writes in *Wealth*, "and have inquired very carefully into the constitution and history of several principle Universities of Europe" (*Wealth* 758). Smith spends the greater part of his focus on the passages that follow this citation on the problems of funding and access, as well as on Roman education at its best. He singles out endowments as being particularly corrupting to the commitment of the sinecured Oxford professoriate, where birth and fortune are more respected than merit (*Wealth* 761). "In the University of Oxford," he writes, "the greater part of the public professors, have for these many years, given up altogether even the pretence of teaching" (*Wealth* 710). Smith himself was reprimanded at Oxford for reading Hume's *Treatise of Human Nature*, which like Locke's work, was banned.[114]

With pronounced distinction placed on the Scottish alternative, Smith continues in the letter to Dr. Cullen: "In the present state of the Scotch Universities, I do most sincerely look upon them as, in spite of all their faults, without exception the best seminaries of learning that are to be found any where in Europe" (*Correspondence* 173). This was not a matter of provincial hyperbole, or the extension of a regional academic turf war. Students at Oxford and Cambridge came and went from the tedious lectures as they pleased and without concern for a coherent course of study. In 1772, Gilbert Wakefield described the intellectual import of London university life as "odious beyond description."[115] One historian of Oxbridge describes the period 1680 to 1780 as in general "one of apathy and torpor," and enrollment between the universities declined by 50 percent during that time.[116] As Thomas P. Miller notes in *The Formation of College English*, the English universities produced a decreasing percentage of recognized men of science, from 67 percent in the seventeenth century, to only 16 percent by the next hundred years. By contrast, university-educated men from Scotland and abroad rose from 10 to 23 percent during the same period.[117]

But what exactly is a specifically literary education, and what value is Smith establishing by using the phrase "literary merit"? Smith and his contemporaries were concerned with the archaic nature of a curriculum based on outmoded scholastic or Aristotelian vocabularies and preferred instead a system that took into account, as we have noted, the apparatus of taste as a way of sorting the incalculable reality of collective experience into its proper form of divided unity. This is the final basis of civil society, a concept introduced to the English by Scottish literary men.[118] As the letter to Cullen continues, we see that literary education gains its value in proportional relation to its success in the emptying out of corporeal concerns; such learning should produce dignity over whatever questions of acquisition and material exchange we must put beneath the pleasure of wonder. "In poetry and philosophy, public admiration . . . is almost the whole . . . of their reward" (*Wealth* 123). "Teaching," Smith continues, is more "honorable than writing for the bookseller . . . ; [or] writing for bread" (*Wealth* 148–149).

Thus, Smith rails against a trade in degrees that inflates profit over science (*Correspondence* 173) and denounces the absurd constitution of the English universities (*Correspondence* 27). Like Kames, Smith calls for "the progress of [Roman] refinement, when philosophy and rhetoric came into fashion" (*Wealth* 759). He also calls for the introduction in the Scottish universities of the seemingly opposite dynamics of free competition (student payment versus monopoly endowments) and the achievement of pleasures in common, the latter of which will be exclusively cultivated within the new specialty of English literary studies.[119] While the *London Times* could write of Smith a few weeks after his death in 1790 that he "converted the Chair of Moral Philosophy into a professorship of trade and finance," before mid-century, as we have noted, the divisions between disciplines on this order would not have been so rigidly or exclusively defined.[120]

Regarding the indictment of the British university system in *Wealth*, Hugh Blair writes in a letter to Smith that "you have raised very formidable adversaries who will do all they can to decry you" (*Correspondence* 188). Blair was appointed Regius Professor of Rhetoric and Belles-Lettres at Edinburgh in 1762, making him the living embodiment of a Kamesian literary educator. Indeed, he was effectively the first university chair of modern literature in the English-speaking world (which incidentally did include royal patronage).[121] And while Blair asked that the phrase *belles lettres* be included in his professorial title in order to give it a more modern air, he certainly found ways around the modest compensation of the Edinburgh system, selling the copyright to his lectures for 1,500 pounds. This was a massive sum by the standards of 1793. Blair's profit on literary studies, in spite of literature's explicitly disinterested and de-corporealizing status, is another example of how the modern disciplines produce value by both narrowing and broadening access to so-called pleasures in common.

It should come as no surprise that, in his capacity as part of the Moderate-wing of the Scottish clergy, Blair fought mightily against popular influence upon the selection of clergyman in the Presbyterian Church. As Miller points out, the "first university professorship dedicated to the teaching of English was founded to reward a leader of the Moderate Party [Blair] for establishing subservience . . . [and] suppress[ing] popular resistance in the Presbyterian Church."[122] In reprimanding certain student societies apt to consider improper subjects of debate, Blair warns against the "promiscuous Societies, in which multitudes are brought together who are often of low stations and occupations, who are joined by no common bond of union, except an absurd rage for Public Speaking."[123] For all the praise given by twentieth- and twenty-first century scholars to the literary clubs of the Enlightenment, it should also be noted that by 1782 the laws of Scottish Philosophical Societies were careful to exclude "religious or political disputes . . . [and debate of] any Warmth that may be offensive or improper for philosophical enquiries."[124] The point to emphasize, and the point we have been developing in various ways throughout this chapter, is that the management of "multitudes"—implicitly, the great majority of (labouring) men and women; the lower ranks—occurs at this moment of epistemic change through a cultivation and peaceable dividing of the kind of knowledge that places new stakes on how tasteful reading and writing align.

In a letter praising Smith for the passages on education in *Wealth*, fellow Scotsman Adam Ferguson remarks, "you have provoked . . . the church . . . [and] universities." More interestingly, Ferguson insists, "you [Smith] are surely to reign alone on these [both commercial and pedagogical] subjects." He quickly adds: "You are not to expect the run of a novel, nor even of a true history; but you may venture to assure your booksellers of a steady and continual sale" (*Correspondence* 193). Again, about the issue of the novel, we will have more to say in Chapter 3. What is important for us in conclusion of this chapter is that the issue of book sales, scholarly reputation, and *intra*-national rivalries between British and Scottish knowledge systems retain an ambivalent quality in these lines from Ferguson. They both praise Smith and reassure him against the *over*-popularity of his own prose.

The stakes of popular reputation were mixed and understandably high. Perhaps this is the way to explain Smith's refusal to publish Hume's writing on religion posthumously, "because of the clamour which I foresee they will excite," against Hume's dying wishes.[125] The delicate capacities of taste are worth having precisely for the way in which they enable the sorting of a wide number and variety of texts, for a readership of the many, cultivated by a few. Being read is worthwhile, but what Smith continued to deride as the arts of popularity (echoing Hume, ghostly practitioners stirring up dissenters and radical Methodists) also meant that the multitude, imagination, writing, and corporeal labor might come together in a relationship "adapted . . . to the disorderly affections of the human frame" (*Wealth* 191). By framing the proliferation of writing in a particular way, establishing its mechanisms of division as well as the divisions between different kinds of prose, the passion and credulity of popular contention is itself divided into regularity and order. What different manners of framing human affection, and what alternative ways to reconfigure the divisions between thinking and work, we leave to the following chapter.

2 "TUMULTUOUS COMBINATIONS"
The Transindividual from Adam Smith to Spinoza

TO SAY SOMETHING NEW about Adam Smith's conception of sympathy would appear to be nearly impossible. Not only does the sheer volume of writing on Smith suggest that what can be said has been said, but the enduring authority of "the Adam Smith problem"[1] imposes on the reader the possible alternative readings of Smith as a thinker of sympathy (as expressed in *The Theory of Moral Sentiments*, hereafter as *TMS*) or self-interest (*Wealth of Nations*), which does not exclude an ingenious mediation between the two to show that they in fact depend upon each other or are the expression of a single human nature. And, as is the case with any system of formal opposition, there can be no *a priori* limit on the utterances it can generate: In this way commentary can function as a kind of shell game in which the commentator reveals an unexpected meaning under a given text, often to the amazement or dismay of readers, as if against all available evidence it is really the *TMS* that contains theory of self-interest, while hidden in *Wealth* lies a theory of sympathy heretofore associated with the earlier text.[2] In addition to the structural or analytic approaches to these questions, readers have found it possible and perhaps necessary to trace the genealogy of sympathy and self-interest in the history of philosophy prior to Smith and decide the extent to which he accepted or rejected his theoretical inheritance. Thus, even the interpretive conflicts that arise around Smith's works operate within a horizon beyond which it seems impossible to go, although the precise nature of this impossibility remains to be explored.

To see, let alone to say, something new about Smith's conception of sympathy will accordingly require more than simple ingenuity or greater celerity of thought. The set of possible readings, with their apparent divergences and oppositions, are so historically sedimented that simply becoming aware of the boundaries it imposes on us will not allow us to escape it. There is only one way out, one way forward: through the text itself, refraining, initially at least, from translating it into our own philosophical idiom, reading it in the original, so to speak, and doing so, to the extent possible, line by line and word by word. Further, while we cannot ignore the relatively few passages cited repeatedly in the studies of the *TMS*, such a practice of reading will force us to confront those passages regularly overlooked (some of which are extremely surprising, and sometimes bizarre) and to consider why they have been overlooked and how these oversights have defined the existing readings of the text.

The great medieval commentators on the Hebrew scriptures who, tired of allegorical readings that claimed to discover the hidden meanings of the text, decided to read it word by word and even letter by letter, setting aside doctrine in order simply to understand what scripture actually said, felt like explorers in an unknown land. Their studies produced extraordinary results that continue even today to disturb readers. And if reading the text (or at least certain passages) word by word reveals contradictions and incoherence, so be it: Perhaps there is more to be gained from following the text wherever it leads than in abstracting arguments from the words in which they are expressed to demonstrate their coherence. Even such a literalist reading, however, will not suffice to explicate the function of the term "sympathy" in the *TMS*.

In order to grasp the meaning of the concept in its textual existence, we will need to contrast Smith with the most powerful expression of the diverse phenomena captured by "sympathy": Spinoza. In introducing a name rarely seen in discussions of Smith,[3] we must confront a fundamental difficulty: There does not exist a single reference to Spinoza in the entire of Smith's *corpus*. And this fact is curious, indeed, when we consider that Smith discusses every other notable philosopher of the period somewhere in his work: Bacon, Descartes, Gassendi, Hobbes, Pascal, Malebranche, Locke, and Leibniz. While this absence is hardly surprising in such texts as *Jurisprudence* or *Wealth*, it takes on considerable interest in the case of the *TMS*, particularly insofar as the latter begins, in every sense of the term, with the concept of sympathy, a term used by Hume[4] and others familiar to Smith to denote the communication of ideas and emotions between individuals. For it was Spinoza more than any other philosopher of the time (or perhaps of any time) who explored what has been called the interindividual (Matheron) or transindividual (Balibar) dimension[5] in which the concept of sympathy is necessarily grounded. By "transindividual," we mean the various irreducible forms of individuality that elude the simple opposition between the person in the juridical sense and the community, society, or state: for example, such entities as couples, groups, and multitudes, as well as the ways in which which the boundary between individuals is permeable, allowing passions or affects to pass between them to such an extent that it is impossible to say to whom a feeling properly belongs or in whom it originated.[6]

It would be possible, of course, to argue that Spinoza is present to Smith's work (if not in it) but at a remove, present in his effects, as it were, by means of certain intermediaries or emissaries through which his ideas are communicated. When Smith, for example, describes the operation of sympathy, that is, the precise mechanism by which it comes into existence (as distinct from its role in human society), the critical reference, while never explicit, to Malebranche, Mandeville, and Hume is unmistakable. Although the first and last of these took great pains to disavow any inheritance from Spinoza, they did so precisely when and where they most borrowed from or merely agreed with him.[7] Mandeville, who could never be accused of concealing unpopular views, made Spinoza's axiom "By reality and perfection I mean the same thing" the foundation of his defense of the market and the individual passions that made "the whole mass a paradise" (*E* II, 6)(the five parts of Spinoza's *Ethics* are hereafter cited with *E* and part number, followed by the specific proposition).[8]

The notion of an indirect reference to Spinoza, however, does not begin to capture the way in which the opening of the *TMS* is a confrontation not so much with a philosopher as with a philosophy, that is, a set of concepts. This confrontation does not take the form of the direct refutation exhibited in the concluding section of the *TMS* where Smith examines in some detail various "systems of moral philosophy." Nearly half a century earlier, Shaftesbury ascribed to the critics of sociability, as he understood it, a far more subtle strategy than refutation:

> According to a known way of reasoning on self-interest, that which is of a social kind in us should of right be abolished . . . that by this means there might be nothing remaining in us which was contrary to a direct self-end; nothing which might stand in opposition to a steady and deliberate pursuit of the most narrowly confined self-interest.[9]

Smith is often read as a theoretician of sociability in the strongest sense, for whom sympathy is the origin and foundation of society itself. Is it possible instead to read him (and in this way situate Smith in relation to Spinoza) as continuing the work described by Shaftesbury of an abolition or demolition that will leave "nothing remaining" of the genuinely social? Further, is it possible to read Smith, for whom society is necessary to human existence, as advancing a paradoxical theory of society without genuine sociality?

To begin to address these questions we might recall Louis Althusser's definition of the positing of origins in philosophy as a double gesture that excludes "that which must not be thought in order to think what one wants to think."[10] If sympathy is both the starting point of his discussion of morality, and posited as an origin by Smith, Althusser's definition allows us to understand the opening of the *TMS*, Part I, Chapter 1, as constituted by a double gesture that preserves the idea, or perhaps merely the term "sympathy," only to the extent that it empties it of any content or significance that would exceed the boundary of the individual. In other words, Smith may be seen as a more cunning practitioner of the strategy described by Shaftesbury, not merely abolishing the transindividual or interindividual dimension, but doing so by means of the very language and lexicon of transindividuality itself.

This is the sense in which the objective of the *TMS* is not so much to refute or disprove the very idea of a transindividual dimension in which a person can (and in fact must necessarily) not only know but feel what another person feels, as to render it unthinkable and even unimaginable. Neither Hume's brief and inconclusive remarks on sympathy from Part II of the *Treatise of Human Nature* or Malebranche's more substantial but nevertheless finally ungrounded remarks in the second book of *De la recherche de la vérité* pose enough of a threat to prompt Smith to undertake an operation of exclusion. It could be nothing less than that of which they represent a brief and equivocal version, Spinoza's thought itself: the ideas immanent in body of propositions and scholia that compose Parts III and IV of *Ethics*, which would provoke as Althusser put it a "ferocious" attempt "to wall up forever and bury deep in the earth"[11] a philosophy that would prove as destructive to Smith's doctrines of society as to the institutionalized forms of superstition and fanaticism to which Spinoza appeared so threatening.

To see Smith's philosophical operation at work, it is necessary to go no further than the first sentence of the *TMS*. The sentence is remarkable in a number of respects, above all, perhaps, because it offers the strongest (that is, the least ambiguous or ambivalent) account of sympathy in the entire work. It is the account of which every subsequent description of sympathy will represent a qualification:

> How selfish soever man may be supposed, there are evidently some principles
> in his nature, which interest him in the fortune of others, and render their hap-
> piness necessary to him, though he derives nothing from it except the pleasure
> of seeing it. (*TMS* 9)

Here, Smith associates himself with a succession of critiques of Hobbes's political anthropology, according to which human beings insofar as they are motivated by self-interest alone are by nature unfit for society, their inclinations leading them not merely to indifference to the well-being of others but to an active enmity. Smith appears, in the first sentence of the work, to align himself with those powerful statements of human sociability mobilized in reaction to Hobbes by such figures as Shaftesbury, Butler, Hutcheson, Hume, and Rousseau. Sympathy as he defines it here is irreducible: No matter how "selfish" (a term that is in this context more descriptive than normative, denoting an exclusive concern for self above others, whatever the extent to which we prefer our own advantage to that of others), there remains something "evident" (in the sense of obvious, unmistakable, undeniable) that must "interest" man "in the fortune of others."

The term "interest" is noteworthy here: It is more than a curiosity about others that might coexist with the desire to promote one's own prosperity, a favorable comparison of oneself to others that might add glory in Hobbes's sense[12] to one's material advantage, thereby compounding one's pleasure. On the contrary, it suggests that one's own interest includes the "fortune" and thus also the interest of others. The happiness of others (in the plural) is "necessary to him," that is, to his own happiness and not because he can calculate some gain thereby (through their bounty or goodwill), but for no other reason than that he derives "pleasure" merely from "seeing" theirs.

The principles in man's nature "which interest him in the fortune of others" interest him, as well, in their misfortunes. If indeed their happiness is necessary to his own, its absence is a sure impediment to his happiness. Thus "we often derive sorrow from the sorrow of others," a "sentiment" that is one of "the original passions of human nature." As such, this sentiment, pity or compassion, is not felt by the "virtuous and humane" alone but even by "the most hardened violator of the laws of society." Here, as a number of commentators have noted,

Smith alludes to Mandeville's devaluation of pity in the "Essay on Charity and Charity Schools" as no less natural, and therefore animalistic, than urges such as hunger or sexual desire and no more productive of sociability than they.[13] We praise no one for feeling the prompting of instinct; wherein, then, lies the virtue of pity, which is nothing more than an involuntary reflex of our nature?

Smith's allusion to Mandeville at the conclusion of the first paragraph of the *TMS* distances himself from the doctrines of Shaftesbury (who was himself the object of Mandeville's criticism in "A Search into the Nature of Society") and from Butler and Hutcheson (both of whom sought to refute Mandeville's position). Nevertheless, he allows us to see a theoretical ground common to all the parties in this particular dispute. Each agrees that, far from being uniformly "selfish," man, for good or for ill, cannot remain unaffected by the happiness or sorrow of others. In this sense, Mandeville is no less a partisan of sociability than the others, even if he conceives its foundations very differently, a fact that would prove crucial in the formation of Smith's own doctrines.

If the first paragraph of the *TMS* not only preserves but foregrounds the concept of sympathy, the second both empties it of the significance it possessed in the work of previous theoreticians and substitutes another, radically opposed, meaning in its place. In this way, Smith's philosophical strategy—that is, not only the content of his thought and its basic propositions, but the concrete ways in which he formulates these propositions and attempts to impose them as truth—appears strangely similar to that of Spinoza. It is nothing less than the "operation of the *sive*" as André Tosel called it,[14] an operation of substitution and translation that, in Spinoza's case, preserves the language of theology while translating each of its terms into its opposite, systematically transforming transcendence into immanence, as in the famous "Deus, sive Natura" (*E* IV, Preface). In addition to the conjunction "sive," (meaning "or" or "that is"), Spinoza has frequent recourse to terms such as "veluti," and "quasi" (both of which are commonly translated as "as if" or "as it were") in order to help the reader understand familiar terms in radically new ways.[15] In the case of the *TMS*, Smith asks us to translate sympathy, previously understood as a "communication" or "transmission" of affect from one individual to another, and therefore a transindividual phenomenon, into one that is purely intra-individual, nothing more than an exercise of the imagination that finally neither depends upon others nor even requires their existence.

The first sentence of the second paragraph of the *TMS* does not refute or address in any way the theories of the communication of sentiments, but rather renders them nonsensical: "As we have no immediate experience of what other men feel, we can form no idea of the manner in which they are affected, but by conceiving what we ourselves should feel in the like situation" (*TMS* 9). No immediate experience: We are encased in our bodies and they, we presume (and can do no more than presume since we can have no direct experience of their emotions), in theirs. We experience our own feelings directly or immediately, which here means without any effort of thought or exercise of the will.

In his early text "Of the External Senses" (in *Essays on Philosophical Subjects, EPS*), Smith seeks to establish the boundaries of experience. When a man

> lays his hand upon the body either of another man, or of any other animal, though he knows, or at least may know, that they feel the pressure of his hand as much as he feels that of their body: Yet as this feeling is altogether external to him, he frequently gives no attention to it. (*EPS* 136)

Similarly, vision presents to us a world that is "only a plain or surface," (*EPS* 151) including the surfaces of others' bodies. If we "know" that other people feel at all (and note that Smith leaves open the possibility that we may not know), it is by virtue of our "conceiving" but not experiencing their feeling. In the absence of an operation of the intellect entirely unnecessary to our experience of our own feelings, we can form "no idea" of what others feel. Further, the "idea" we form not of the situation of their bodies but of what they feel within an inaccessible interior is not strictly speaking derived from them at all but from ourselves. We must conceive "what we ourselves should feel in the like situation" (*TMS* 9). There can be no determining of the adequacy of our conception of the other's feeling except in relation to ourselves.

To illustrate his point, Smith adduces an extreme example that has all the appearances of a deliberate provocation: "Though our brother is upon the rack, as long as we ourselves are at our ease, our senses will never inform us of what he suffers" (*TMS* 9). This is the first in a series, quite unusual to say the least in the history of philosophy, of references to torture, corporal punishment, and execution; indeed, the chapter will conclude with an encomium devoted to capital punishment.

The term "brother" is intriguingly ambiguous itself. Is it a generic term, similar to the biblical "neighbor," or is it to be taken literally, the male child of one's own parents and therefore a member of one's own family, a "blood" relative who has grown up in the same affective world? It is as if Smith seeks to dissociate individuals even from those closest to them, suggesting that the feelings even of another individual to whom we are tied by the most intimate bonds and who is "upon the rack" and therefore experiencing excruciating pain, the signs of which present themselves unequivocally to our visual and auditory senses, remain inaccessible to us (although he curiously adds the qualifying phrase, "as long as we ourselves are at our ease," as if a shared physical situation opens the possibility of shared feeling, a possibility he pursues no further here).

Our senses, Smith reaffirms, "never did, and never can, carry us beyond our own person" (*TMS* 9). Here, he invokes not only an inductive conclusion drawn from the fact that our senses have never thus far carried us not only to another, but more importantly beyond ourselves, but also a deductive conclusion: Reason tells us that our own person is an absolute horizon. When, therefore, we speak of our sympathy for our brother as he undergoes torture before our eyes, we mean nothing more than that "by the imagination, we place ourselves in his situation, we conceive ourselves enduring all the same torments, we enter as it were into his body and become in some measure the same person with him" (*TMS* 9). The "as it were" is crucial here; Smith allows the reader familiar with the lexicon of sympathy to begin to translate the transindividual into the intra-individual, to understand that what is meant by such phrases as entering into or sharing the feelings of others, experiences he has just ruled out as impossible, can now be understood as acts of the imagination by which we consider what we ourselves have felt, or more problematically might feel, had we never experienced ourselves in a similar situation, which in no way involve any contact with the internal world of another.

This act of the imagination—of which we are simultaneously the subject and the object, and only secondarily referring what we thus begin to feel to what we know, or may know, as another person—is, of course, anything but immediate or spontaneous. Indeed, sympathy now understood as the act of will by which we conceive what we ourselves might feel in a given situation means that even the spectacle of our brother on the rack will only "begin at last to affect us" when the agonies he appears to us to suffer "are thus brought home to ourselves" (*TMS* 9). The passions, which "upon some occasions may seem to be transfused from one man to another, instantaneously, and antecedent to any knowledge of what excited them in the person principally concerned" (*TMS* 11), can in reality never pass from or go beyond the boundary of one's own person. Transfusion, transmission, and communication of feeling between individuals exist only at the level of appearance. They are in fact nothing more than acts of what Kant called imputation (*Zurechnung*).

In certain ways, Smith's conception of sympathy takes as its starting point Hobbes's much-contested definition of pity in *Leviathan* as "Griefe, for the calamity of another," which arises not from any direct or indirect experience of another's distress at the calamity he suffers, but "from the imagination that the like calamity may befall himself."[16] If the calamity is the consequence of the wickedness of the other, our pity is less than if the sufferer is innocent (which suggests that such a calamity could befall anyone, including ourselves). Thus, even Hobbes who, to recall the opening line of the *TMS*, supposes man to be as selfish as may be supposed, admits that under certain, far from uncommon, circumstances we may be aggrieved by the sufferings of another, our contentment disturbed by their misfortune. But, and this is crucial for Smith, this grief arises from no other source than our imagination and refers finally to no one other than ourselves.

In fact, Hobbes as Smith reads him is Hobbes read by Joseph Butler, who devoted a long note in his sermon "Upon Compassion" to Hobbes's discussion of pity in *De Homine* (nearly identical to that which figures in *Leviathan*). First, Butler accuses Hobbes of attempting to preserve the words "pity" and "compassion" while redefining them in a way that is completely at odds with "common language."[17] Pity for another, according to Butler's account of Hobbes, does not concern the other at all, but the self, which from the example of another's misfortune fears for its own sake. Pity then, as Butler contemptuously remarks, would be no more than a species of "cowardice"[18] that is neither noble nor even social. Of course, Smith, who evinces, if anything, greater contempt for cowardice than Butler, nowhere endorses the idea that in pity our imagination causes us vividly to feel only what we fear may happen to us. Like Butler, he insists that sympathy is an act of the imagination stimulated by a variety of affects we see, or think we see, in the other and not simply the sentiment of sorrow. It is perfectly possible to sympathize in Smith's sense with the joy as well as the unhappiness of others.

More significant for our purposes, however, is Butler's insistence on a discrepancy central to Hobbes's account of pity:

> If there be really any such thing as the fiction or imagination of danger to ourselves from the sight of the miseries of others, which Hobbes speaks of, and which he has absurdly mistaken for the whole of compassion; if there be anything of this sort common to mankind distinct from the reflection of reason, it

would be a most remarkable instance of what was furthest from his thoughts, namely, of a mutual sympathy between each particular of the species, a fellow-feeling common to mankind. It would not indeed be an example of our substituting others for ourselves, but it would be an example of our substituting ourselves for others. And as it would not be an instance of benevolence, so neither would it be any instance of self-love.[19]

What is remarkable here is Butler's endorsement of Hobbes's grounding of compassion, of "fellow-feeling," in the imagination alone of what Smith would call the spectator; the idea of sympathy as a communication or transmission of affect across individuals disappears without comment, replaced by a notion of irrevocably separate persons, each confined to the horizon of his or her sole self, substituting themselves for others by means of the imagination. It is this foundation that Smith adopts as his own and from which he will draw a series of unprecedented conclusions. In fact, his transformation of sympathy into an intra-individual experience leads him far beyond Hobbes or Butler.

Because he argues that a man's senses cannot carry him beyond his own person and because he can never form any conception of another's sensations, Smith must move to formalize the necessary discrepancy between what a man imagines and what the other feels by resolving the sympathetic relation into separate and unequal roles: that of the spectator and the person principally concerned. To be a spectator, of course, is to be distinguished from the role of participant; I cannot participate in the sorrows or joys of others; I can feel only my own sentiments. Those experienced by others (or rather those I conceive others to be experiencing) I can only approximate (without ever possessing the means to judge the adequacy of the approximation) in an act of the imagination.

The fact that our senses "never can carry us beyond our own person" means that it is perfectly possible for us in the act of sympathy to be "spectators" of a scene entirely of our own invention. We may, like the mother of a sick infant cited by Smith, impute both a form and a degree of suffering not found in the person principally concerned. At the extreme, sympathy does not even require the existence of another human being. Thus, "we sympathize even with the dead," and such sympathy has nothing to do with our sense of their living on in that "awful futurity which awaits them" (*TMS* 12). We sympathize not with their person, insofar as they constitute thinking and feeling beings, but precisely with a rotting corpse and therefore a thing. We imagine ourselves, according to Smith, in the place of that lifeless body "laid in the cold grave, a prey to corruption and the reptiles of the earth" and soon forgotten by "their dearest friends and relations" (*TMS* 12). This particular form of sympathy, which Smith does not hesitate to call an "illusion of the imagination" (*TMS* 13), produces

> one of the most important principles in human nature, the dread of death, the great poison to the happiness, but the great restraint upon the injustice of mankind, which while it afflicts and mortifies the individual, guards and protects the society. (*TMS* 13)

Paradoxically, our sympathy with the dead, if it indeed "afflicts and mortifies" with the intensity that Smith ascribes to it, would constitute the most potent form of sympathy we can experience. In the case of living persons, however powerful the "illusion" that consists of "our putting ourselves in" the place of another may be on certain occasions, it is in the vast majority of cases surprisingly faint. On "frivolous occasions," such as that of a man who endeavors "to divert the company," the pleasure he feels in their "mirth" or the dejection he feels when "he sees that nobody laughs at his jests but himself" (*TMS* 14) is instantaneous (a fact that Smith cites against the contention that all such sentiments are derived from a calculation of self-interest).

In general, though, the more powerful or "violent" the passion of the person principally concerned, the less likely the spectator is easily or spontaneously to sympathize with their passion. If, for example, we are told that the stranger "who passes by us in the street with all the marks of the deepest affliction" has just learned that his father has died, while we "approve of his grief" as proper, we "scarce conceive the first movements of concern upon his account" (*TMS* 17). As spectators to a sorrow that we cannot help but approve, we will nevertheless feel not the slightest sympathy without the most deliberate act of will: We must "take time" from our other employments and attempt "to picture out in our imagination" his distress and "consider his situation, fully and in all its parts." This, Smith will call "conditional sympathy" (*TMS* 18).

The conditional nature of sympathy, or even the possibility of a sympathy that is never actually experienced by the spectator, does not simply rest on an original judgment according to which the propriety or impropriety of the other's emotion is determined. In many, perhaps most, cases, passions cannot be deemed "consistent with propriety" either in themselves—pride, ambition, anger, resentment, fear, and the full range of passions "which take their origin from the body" (*TMS* 28), pain, hunger, sexual desire—or by virtue of their immoderate degree (sorrow or joy). Even, however, in those cases in which the legitimate passion of the person principally concerned exhibits the proper "mediocrity" (*TMS* 27), the spectator must work and work hard to produce what he imagines (but can never know) is "some correspondence of sentiments" between him and the person principally concerned. He must

> endeavor, as much as he can, to put himself in the situation of the other, and to bring home to himself every little circumstance of distress which can possibly occur to the sufferer. He must adopt the whole case of his companion with all its minutest incidents; and strive to render as perfect as possible that imaginary change of situation upon which his sympathy is founded. (*TMS* 21)

Even if the spectator is able to accomplish the arduous task that we may justly call the work of sympathy, her emotions will most likely "fall short of the violence of what is felt by the sufferer" (*TMS* 21). For the product of the labor described above, even if it is diligently executed, will be "but momentary. The thought of their own safety, the thought that they themselves are not really the sufferers continually intrudes itself upon them" (*TMS* 21), more or less quickly dissipating the illusion that is sympathy.

The conditional and fleeting character of even the most carefully wrought sympathy compels Smith to focus his discussion primarily on the person principally concerned. It appears that the burden of sympathy is on his side rather than the side of the spectator. It is a double burden: Not only must the sufferer "moderate" his grief no matter how catastrophic the events that produced it so as not to "disgust" or "exasperate" (*TMS* 11) the spectator and thus lose any hope of a sympathetic response, but to do so, he must also himself engage in the work of imagination and "assume the circumstances" of the spectator and "imagine in what manner he would be affected if he was only one of the spectators of his own situation" (*TMS* 22). Accordingly, it is precisely the individual afflicted with the greatest sorrow who is well advised to recall Smith's maxim that

> We are disgusted with that clamorous grief, which, without any delicacy, calls upon our compassion with sighs and tears and importunate lamentations. But we reverence that reserved, that silent and majestic sorrow, which discovers itself only in the swelling of the eyes, in the quivering of the lips and cheeks, and in the distant, but affecting, coldness of the whole behavior. (*TMS* 24)

But the moderation of one's grief, for Smith, is not reducible to the self-interest that is gratified when the sufferer is able, however briefly, to procure the sympathetic approbation of another. Evoking the Stoic tradition, Smith finds the greatest virtue "in that degree of self-command which astonishes by its amazing superiority over the most ungovernable passions of human nature" (*TMS* 25).

Sorrow is no doubt only one of these "ungovernable" passions and is far from the most difficult to master: There exist in our breast those "unsocial passions" of resentment, hatred, and anger, which are "necessary parts of the character of human nature" (*TMS* 34). Such passions are not only natural responses to injuries, real or imagined, done to us by others, they even possess a certain utility. Resentment of ill usage "is the safeguard of justice and the security of innocence. It prompts us to beat off the mischief which is attempted to be done to us, and to retaliate that which is already done" (*TMS* 79). The desire for retaliation is "the great law which is dictated to us by Nature," the social consequence of which is that the violator of justice who has "no regard to the sufferings of his brethren" will "be over-awed by the fear of his own" (*TMS* 82).

Thus, man who is "naturally endowed with a desire of the welfare and preservation of society" is equally endowed with "an immediate and instinctive approbation" (*TMS* 87) of the punishment of unjust actions. When a man "looks upon the just punishment of an ungrateful murderer or parricide," he "applauds with ardor, and even with transport, the just retaliation which seems due to such detestable crimes, and which, if by any accident, they should happen to escape, he would be highly enraged and disappointed" (*TMS* 90–91). In fact, the desire for retaliation and punishment, and the "transport" that the gratification of such desire produces, constitute to a far greater degree than any social passion, such as sympathy, the "great safe-guards of the association of mankind" (*TMS* 86).

We can now understand why sympathy could never provide the foundation of morality or justice. Sympathy with the distress of others, including, and perhaps especially, the distress that we ourselves inflict or contemplate inflicting upon others, requires significant effort on the part of the spectator who must master feelings of indifference or even contempt to "bring home to himself" the case of another. On the other side, the person principally concerned must exert all her will in precisely the most unpropitious of circumstances to stifle any outward expression of grief or pain in order not to incur the contempt of the spectator.

Pity, for Rousseau, prior to law or custom, is a natural desire to refrain from hurting another and, as such, leads to the mutual conservation of the species and serves as the foundation in or out of society for human coexistence. The following passage may be read as a direct response to Rousseau's *Discours sur l'origine et les fondements de l'inégalité parmi les hommes*:

> Men, though naturally sympathetic, feel so little for another, with whom they have no particular connection, in comparison of what they feel for themselves; the misery of one who is merely their fellow-creature is of so little importance to them in comparison even of a small conveniency of their own; they have it so much in their power to hurt him, and may have so many temptations to do so, that is this principle did not stand up within them in his defense and overawe them with a respect for his innocence, they would, like wild beasts, be at all times ready to fly upon him; and a man would enter an assembly of men as he enters a den of lions. (*TMS* 86)[20]

However useful and indeed necessary the sentiments of resentment, anger, and vengeance may be in both correcting and preventing wrongdoing, the sentiments themselves, like those of grief, tend to provoke antipathy rather than sympathy. Even in the case of manifestly undeserved misfortune and utter ruin, we can only sympathize with the person principally concerned to the extent that he does not manifest the smallest external sign of the rage, fear, or sorrow that he must feel:

> If he should be reduced to beggary and ruin, if he should be exposed to the most dreadful dangers, if he should even be led out to a public execution, and there shed one single tear upon the scaffold, he would disgrace himself forever in the opinion of all the generous and gallant part of mankind. (*TMS* 49)

As for those who have fallen a lesser distance or perhaps not at all, but suffer from a "mere want of fortune, mere poverty," their example

> excites little compassion. Its complaints are too apt to be the objects rather of contempt than of fellow-feeling. We despise a beggar; and, though his importunities may extort an alms from us, he is scarce ever the object of any serious commiseration. (*TMS* 144)

Indeed, poverty does not in and of itself merit any compassion on our part. The "wages of the meanest laborer" in England are sufficient to supply him with "the necessities of nature" (*TMS* 50). Not only do they supply him and his family with food, clothing, and shelter,

> If we examined his oeconomy with rigor, we shall find that he spends a great part of them upon conveniencies, which may be regarded as superfluities, and

that, upon extraordinary occasions, he can give something even to vanity and distinction. (*TMS* 50)

In Smith's England there is no hunger or malnutrition, and certainly no famine, and thus no cause for commiseration with the poor. We will have occasion to discuss this in more detail in a later chapter.

Further, Smith repeatedly recommends the perspective of that philosophy of the "most heroic magnanimity," Stoicism.[21] The wise man, according to Stoic doctrine as Smith understands it, never complains or "whines" (a word, it must be admitted, seldom seen in philosophical works) about his fate, whether it be poverty or exile (*TMS* 139):[22]

> He does not look upon himself, according to what self-love would suggest, as a whole, separated and detached from every other part of nature, to be taken care of by itself and for itself. . . . Assured of the wisdom which directs all the events of human life, whatever lot befalls him, he accepts it with joy, satisfied that, if he had known all the connections and dependencies of the different parts of the universe, it is the very lot which he himself would have wished for. (*TMS* 59)

At the same time, Smith's version of Stoicism is far from advocating a passive fatalism. First,

> every animal was by nature recommended to its own care and was endowed with the principle of self-love, that it might endeavor to preserve not only its existence, but all the different parts of its nature, in the best and most perfect state of which they were capable. (*TMS* 272)

Such an endeavor required that the individual undertake acts of will, "choice or rejection," to "support this state of existence" (*TMS* 272). Virtue consisted precisely in "selecting always from among the several objects of choice presented to us, that which was most to be chosen" (*TMS* 273).

According to Smith, the Stoics regarded human life

> as a game of great skill; in which, however, there was a mixture of chance, or of what is vulgarly understood to be chance. In such games the stake is commonly a trifle, and the whole pleasure of the game arises from playing well, from playing fairly, and playing skillfully. If notwithstanding all his skill, however, the good player should, by the influence of chance, happen to lose, the loss ought to be a matter, rather of merriment, than of serious sorrow. (*TMS* 278–279)

If human life in its natural state can be considered a kind of game of skill, so can the life of an individual in society. There, the endeavor to preserve oneself can be likened to a "race for wealth, and honors, and preferments" (*TMS* 83).

Other individuals are "competitors" whom "he may run as hard as he can, and strain every nerve and every muscle, in order to outstrip" (*TMS* 83). Those who lose the game of life or the race for wealth must understand that the rigors to which they must submit are like a painful course of treatment ordered by a physician, "indispensably necessary," not to their individual well-being, but "to the health, to the prosperity and happiness of the universe, to the furtherance and advancement of the great plan of Jupiter" (*TMS* 289) the workings of whose "invisible hand" may be seen in the movement of the stars, as well as the oeconomy of that harmonious system of commerce.[23] Thus, poverty, the particular rigor that falls to those (the great majority of any prosperous society) who have lost the race for wealth is not in any sense an evil and certainly does not merit the work required to produce a feeling of compassion. It neither denies us what is necessary to life (and Smith, like Locke[24] and Mandeville,[25] never ceases to remind the reader that the poor live better than the rich once did in Europe or do, at present, live in Africa or the Americas), nor is it some sort of failure or fault of a given society. On the contrary, it is a necessary part of its harmonious order. These arguments will serve Smith well in *Wealth*.

Why then do we "regard it as worse than death" (*TMS* 50) to be reduced to such a life? The answer lies in the fact that although the rich do not sympathize with the poor, the poor, in contrast, sympathize with the rich—namely, with the contempt that the rich feel and which the poor, by putting themselves in the place of the wealthy spectator of their own poverty, can feel toward themselves. The poor man

> is ashamed of his poverty. He feels that it either places him out of the sight of mankind, or, that if they take any notice of him, they have, however, scarce any fellow-feeling with the misery and distress which he suffers. (*TMS* 51)

The rich

> turn away their eyes from him, or if the extremity of his distress forces them to look at him, it is only to spurn so disagreeable an object from among them. The fortunate and the proud wonder at the insolence of human wretchedness, that it should dare to present itself before them, and with the loathsome aspect of its misery presume to disturb the serenity of their happiness. (*TMS* 51)

For the poor, indeed, the poorest of the poor, those who by fortune have been reduced to beggary or even slavery, to express their misery can only heighten the contempt of the fortunate; in fact, any voluntary manifestation of their suffering becomes a "whine," an attempt to extort from the happy relief— if not material, a sign, however slight, of commiseration.

At this point, however, Smith appears to have reached an impasse. In his desire to warn the poor and oppressed that they can expect little from the fortunate other than contempt and that to call attention to their condition will only aggravate the antipathy that the rich feel toward them, he appears to have forgotten for a moment how difficult it is, according to his own argument, to sympathize with the violent emotions of contempt and hatred, and all the more so when these violent and unsocial passions are directed against the spectator herself. If it requires great exertion of the will and powers of concentration to imagine what another may feel, even when we approve of the other's emotions, how can a person, however powerful her mastery of her own inclinations, exert herself to sympathize with another's contempt of her, when she is guilty of nothing more than suffering poverty?

It was perhaps Smith's awareness of the improbability of a man sympathizing with the hatred and contempt that another might feel toward him, the implausibility of his working to bring home this hatred and contempt to himself, to transform these passions into self-hatred and self-contempt, that necessitated the expansion in the second edition of the *TMS* of the concept of the impartial spectator.[26] The fact that we are separated from others by an abyss and can only imagine what they feel means that the spectator can never exert sufficient influence upon us to persuade us to alter our conduct, let alone our feelings. Given that the spectator is nothing more than a product of the imagination of the person principally concerned, the latter, if he is to be subjected to moral judgment at all, must become his own spectator.

> When I endeavor to examine my own conduct, when I endeavor to pass sentence upon it, and either to approve or condemn it, it is evident that, in all such cases, I divide myself . . . into two persons; and that I, the examiner and judge, represent a different character from that other I, the person whose conduct is examined into and judged of. (*TMS* 113)

In this way, we add a supplement to our sympathy with others' view of ourselves. The pleasure of imagining that they love and esteem us is compounded by the sense that we ourselves approve of what we imagine they feel as deserved, and in this our pleasure is increased. Similarly, "what so great misery as to be hated," that is, to imagine that others hate us, "and to know that we deserve to be hated" (*TMS* 113).

The work of creating within oneself an impartial spectator might appear to be even more difficult than the work of sympathy, but for Smith self-judgment and particularly self-condemnation are involuntary passions. The most hardened criminal, indeed, the murderer, fears being hateful and despicable more than "the thought of being hated and despised" (*TMS* 117). A man esteemed by the community, but who has committed a dreadful crime that will never be discovered, will be prey to involuntary imaginings of "the manner in which mankind would look upon him, of what would be the expression of their countenance and of their eyes, if the dreadful truth should ever come to be known" (*TMS* 118). Such men have been driven to reveal "of their own accord, what no human sagacity could ever have investigated" (*TMS* 118) and to endure punishment in order thereby to imagine themselves objects "rather of compassion than of horror" (*TMS* 119). The fact that we can never move "beyond our own person" in this sense imprisons us: We cannot escape the confines of the self and the play of the imagination to which we are subject. We are perpetual exiles from a world we can imagine but never know. The compassion, esteem, or contempt we impute to others is never anything other than the judgments we apply to ourselves, the images of the faces and eyes of others that present themselves spontaneously in our mind.

But what of those who are the objects of undeserved contempt, who know they are blameless but who nevertheless imagine, more or less accurately, that others view them with horror or disgust? Smith cites the case of the Calvinist Jean Calas, "broke upon the wheel and burnt at Tholouse for the supposed murder of his own son, of which he was perfectly innocent" (*TMS* 120), and who refused to confess to a crime he did not commit. Such a spectacular example, however, may only be an extreme case of the unmerited contempt the poor, indeed, the laboring poor, face every day from their "betters," as Smith has explained in great detail. In such circumstances, our inescapable interiority, the internal exile that marks the condition of our own person, becomes both a refuge and the site of our irreducible freedom.

It is here that Smith, so often a partisan of self-interest and the champion of the self-seeking of all living things, departs not only from the rational choice theory of our own time, but from the philosophies of self-love and self-interest represented by such diverse figures as Hobbes, La Rochefoucauld, and Mandeville.

Taking the example of Epictetus, Smith argues that a man's own person, encased in the body but separate from it, is a refuge. We may bear with equanimity not only opprobrium but the most exquisite tortures if we judge ourselves, by means of the impartial spectator, innocent of the charges against us. Smith exhibits in this regard great admiration for the degree of self-mastery found in savage nations, declaring their "magnanimity and self-command . . . almost beyond the conception of Europeans" (*TMS* 206). Smith's savages live in a world of constant hunger and deprivation and frequently die "of pure want" (*TMS* 205).[27] Thus,

[A]ll savages are too much occupied with their own wants and necessities to give much attention to those of another person. A savage, therefore, whatever be the nature of his distress, expects no sympathy from those about him, and disdains, upon that account, to expose himself by allowing the least weakness to escape him. (*TMS* 205)

Smith characteristically elaborates a detailed fantasy of the torments a savage may expect to suffer, not as a result of mere want, but at the hands of his enemies:

After he has been scorched and burnt, and lacerated in all the most tender and sensible parts of his body for several hours together, he is often allowed, in order to prolong his misery, a short respite, and is taken down from the stake: he employs this interval in talking upon all indifferent subjects, inquires after the news of the country, and seems indifferent about nothing but his own situation. (*TMS* 206)

What might by others be regarded as a brutish state from which the advances of civilization have delivered us assumes for Smith heroic dimensions: Indeed, it furnishes the basis for Smith's denunciation of modern slavery. What renders the African superior to his master is not his love of liberty or refusal to submit to captivity:

[T]here is not a Negro from the coast of Africa who does not, in this respect, possess a degree of magnanimity which the soul of his sordid master is too often scarce capable of conceiving. Fortune never exerted more cruelly her empire over mankind than when she subjected those nations of heroes to the refuse of the jails of Europe, to wretches who possess the virtues neither of the countries which they come from nor of those which they go to, and whose levity, brutality, and baseness, so justly expose them to the contempt of the vanquished. (*TMS* 206–207)

The ability to prevent the slightest murmur of complaint or the slightest outward expression of pain or sorrow from escaping, a capacity that links savage
nations and Stoic philosophers, slaves modern as well as ancient, exceeds in the
former the mere self-government of the passions to lead to

> habits of falsehood and dissimulation. It is observed by all those who have been
> conversant with savage nations, whether in Asia, Africa, or America, that they
> are all equally impenetrable, and that, when they have a mind to conceal the
> truth, no examination is capable of drawing it from them. (*TMS* 208)

Savages differ from Stoic philosophers in that they have not succeeded in mas-
tering the passions, but merely their outward expressions. Their passions, in
fact, which "lie concealed in the breast of the sufferer are, notwithstanding, all
mounted to the highest pitch of fury" (*TMS* 208).

In the case of Epictetus, it cannot be sympathy with what he imagines
would be the response of his persecutors that allows him to master his outrage
at the injustices done to him, or reject the admonitions of the other within.
On the contrary, his degree of self-government is such that he has mastered
perhaps his most powerful passions: the fear of death and the desire to persist
in his own being. This degree of self-mastery always procures for the individual
able to exercise it the ability to face any calamity that fortune may visit upon
him with equanimity and tranquility.

> I am ordered, says Epictetus, not to dwell at Nicopolis. I do not dwell there. I
> am ordered not to dwell at Athens. I do not dwell at Athens. I am ordered not
> to dwell in Rome. I do not dwell in Rome. I am ordered to dwell in the little and
> rocky island of Gyarae. I go and dwell there. But the house smokes in Gyarae.
> If the smoke is moderate, I will bear it, and stay there. If it is excessive, I will go
> to a house from whence no tyrant can remove me. I keep in mind always that
> the door is open, that I can walk out when I please, and retire to that hospitable
> house which is at all times open to all the world; for beyond my undermost gar-
> ment, beyond my body, no man living has any power over me. (*TMS* 280)

Thus, at the heart of our person, grounded in the voluntary act by which
we remain alive, lies that "asylum which takes away from every man every
pretence of complaining" (*TMS* 280), the irreducible freedom to bring about
one's own death, an act that simultaneously expresses our contempt for those
who unjustly oppress us and our acquiescence in the order that governs all
things.[28]

But this freedom to retire to one's last refuge, the contemplation of which alone may allow a person to bear great suffering and injustice, is not all that sustains the laboring poor in the face of relative deprivation and the open contempt of their superiors. Fortunately their sympathy for the rich does not solely deliver them to the disapprobation of the latter.

As difficult as Smith has demonstrated it to be to sympathize with the sorrows of others, so it is easy and natural to sympathize with their happiness (which, for Smith, can mean no more than what we imagine, rightly or wrongly, to be their happiness): "[M]ankind are disposed to sympathize more entirely with our joy than with our sorrow" (*TMS* 53). This sentiment is in fact the origin of our "natural disposition to respect" (*TMS* 53) those we deem superior to us. Such respect, Smith argues, is not a matter of utility: We admire even and perhaps especially those whose distance from us insures that we can have no

> expectations of benefit from their good-will. Their benefits can extend but to a few; but their fortunes interest almost every body. We are eager to assist them in completing a system of happiness that approaches so near to perfection; and we desire to serve them for their own sake, without any other recompense but the vanity or the honor of obliging them. (*TMS* 52)

In addition to what we imagine is the happiness of the rich and powerful, the means to this happiness does not fail to win our sympathy and admiration. According to Smith, who here departs without noting that he does so, from ancient Stoicism, we pronounce the vanity and worthlessness of palaces and possessions of the rich only when we ourselves are prey to pain and sorrow, and our imaginations remain "confined and cooped up within our own persons" (*TMS* 183). In times of "ease and prosperity," our imagination

> expands itself to everything around us. We are then charmed with the beauty of that accommodation which reigns in the palaces and oeconomy of the great; and admire how every thing is adapted to promote their ease, to prevent their wants, to gratify their wishes, and to amuse and entertain their most frivolous desires. (*TMS* 183)

If, however, reason supplants imagination, and we consider the utility of such things, "the real satisfaction which all these things are capable of affording, by itself and separated from the beauty of that arrangement which is fitted to promote it, it will always appear in the highest degree contemptible and trifling" (*TMS* 183). But reason rarely supplants the imagination, and all "The pleasures of wealth and greatness" not only appear beautiful, but their very beauty and the pleasure it inspires in us serve to convince us that the achievement of these otherwise trifling things "is well worth all the toil and anxiety which we are so apt to bestow upon it" (*TMS* 183).

Were the laborer content merely to satisfy his basic needs and perhaps those of his family, there could be no progress. Smith imagines a "poor man's son, whom heaven in its anger has visited with ambition" (*TMS* 181). To rise to the condition to which he aspires, to acquire the accommodation and ease that he dreams will bring him true contentment, "he submits in the first year, nay in the first month of his application, to more fatigue of body and more uneasiness of mind that he could have suffered through the whole of his life from the want of them" (*TMS* 181). Smith's tale, however, is no success story: The poor man's son spends his whole life in pursuit of "the idea of a certain artificial and elegant repose which he may never arrive at," only "at last to find that wealth and greatness are mere trinkets of frivolous utility" (*TMS* 181).

But here Smith cautions us against adopting the perspective of a "splenetic philosophy" that "depreciates those great objects of human desire" (*TMS* 183). For if it is true that "in ease of body and peace of mind, all the different ranks of life are nearly upon a level" (*TMS* 185), the deception that leads us to believe otherwise, that impels us to imagine the happiness of the rich to be immeasurably superior to our own and that this superior happiness derives from their possessions, is necessary to society:

> It is this deception which rouses and keeps in continual motion the industry of mankind. It is this which first prompted them to cultivate the ground, to build houses, to found cities and commonwealths, and to invent and improve all the sciences and arts, which ennoble and embellish human life; which have entirely changed the whole face of the globe, have turned the rude forests of nature into agreeable and fertile plains, and made the trackless and barren ocean a new fund of subsistence, and the great high road of communication to the different nations of the earth. (*TMS* 183–184)

It is at this point that the political stakes of Smith's discussion of sympathy become clear. Sympathy is our imagination of what another feels by conceiving what we ourselves would feel in a similar situation without the slightest communication or transmission from another to us, given that our senses neither carry us beyond our own person to another, just as their senses cannot, we presume, carry them beyond themselves. For this reason, the apparition of another's suffering is always too faint, too wavering, and our will to undertake the work of imagination necessary to "bring home" their case to us too weak, beset on all sides with distractions, weighed down by the sense of our own ease, for this sentiment to serve as a reliable foundation for social conduct. For the very same reasons, we tend quite easily and effortlessly to sympathize with the happiness of others: The mere imagining of ourselves enjoying the luxuries of the rich brings by itself a degree of pleasure that is only heightened when we add our disinterested admiration of the beauty and magnificence of their possessions.

Further, if Smith has limited our ability to sympathize with the suffering of others, so he has also restricted the number of conditions that legitimately deserve the name of misfortune. Most notably he has eliminated poverty and want from the list—both because they are not absolute but only relative ills and because our inability to sympathize with them serves the society as a whole, as does our ability and even willingness to picture ourselves in the palaces of the great.

Thus, while the laboring poor promote the ease of the rich with as much or more assiduousness as they do their own and sacrifice their happiness for the illusory promises of wealth, the rich in no way reciprocate. And why should they? What regard is owed to those who competed for riches and honors and lost? What about their condition merits an undertaking of the work of sympathy? It is here that Smith transforms the concept of natural sociability as radically as he does the concept of sympathy. While Shaftesbury, Butler, and Hutcheson insisted on the existence of social instincts—often taking the form of benevolence without which society could not exist, let alone prosper—Smith, following Mandeville but more radically than he, predicated human sociability not on the presence of pity, but on its absence. "The proud and unfeeling landlord" who is "without a thought for the wants of his brethren" (*TMS* 184) may wish to consume himself all that his limitless desire confronts, but "the capacity of his stomach bears no proportion to the immensity of his desires" (*TMS* 184) and consumes hardly any more than the poorest of his dependents. The rest—that is, most of what his lands produce—must either go to waste or be sold upon the market so as to gratify the needs of others, while securing the landlord the money he needs to lead a life of magnificence.

Their "natural selfishness" (*TMS* 184) and vanity not only does not prevent them from making "the same distribution of the necessaries of life, which would have been made, had the earth been divided into equal portions among all its inhabitants" (*TMS* 185), but it is the cause of this distribution. The hand that thus leads them to make this distribution, and thus to a form of charitable giving, is necessarily invisible: They will produce and distribute these necessaries only on the condition that they neither intend nor know that they have helped insure that "the beggar, who suns himself by the side of the highway, possesses that security which kings are fighting for" (*TMS* 185).

This last bit of hyperbole concerning the "security" of the vagabond is revealing: Smith insists repeatedly that the poverty of the laboring classes is relative and that in absolute terms they are quite well off; even his vagabonds are secured from starvation and violence. Further, not only is their material condition more than sufficient to their happiness, but the very rigors of their lives—the uncertainty of employment and therefore of their living—provide them with the opportunity to display whatever courage of which they are capable:

> Can there be any shame in that distress which is brought upon us without any fault of our own, and in which we behave with perfect propriety? There can, therefore, be no evil, but, on the contrary, the greatest good and advantage. A brave man exults in those dangers in which, from no rashness of his own, his fortune has involved him. They afford an opportunity of exercising that heroic intrepidity, whose exertion gives the exalted delight which flows from the consciousness of superior propriety and deserved admiration. (*TMS* 278)

The contempt of the rich for the poor is thus all but negated: The poor derive through sympathy perhaps more enjoyment from the possessions and pleasures of the rich than the latter do themselves, a fact that neutralizes the effects of their relative deprivation. Further, if they satisfy the expectations of the judge within and understand and accept their place in the design of providence, they may not only lead satisfied lives but may even be transported by the beauty, that is, the order and harmony of the system in which they admittedly occupy a subordinate place.

Indeed, in the case of the patriot who sacrifices his own interests to advance those of the whole society, "his conduct does not always arise from pure sympathy with the happiness of those who are to reap the benefit of it" (*TMS* 185). Rather,

> The perfection of police, the extension of trade and manufactures, are noble and magnificent objects. The contemplation of them pleases us, and we are interested in whatever can tend to advance them. . . . We take pleasure in beholding the perfection of so beautiful and grand a system, and we are uneasy till we remove any obstruction that can in the least disturb or encumber the regularity of its motions. (*TMS* 185)

The laborer may be thought of as the patriot of the market, pleased with the perfection of the law of supply and demand, as well as the regularity of its motions, even as it triples the price of provisions while raising wages by a mere 10 percent, leaving him and his family to starve.

We may now see the full extent of the theoretical revolution that Smith carried out, a revolution that boldly redrew the line between the thinkable and the unthinkable: He not only executed as complete an affective separation of individuals as could be imagined in a social world, but he did so while retaining and redefining the language of sympathy, heretofore the very name of affective communication and therefore of transindividuality. But we must be very clear about Smith's conceptual operation: While it might appear, as it did to Foucault, for example, that he so completely disentangles individuals and their interests in order to produce the *homo oeconomicus* that one admittedly finds in certain passages in *Wealth*, the individual is immediately aware of his interest, his "utility," and with little or no forethought calculates the most efficient means to maximize it, proceeding in a manner that no contravening passion, however powerful, can contain to realize this interest.[29]

While it is undoubtedly true, as Albert O. Hirschman has argued,[30] that Smith helped transform the passion of selfishness into rational self-interest and helped make the latter the paradoxical foundation of a material sociability that no agent intends or desires but from which all derive benefit, to stop our analysis there would be to fail to see the truly moral dimension of the *TMS* and the way in which it inaugurates a new subject form. The solitude of the individual who can never think or feel beyond her own person is the ground of a freedom that those possessed of sufficient strength of will can realize, and this freedom confers far greater moral worth on the acts predicated upon it than the social conduct to which (according to Shaftesbury, Butler, and Hutcheson) we are driven by the force of instinct. This freedom, however, is not merely determined by our solitude, but perhaps even more by the apprehension, which our solitude in a certain way permits, of the possibility of an absolute self-mastery whose fullest expression (however rare it may be) consists in our genuinely desiring and bringing about our own demise, that is, in "voluntary death" (*TMS* 283). Under certain circumstances we will take this step to avoid the disapprobation not of others, whose responses we can only imagine, but of the judge within who permits neither whining nor protest at the fate that fortune, or the market, has allotted to us.

Obviously, Smith's reworking of Stoic doctrine and his stated preference for that system above all others put him at odds with many Christian apologists for whom the "Stoic's pride," as Alexander Pope called it,[31] was incompatible with the humility demanded of Christians. No critique of Stoicism, however, was more relevant to Smith's reading than that of Malebranche. Writing of Seneca, he denounces the very persuasive power, both irrational and unfortunate, of Seneca's elegant writing, whose every word "flatters the concupiscence of pride"[32] and that confuses arrogance with courage and separates patience in the face of suffering from the element of humility that justifies it. He is one of those authors who "makes us believe without knowing what we believe," and at the center of his thought is a species of what Malebranche does not hesitate to denounce as madness:

> There are many kinds of visionaries [*visionnaires*, a term which here denotes those suffering from delusions about their present condition rather than those with a "vision" of the future in the current sense of the term in English]: Some imagine that they are turned into roosters and chickens; others believe that they have become kings or emperors; still others have persuaded themselves that that they are independent and like gods.[33]

By "independence," Malebranche refers to the Stoic claim, cited by Smith, that one can separate oneself not only from the emotions and passions of other human beings, even friends and family, but even from one's own body whose pains one may, like the savages of Smith's time, learn to bear with equanimity. To imagine oneself a god is to imagine that one is determined by no other source than one's own will, dependent on nothing or no one.

A generation after Smith, Hegel would not so much denounce Stoicism as explain it historically as the mode of thought proper to "a time of universal fear and servitude,"[34] an attempt by consciousness to recover within itself the freedom it had lost in the external world. What sort of a world was this? A world "where one cold rule was extended over all the civilized world," where "the living individualities of national spirit . . . [were] stifled and killed," where "a foreign power, as an abstract universal, . . . pressed hard upon individuals."[35] Hegel, of course, had in mind the slavery of antiquity and brutal rise of the Roman empire. The virtue of Smith's narrative is to remind us that his own time was itself a time of empire, when half a continent was enslaved and the populations of others slaughtered, while the cold rule of the market deprived millions of their livings and lives, an abstract universal that set about to destroy every culture it arrived to liberate. Perhaps this philosophy of inwardness, of self-sufficiency and self-government, in which one is enjoined to become as inured to the sufferings of others as to one's own, which devalues all that is out-side, even the body itself, is indeed the most fitting doctrine of the time of fear and servitude that we have yet to leave behind.

One of the most thorough and devastating critiques of Stoicism (or, more precisely, the early modern reclamation of Stoicism) came not from one of its many Christian critics but from Spinoza who, nearly a century before Smith, carefully dismantled its foundations in his major work, the *Ethics*.[36] Spinoza rarely mentions Stoicism, and when he does so in the Preface to Part V of *Ethics*, he qualifies his description of its doctrine with the phrase "*si recte memini*," or "if I remember correctly" (*E* V, Preface), as if it were not worth the effort to consult their works again, at least when their arguments concern-ing human freedom and the potential power of the mind over the passions are more forcefully elaborated by Descartes in the *Passions of the Soul*.

This, like so many other similar gestures in *Ethics*, should be taken with a grain of salt. It might well be argued that the primary object of Spinoza's cri-tique is precisely the Stoic tradition as it was reread and reconstructed in his own time. The Preface to Part III, the center of *Ethics*, begins with a denun-ciation of what Malebranche called the delusion of the independence of the individual. For the Stoic dream of the mind's absolute mastery over the pas-sions, a mastery whose triumph is its own extinction (that is, a freedom that fully reveals itself only in self-destruction), rests on the illusion that man is an empire within the empire of nature, by his nature outside of the jurisdiction of its laws. The notion of man existing "outside of nature" (*E* III, Preface) permits a second illusion erected upon the first: that "He has absolute power over his actions and . . . is determined by nothing other than himself" (*E* III, Preface). This in turn converts the consideration of human actions from knowledge into moral judgment, and we praise or denounce passions as the free choices of individuals determined only by their will, instead of understanding them as determined by the "same necessity and power of nature as all other singular things" (*E* III, Preface).

But this is merely the starting point of Spinoza's critique of the illusion of independence. Central to the Stoic doctrine, especially as Smith understood it, is the idea that the mind remains separate from the body, the latter being no more than the house in which the mind or soul dwells. As such, the mind could be trained to ignore and transcend the rigors and sufferings of the body. In fact, as Hegel remarked of Stoic consciousness, the constraint of the body in chains is the perfect opportunity to realize that freedom of which no tyrant or master can deprive oneself, the freedom of an interiority that will always remain inaccessible to anyone other than oneself. The weaker the body, the less it can interfere with the workings of the mind and the quest for virtue.

Against these notions, Spinoza develops an entire chain of arguments. First, there can be no separation of mind and body: "The order and connection of ideas is the same as the order and connection of things" (E II, 7). In the scholium to the same proposition, Spinoza rules out even a separation of mind and body that would render them parallel, that is, in Cartesian terms, "thinking substance and extended substance are one and the same substance" (E II, 7, schol.). This in turn leads to two further arguments. The "mind cannot determine the body to movement or to rest, or to anything else," and, directly against Stoicism, "anything that increases or diminishes, helps or hinders the power of our body to act, the idea of that same thing increases or diminishes, helps or hinders, the power of our mind to think" (E III, 11). For Spinoza, the constraint or weakening of the body can only constrain or weaken the mind to the very same degree. The slave's belief that he retains an internal freedom is the effect of his servitude, an adaptation to and affirmation of his own oppression.

The implications of declaring the mind and body to be one and the same thing for Spinoza's theory of the "affects" (a term that he employs in place of "passions" as free from the theological and philosophical history of the latter term)[37] are tremendously important, even if there can be no possibility of reconstructing that theory here. Suffice it to say that Spinoza's elimination of the separateness and interiority of the mind radically calls Smith's positions into question.

Let us take the phrase, cited earlier, in which Smith describes the conditions of possibility of the operation of sympathy as well as its limits:

[T]hat there may be some correspondence of sentiments between the spectator and the person principally concerned, the spectator must, first of all, endeavor, as much as he can, to put himself in the situation of the other, and to bring home to himself every little circumstance of distress which can possibility occur to the sufferer. . . . After all this, however, the emotions of the spectator will still be very apt to fall short of the violence of what is felt by the sufferer. Mankind, though naturally sympathetic, never conceive, for what has befallen another, that degree of passion which naturally animates the person principally concerned. (TMS 21)[38]

It is instructive to compare this passage to Proposition 27 of "Of the Affects," perhaps the center of the third of five parts and of which Smith's account of sympathy is a reworking and a translation into the idiom of separated individualities: "From the fact that we imagine a thing similar to us about which we have had no affect, affected by a certain affect, so we will be affected by a similar affect" (*E* III, 27).

There is a sense in which the passages appear to exhibit a similarity. For Spinoza, as for Smith, the correspondence of feelings between two individuals originates in an act of the imagination. Is it then the case that sympathy, as understood by Smith and what Spinoza will call in the scholium to this proposition an "imitation of the affects" (*affectuum imitatio*), are similar, if not identical operations? To begin to answer this question, we must first determine if by the term "imagination" they mean the same thing.

As we have seen, Smith assigns a very important and quite specific role to the concept of imagination in the opening of the *TMS*, where it serves to take up where the senses leave off, namely the boundary of "our own person." The imagination allows us to "conceive" not what the other person feels, but only what we ourselves would likely feel, based on our own past experiences, were we to suffer a similar misfortune. Imagination, then, is not so much a "picturing" of the other, as of ourselves, or rather a relating to the other only through a hypothesizing of what we assume we might feel in a given circumstance and then attributing the results to the other. Of course, and herein lies one of the constraints upon sympathy, if we have never suffered in such a way (let us say, on the rack), it will be difficult to sympathize fully with one in such a condition. Further, Smith's imagination depends upon the operation of the will: We must want to sympathize and work quite hard mentally to achieve and maintain a state of sympathy.

For Spinoza, in contrast, imagination is neither an act of will nor does it strictly speaking take place within the confines of our own person. In the Demonstration that follows Proposition 27, Spinoza briefly recapitulates his account of the imagination in Part II of *Ethics*: The verb "to imagine" refers to the production of images in the mind by the ceaseless and innumerable encounters between our body and other bodies in a way that is absolutely independent of the will. Because these images were produced by such encounters, they are not in and of themselves false and become the source of error only to the extent that we believe that the bodies that engendered them are present to us. Interestingly, this belief can never be overcome by the will or by the force of reason, nor should it, according to Spinoza. The "power to imagine would be a virtue" of the mind if we, "at the same time knew that these things in fact did not exist" (*E* II, 17, schol.).

The imagination is thus itself perfectly "objective": It consists of the images produced by the encounters between things and is the source of error only if these images are not accompanied by an idea of their nonexistence. We see or imagine a stick bending in the water but know as we thus see or imagine that the stick remains unbent. To imagine that another is suffering literally is then to be presented with, to "suffer" the image of this suffering, an image that is the effect of the encounter with the other. We have then an experience of the other, of the other's affects, which are in no way hidden or walled off from us. Far from our having to "picture out" in our mind what we would feel were we on the rack ourselves in place of our brother, to witness such a scene would be necessarily to suffer from the pictures or images of excruciating pain, images that, by their number and the intensity of the affect they produce within us, threaten to overwhelm our reason (and this would be the case, Spinoza emphasizes in Proposition 27, even if the other were unknown to us) independently of our will and contrary to our desires.

But Spinoza does not here refer literally to our imagining another person affected in a certain way, but only "a thing similar to us" (*rem nobis similem*). Up to this point in his discussion of the affects, Spinoza has referred to the things that affect us with joy or sadness and for which we accordingly feel love or hate. Only in Proposition 21 does he speak for the first time of the things we love being themselves affected by joy or sadness. In part, Spinoza's insistence on employing the word "things" well into the discussion of affects forces us to reflect upon the distinction between persons and things and to consider whether it is possible to understand the specificity of the human without separating it from the rest of nature, without separating body and soul into different substances according to which the soul would remain at least potentially free of the body, and therefore of physical nature.

By defining "us" (things like us) as things affected by affects, and by using the term "affects" with its suggestion of interaction (with other things that affect us), he eliminates any notion of an internal world that separates us from nature and from each other, that is, from all other things. We are no longer immured in an interior realm inaccessible to others as they are in theirs; there is no solitude of consciousness or the refuge of one's own person. It is at this point that Spinoza's notion—that whatever increases or diminishes the power of the body to act necessarily, simultaneously, and to the same degree, increasing or diminishing the power of the mind to think—takes on its full significance. Joy is the affect that accompanies an increase in our powers, and sadness is the affect that accompanies a decrease.

Spinoza's refusal to raise human beings not only above their bodies but even above their existence as mere things proves extremely inconvenient to the very philosophical and theological traditions upon which Smith drew in the *TMS*: There exists not the slightest internal refuge into which we might, with the proper exercise of the will, flee—no safe harbor within, beyond the violence of the political and social storms raging around us, no possibility that the mind will not suffer from the least degradation inflicted upon the body. Even more importantly, there is no wall or abyss separating and protecting us from the intrusion of others' desires and hatreds that without our knowing it supplant and become our own.

In fact, the specificity of the human, according to Spinoza's argument, renders us more rather than less prey to the play of forces in which we are immersed. Unlike other things, we are things affected by affects, including the affects that affect things similar to us. Thus, there is nothing about the things like us that would render their feelings inaccessible to us or ours to them. More importantly, however, there is nothing to protect us from their affects, which pass from individual to individual with the ease of a virus, carried by a constant flow of images that is itself the consequence of our being a thing interacting with other things that we can neither escape nor hope to control.

This being affected by the affections of others, carried by the images to which we are constantly subject, Spinoza calls "imitation." The term, also used by Malebranche, probably derives from Descartes's argument that animals exhibit the capacity to imitate human beings even though they are nothing but machines: Descartes's machines imitate other machines.[39] Why "imitation" instead of "transmission" or "communication" of affects, when there clearly exists a replication of the other's affect? In part, Spinoza's use of the term "imitation" suggests the physical, external nature of our assuming other's affect: We do not simply "feel" it, but are altered by it in body as in mind and adopt it as our own.

To emphasize that the imitation of the affects is not an act of will, Spinoza insists that even if we have felt nothing from or for this thing in the past, we will automatically (*eo ipso*) be affected by a similar affect. Imitation here refers to an instantaneous and involuntary mimicry, even to what Malebranche called a contagion of the affects, over which neither the one affecting nor the one affected have necessarily any knowledge or control. We imitate the affects of others without knowing why or what we imitate or, in many cases, even that we imitate their affects. The image of the sadness of the other saddens us, while the image of the other's joy renders us joyful. Affects arise from encounters between things, and the imitation of the affects is the communication of a force that transforms to a certain degree the thing affected. It is impossible to speak, under such circumstances, of a division between a spectator and a person principally concerned. There are no spectators in the realm of the affects, and everyone risks becoming "principally concerned" as affects spread far beyond the point of origin, which becomes lost in the flow. The affects are therefore not intra-individual phenomena, nor can they belong in an analogous way to that supra-individual: the state or society. They are by their very nature *transindividual*, forming compositions of a number of individuals.

It is not difficult at this point to see the political stakes of Spinoza's account of the affects. The fact that another's misery is immediately reproduced in us leads inescapably and, again, automatically to certain actions. The pain that accompanies the image of the suffering of the other prompts us without reflection or the intervention of the will "to endeavor to free them" (*liberare conabimur*) to "the extent to which we are able [*quantum possumus*]" from their misery.

And this is the beginning of wisdom: Pity "is in and of itself bad and useless" (*E* IV, 50) in that it saddens and therefore diminishes our ability to think and to act. In the grip of the pain of the other's misery, we may act irrationally, hating and even attempting to destroy those who have brought us such pain (we might think of Smith's beggars whose misery is lived by its spectators as "extortion"). Those who live under the guidance of reason, however, will follow the dictum that Smith's contemporary William Blake would articulate so well: "Pity would be no more / If we did not make somebody poor / And Mercy no more could be / If all were as happy as we."[40] Those who do not address the misery of others, whether on the basis of reason or pity, "are justly called inhuman. For they are no longer similar to men" (*E* IV, 50, schol.).

Further, Spinoza noted earlier that our tendency to be affected by the affects of another leads from a binary relation to triadic and finally social relations. We will feel a certain love, which Spinoza calls *Favor*, to the one who "does good to the other"(*E* III, 22, schol.) thereby affecting him, and by extension, us, with joy. And we will feel hatred toward "one who does evil to another," an affect Spinoza calls *Indignatio*. In the same way, we will feel joy if we imagine we have been the cause of another's joy and pain if we imagine that we have been the cause of another's pain. The first is glory (*Gloria*) and the second shame (*Pudor*). Hatred and its derivatives, indignation and shame, which are both in some measure justified by the acts of the one toward whom we feel hate (even in the case of oneself), will be accompanied by some measure of sadness, whatever the joy that arises from the image of the hated one destroyed (*E* III, 47). The destruction of the most vicious evildoer, far from leading to "transport," will lead to a "fluctuation" of the mind in which joy and sadness, hatred of the other and self-hatred, alternate. We might say that Spinoza has inverted La Rochefoucauld's famous maxim: "In the adversity of our best friends, we always find something that does not displease us."[41] For Spinoza there must always be something in the adversity of even our worst enemies that does not and cannot entirely please us. A society, then, whose order depends on fear and hatred and on the ever-present threat of death will be condemned itself to fluctuation and disorder, weakened and divided against itself.

Significantly, Spinoza's notion of the imitation of the affects explicitly rules out any imitation of the affects of the rich by the poor majority who might otherwise be satisfied with a vicarious enjoyment of pleasures they can never physically share that would provide the foundation for the reverence for authority necessary for social order. For we imitate not simply the affects of others but also their desires: We come to desire what others' desire and not simply for others but for ourselves. In fact, "if we imagine that someone enjoys a thing that only one may possess, we will endeavor to bring it about that he will no longer possess it" (E III, 32). A society based on significant inequalities in wealth and property will thus perpetually engender conflict.

Spinoza singles out the imitation of desire from all the other forms of affective imitation: It is that which can condemn a society to perpetual conflict or unite its members. The envy that arises with the inequality of possessions engenders a cycle of hatred and destruction that no state will be able long to contain. But the imitation of desire also produces what Spinoza calls emulation (*Emulatio*): It is "the desire of a certain thing engendered in us by the fact that we imagine that others similar to us [*alios nobis similes*] have the same desire (E III, 27, schol.). Throughout Proposition 27, as we have noted in our analysis, Spinoza has referred to our imitating the affects of *a* thing similar to us, in the singular. Here alone, in the case of emulation, he uses the plural: We imitate *the* desire (in the singular) of others (who all thus have the same desire).

The specific use of the plural and the singular in this proposition raises a series of questions. Can we imitate the desire felt by a number of things similar to us simultaneously? Would this, in turn, not imply that they were all affected by the same desire, and how, if not by imitation? These are interesting and indeed troubling questions, especially when we consider them in the light of Spinoza's account of desire in the preceding portion of Part III of the *Ethics*. As he explains in the scholium to Proposition 11, desire (*Cupiditas*), joy (*Letitia*), and sadness (*Tristia*) form the three "primary affects" (*affectum primarium*) of which all others represent variations. Joy is the affect that affects us when our power is increased, while sadness affects us when our power is diminished. If I imitate the joy (or any of its variations) of another, my power to think and act increases, while my imitation of the other's sad affects weakens me.

What then is the place of desire in this play of forces? In a certain sense, desire may be said to be the condition of the other primary affects insofar as Spinoza defines it as the "consciousness" of an individual's endeavoring to persist in its being; this striving in relation to the mind is called will (*Voluntas*) and in relation to mind and body appetite (*Appetitus*). Desire is the consciousness of this appetite, that is, of our endeavoring to persist in our being. "Endeavor" is, of course, the translation of *conatus*, the "actual essence" (*E* III, 7) of a singular thing that by virtue of existing is endeavoring (a word that Spinoza empties of any connotation of intention, since he speaks of the *conatus* of any singular thing) to be itself.

A singular thing: It is here above all where Spinoza approaches Smith, and the stakes of their divergence become clear. Let us leave to the side Spinoza's militant theoretical antihumanism, his categorical refusal to separate the human thing, the human individual, from any other thing. While Spinoza does use the term "individual" (*Individuum*), he prefers the term "singular thing" (*res singularis*), a term that cannot be restricted to human individuals alone. Even in those cases in which he uses the term "individual," however, he refers to individual things of which human beings would be but a part. His preference for "singular thing" works against a theoretical humanism or anthropology in yet another way, though. It forces us to conceive of human beings not as expressions of one essential nature, self-interested or benevolent (or the two simultaneously), but as singularities. The human individual is neither an original nor final point, but is a composite, composed of other individuals. As Pierre Macherey has argued,

> The individual or the subject does not exist by itself in the irreducible simplicity of a unique and eternal being, but is composed through the encounter of singular beings which conjuncturally unite in it, that is, which coexist in it, without this unity presupposing a privileged relation, the unity of an internal order at the level of their essences, which would persist in their identity.[42]

Spinoza's notion of the human individual as a composite singularity thus renders individual identity unstable and liable to change, even dramatic change, according to the way it is affected by other individuals. Nothing restricts the boundaries of the individual, as established in law, or as the subject of interest, from expanding beyond what Smith refers to as the person. It is at this point in Spinoza's thought that the dimension of transindividuality opens up: the possibility of imagining forms of individuality or human singularity between the juridical categories of the individual and the state or society (conceived in organicist or "holist" fashion as a supra-individual, endowed with a will to realize the ends it has designated, or in individualist fashion as nothing more than the sum of the irreducible separate individual wills of which it is composed).

We can never withdraw from others into a world of material or even affective self-sufficiency; "commerce with many things external to us" (*E* IV, 18, schol.) is necessary to the conservation of our being. But this very commerce brings risks as well as opportunities. We may be overwhelmed by external causes antagonistic to our singular essence, as is the case with those who "choose" voluntary death.[43] But we may encounter things not only useful to our conservation but things that agree (*convenient*) with our nature. For Spinoza it is possible for two such individuals "to compose an individual twice as powerful as each one taken separately" (*E* IV, 18, schol.). Thus the surge of affects across individuals may disrupt the relation of agreement between the individuals of which we are composed, weakening us and setting us against ourselves as well as others. But it may also unite us with others in a relation that increases our power to think and to act. Emulation, the imitation of the desire of the other, is the affect that accompanies such a unity; it is the consciousness of a singular thing composed through the conjunctural agreement of individuals endeavoring to persist in its being. As such, as an individual in Spinoza's sense of a singular thing, it is as real and as irreducible as the parts of which it is composed.

Interest—for Hobbes, Mandeville, and Smith—functioned as a principle of individualization; interest was the expression of the individual's tendency to self-conservation, a tendency that, at least initially, separated every one from every other one, even if the very principle would lead these essential separate individuals enthusiastically or reluctantly, wittingly or unwittingly, into society. In Spinoza's hands, however, the principle of self-conservation, or *conatus,* tends to transindividualize the human world, leading individuals to combine into new, more powerful individuals: couples, groups, even mass movements of a multiplicity of bodies in agreement, moving and speaking in unison, moved by a new *conatus* and a new desire. Such mass movements, which Spinoza theorized in his last work, the *Tractatus Politicus,* as the figure of the multitude, often begin in a moment of collective indignation[44] at the cruelty of masters—

visible or invisible, a monarch or a world bank—only to discover at the moment a new more powerful individual is formed, a tremendous power to think and to act, the power not simply to destroy a world of servitude and deprivation but to make another world in its place.

It is this strain of thought that must be buried deep in the earth, its very memory effaced. As was often remarked about Spinoza, such doctrines are not to be refuted because their refutation allows them to spread. Only when they have been rendered unthinkable and unimaginable can the books that contain them be read again as safely as if the offending parts had been removed by a censor.[45] The TMS was but one of the many spade-fulls of earth that covered Spinoza's thought, refusing even to name that which was buried in its opening gestures. But the text, if not the man, remains haunted by the image, even if not the thought, of that which it buried and, like the criminal consumed by remorse whose tortures Smith so carefully details, cannot fail to remember that which its happiness depends on forgetting. What are these images or reminiscences from which the text suffers and what allows us to connect them to the repression of the transindividuality that Spinoza theorizes? In what sense can we say, as Smith does of the criminal, that "the thought of this perpetually haunts him, and fills him with terror and amazement" (TMS 84)?

We will recall that the strongest version of sympathy in the TMS appears in the first sentence of the first paragraph, while the most detailed, if succinct, refutation of the common notion of sympathy as a communication of feeling immediately follows it in the second paragraph of the work. We need go no further than the third paragraph of the TMS to find a striking image that, although meant to serve as an example of the fact that we sympathize with others only "by changing places in fancy with the sufferer" (TMS 10), raises serious questions about the very restrictions Smith has placed on sympathy, questions that he neither addresses nor even acknowledges:

> When we see a stroke aimed and just ready to fall upon the leg or arm of another person, we naturally shrink and draw back our own leg or our own arm; and when it does fall, we feel it in some measure, and are hurt by it as well as the sufferer. The mob, when they are gazing at a dancer on the slack rope, naturally writhe and twist and balance their own bodies, as they see him do, and as they feel that they themselves must do if in his situation. (TMS 10)

The sentences exhibit the parallelism that is a hallmark of Smith's writing. Both illustrate not only that changing places in fancy of which Smith has spoken in the preceding sentence, but illustrate, perhaps to assuage the reader's skepticism, the power that the fancy or imagination can have over us. In the first case, although "we" (let's pay attention to his pronouns) know that it is not our arm or leg at which a stroke is aimed and ready to fall, despite our certainty on this account, we cannot help rapidly and powerfully to imagine what we ourselves would feel and for a moment respond to the sight before us by drawing back as if we were the target. We do so, Smith repeats in both sentences, "naturally," suggesting both the commonality of such a response and the near spontaneity of our physical reaction (as if it were a matter of instinct rather than volition). Both the near spontaneity and the power of our sympathy, in this case, appear quite at odds with Smith's later account of the difficulties that the spectator must face in sympathizing with even those sentiments he views with approbation. In fact, the first sentence here is ambiguous: The stroke is aimed, but the passive voice denies us any knowledge of by whom; it falls upon another person, but we do not know if he is about to suffer an undeserved assault or just retribution for criminal acts (the image in certain ways suggests corporal punishment, such as caning or flogging).[46]

Irrespective of our judgments concerning this man and the acts about to be carried out against him, our sympathy is immediate and strong; it involves our body as well as our mind and impels us to act as well as to feel. In fact, the work's third paragraph poses a problem to which Smith devotes little attention and to which in a certain sense his argument is designed to minimize: the problem of excessive, unreasoning sympathy that can overpower one's reason and cloud one's judgment, spilling over from the mind into the body; this is a problem, Smith suggests here, perhaps restricted to "persons of delicate fibers and a weak constitution" (*TMS* 10). The use of the second person plural, "we," in the first sentence, together with the repeated term "natural," however, implies that such reactions are common—even, in however diminished a degree, universal.

The next sentence appears to repeat the assertion, contained in the first, that a kind of imitation as a result of a vivid action of our imagination can, under certain circumstances, be perfectly "natural." But it proceeds to complicate this already complicated idea in certain ways. The subject of the sentence and the agent of the action is "the mob," which Smith immediately reduces to the individuals that compose it by substituting for it the pronoun "they." It is perfectly consonant with the preceding sentence: Individuals watching a "dancer on the slack rope" (not a euphemism for hanging, although this has surely crossed the mind of many readers, but a balancing act). What is remarkable here is that a number of individuals simultaneously feel the same feeling and physically react to the spectacle before them with the same bodily movements.

Smith has thus described what we have no choice but to call an imitation of the affects, a kind of affective contagion that simultaneously afflicts the mind and the body and to the same degree. The imitation of the spectacle before them, and perhaps of each other, has united them; they are no longer a collection of dissociated individuals, each sealed off in his or her own person. They feel and do the same things, and it is this that constitutes them not only as *a* mob, but also as *the* mob. The term "mob" in the eighteenth century is not merely a synonym for crowd. The mob, an abbreviation for *mobile vulgus* or "changeable masses," appears often in Roman historical writing as that force that often decides the outcome of political struggles, and *vulgus* was often used interchangeably with *multitude* (Spinoza himself uses the term in both the *Tractatus Theologico-Politicus* and *Ethics* to denote "the masses").[47]

The mob, for Smith in this particular passage, does not simply exemplify the innocence and ignorance of the vulgar; it demonstrates that even in (or perhaps because of) their innocence and ignorance, a significant number of individuals unite in the simultaneity not only of sentiment, but of bodily action to become a singular thing, the mob. We might recall here Spinoza's remark: "If several individuals concur in the same action such that they are all together the cause of the same effect, I consider them all in this way one and the same singular thing" (*E* II, 7). Such a notion would appear to take us far away from the solitary individuals who populate the bulk of the *TMS*. It will take us as far, in fact, as *Wealth*, where masses, the very possibility of whose unity is never explained, struggle for wages or simply for food.

In Chapter 2 of *The Wealth of Nations*, Smith ascribes a certain "propensity" to human nature: the propensity to truck, barter, and exchange one thing for another. Although Smith cannot decide whether this propensity is "one of those original principles in human nature" or whether (and it is to this explanation that he is inclined) it is the "necessary consequence of the faculties of reason and speech," he nevertheless finds it to be "common to all men" but absent in every "other race of animals" (*Wealth* 25). The absence of such a propensity in animals means, for Smith, that they

> know neither this nor any other species of contracts. Two greyhounds, in running down the same hare, have sometimes the appearance of acting in some sort of concert. Each turns her towards his companion, or endeavors to intercept her

when his companion turns her towards himself. This, however, is not the effect
of any contract, but of the accidental concurrence of their passions in the same
object at that particular time. (*Wealth* 25–26)

In *Jurisprudence* (*LJ*), Smith takes the argument further. Even an "accidental
concurrence" of animals' passions and actions must give way by virtue of their
physical proximity to violent competition: "Monkeys, when they rob a garden,
throw the fruit from one to another, till they deposit it in the hoard, but there is
always a scramble about the division of the booty, and usually some of them are
killed" (*LJ* B, 494). What is remarkable here is that in both the human and the
animal world private interest separates individuals and sets them against each
other. In the human world alone private interest may, under certain circumstances, furnish the basis for the only kind of communion there can be between
separate individuals: a contract based on the expectation of gain. As we have
seen, this affective isolation and pursuit of one's own interest at the apparent
expense of all others paradoxically produces the material community without
which humans cannot long subsist.

In a certain sense, the move to differentiate man from all the other animal
races is a feint that draws our attention away from what the passage says about
the human world. For, if human beings alone possess a capacity for cooperation, this cooperation has a single origin: the private interest of each individual
who "trucks and barters" not simply with a view to mere utility, but who seeks
to get better than he or she gives in return. Individuals, thus, enter into cooperation for the sake of interest and interest alone, and such cooperation can
only take the form of a contract whose parties have calculated what is to be
gained from such an exchange. No form of cooperation and community can
emerge immediately, spontaneously, or by any other means than the hope of
increasing one's holdings.

Smith will go even further than Hobbes (who ascribed to bees and ants
a sociability that he argued was absent in human beings)[48] to deny any form
of association outside of the contract: Rather than content himself with a
demonstration of the necessity of the contract to any union between human
individuals, given the potential violence of competition outside the law, he will
exclude any form of cooperation in the animal world for the obvious reason
that animals cannot make contracts; their apparent cooperation will in fact give
way to a fight to the death over the desired object. Such an extravagant view
of human nature is, of course, absolutely necessary to the conception of the
market, its functioning and rationality, which Smith will develop in the ensu-

ing chapters of *Wealth*. To be able to "consult his interest" (as opposed to that of others) and to seek his own advantage, the individual must be made separate and solitary, impervious to the affects and desires of others, indifferent to or contemptuous of their suffering and deprivation, immune to the affective contagion whose effects other authors so feared.

It is all the more surprising then that it is in *Wealth*, the work in which Smith's reduction of transindividuality is most complete, that he demonstrates the existence of what can only be called solidarity: the constitution of a group whose members are not united solely through the mediation of a contract. Smith will go so far as to demonstrate what Spinoza called the imitation of desire and the transindividualization of interest, such that individuals unite to form a singular thing and all together become the cause of a single effect. In civilized society, where the produce of the laborer is no longer his but belongs to his master or landlord, and a great many workmen are united under a relatively few masters, the rate of wages no longer takes the form of a contract between an individual laborer and his master or even between a number of laborers and a master. Rather, the "contract" (the term Smith uses even though it will appear increasingly inadequate to describe the changeable nature of wages) is made between two "parties": masters, as a group, and workmen. It appears that the latter so readily and easily unite (and thus overcome with surprisingly little difficulty the whispering within of self-interest that urges each worker to compete against his or her fellows, or at least to calculate the return on the expenditure of time and energy that such unremunerated activity demands) to extract raises from their masters. Laborers have so commonly and automatically resorted to such action that, Smith reminds us, governments have been compelled repeatedly for nearly a century to enact legislation against "combinations" of laborers to raise or even simply maintain their wages against a reduction.

While no such legislation has been enacted to prevent combinations of employers, Smith cautions the reader: "[W]hoever imagines, upon this account, that masters rarely combine, is as ignorant of the world as of the subject" (*Wealth* 84). Smith's account of the masters' combination (about which he has much more to say than about that of the workmen) is extremely interesting: "Masters are always and everywhere in a sort of tacit, but constant and uniform, combination, not to raise the wages of labor above their actual rate" (*Wealth* 84). The term "tacit" here stands out. This combination is manifestly not the consequence of a contract in the usual sense of the word. No promise has been made in the expectation of exchange for gain: There is no need for such a promise to unite with other masters, because there has never been a time of disunity that would have to be transcended through the mediation of a contract. There is "always and everywhere" (or always-already) combination that therefore never originates in the will of separate actors but is the very condition of their being masters. There is no foundational act undertaken by originally separate individuals who decide one by one to come together but a "constant" collectivity whose desires and interests are the same.

But what of the laborers? Their combination appears, if anything, more tenuous and inconstant than that of the masters. Sometimes, when masters collectively "sink the wages of labor" even though the wage reduction is "severely felt" by the workers, they sometimes yield without resistance. Even in the face of the deprivation that they and their families will feel, they fail to combine. Want and the specter of destitution, as well as fear of punishment, prevent them from uniting. However, sometimes—in fact, more frequently than not—even in the face of threat of destitution and state violence, workers resist "by a contrary defensive combination" (*Wealth* 84). In such cases (and not only according to Smith's account) these combinations are not undertaken with a calculation of interest, and there is something manifestly irrational in them. Not only is their goal unattainable according to Smith, but they arise from what we can only call the effects of hatred and indignation: hatred for the rigor imposed on the individual himself and indignation for the fact that this rigor has been imposed on his family and his fellows.

The effects of individualization and separation produced by the market, as well as the state, are thus opposed by countereffects: The combination of workers is constituted by shared affects themselves determined by the conjunction of bodies and minds "collected into the same workhouse" (*Wealth* 14), subject to the same conditions and discipline. Alongside the product of industry, in such workhouses is produced a new singular thing, united and powerful, capable of "the most shocking violence and outrage" (*Wealth* 84).

"The mob is terrifying when it is not afraid" (*E* IV, 54, schol.). Smith's project is not so much to condemn the mob as to demonstrate its impossibility: Combination is not so much wrong as an illusion, at most "an accidental concurrence of . . . passions" that one finds in various races of animals. Smith's work as a whole is marked by an extraordinary effort not only to separate individuals in terms of affects, desires, and interests, but to translate the language of sociability into the idiom of individuality. What we thought were relations between individuals were, in fact, intra-individual relations between us and what we imagine we would feel in the place of the other. The elaboration of the individual necessary to the market, the individual who consults and acts on self interest alone, could only take place on the basis of a refusal and forgetting of all that is contained in Spinoza's theory of the imitation of the affects, the trans-individualization of even interest itself. In fact, can we not say that the illusion necessary to Smith's system is that we cannot experience others' feelings, that we will never confuse their interest for our own, and that all suggestions of a genuine transfusion of feeling and a complication of identity beyond the individual's imagination is a threat to the rational foundation of society?

The attempt to individualize the social field was not merely aimed at the ancient and medieval notion of the human being as *zoon politikon*; it was also and increasingly an attempt to counter in theory and in philosophy the rise of the urban masses and the new collectivities of labor, "free" as well as unfree, the inescapable byproduct of the very division of labor that lies at the origin of economic progress. If Smith's texts are haunted by what they have forgotten, it is not merely the power of Spinoza's thought that disrupts them and sets them against themselves. It is that from which Spinoza's thought cannot be dissociated, the "tumultuous combinations" whose destructive violence is finally less frightening to Smith and his heirs than their power to make a world.

3 "NUMBERS, NOISE, AND POWER"
Insurrection as a Problem of Historical Method

This is a dreadful Discouragement to all Men of true Genius, who are often contented to bury their Talents under a Bushel, rather than by producing them in Public, to Trust the Decision of their Merit to a Tribunal, where Numbers, Noise, and Power, too often carry the Question against Sense and Reason.

Henry Fielding, *The True Patriot*[1]

THE DEMONSTRATIVE ARTICLE "this" in the epigram from Fielding could refer to any number of problems in the context of his split professional life, which no matter how varied, was concerned, like our own focus in this chapter, with the "noise" of "numbers." Of course, Fielding is known in traditional histories of the novel as one of the key originators of formal realism. And apposite to Fielding's worry above, the eighteenth-century novel is well-established as a mode of writing that is, on the one hand, problematically numerous—dangerously popular, especially to the lower ranks—and, on the other hand, particularly well suited to sorting the masses of experiential data along individualistic and more or less reasonable lines. The modern novel's business was one of sorting the apparently capricious "tribunal" of "numbers and noise" into more or less probable outcomes, an important corrective in an age of popular contention, exuberance, tumult, riot, and even insurrection.

That the overproduction of novels could be addressed as a similar problem of numeric excess is an important point to add to Fielding's complaint about too many readers in general. Indeed, Adam Ferguson chided Smith over the popularity of *Wealth*, as if the book's immediate and wide prevalence would diminish its significance, remarking to his colleague, "You are not to expect the run of a novel."[2] And with regard to insurrection, we should remember that Tom Jones, the protagonist of what was for generations regarded as the English novel's foundational work, made his way from being an impoverished foundling toward adulthood, family, and wealth in the context of the Jacobite invasion of 1745.[3] *Tom Jones* was published just four years after that event.

Such timing invites us to seek out connections between the history of the English novel—a "new species of writing," as Fielding famously proclaims, and the original pop-literary form—to both the history of Jacobitism and the history of *history* itself: Novels and historical writing in the eighteenth century were commonly beset with the problem of mass readership and were themselves focused on working out popular contention according to a progressive and probabilistic understanding of time. This understanding was also supposed to be a nationally coherent one, linking temporal experience to the security of property and to the forms of patriotic belonging that underscored the durability of British/Scottish union in 1707. The kind of patriotism achieved by the promotion of such temporal experience was designed to foster virtues—as we shall see, sometimes ambivalently—that perpetuated domestic peace while never quite completely sidelining popular contention.

In order to delineate this process, we want to begin this chapter with an account of popular Jacobitism. We realize of course that organized military rebellion on behalf of the Stuart cause should not be flatly equated with popular contention writ large. But they crossed over in important ways that for eighteenth-century thinkers were subsumed under the protean heading of the "multitude." In our account of unrest around the Stuart cause, we want to show how descriptions of Jacobite and other "mobs" as being antithetical to stadial historical progress bear comparison with Hume's rejection of *a priori* notions of cause and effect. From here, we move from popular Jacobitism and kindred activities to an account of eighteenth-century historiography proper: How was the social and political concern with insurrection—for Hume, Robertson, and others, reaching back to the precarious union of crowns under James VI and I in 1603—addressed by epistemic debates over so-called conjectural thought?

Our next move delves in a more focused way into the relationship among multiplicity, novels, and history. At issue in this section is how the unprecedented amassing of novels themselves presented a problem of "numbers" in the form of literary overproduction akin to the one that designates the fear of insurrection in eighteenth-century historical writing.

Finally, we develop the ambivalent value that Scottish historians gave to what they called "martial virtue," a way of canalizing insurgency on behalf of the state's monopoly on violence that was also supposed to stem the deleterious effects of capitalist luxury. Here popular contention presents a permanent problem—sometimes governable, sometimes leading to riot, insurrection, and war. As such, what Hume called "the fury of the multitude" signals the dangers of popular resistance to historical progress and complicates the ability to produce effective historical narrative written in stadial terms.[4]

But for now, think of Henry Fielding before his bestseller, *Tom Jones*: the pitiable (and relatively poor) dramatist, whose play *The Golden Rump*, harshly critical of Walpole, may have also initiated the censorious Theatrical Licensing Act of 1737. (His play *The Tragedy of Tragedies* was one of the most popular productions of the eighteenth century.) To the conflict between "numbers" and "reason" add the other keyword: "power." Fielding was not only an Enlightenment critic and literary innovator, characteristically focused on the relationship between social order and good taste, but a political antagonist turned pensioned scribbler, a barrister, a fierce anti-Jacobite, and, not least, the first modern Justice of the Peace for Westminster and Middlesex.

Fielding's tour in political journalism (after his defense of Pelham's "patriot" government) started formally with *The True Patriot*, which, like its successor (satirically titled *The Jacobite's Journal*) was written in the context of the notorious uprisings of 1715, and especially, of 1745. Whether or not Prince Charlie's army under Lord George Murray had any real chance of taking London—to make his father, James VIII of Scotland, III of England—for Fielding and so many others the threat of Jacobite insurrection was a proximate one. That Charles made it as far south as Derby, where the Manchester unemployed joined him, is a tribute to Jacobite surprise.[5] In *Lectures on Jurisprudence* (hereafter *LJ*, with A or B indicating which manuscript), Smith remarks,

> In the year 1745 four or five thousand naked unarmed Highlanders took possession of the improved parts of this country without any opposition from the unwarlike inhabitants. They penetrated into England and alarmed the whole nation, and had they not been opposed by a standing army, they would have seized the throne with little difficulty.[6]

Smith's point was both to mark the so-called barbaric stage of Highland underdevelopment as well as to contrast their skills at war with the relative weakness of those ahead of the historical curve. Later historians have confirmed that most of the territory gained in the "Forty-Five" occurred as the invading Scottish army walked from Glenfinnan to Edinburgh. This was made possible thanks in part to English improvements of the northernmost road systems under General Wade, improvements that were made, ironically, as part of an act in 1725 meant to disarm the Highlanders.[7] (Indeed, regarding the North of Scotland, the ironies of disarmament tend to stack up: In 1682 James VII and II—a Stuart king—appointed a commission for securing peace in the Highlands.)

The point we want to begin with is that, in the years between the time Charles sailed out of Moidart to France (the same way he came in) and the arrival of William in 1688, displacing the Stuart dynasty once and for all, Jacobitism signaled crisis as well as opportunity. In the years immediately following the so-called Bloodless Revolution, England was beset with unprecedented episodes of riot and sedition—some thirty towns and villages reported riot on William's coronation day.[8] For Fielding, as for most moderate Enlightenment thinkers, allegiance to the Stuart cause was connected to the question of insurgency as a general social problem.

From William's ascension to the throne in 1688, through the subsequent uprisings of 1715 and 1745, Jacobitism provided a heading under which a spectrum of popular contention could be organized, from the most spontaneous and harmless to the most organized and violent. Studies show that a full 90 percent of the Scottish population was against the merger with a newly created Great Britain 1707; and in the years leading up to and immediately following that event, two-thirds of all prosecution for public disturbances in the Midland counties were associated with Jacobite sentiments. This contrasts revealingly with the figure of one-third of popular disorders being Jacobite inflected in London during the same period.[9] And though Jacobitism signals a direct challenge to established British sovereignty in the form of marching armies, it should not be seen as equivalent with them. Nicholas Rogers (in "Riot and Popular Jacobitism in Early Hanoverian England," hereafter "RP") notes the "lack of correspondence between riot and armed insurrection," and that "even in the West Country, while rioting was especially prominent in the early month's of [William's] reign, there is a decline in violence prior to the projected uprising there" ("RP" 72).

Indeed, given the myriad examples of popular contention on behalf of the exiled Stuart monarchy between 1680 and 1720, local recruitment for the formal Jacobite uprising of 1715 was disappointing. Popular disaffection peaked before the "Fifteen," according to Rogers, though roughly 700 English men (mostly gentlemen) did join the Scottish army at that time. Rogers cites (in *Crowds, Culture, and Politics in Georgian Britain*, hereafter *CCP*) that the invasion of 1745 was little better in this regard, with only 200 Jacobite rebels officially recruited in disaffected Manchester out of a population of 30,000 (*CCP* 37, 54).

The "tributaries of disaffection" susceptible to Jacobitism were, to extend Rogers's metaphor, "too diverse" (*CCP* 37) to flow through the narrow channels of military violence.

Thus, rather than seeing popular Jacobitism as a seamless extension or spontaneous mirroring of organized military rebellion, Rogers's point, consistent with our own, is to regard the *popular* itself as a form of contention that exceeds the reductively oppositional dynamics and traditional binaries circumscribed by purely oppositional notions of categorical—in this case, *national*—difference. The mode of "diversity" we might extract from Rogers's use of that term refutes reduction to prevailing social and political dyads. Rogers therefore rejects the classical social oppositions underwriting the important work in eighteenth-century crowd studies stemming from George Rudé and others and inserts instead a regard for popular contention as "a field of force" (*CCP* 11, 13).[10]

Similarly, he dismisses the rendering of the crowd of Gustave le Bon and Robert Park of the Chicago School as "the atavistic residuum of the instincts of primitive man" (*CCP* 34). Here, we would emphasize, the crowd becomes as much a problem of historical method as it is one of historical analysis—less an object ripe for diachronic anatomical description over linear trajectories of time than a unique temporal-spatial enigma in its own epistemological right. Though popular Jacobitism was an object of eighteenth-century thought across the emerging disciplines, to the extent that such crowd events variously resisted dominant forms of Whig objectification, popular contention was also an obstacle to history writ as unimpeded narrative of Enlightened social progress.

In 1737, one British MP dubbed the Jacobite crowd (or here, the "mob") "a horizontal kind of beast" (*CCP* 16). That it was "horizontal" speaks to the crowd's ability to complicate dominant structures, or better, speaks to its irreducibly "plural," "protean," "mobile," "ambiguous," "unpredictable," and "*sometimes* subversive" positions within presiding oppositional norms. That the so-called mob was "a kind of beast" is indicative of the categorical disruptions that popular contention brought to predominant notions of the progress of civilized man (emphasis ours; *CCP* 21, 22, 55, 57). A Newcastle keel-man could, for example, vandalize pictures of Kings James I and Charles I during a strike or food riot, yet ten years later proclaim Charles II his rightful sovereign during the occasion of a subsequent strike. In the words of one Bristolean cited by Rogers, the plebian wearers of Oak Sprigs for the memory of King James's exile resented judgments "passed upon their Thoughts, Innuendo's drawn from Gestures of the Body and Motions of the Fingers" ("RP" 80).

In this world of profanity and blasphemy, such behavior as "oaths, portents, riddles, revels," and so on presents a peculiar archive—one that, because intensely local, belies an adherence to general social norms. Under the heading of popular Jacobitism, we may thus find all sorts of seditious activity: "A band of Jacks on a drunken spree"; the "bawling out . . . of Pye-Corner pastorals on behalf of dear Jemmy, lovely Jemmy"; whistling airs in the street; reciting riddles; speaking "Free Language"; making the irreverent huzzhah; poaching; sending incendiary letters; any number of other forms of unrest that harnessed the dissatisfaction of common people in what Rogers calls "an idiom of defiance" (*CCP* 40, 41; "RP" 71). Government and organized political partisans had to live with, as well as attempt to contain and/or mobilize, a form of collective agency that was both an obstacle to the emergence of the public sphere and a force immanent within it.

The *non*-exclusively linguistic idiom of popular Jacobitism presented by Rogers thus broadens our understanding of Stuart association (if not also overt allegiance) beyond the dualistic sense of clashing armies and opposing political orthodoxies. The interesting point about popular discontent as manifest within and around the term "Jacobitism" up until mid-century was its ability to work with its own internal dissonance, its propensity to affirm what looks in retrospect like an error of category, or to cite Cairns Craig (in *Intending Scotland: Explorations in Scottish Culture Since the Enlightenment*, hereafter *IS*), its uniquely "*intra*-national" quality (emphasis ours).[11] Craig critiques not only the ahistorical idea of treating union history as the example of a failed nation, as committed unionist H. R. Trevor-Roper and others would have it, but also the "failure of national theory to account for the nature of the nation" (*IS* 52). What most theories of nationalism miss is that features other than national identity were also important to popular Jacobitism, even though at one crucial historical moment, it put Scotland on the threshold of national self-recognition.

But even at an organized political level, as Colin Kidd points out, a close reading of the document securing union belies its supposed coherence as a legally binding contract. Was it

> a Treaty or an Act of Parliament—or even two Acts of separate and equally sovereign Scots and English parliaments? If the Union was a Treaty, did the parties to the Treaty continue to exist after 1707 and is the Treaty justiciable in international law?[12]

Kidd continues (in *Union and Unionisms*, hereafter *UU*), "There is no agree-ment in the current academic literature as to whether post-1707 Britain was a brand new state or . . . embodied continuities from the pre-1707 states out of which it was formed" (*UU* 85).

Here the Act of Union signifies a promise that paradoxically dissolves the unity of one party in the very act of promising. And in the new form of a sup-posedly unified entity, older continuities that attenuate supposedly bygone di-visions are still traceable: The past betrays the present in this way, cross-cuts the history of a new state of Great Britain that is not yet completely actualized on the ground. In addition, what remains after that promise of national unity in 1707 is both a state of absence and—as Kidd's provocative book title *Union and Unionisms* intends to underscore—a condition of multiplicity not reduc-ible to the prospect of unification then being proposed. The key complication is summed in Kidd's title as "unions," with an indomitable emphasis on the plural. Defoe knew the stakes, as he put them in a poem from 1704: "Union's the Nation's Life, Peace and the Soul,/ Union preserves the Parts, and Peace the Whole."[13] His play on the words "peace" and "piece" show the close connec-tion between plurality, national coherence, and popular disorder. Queen Anne's Alien Act of the following year speaks very much to this point, as it would have made the Scot in England a foreigner at home.

Thus to speak of achieving Scottish sovereignty in the eighteenth century as if it could be applied to an entity not already internally cohesive falsely positions "unionism and nationalism as opposites" (*UU* 6). In Penicuik, Midlothian, a clerk thus reports: "In a corner of the street you may see a Pres-byterian minister, a Popish priest, and an Episcopal prelate, all agreeing in their discourse against the Union, but upon quite different views and contradictory reasons."[14] The observation is consistent with Kidd's point: "The fluidity of older strains of Unionism [has been] obliterated . . . from popular memory" (*UU* 5). The kinship between *Jacobitism* and other forms of anti-Unionist parti-sanship—not least among the religious sects—is something lost to history and is precisely what we need retrieve by attaching the term "popular."

In his magisterial six-volume tome *The History of England* (hereafter *HE*), Hume is uniquely keen to examine the divergent forces of the so-called people's rage as a decisive factor of historical change. Scottish insurrection around the ascension of Stephen, the defeat of King William, and the rise of Henry II are key events that begin this history; and in the wake of Scottish defeat and forced union under Cromwell, the fitful end of the Stuart kings, followed by a more peaceable (if still precarious) placing of William of Orange on the throne, are the events that end it. Pursued by a "mutinous populace" bent on "leveling all mankind," Richard II is forced to take shelter in the tower (*HE* II); King Edward works to master the "popular arts" against the ever-present force of "Scots . . . resistance" (*HE* II, 65); Henry's "natural arrogance" produces "insurrection [among a] licentious populace" (*HE* III, 161); a virtuous but hypocritical Mary, Queen of Scots, "seize[s] the opportunity of . . . rebellion" to commit Lady Elizabeth, her sister, to the Tower (*HE* III, 419); and Cromwell, though his "genius" was "guided by events, and did not, as yet, foresee," showed "profound[ly] . . . artful conduct" in using both "delay" and "celerity . . . to combine the most contrary interests in a subserviency to his secret purposes." "Nothing could be more popular," Hume continues, than inspiring an army of "tumultuary peasants" to march on Parliament in this way (*HE* V, 450, 470, 499, 510).

A survey of the table of contents of Hume's *History of England* shows that the most common terms among its subtitles are words like "insurrections" or "new insurrections" (used five times as headings in volume I alone); "popular insurrection," "insurrection of the common people," or "domestic disturbances" (six subheadings in five chapters in volume II); "insurrection," "revolt," or "war" (ten subheadings in volume II); and so on, through the "suppression of the Levelers," "Jamaica conquered," and the "Treaty of Westphalia" in the final volume.

Though *The History of England* in its entirety covers the period from the Norman invasion of the eleventh century through the Glorious Revolution of the late seventeenth century, Hume chose as his starting point the first Stuart monarchy of James VI and I, following Elizabeth in 1603. He then proceeded to write, in a sort of oscillating way, about the later Stuart reigns (volumes V and VI), then returning to the Tudors (volumes III and IV), ending with the "barbarous times" (*HE* I, xii), the period before Henry VII (volumes I–III).

Hume decided to start with the Stuarts and, by implication, with the origins of mid-eighteenth century Jacobitism, for the revealing reason: It was the period "when . . . the misrepresentations of faction began chiefly to take place" (*HE* I, xi). In a separate letter to Smith, Hume puts his focus on "the *continual* struggle between the Crown and the people" as a specifically Jacobite-oriented "Quarrel between Privilege and Prerogative" (emphasis ours, *HE* I, xii). This struggle for Hume had a lasting presence throughout so-called *English* history (the titular slighting of Scotland, Ireland, and Wales should not be missed here), even though it varied in consequence and intensity until the presumed moment of peace established with William's elected ascension. The "continual" clashes of the "people"—an anachronistic term given Hume's more typical use of terms like "licentious multitude" (*HE* II, 47) or "the ignorant multitude" (*HE* VI, 170), from beginning to end in his *History*—coalesced into its most threatening form the moment the Stuarts assumed the throne (though riotous activity and insurgency would reach its apex some decades later with the Puritans and Levelers of the English civil war).

Given Hume's preoccupation throughout all six volumes of the *History* with what Hume elsewhere calls the "many latent claims . . . of popular principles" (*HE* VI, 530), we might be tempted to add a "latent" but more descriptive subtitle to his work, such as *The History of England, Through Six Centuries of Popular Contention and Revolt, with a Special Emphasis on Scotland*. Indeed, the word "many" is as important as the word "latent" in connection to "popular principles." This is because what was missing or is barely traceable in history before the Scottish school was an account of England from the perspective precisely of the many—of popular disorder, insurrection, riot, the so-called multitude, the vulgar, Jacobites, Puritans, republicans, savages and barbarians, alike.

It is also significant that, for Hume, Smith, and the rest of their intellectual kin, Scotland is the location where this form of historical agency originally resided, and less happily, retained a residual presence in their own day. But it is significant less for reasserting ancient claims to national identity than for remarking upon the complexities that Scotland brings to the very question of nation, especially insofar as those questions are also ones of popular contention. One of the most important developments in Jacobite studies has been to complicate presumptions about Scottish identity in the early modern period, which is too often viewed against the oppositional foreground of purely English dominance. Leith Davis summarizes this development as the recognition instead of an encounter "between heterogeneous elements."[15] This is not at all to underemphasize the question of English dominance, of antiunionist political struggle up to and after the "Forty-Five." But it does force us to think about such conflict according to a more complex grid than the simple bifurcation of Scotland-Jacobite-Highland-Catholic insurrection on the one side, at the margins, versus England-Whig-Lowland-Protestant on the other.

It is revealing that of the 20,000 soldiers organized by the Earl of Mar in the "Fifteen," only 4,100 were Highlanders. It should also be noted that the definition of "Highlander" was by no means a consistent one. It could mean the mountainous region of northern Scotland at one time, and of Britain north of

Inverness, including the western islands, at another. Some were called Highlanders even if they moved, especially if they spoke Gaelic. Highland status
could be inherited, without stepping foot in northern Scotland, as there were
Highlanders native to Glasgow in the eighteenth century. Notably, the Earl of
Loudoun, identified as a member of the powerful Campbell clan, led English
regiments *against* the Jacobites in 1745. And many descendants of prominent
Highland families did not self-identify as such.[16]

In a more recent overview, which we will not rehearse here, Davis explains
current challenges to the notion of a Scottish periphery and argues instead for
the unique status of Scotland as neither reducible to the circumscriptions of
alterity that underlie other episodes of imperial occupation (which, as the Darien
disaster shows, some Scots were happy enough to foist upon others), nor simply
a notion of Scotland as an objectified "other," against which an internally coherent British subject emerged.[17] Of her many important citations, Davis glosses
Murray Pittock's term "altermentalities" to signify the entirely immanent—if also
historically occulted—proximity of Scotland to the English national imaginary,
rather than its being cordoned off from it. Pittock's work is important because
he is consistently keen to reject the notion of pure Scottish aggression to a facile
dualistic equation with undivided English defense. He notes that when William
landed by invitation with his 15,000 soldiers in the so-called glorious year of 1688,
he did so not only with some cooperative Catholics (75 percent of all English
Jacobites were Catholic) but also, as one witness describes, "with 200 negroes
wearing embroidered caps . . . and 200 Finlanders in bearskin and black armor."[18]

Robert Ferguson, whose 1715 pamphlet *The History of All Mobs, Tumults,
and Insurrections in Great Britain from William the Conqueror to the Present
Time* (it also included a copy of the 1714 Riot Act), is as remarkably short at
sixty-eight pages as Hume's *History* is long and is an interesting case in point.
A Scottish Presbyterian minister known as "the plotter" for his implication in
the Rye House Plot, he changed allegiances wherever nonconforming opportunity led. Ferguson was at one point an anti-Jacobite pamphleteer who wrote a
manifesto against King James II and plotted against Charles II. He returned to
England after exile with the rest of William's diverse crew in 1688. But he later
also corresponded sympathetically with the Jacobites in France and turned on
William through various plots and violent pamphlets. If it is true, as Ferguson writes (well before Hume), that "in all our Histories of Great Britain . . .
we meet with nothing more frequent than Mobs and Insurrections," then he
clearly also took advantage of the strange "disorders" and endless "outrages" of

"the Rabble" as they took liberty to express whatever form of antigovernmental violence was expedient at the time.[19]

The characteristics of the Jacobite elites were also decidedly more fluid than we may tend to assume. Many wanted toleration, the end of the enclosures of land, or to challenge corrupt Whig property rights, all of which gained support among the poor.[20] As Pittock also reveals, and as we have already seen Hume puzzle over, some of the radical Presbyterians, though attached within memory to the leveling tendencies leading up to Cromwell, could also support the Jacobites. To the extent that Jacobitism signified outsider status after 1688, the term "tended to draw together (if only temporarily) disaffected groups, and to criminalize those ideologically opposed to the Hanoverian regime, thus driving them into cross-class alliance with criminals who themselves became politicized as a result of the connection."[21]

Further challenging the idea of a strict Highland versus Lowland divide, Pittock notes that some 25 percent of the English country gentry had Jacobite inclinations during the first two Georges (one person in ten in Sussex; up to 40 percent in Lancashire), and that at their zenith more than 140 Jacobite clubs existed in England, over 90 percent of them *outside Scotland*.[22] A volatile combination of "high cultural patronage and folk cultural practice sustained the network of Jacobitism . . . [,] promoting some of the most difficult public-order issues that the British government have ever had to deal with."[23] Indeed, the word "network" in this citation is an apt way to think of the insurrectionary dynamic of so-called mob activity, not least because it forbids the too-easy equation between riotous activity and simple party politics. A net-centric notion of popular Jacobitism invites us to think of such agency as specific and provisional, temporary and opportunistic, productive of singular combinations of opposites, experimental, and above all subject to chance.

Taken with these aspects in mind, popular Jacobitism is "linked to contemporary social and technological change . . . [;] its own early version of virtual reality."[24] Such an interest in Jacobite material culture offers a theory focused on the vitality of Jacobite objects as they pronounced disruptive forms of articulation beyond traditional forms of speech. Their most profound significance was to make "oblique reference to more explicit public political sympathies [while] occult[ing themselves] in privacy and silence."[25] Pittock argues that this notion of Jacobite "thingness" "exceed[ed] the merely objective," and therefore existed not as a public sphere, but as a "counter-public sphere, whose ingenuity allowed a degree of openness essential to communication but opaque to law."[26]

Others have sought in the eighteenth century a lost history of "thing theory," erased in part by the Scottish legal division between "corporeal" and "incorporeal" property that we addressed regarding copyright in Chapter 1. In a corresponding vein, Pittock's notion of a Jacobite materialism is based on both the nonsubjectively reducible agency of objects and on the limits of representational notions of language under conditions of state surveillance and popular political practice. He suggests not only that the "thing" animates initiates' encounters with uniquely loaded episodes of silence but also that it generates previously unspeakable forms of multiplicity. We might recall here Hume's idea of the *many* claims of popular contention throughout history as also necessarily *latent*. Jacobite materialism conceived in this matter displaces subject/object alignment and replaces this connection to ever more connections, over which a subject—especially, the subject of commercial exchange—does not have prescriptive control.

Thus, insofar as popular Jacobite activities were *virtual*, they allowed opportunities for the poor, landless, and illiterate majority to assert plebian birthrights against Whig interests, often without direction from above. E. P. Thompson has famously recorded Jacobite involvement in riots on turnpikes, demolitions of mills, seizures of grain, and game poaching on the order of the Blacks of Waltham of 1723.[27] And lists of arrests presented by Paul Monod reveal that the ranks of gentlemen among the sorts who rioted in the period from 1715–52 were greatly diminished from the preceding period beginning with 1689. In addition to clergy, the status of the accused after the "Fifteen" was comprised largely of the lower orders.[28] Here was an unruly amalgam of preindustrialized labor and laboring poor, or to use Defoe's eighteenth-century language, the "saucy, mutinous, and Beggarly."[29] Further recalling Rogers, these primarily anti-Whig rioters were often masterless men from the industrial hamlets: nailers and buck masters, colliers, apprentices, weavers, keel men, poachers, or simply the "younger sort of people" who were rightly suspicious of Hanoverian wars leading to widespread impressments ("RP" 74, 80).

It is worth noting on this count that the celebrations of James VII and II's birthday coincided with anti-impressment riots in 1695 (*CCP* 27, 35). Regarding popular hostility toward the derogatorily named "military ministry" as it was—*pace* establishment historians—known at the time in popular circles, we should note that William's reign began a period that was anything but bloodless. In addition to myriad riots and later Jacobite invasions, it ushered in a time of almost continuous war with France.[30] For example, in the nineteen years between the revolution and union, there were only five years of peace. The bread riots of

1756 were led by Midland miners, who warned that "the pretender would soon come and head" them ("RP" 84).

But discord over commercial interests also played across ranks, as Lord Belhaven's high rhetorical speech at the final session of the Scottish parliament before union would suggest. His famous "vision" monologue, which Parliament did not take altogether seriously, and at which he was said to have shed a theatrical tear, was knocked for being "contrived to incense the common people."[31] Striking the pose of an ancient prophet, Belhaven proposed an apocalyptic vision of the future as "our Ancient mother, Caledonia . . . [,] attending the final blow." This comes about, among other forms, in the guise of the "petty English Excise-man," which reduced the law-abiding Scot to "an equal level with Jews, Papists, Socinians, Armenians, Anabaptists, and other sectaries."[32] About the issue of English taxation, Belhaven was at least initially right: The Malt Tax of 1713 predictably incensed the Scottish populace.

The association of a disenfranchised Scotland with the status of the Jews— both depicted as "vagabonds over the whole earth"—was not an uncommon one.[33] The literary Jacobite often took on the guise of an ancient prophet of Israel. This held a cataclysmic flavor apposite to *virtual* reality, injecting a different connotation of *Jacob* (as in the grandson of Abraham, renamed Israel by God in Genesis 32: 28–29) into *Jacobitism*, where defeat and promise could be lamented and celebrated proleptically and at the same time. In a way also conjuring sore feelings over Scotland's national commerce, the Porteous Riots of 1736 (where smugglers were freed by an Edinburgh mob) were based on the question of illicit trade, turning Robin Hood sensibilities into direct street actions, now regarded as politicized crime.[34]

During the 1781 Gordon Riots, London's lower sorts took to the streets to attack the Old Bailey, free debt prisoners, and destroy the house of Lord Chief Justice Mansfield. Notably, Mansfield was born to aristocracy in Perth, with both parents supportive of the Old Pretender's cause. But Mansfield's position against the crowd was thoroughly updated. "It appears most clearly to me," he remarked, "that not only every man may legally interfere to suppress a riot, much more to prevent acts of felony, treason, and rebellion, in his private capacity, but he is bound to do it as an act of duty."[35] Perhaps this emphasis on personal duty rather than political ire is why Mansfield helped soften the punishment of Edinburgh after the Porteous Riots.

By contrast, the goal of the statutes for disarming the Highlands after Cumberland's brutal victory in the "Forty-Five," the long-term residence of the British army there, and the annexing and redistribution of land were based partly on putative vengeance and partly on promoting such behavior by the example of overwhelming force. But the British garrisons constructed North of the Tweed between 1745 and 1759 also expressly promoted a civilizing mission: The circulation of money in the region, the spread of the English language, Protestantism, and a focus on the commercialization of coal mining and farming went hand in hand with the fight against riotous behavior nationwide.[36]

We have already noted the importance of the Society in Scotland for the Promotion of Christian Knowledge (SSPCK) in Chapter 1.[37] Related to such efforts, Duncan Forbes recommended that the government establish schools near Highland military outposts, including "spinning schools to draw the idle females of these countries into the manufacture."[38] Pittock further develops the historical record of gendered Jacobitism (notably, Prince Charlie escaped disguised as a woman) associated with early feminist writers such as Mary Astell, Anne Finch (Countess of Winchelsea), and Delarivier Manley.[39]

Even before the Culloden massacre, the rape and molestation of Highland wives was perceived to be an effective way of curbing men to abandon the Jacobite cause. One Jenny Cameron, a fierce Jacobite alleged to have had a brief affair with Prince Charlie, was described as "hot and violent" and said to have gone to Edinburgh "dressed as a man, picking up women of the town, with whom [she] sometimes went to the bawdy-house, and carried the frolic as far as their sex would permit them."[40] It might also be added that Tom Jones's love interest, Sophia Western, is at one point in Fielding's novel of accident and sexual mishap (often, they are one and the same) mistakenly identified as Jenny Cameron.

What can be highlighted in this and in previous examples of Jacobite defiance is a form of popular contention that is both physical and phantasmal, something that served as a means of purveying symbolic, massively diverse forms of popular *qua* political license. Regarding such ghostly qualities of Jacobitism in England, as a French ambassador noted in 1712, "everyone is afraid to declare himself, [which is] a matter of losing your head and your property."[41] As we have seen though, owning property was not a prerequisite for Jacobite tendencies, which took place in a way that appealed strongly to the property-less majority:

> "[I]n peacetime [i.e., in times of popular tumult rather than overt war] the poorer Jacobite was more likely to be prosecuted; at times and in places affected by Jacobite war [such as during the "Fifteen" and the "Forty-Five"], the officer class . . . [was] more likely to find themselves in the dock.[42]

And according to Eveline Cruickshanks, we should not assume that only Jacobites rose up in rebellion, because records of court proceedings against lesser, symbolic kinds of Jacobite activities lack political detail. Moreover, because arrest warrants for public disturbances were written on more general grounds, "contemporaries preferred to draw a veil of silence over the matter."[43] Pittock points out the way in which the boundaries between sedition and treason became frayed in the first decades of the eighteenth century, a process: "conjoining . . . 'seditious libel' [with] 'treasonable words.'"[44] Indeed, an act of 1704 against "traitorous correspondence with her Majesty's enemies" extended the definition of treason into private letter writing.

The slippage between sedition and treason around Jacobite letter writing is only one example that troubles more idealized notions of eighteenth-century civil society. Related to it, we might recall that Habermas's public sphere theory is famously based on the rise of the epistolary novel.[45] But Jacobitism's treacherous objects (not only its letters, but secret signs, incendiary toasts, clothing, implements for drinking and eating, physical gestures, room interiors, and so on, as listed by Pittock in the Jacobite network of "things") are linked to recognition of the past in a different way than the civil society activities that Habermas continues to endorse. Pittock suggests that the

> tokens of the success of . . . treacherous objects . . . [lie] in concealing what was being communicated and inflecting what was being memorialised towards the very condition in which it is now remembered: their secrecy has triumphed over the language absent from the means of its own memorialisation.[46]

From these citations about performing memory, three points are worth developing. First, popular Jacobitism, writ here as sedition that slips into treason, is unrecognizable as the idealized, intersubjective consciousness found in either Smith's impartial spectator or in Habermas's similar notion of communicative reason. Memory as a Jacobite activity supersedes public consensus, resists connections with the past that are flatly mimetic, and forbids anthropocentric, overly volunteeristic renditions of intersubjectivity.

Second, a practice of popular memory such as this is founded by a more fluid and proximate relationship between people and things, between the subject knowing and the object present to be known, than are available to traditional notions of how meaning is produced. For reasons we will make clear just below, the keyword we would glean from Pittock is the word "means," as in *how* memory is mediated and to *what effect*, rather than what Hume would controversially reject as *a priori* assumptions about the causal relations between objects.

Therefore, a third lesson from popular Jacobitism is that the meaning of an object is based on an experience of time that is, paradoxically, both localized and experienced *en masse*, which is to say, time experienced in a way that neither confirms nor proscribes what is available to individual memory, let alone the established historical record. Things and actions (or better, things *as* actions) are neither distant nor objectifiable in relation to consciousness. Rather, like Scotland to England, they are immanent to one another, bearing agency initiated by a multiplicity of sources that are not reducible to a prescribed chronological outcome. Time is less a matter of connecting with a past fully legible in the present, less a matter of seeing easy transitions between the old and the new—recall Hume's keyword "latent"—than it is an encounter with archives that, because they are so *numerous*, are contingent and remain to be seen.

We would argue that these three points, lifted from Jacobite memory work—the displacement of individual reason by a network of things, the related emphasis of means over ends, and the troubling abundance of chance—are what preoccupied Hume in his philosophical works. To begin with, in his *Treatise of Human Nature* (hereafter *THN*), Hume gives us the premise that "all reasonings concerning matters of fact seem to be founded on the relation of cause and effect."[47] His endorsement of inference is therefore explicitly based in the temporal foundations of experience. "It seems the duty of an historian," he writes, to make the "proper inferences and conclusions" about the past (*HE* VI, 140). Further, in his *Abstract of a Treatise* (hereafter *AT*), he gives us a distinction with the same attachment to time between sense *impressions*, "feeling a passion of emotion," or as he also calls it, an image "conveyed by our senses," on the one hand; and *ideas*, which we form "when we reflect on a passion or an object which is not present" (*AT* 408), on the other.

Both *impressions* and *ideas* are time bound, as we move from the present-tense sensation of the former—what *is* that?—to the past-tense recognition of the latter—not only what *was* that, but *how* in its current absence does it compare to like objects the way we habitually categorize them? We have seen this sequence already in Chapter 1 where we discussed Smith's "pleasing wonder of ignorance," the movement from the shock of an object's mis- or non-recognition, to its categorization next to this or that similar object, which at least ideally should produce the more pleasing and settled effect of admiration.

Hume uses the same terms in the *Treatise* (*THN* 75). But for him, the pleasure is often overridden by worry because the mis- or non-recognition of an object, its *latent* meanings, its capacity for multiple and even contradictory evaluation, is more liable to confront us than we would like to think. We noted some, very carefully measured, room to maneuver in Smith's will to categorize. The surprising object can on rare occasion retroactively rearrange the categories that we would otherwise be bound to fit it within. Hume's more pronounced skepticism makes him both more cognizant of, and more anxious about, the tenuousness of the object/category relation than others in his cohort. He is therefore also more dubious than Smith about what the subject can and cannot know, or better, more focused on the—again, for Hume, explicitly temporal—episodes of disruption that *not* knowing can produce.

Hume, for example, was notorious even in his day for suggesting that past experience is connected to the future by "supposition" and is therefore "a proof of nothing for the future" (*AT* 409). This proposition brought scandal to the *Treatise* and forced him to defend and further explain "this very skeptical book" anonymously, and in the third person, in the *Abstract* that followed shortly after. But here Hume emphasizes, rather than explains away, the main point of the *Treatise*, underscoring the central issue of time for the production of meaning: "It is not anything that reason sees in the cause," he writes, "which makes us *infer* the effect. . . . The mind can always *conceive* any effect to follow from any cause" (emphasis in original, *AT* 410). And indeed man has, as conceived by the negative examples of barbarous superstition, Jacobite memory, and Puritanical prophecy that Hume will describe at length in *The History of England*. "May I not conceive that a hundred different events might as well follow from that cause," he continues in the *Enquiry Concerning Human Understanding* (hereafter *ECH*): "There are always many other effects."[48] Therefore, "we can give no reason for extending to the future our experience in the past, but are entirely determined by custom" (*AT* 411, 412). The propensity of knowledge to settle on this or that cause is essentially "arbitrary," though meaning is governed—*tentatively*—on the "habits" of anticipation that we either institutionalize in the annals of scholarship, or more precariously, attempt to promote among a "people," themselves always liable to "rage."

Our point here is thus both epistemological as well as ontological; and both aspects are connected to the problem, in the specific sense we have been using the term, of "numbers." At the limits of knowledge for Hume is not a simple notion of oppositional otherness, or the smooth continuum of time, but is rather about the immediate force of multiplicity itself at the moment of a first impression. While in the *Abstract* Hume remarks upon the difficulty of choosing among "hundreds" of different events, in the earlier *Treatise* he writes, there are *"millions* of causes and effects" (emphasis ours).[49] Perhaps Hume was forced after the ill reception of his book to hedge his bets. In any case, common to both the *Treatise* and the *Abstract*, "impressions . . . are . . . lively and strong . . . ; ideas are the fainter and weaker." This distinction is akin to "that betwixt thinking and feeling" (*AT* 408). And to the extent that ideas may fade, to the extent that epistemic "habits" may be broken, that categories will mutate, and subjects change in relation to a multitude of objects over which they have limited control, philosophy must be open to the unexpected.

Chance is not a wholly dismissible force for Hume. To the contrary, he parses this further and links it to the keyword for eighteenth-century historiography of "conjecture": "Probability or reasoning from conjecture may be divided into two kinds, *viz.*, that which is founded on *chance*, and that which arises from *causes*" (emphasis in original, *THN* 175). "Chance can only destroy this [causal] determination of the thought, and leave the mind in its native situation of indifference" (*THN* 176); "chance is nothing real in itself" (*THN* 175).

Hume then connects the effect of chance to produce that sense of absence to its appropriate social coordinates: "'tis commonly allow'd by philosophers, that what the vulgar call chance is nothing but a secret and concealed cause" (*THN* 181). The "indifference" mentioned here can be explained in a number of ways. First, chance means the disruption of the "habits" at work in the always tenuous "supposition that the future resembles the past" (*THN* 184). It means the inability, at least in the moment, to *differentiate*. Second, at the moment of chance disruption, philosophy becomes aware of its own limits. All that thought can articulate, at least in the initial encounter with chance, is "nothing"; and this is because philosophy, as Hume is quite clear in repeating, can never articulate the infinity of factors that may go into a given event despite what it looked like in the past—that is, philosophy can never say it *all*. And third, the rejection of *a priori* presumptions regarding causality is associated, dubiously for Hume, with the immediate; in other words, the insufficiently habituated influence of the "vulgar," which Hume also implies by the term "indifference," should hardly be an influence at all.

To sum up, and in line with our first point about Jacobite memory, in-the-moment sense experiences, not protracted customs of reason, orient the subject, situated as it is among a network of nonhabituated "things"; and from that proposition, the subject's orientation is irreducible to individual will. Further still, the process of habituation that controls meaning is, as Hume remarks, "arbitrary," or at least, dependent on a mass of animate and inanimate factors that are never simultaneously available to the philosopher but are provisionally open to change. The nature of that opening to change is important to surmise in Hume, because doing so will allow us to address debates over historical method, and the place of chance within it, in a more precise way than most of the historians of Hume's time will do. He is clear that foresight is not a valid option for a philosopher, though "we must be conscious of the inability . . . of foretelling" (*AT* 20; *THN* 223).

Related to the recognition of this limit, we have quoted above only the first part of an oft-cited sentence from the *Treatise* where Hume links reason to the "relation of cause and effect." But what we left out is the second clause of that sentence, where Hume says, "we can never infer the existence of one object from another, unless they are connected together, either *mediately* or *immediately*" (emphasis ours, *AT* 409). What to make of the unusual adverbial use of the first term? For a start we can take it to be consistent with what Hume says of the distinction between *ideas* and *impressions*. The *immediate,* as we have said, happens in the sensory present and tends to be the *de*-differentiating province of the vulgar. But the *immediate* encounter with a surprising object or event is also, according to Hume, a more forceful and more vital force than an extended train of reflections on the past, which are relatively weak and subject to fade over time. Thus, in the first instance, *mediate* denotes the necessary second stage of how meaning is both stabilized and shared: thinking about the past, comparability, and habitual philosophical order.

But there is a second way to understand the adverbial sense of the word "mediate" by putting it into noun form, as in "mediation." We have intimated already the significance of this word in light of Pittock's suggestive account of a Jacobite virtuality: his network of "things." For the purposes of understanding Hume on *mediation,* we can extend his repeated dismissal of philosophical foresight to a fuller account of inductive historical reasoning (*ECH* 7, 20, 24). "There is required a *medium,*" he writes, "which may enable the mind to draw such an inference [between past and present propositions], if indeed it be drawn by reasoning and argument" (emphasis ours, *ECH* 25). And again, "Where is the *medium,* . . . which join propositions so very wide of each other?" (emphasis ours, *ECH* 27). Without it we are faced with that crucial problem of multiplicity, mere sensory experience, "an infinite number of real parts of time, . . . [which] no man would ever be able to admit" (*ECH* 115).

In Clifford Siskin and William Warner's use of the term "mediation," *medium* has a technological import, specifically, in reference to the technology of print. This is significant, because during Hume's life the numbers of readers and the amount of material to be read—that is, *media*, more precisely, the *popular* media—proliferated at an unprecedented rate and on an unanticipated scale. In more exacting terms, Hume calls this media event "a *sudden* and *sensible* change" (emphasis ours).[50] We have seen evidence of how this change was recognized already in Fielding, how the threat of "numbers" regarded as literary overproduction created anxiety for the producers that they could never have prepared for in advance. Indeed, logic would dictate that any such printed preparation would only extend and exacerbate the problem of so many literary "numbers." There was not a quick philosophical fix for the explosion of print culture in the eighteenth century, and so new habits of criticism, of taste, and of education had to be formed.

Hume, too, is explicit on the importance of "the republic of letters, and the art of printing" (*THN* 195), insofar as writing should maintain a specifically *mediated* account of the past that would, at least he hoped, buffer the relative weakness of ideas against the *immediate* force of sensation. Hume's unforgiving suspicion about philosophical habit is seconded only by his skepticism about the popular media. Under decades of Whig rule, Hume complains, "Compositions the most despicable, both for style and matter, have been extolled, and propagated, and read; as if they had equaled the most celebrated remains of antiquity" (*HE* VI, 533). We have seen examples in Chapter 1 of Hume's unabashed elitism regarding the standards of taste.

Hume is supportive of freedom of the press but is clearly also worried about its subversive potential. "Liberty of the press" is described as particularly "subversive of civil society" as the Puritans continued to antagonize both Elizabeth and James, threatening the union of the crowns in 1603 the very moment it was established (*HE* VI, 130). The reason Hume opposed "the religious spirit" of Puritanism as spread through the press is a decidedly temporal one of its promoting assemblies and "factions" in order to make what they called "prophesyings." This "social contagion," Hume repeatedly reminds, is particularly effective among the "more turbulent, and less . . . submiss[ive]" Scottish nation, whose "populace . . . [is] more uncultivated and uncivilized, . . . [and exhibits] a higher degree of ferocity" (*HE* V, 250, 252). Puritanism as such "contains in it something supernatural and unaccountable; . . . its operations . . . correspond less to their known causes than is found in any other circumstance of government" (*HE* V, 12, 67). Getting time wrong on a popular scale, as the word "prophesy" suggests, has the far greater dangers of producing social unrest than the more affirmative experiments of philosophical reflection.

Alternatively, in *A Dissertation on the Passions; The Natural History of Religion* (hereafter *NHR*), Hume describes the "precipitate march of the vulgar" (*NHR* 57); he argues that history provides a narrative of "visible gradation, 'til we arrive at those who were eyewitnesses and spectators of the event" (*THN* 131).[51] Hume also remarks that historical evidence and proof "depend on the fidelity of Printers and Copyists" (*THN* 196), which is an important part of the "circumstance that preserves the evidence of history" (*THN* 197). He also qualifies his own historical accounts of ancient times with phrases like "as far as writing or history reaches" (*NHR* 34). And he delineates clearly between "traditional," meaning oral, and the "scriptural" historical epochs. Without the aid of writing, the ancient religions were not only "complex and contradictory," but more revealingly for our purposes, the "stories of the gods were *numberless*, like the popish legends" (emphasis ours, *NHR* 72).

Hume's faith in writing is telling. Ironically, it is *numberless-ness* that became a print media event at precisely the historical moment of Hume's writing. The problem here is one of having to both solve the problem of "numbers" at the level of sorting "millions" of causes, while at the same time contributing to the overabundance of print. Thus, in *Enquiry Concerning Human Understanding* the sentence that follows Hume's reference to a "required medium" is crucial: "What that medium is, I must confess, passes my comprehension" (*ECH* 25). Mediation as such denotes a vital nexus between expected philosophical outcomes (habit) and processes of change that circumvent expectation and appear to arrive, at least before they make categorical sense, on the order of chance. Our purpose here, in advance of a more focused account of historical method, is simply to develop the connection between causality and "numbers." If we can begin to associate *mediation* in the Humean sense with his rejection of *a priori* assumptions about cause, and if—against philosophical "habit"— we can advance the alternative of putting the "hundreds" (if not "*millions*") of cause/effect relations back into the question of history, then we have gone the right distance at this point in our argument.

Benedict Anderson has influentially explained the invention of "homogenous, empty time," which we would suggest is akin to Hume's mixed assessment of "habit," only here, in a social rather than an exclusively philosophical register.[52] Anderson's thesis is a differently motivated version of Habermas's influential passages on "*trans*-temporal continuity."[53] Both theorists emphasize the promotion of "calendrical" time as a way of mediating not only individual differences but also—and this is crucial—of putting popular agency into publicly presentable order. By suspending those differences through the media activities of criticism, epistolary novels, and newspapers, time can be sorted into a template of oppositional differences, the shared time of the progressive sequence, seriality, and consensus, which work to produce what Anderson calls "hypnotic confirmation of the solidity of a single community."[54]

Anderson's evocation of Ernest Renan's remark that imagining the nation relies as much on remembering as on forgetting is also important. The idea of lost time underscores the point that the experience of heterogeneity displaced by homogeneous time is occurring as an encounter with—to use Smith's term—unavoidable "gaps" in print capitalism's various mnemonic registers.[55] For example, the pamphlet wars that broke out in the roughly 60-year time frame of Jacobite threat—from Dundee's Highland infantry at Killiecrankie in 1689, to the ghastly annihilation of the MacDonalds at Glencoe, through the homicidal slaughter, rape, and proposed starvation of Highland noncombatants at Culloden moor in 1746—show an episode of turmoil arguably more relevant to mass social behavior that one might gather, say, from considering Habermas's "blissful" (his term) account of civil society, which emerged in his blueprint of the public sphere in part by reading Fielding.[56] Dr. Henry Sacheverell's tract of 1709, which celebrated the delivery from Catholicism by the arrival of William in 1688, sold 100,000 copies—clearly a *mass*, if perhaps not finally a *public*, media event. As the subsequent High Church riots would show, this episode in the history of print culture was not conducive to the maintenance of civil society.

Nathanial Mist, conversely, was frequently tried for sedition by Walpole's Whig administration for his staunchly Jacobite *Weekly Journal*. Mist's seditious editorials in the *Norwich Gazette* were also popular. Indeed, Jacobite journalism was in the vanguard of the advance of commercial writing, which can be estimated at about 200,000 readers a week at its zenith.[57] The government was sufficiently worried about the unrest attached to this form of reading that it eventually assigned Daniel Defoe to spy on Mist (as well as do some writing for him). In 1727, Mist was tried for libel against George I, and he was sentenced once again to prison. He soon fled to France to join a growing Jacobite diaspora.[58] The last Jacobite rebel, Dr. Archibald Cameron, was taken from the

Highlands and hanged as late as 1753, and there was even a final armed attempt at insurrection in 1759.[59] These are largely forgotten events that are disturbingly concurrent with the invention of the public sphere. And they are forgotten on account of particular ways of remembering. Our task is to elucidate the twists and turns of mass agency outside—or at least partially outside—that overly idealized zone of homogeneous time, to the extent that it ever really existed.

If "numbers" bother Fielding in the sense that too many people are prone to judge cultural artifacts differently, it should also be said that the way in which "numbers" manifest "power" is through vicissitudes specifically to do with making or prohibiting social and historical change. Time matters to Fielding as much as it does to the differently motivated Jacobite memorializers affirmed by Pittock above. The phrase "too often" in our epigram signifies a problem of explaining—or *too often*, explaining away, as in forgetting—certain forms of change where history and *non*-homogeneous "numbers" of people and things intersect. This accords with Hume's observation of the *mediate* (or mediated) idea grounding the *immediate* sense impression and complicates his investment in the preservative function of print.

Fielding writes, "There are no human Productions [other than writing] to which Time seems so bitter and malicious an Enemy, . . . Art must sooner or later yield to this great Destroyer."[60] In contrast to statues and painting, the moment when print becomes the dominant medium signals for contemporary writers the acceleration of what would have been an earlier—and slower moving—form of experience, contained within a more limited zone of contact than could be designated by Fielding under the fragile heading of the "public." Thus, in defending the poorly received *Amelia*, he proclaims, "habitual and inveterate Evils are to be secured by slow alteratives, and not by violent Remedies."[61] The problem implicit in this equation between "slowness" and "violence" is telling in that this increase in velocity is combined with novel writing as it tends to be experienced in a popular way. In the same way, time threatens to keep the best writing from lasting for a "reasonable period of existence."[62] This is a form of creativity that threatens to "destroy" the few gems of eighteenth-century writing while also producing an excess of it, most of which should be discounted if counted at all.[63] Writing therefore initiates a form of temporal disruption as a *mass*—but decidedly not a *public*—experience, those "cunning Methods [invented by] the Malice of Time."[64]

This is not to say, with popular memory in mind, that there is a simple division here between linear and nonlinear chronological order. Dipesh Chakrabarty's introduction of the term "heterotemporality" is useful for thinking about alternative forms in popular memory. For him the term marks not only "the plurality of times coexisting in the common space of the present" but also—crucially for our purposes—the idea that the present is non-totalizable.[65] Indeed, both temporal connectivity and conflict are at work and on all sides in the struggles over the centralization of the British state. The Scottish parliament accepted James in 1685 to establish an "uninterrupted line of one hundred and eleven kings [so that] our civil commotions [will be] brought into wished events."[66] And this line of thinking held sway in later Jacobite appeals to the future in need of repair with the past.

The different point we want to add beyond Anderson and Habermas, and more in line with Chakrabarty, has less to do with linearity and rupture than it does with the way in which different kinds of continuities and discontinuities happen at the same time. This is a matter of the way "numbers" are managed by the very notion of placing them into distinctions of *kind* (disciplines, genres, categories of affective response, national character) so that they are sifted from so much irredeemable "noise." Contested tradition portends unknowable futures. We would argue therefore that the particular "malice" described by Fielding as an "Act of Violence"—time experienced as a "cruel Tyrant daily execut[ed] on us writers"—is the same creative malevolence exercised by popular disorder.[67]

As we have noted, Fielding's experience as a playwright in the late 1730s brought him up close not only with errors in taste but also with dramatic performance as fully the concern of social confrontation. It is logical then that the dramatist-journalist-novelist *cum* chief law enforcement officer should theorize the problem of corrupted taste and population management in consistent ways. To stay within Fielding's terminology, consider his use of the *nomen collectivum* concept, which is referenced in the same article in the issue of *The True Patriot* following the "Forty-Five" that we have quoted from above. Here Fielding contrasts the difference between the "ancient privileges" of theatrical response aligned somehow with "critics like the Mohocs of old"[68]—groans, hisses, catcalls, restless movement, and the like, "noise" to the point of in-house violence—with contemporary authorial prerogative, "the Right of disturbing an Audience," which Fielding insists ought to be established without the worry of riot.[69]

In a satirical sendup of popular spectatorship in its *noisy* mode, a problem Fielding simply dubs "the Town," he recites a story told to him by a young gentleman of dramatic performance gone decidedly wrong. Here "one of their [the *Town's*] *Number*" escalated audience response from a simple hiss to the point where "the *Town* presently took up an apple and flung it at his [the young gentleman's] head."[70] The grammatical impossibility of the collective noun "the *Town*" partaking in an individual act like throwing fruit in the direction of the stage is exactly Fielding's point, as is the fact that the storyteller turned out to be (of) the *Town* itself—paradoxically, both the offending apple thrower and its accidental target.

In that sense, this nefarious form of spectatorship, its riotous quality, and by implication the entirely *un*-patriotic way of watching make the audience both a witness of performance and performance in itself. In hearing the story for the first time from the young gentleman, Fielding assumed that the apple came from "some impudent Rascal" whose name was *Town*. But he realizes upon retelling the story that "the *Town* was *Nomen Collectivum*."[71] The time that it took between Fielding's hearing the story and its reiteration, an example in microcosm of his worry from our epigram that artistic value should exist for a *reasonable* (if not an absolute) period of time, allows him to satirize the enigmatic predicament of one being hit by the apple that one may also have thrown. The term *"nomen collectivum"* is the paradoxical trajectory of the apple thrown both *by* and *at* the *Town*. In that sense, it signals a crucial interaction between the two dynamics at the core of this chapter: multiplicity and time.

Nomen collectivum is a suitably disturbing concept for a law enforcement man, and the tradition of seventeenth-century natural law, which finds its way into the writing of Smith and his cohort, has been well enough covered in past scholarship on Enlightenment jurisprudence.[72] In broad terms, *nomen collectivum* is an expression simply meant to explain how a word that is used in the singular might also be understood in the plural: The word "misdemeanor," which is the same whether or not you have committed more than one, is the standard example used in legal dictionaries. "Town" is also such a term; so too, "Parliament." It was a term also used in debates over sovereignty, specifically, as those debates played out in the wake of the Puritan revolution, Cromwell's protectorate, the return of Charles II to the throne by the same army that exiled him, and the restoration of the Stuart line up to the so-called *bloodless* arrival of the new *stadholder*, William of Orange, in 1688.

An anonymous tract published in the tumultuous time of 1683 uses *nomen collectivum* not as an indication of Stuart angst but on behalf of Whig suppression. In the same year of the Rye House Plot (an attempt to assassinate both Charles II and James), the anonymous author of the 1683 tract insists "the word *Parliament* is *Nomen collectivum,* and means the King, Lords and Commons; for it is they jointly that can make Laws." The chapter in which this citation appears is aptly titled: "Whether the Name of *Parliament* can properly be given to any Part or Parts of this Body, not being the Whole?"[73] At stake in that word "whole" is the connection between partiality and unity in achieving social order—the connection between "numbers," on the one hand, written off by Fielding as so much indiscriminate "noise," and the invention of a public sphere, on the other hand, that is more manageable than the one Fielding derides as lacking theatrical good taste. The connotations of *nomen collectivum* are unmistakably oriented toward making the population governable, toward processing "numbers" into comprehensible units assumed to be unique and unified at the same time: society, the people, the public. The concept of *nomen collectivum* in Fielding's story of popular license indicates not only the contemporary persistence of early-modern public discord but also of temporal experience, theorized to produce a unified *philosopheme* that joins civilization with commercial life. The "ancient privileges" of riot to which Fielding refers evoke the abolition of the heritable jurisdictions (which was guaranteed by the Act of Union) after the last Jacobite insurrection, thought from a Whiggish perspective to be an anachronistic remnant of tyrannical times.

When Samuel Johnson criticizes the Wilkes riots, which took place in response to John Wilkes's arrest upon the publication of *The North Briton* (number 45) in 1763, he describes the Wilkite crowd in ways that compare well with Fielding.[74] Because he accused King George III of lying in a royal speech praising the treaty of Paris, Wilkes was charged with seditious libel, fled to France in 1764 to avoid trial, and subsequently sought a seat in Parliament while *in absentia.* (He was also seriously in debt and had a penchant for public scandal in the press, as his interest in pornography would suggest.) Here, like Fielding, Johnson sees an "epidemic [of] patriotism" gone wrong, a misfire in the *nomen collectivum* writ on too large a social scale to contain the singular within the plural.

Samuel Johnson writes in "False Alarm" (hereafter "FA"), somewhat suspiciously, "he [who] hitherto cared only for himself, now cares for the public."[75] In Fielding's vein, this produces a serious concern about how "numbers," under conditions of riot, no longer adhere to divisions of rank. Indeed, as we have seen, the subordination of servants, the irregularity of labor, the tetchy sensibilities of the workman—these complicate progress toward the public sphere ideal. Johnson continues,

> the taylor slips his thimble, the drapier drops his yard, and the blacksmith lays down his hammer; they meet at an honest alehouse, consider the state of the nation . . . are alarmed at the dreadful crisis, and subscribe to the support of the Bill of Rights. ("FA" 335)

In line with Fielding's concerns as a magistrate, Johnson thus proposed rerouting the procession for George III's coronation so that it would not be "rendered dangerous to the multitude" ("FA" 300). This is not to say that Johnson was unwilling to enjoy an occasional tipple on behalf of insurrectionary change, having allegedly shocked the Oxford dons by toasting past and future uprisings of West Indian slaves.

Regarding inequality at home, however, it is important to point out that in the years immediately following the start of Whig ascendancy—which made Scottish shipping particularly difficult because of the long period of the French wars—about 200,000 people were reduced to begging.[76] The Hanoverian succession alienated the unpropertied masses. The presumption that union would benefit the majority of Scots was by no means self-evident, though upon suspension of the Navigation Acts it did produce a new and ostentatiously rich class of tobacco barons.[77] What is important to point out is that commentators like Fielding and Johnson held a common believe that popular discontent was (a) a form of agency that was at its most dangerous when it brought into the mix riot of the plebian ranks, and (b) the legitimacy of the multitude to effectuate political change was best addressed as something embedded in a past that Great Britain would best do without.

Let us not forget that Wilkes was a Scot (but then again, so was the ambivalent historian-novelist Tobias Smollett, whose progovernment journalism Wilkes was writing against). In the hyperbole characteristic of the mid-century pamphlet wars, Johnson writes,

> Every one knows the malice, the subtlety, the industry, the vigilance, and the greediness of the Scots. The Scotch members are about the number sufficient to make a house. I propose it to the consideration of Supporters of the Bill of Rights, whether there is not reason to suspect that these hungry intruders from the North are now contriving to expel all the English. . . . For who can guess what may be done when the Scots have the whole House to themselves? ("FA" 333)

The irony here—and this is a key point for understanding the complex, shifting oppositional dynamics of Anglo-Scottish politics of the day—is that anti-Scottish abuse of Wilkes's *North Briton* was written against George III's Scottish advisors (specifically, Lord Bute).

We should thus hesitate in calling these politics oppositional in any facile sense of that term, which is not to say that Scottish insurgency was any less powerful for being called, as Johnson says, "the rabble, [who], whensoever they come, will be always Patriots, and always Supporters of the Bill of Rights" ("FA" 333). In the case of Wilkes, he is both dismissive of the "mingled masses" and condemning of their initiative in seizing "the offices that chance allows them." "Plebeian grossness" is here equal to "the desire of leveling" ("FA" 341). But Johnson also remarks that "impatience of the people, under such immediate oppression [as servile authority, will] produce quarrels, tumults, and mischief."[78] The word "whensoever" suggests that the uncertainty of social order as brought about by the intermingling of North and South (an "intrusion")—generations after the union—is experienced partly as a problem having to do with the experience of time. "A true Patriot knows that futurity is not in his power. . . . He knows the prejudices of faction, and the inconstancy of the multitude."[79] The problem with the multitude is not that they pretend to know the future, though "inconstancy" is how the multitude is most likely to be characterized from an external philosophical perspective. About futurity, they are as much in the dark as "true Patriots," whose position is by implication social quietude if not also political stasis. Instead of leaving the future alone to take care of itself, Johnson's rabble is more likely to produce and then seize the exigencies of chance from some place both within and without the national imaginary.

There is a distinction here about how to mobilize a condition of political immanence—that is, of both belonging and not belonging to Britain—of acting with great vulnerability, but in a collective way, with a future no individual could know in advance. To cite Johnson again, "the people is [sic] a very heterogeneous and confused mass of the wealthy and the poor, the wise and the foolish, the good and the bad."[80]

> Ale and clamour unite in their powers; the crowd, condensed and heated, begins to ferment with the leaven of sedition. All see a thousand evils, though they cannot show them, and grow impatient for a remedy, though they know not what. ("FA" 337)

Unlike the *nomen collectivum* when it is working effectively, in the Wilkes riots, among other episodes of that kind, the *singular* will not converge in a seamless way with the *plural*. In that sense, to use a bygone but nonetheless legitimate verb, to be "rabbled" is partly to experience historical change, especially where the consequences of that change are in no way conceivable until after the event.

The notion of "rabbling" originates in the early 1660s, in the wake of the Puritan revolution (recall Johnson's fear of "leveling" above), a major point of contention for Scottish historians, as we will see, and one related to the advance in the circulation of writing among the lower ranks. To cite a Scottish text from 1714, which covered the life of one ejected Church of England curate, it was a still a problem that Presbyterian ministers of Scotland could "*rabble against the Episcopal ministers*" (emphasis ours). Moreover, the "persecuting spirit of the Presbytery, which in the unhappy Times of the Covenant, made havock of all things . . . did greatly surprise our neighbour nation."[81] English eyes upon Scotland, and indeed, the lack of an appropriate national equation found there, is what generates the surprise.

This is not, of course, to say that Jacobitism was coequal with the leveling tendencies of Covenanters ("Nea King but Christ," the revolutionary phrase would go). Although King James VII and II repealed the penal laws for Catholics in 1686 before his later exile, indulgence did not extend to field conventiclers. Indeed, a minister was executed in 1688, the same year as the so-called Bloodless Revolution, which ended the Stuart reign. Charles II was notoriously brutal in trying to stamp out the National Covenant Movement during the preceding period of the Restoration. Our noting the elision above between Scottish Presbyters and making "havoc," as it was later described regarding popular Jacobitism, is to indicate the complexity of oppositional politics during the period insofar as they took the form of temporary alignments and unexpected combinations of allies. Though acts against bearing arms and wearing traditional costumes intensified after the "Forty-Five," Highlanders would shortly become the backbone of the British army in the form of the Black Watch, deployed in 1756 in North America under the command of the Butcher, Lord Cumberland. And the sons and daughters of Jacobites fought on both sides of the American War of Independence. "Surprise," it might be said, is the most critical—and for the "true Patriot," the most condemnable—feature of *rabbling* as the term was used to describe an essentially Puritan or Jacobite tendency.

Not surprising then that the condition of so being *rabbled* for Fielding and Johnson involves a temporal event that interrupts standard protocols of homogeneous time. Johnson describes that interruption as the crowd's "impatience," a matter of acting effectively, and collectively, without knowing the result of that action. E. P. Thompson—whose work is the *locus classicus* for theorizing the eighteenth-century crowd—has noted in "Patrician Society, Plebeian Culture" (hereafter "PS"), that plebian agency (recall above that Johnson uses the term "plebian" well before Thompson, though Smith regards it as an archaic term) does not reduce to individual consciousness in the traditional sense of attaching action to outcome: "A plebs is not, perhaps, a working class. The plebs may lack a consistency of self-definition, in consciousness; clarity of objectives; the structuring of class organization."[82] Thompson is inarguably correct to insist that for all that, the inconsistency of the mob, crowd, riot, and so on has a distinct political presence. Its "fleeting expressions of solidarities . . . [are] *sui generis*" ("PS" 398).

Chance is *rabbling*'s virtue. This does not of course mean that being *rabbled* is commensurate with the form of individualist spontaneous order alleged to be ushered in without coercion (never mind repressive state action, like Highland genocide) by the invisible hand for which Smith later became famous (about this, a good deal more in our next chapter). Smith's famously self-interested and socially beneficial butcher, celebrated for the way he spontaneously contributes to economic welfare, is decidedly not the same one as Fielding's. "It is not from the benevolence of the butcher, the brewer, or the baker that we expect our dinner, but from their regard to their own interest" is the oft-repeated quote from Smith.[83] Fielding writes in "An Enquiry into the Causes of the Late Increase of Robbers" (hereafter "LIR") instead of "every *riotous* independent butcher or baker, with two or three thousand pounds in his pocket, [who] laughs at [the magistrate's] power," while "every petty fogger makes him [the magistrate] tremble" (emphasis ours).[84] The relation between "numbers" and time in the "riotous" sense are not supportive of commercial interests but instead produce an occasion for Johnson to remind us that the proper duty of socialization is "to lead back the people to their honest labour; to tell them, that submission is the duty of the ignorant, and contentment the virtue of the poor."[85]

As Fielding indicates in linking the *other* butcher's laughter to the pettifogger (an inferior legal practitioner who pursues trivial cases just for money), the embedded nature of riot within the uncertain world of markets and profit should not be dismissed. Nor, as we have intimated, should we underestimate the activity of riotous behavior assigned to Jacobitism, at least up until midcentury, a connection the magistrates both exploited and feared. As Robertson notes, the Riot Act of 1714 was a law pushed through by the Whig government to supplement the common law definition of riot "in ways that struck hard at customary practices, facilitating repression of popular assembly by ignoring the causes of riot and strengthening magisterial authority" ("RP" 80). Indeed, rioters were hanged under the act on the first day of its enforcement, which was just one year before the uprising of the "Fifteen."

The Riot Act was also associated with the highly controversial Septennial Act, which increased the maximum length of a Parliament (i.e., of the time between elections) from three years to seven. This had the effect of keeping the Whig party in power for a longer period of time, a reason to regard both acts, as they were known in the period, as Hanoverian Proclamations ("RP" 80). The full title of the Riot Act was "An Act for Preventing Tumults and Riotous Assemblies, and for the More Speedy and Effectual Punishing the Rioters."[86] As a spy in Scotland directly after the union, Defoe gives a sense of how tumultuous Jacobite street activity could be. "I heard a Great Noise," he writes, "and looking Out Saw a Terrible Multitude Come up the High Street with a Drum . . . shouting and swearing and Crying Out All Scotland would stand together, No Union, No Union, English Dogs, and the like."[87]

Notable in the Riot Act's longer title is one of Fielding's major concerns as London's magistrate: to curb the apparently spontaneous riotous activity by the regular and eternal application of the law. In language mirroring that of the Riot Act, which is singled out by Fielding as the *only* new statute adequate to enforcing "the business of justice" ("LIR" 345), he laments: "under an Absolute Monarchy . . . [there are] more speedy and efficacious remedies against . . . political disorders, than can be administered in a free state, whose forms of correction are extremely slow and uncertain" ("LIR" 348). The ultimate test in the fight against tumultuous activity was to replace Johnson's "impatience" of crowd activity with what Fielding calls the "impatience of rule" ("LIR" 344). But under "civil power" as such, new techniques of policing must be administered to the multitude conceived as a manageable population. They are techniques, as Foucault has described, that are entirely apposite to confronting the spontaneity of crowds (their connection to chance, their refusal, like Johnson's wayward paradegoers, to circulate in predictable ways) as an obstacle to public security.[88] As Fielding says, seek the "way of prevention" as "a way of remedy" ("LIR" 427).

It is logical that Fielding would be disturbed by gaming, specifically, "gaming in the lower classes of life" ("LIR" 371): "The loss of time, and neglect of business" are finally what is at stake in the pursuit of "luxury" by chance instead of work. As such, "luxury should be confined to the palaces of the great" ("LIR" 350). Jesse Molesworth has noted the laws of chance played out among the masses of wage earners "where the laws of state had failed."[89] Almost every English monarch between 1500 and 1800 pushed legislation against or restricting gambling. Hogarth depicted the popularity of gambling clubs like White's in picture six of the *Rake's Progress*. In 1541, Henry VII prohibited day laborers in particular from gaming at the feast of St. John the Baptist. Charles II, Queen Anne, and King George all passed similar kinds of gaming acts, during their respective reigns.

At the center of that string of legislation, we find heightened concern over the moral fiber of the lower ranks that are concurrent with a perceived stadial advance from agricultural to commercial kinds of labor.[90] Indeed, landless workers went from about 25 percent of the population at the beginning of the period to closer to a definitive 60 percent at the end.[91] This change in the nature of work concurred with major shifts in conceptions about futurity and time, where ideas about laying *wagers* and making *wages* tended to collide. Though clearly related, this was not exactly the same change regarding time that Ian Hacking identifies as having occurred in the late seventeenth century, for him around 1660, when Renaissance knowledge writ as authoritative opinion was displaced by the forms of statistical inference as developed by Pascal, Leibniz, Huygens, and Bernoulli.[92] Fielding's worry about the persistence of games of chance among the lower sorts testifies to gambling's vogue in the eighteenth century and is circumstantial evidence that myriad attempts at restrictive legislation failed to curb this popular practice. But as a development distinct from the mathematics of casuistry found in the debates of the Port-Royal Jansenists, the softer capacities of moral restraint and good character among the so-called generality of mankind, superintended by trained aesthetic sensibility among philosophers, was needed to deal in socially responsible ways with the problem of "numbers."

In an *excursus* on the eighteenth-century novel to come later in this chapter, we will see that the domestication of chance was both resolved and further exacerbated by the reading and writing of novels. The point to establish in leading up to that exceedingly popular—and therefore, similarly problematic—phenomenon, is that *qualification* displaces *quantification* such that chance is reduced to a morally calculable, or better, a socially normative ideal. That gambling was a *mass* problem among the lower orders, alongside a problem of *amassing* numerical outcomes, is more to the point of understanding the sociology of time in the eighteenth century as we want to apply it to popular contention and, especially, to narratives about the past. While the arithmetic of probability sought formulaic solutions for the "art of *conjecture*"—a term that would go viral in the decades following Bernoulli's use of it as the title of a posthumously published 1713 text—his followers contrived to have accident work whenever possible on behalf of subjectively restrained, commercially motivated, and nationally coherent ideals that if not finally settled by reason would be best dismissed as "noise."[93]

Fielding's early play *The Lottery* depicts the blind pursuit of lucky numbers, as a fortuneteller convinces the heroine that she will win the £10,000, heightening the drama of an aleatory contract. But lottery, too, was a most convenient way for the state to raise money, especially in times of war, which in the Enlightenment was almost all the time. We might note here, too, that those captured from Prince Charlie's defeated army were subject to different kinds of punishment by lottery. According to Fielding, gambling is first a problem of misspent leisure; second, it is a general correlate to antisocial behavior. Fielding thus continues: "the greater part of mankind must sweat hard to produce . . . the fruits of the earth." When the "vice [of luxury] descends downward to the tradesman, the mechanic, and the labourer, it is certain to engender many political mischiefs." The wrong use of the laborer's time, Fielding complains, is "the parent of theft and robbery" ("LIR" 350). Moving away from the central role of bishops and the ministry, those "cousins of the gentry" ("PS" 391) who may once have minded poor and working people better than they could themselves, Fielding's turn toward political mischief as an issue of managing time marks the advent of a secular temporal guardian: the magistrate himself. He is therefore focused not on whatever future rewards the lower orders used to bank on in the afterlife, but on the virtues of paid work, day after tiresome day.

We have commented already on the issue of time having to do with Jacobite performances of memory, the way according to Pittock that things are apt to supersede dominant forms of consciousness and produce alternatives for identifying both across ranks and *en masse*. And we have described the way in which the mixing of ranks within popular discontent remained linked in the eighteenth century to *rabbling*. Before moving ahead to our discussion of stadial history, of novels, and finally, of war, let us close this section by introducing a different kind of theatergoing than the official one Fielding has in mind. When Thompson notes the relative weakness of the British state, its struggle to centralize itself against Jacobite and other forms of localism following the Whig revolution, he is marking an—as yet—open opportunity for the license of the crowd. He is provocative in repeating that such license "depended on theater," specifically, "the theatrical effects of popular Jacobitism" ("PS" 390, 400, 403).

Nowhere is the theatrics of popular agency more evident than in the celebration of the maypole, which engaged what Thompson calls "the emotional calendar of the poor" ("PS" 392). Rogers too identifies traditional Mayings as distinctly tending to break out in celebratory drinks to the Pretender's health, citing the relatively late recording in 1750 of a Walsall maypole decked out with rose garlands in honor of James II's birthday (*CCP* 47). And while the strand maypole disappeared in 1717, the likes of milkmaids and chimney sweeps continued to engage in typical May Day activities.[94] Rogers, in *Whigs and Cities: Popular Politics in the Age of Walpole and Pitt* (hereafter *WC*), further reveals that the establishment of a political calendar dating back to the Tudor reign was later transformed into an upsurge in popular contention in the four decades after 1680. With the advent of the Hanoverian reign, "the political calendar became a calendar of riot" (*WC* 366). And as the "crowd [came] of age" at this time, so too, the boundaries of the political nation became strained with wider swaths of the labouring population (*WC* 371). Through traditional Mayings, or Oak Apple day, and other forms of royalist folklore, the insurrectional indolence of popular Jacobitism "transformed the official calendar into a carnival of sedition and strife" (*WC* 368). Defoe notes more than 6,300 maypoles erected after 1660, which appeared to Whigs and Puritans alike as "Hell broke loose" ("PS" 393–394). He cautions elsewhere that if the plotters of Jacobites and papists had their way in murdering Queen Anne, "my boys, you [will have] forever lost all the pleasures of Easter, Whitsontide, and Christmas."[95]

It is apposite then in the context of these calendrical wars that the more specific date for the 1707 Act of Union was also May 1, a day traditionally associated with an agrarian seasonal calendar that continued to hold ritual authority after the unification of Scottish and English parliaments. (We might also note here that May Day is related to the festival of Beltane, of Celtic origins; never mind the socialist demonstrations of May Day proper, which started in 1919, in Cleveland, Ohio.) The persistence of the May Day celebration was part of a general practice of putting into rivalry mass demonstrations on behalf of *both* Hanoverian and Stuart anniversaries.

As a similar example of how "the great mob [of] lower class people" (quoted in "PS" 401) worked historical coincidence into chance opportunity, King George's birthday happens to collide with Restoration Day, which of course ironically celebrates the return of the Stuart dynasty in the figure of Charles II.

At the start of the 1700s the official political calendar was already overpopulated with the government's official, as well the crowd's unsanctioned, days of recognition. Indeed, Queen Elizabeth's birthday of November 7 was celebrated until the 1730s. And as Rogers points out, by 1715 there were thirteen royal and state anniversaries celebrated, leaving only three months in the year free from such events (*CCP* 24). That year, which also saw the failure of the latest attempt at Jacobite invasion, began with the contradictory celebrations of King Charles Stuart's martyrdom; followed by the celebration—also in May—of the Hanoverian King George's birthday; and then moved on with the unofficial but all the more explosive celebration of the Pretender's birthday a month later in June. It would have been common at these and other street festivals not only to hear rough music of objectionable nature but also to see working people disguised as King George-the-cuckold (his effectively imprisoned wife having infamously slept with Count Königsmarck), and paraded to the Mayor's door so that the Hanoverian caucus "might kiss his arse" (quoted in "PS" 401).

Monod describes the most alarming Restoration Day as initiated by the Black country buckle makers, who were from an area soon to become one of the most industrialized parts of Britain. In the vein of Thompson, he charts further examples of food rioters refusing to disperse "'til the Pretender came to stop them."[96] What could appear as antic frivolity within plebian Jacobitism was also a serious attempt to enforce a calendar of popular contention against commercial markets, and in resistance to the form of British-state centralization necessary to accommodate it. Such activity served up a politics of commemoration that resonates with the way Pittock theorizes the "virtual" reality of Jacobite "things," manifest at its most effective in the form of promises and historical crises.

To this evocation of the latest development of the Enlightenment age, we might add John Bender and Michael Marrinan's conclusion that in ways similar to opportunities for public contention, "The descriptive regimes of our digital age . . . means that we have all become creatures of chance."[97] Similarly, and apposite to the net-centrism of riotous behavior, the Mayday festival and its attending activities took place in what we might call *real* time, where (a) the outcome of crowd activity, often enough improvisational, was only knowable through its effects—a tipple for Jemmy is only treasonable after you have been identified by the law; and (b) the *real* here is defined as a zone of multiplicity where singular forms of connection are not comfortably reducible to classifications that exist before the action.

J. C. D. Clark critiques the preoccupation with adversary systems, a tendency within English historical scholarship on riot and crowds traceable to Thompson's work, as being based on an overly simplistic "desire to see the past as a debate between two 'sides' . . . which implicitly shapes so many of the historian's results."[98] In this manner, he attempts to pin Thompson with the charge of economic reductionism. Clark suggests, "the replacement of class warfare with popular Jacobitism misses the heterodoxy of dissent."[99]

But Thompson is clear that crowd politics in the early eighteenth century are not (or not yet) flatly oppositional, programmatic, or positioned against any unified state or clearly codified ruling-class opponent because no such opponent existed at the time. On the order of Pittock's (and Monod's) complication of national politics that exceed what Clark calls "the existence of national ideological polarity,"[100] we have tried to describe Jacobite political performance as a mixed media event, and one of an often nonlinguistic nature. Moreover, even while such a performance crosses over to plebian expectations, it also manifests itself across borders and ranks. Thus we have emphasized the multiple, and often contradictory, status of a unique form of eighteenth-century agency, too simply called "riot."

Historical records show also that the tradition of the Jacobite festival was a local affair, resilient especially in the West Midland counties.[101] But its localism existed in a peculiarly wide-scale way, one that put fear into the magistrates of central urban centers beyond the immediate geography of crowd action. Such a phenomenon of what we might call mass localism—Penny Fielding calls it "the singularity of the local . . . [or] an asymptotic position"—speaks very much to the point of Henry Fielding's unruly *Town*, failing as it does to obey the rule of *nomen collectivum*.[102] We have also highlighted a chronological dimension to riot. One Whig diarist writes of counter-festivals mocking the Hanoverian dynasty as "turning day into night and night into day" (quoted in "RP" 78). This was literally true in that Jacobite crowd activity ignored the division, so crucial to magistrates like Fielding, between work and leisure hours enforced upon the lower orders. More than this, the calendar of riot countered the official expectations to honor particular days with particular kinds of activity. This countering of expectation in turn should allow us to look for the ways in which plebian Jacobitism and other forms of popular contention might be linked to the key motif of stadial (or stage-based) societal progress within the context of eighteenth-century historiography.

Enlightenment Chronologies of State

If we believe some historians, they [suspected allies to Mary] were convicted
by sufficient evidence. If we give credit to others, their sentence was unjust,
and they denied, with their last breath, any knowledge of the crime for which
they suffered.

William Robertson, *The History of Scotland*[103]

This passage from the eminent Scottish historian William Robertson (hereafter *HS*) addresses the deliberation of the nobles concerning Mary's incarcera-
tion at Lochlevin in 1567. At issue here is the incurable attachment of the Queen
of Scots to James Hepburn, fourth Earl of Bothwell, a leading Catholic, who
was perceived by Queen Elizabeth, Mary's first cousin and monarchical rival,
as a threat to the English church and state. After more than eighteen years in
prison, as the well-known historical drama plays out, an opportunistic Tudor
quorum found Mary guilty of plotting to assassinate Elizabeth.

Mary's relevance to eighteenth-century historians as the penultimate source
of Jacobite factionalism is crucial here. She was the only surviving legitimate
child of King James V of Scotland and was mother of King James VI of Scotland, who would become King James I of England, after Elizabeth's reign. The
union of the crowns under James in 1603—he began his Scottish reign in 1567—
remained a fully loaded reference point for debates leading up to and after the
union of 1707. Cromwell's success in achieving Scotch, English, and Irish unity
was well enough chalked up by eighteenth-century historians as part and parcel
of the Wars of the Three Kingdoms, from 1637 to 1651. The memory of Puritan
insurrection played fundamentally into the sense that Scottish wars of religion
were not yet complete. Catholic Mary would escape Lochlevin Castle in 1568
and raise an army of 6,000 men, only to be defeated in the Battle of Langside
and reimprisoned two months later.

The historical intrigue of Tudor politics has been well enough rehearsed
and remains the stuff of popular memory to this day. What is compelling about
the rivalry between Mary and Elizabeth for our purposes is how it played out
in the later context of Jacobitism up to and in Robertson's time. What we want
to argue below, to begin with, is that this rivalry served to demarcate divergent
styles of sovereignty (particularly in relation to what Hume called the "people's
rage"), which were commensurate with methodological changes in the writing
of history itself. Robertson is not atypical when he pauses in the epigram to
comment on the differences and contradictions attending the evaluation of evi-

dence for evaluating the past. His attempt to mediate the varied and conflicted evaluations about Mary's guilt (were the casket letters happened upon at Edinburgh condemning Mary to death real or not, and how can we know?) belies the presumption that historical narrative is neutrally based on self-evident facts and exclusive of politics and power.

About Mary, who can say? For Hume, as we have already alluded, the reign of James VI and I, the period of King Charles I who followed him, and Puritan revolution that lead to regicide constituted "a permanent historical minefield." That a period of unrest such as this—regarded both as being in the past but also very much as in the eighteenth-century present—was worrisome. What is historically "permanent" is the risk associated with popular discontent. The "minefield" that eighteenth-century historians like Hume were self-conscious about wanting to tiptoe through was "insurrection." They therefore sought to present what they would argue, with certain ambivalent qualifications, was ostensibly *impartial* rather than overtly *imperial* history. Theirs was a task meant to contrast with medieval accounts of British government—for example, Geoffrey of Monmouth's *Historia Regum Britanniae* of 1136, where historical progress was measured according to the absolute and unshakeable influences of royal authority backed up by divine order.

Informed by anthropological speculation and the individualistic premises of earlier writers (such as Hobbes and Locke, Grotius and Pufendorf), as well as the stadial (sequential or stage-based) narrative structure of Montesquieu, the goal of writers akin to Robertson—Kames, Ferguson, Smith, and Hume, to name only the select list of the influential Scottish historical school—focused on what appear to be the generic concerns of social progress, universal human tendencies, and natural law. This line of historical thinking, according to Colin Kidd (in *Subverting Scotland's Past*, hereafter *SSP*), proposes the "eschewal of partisanship . . . [and] reject[ed] a native political culture associated with armed resistance and religious fanaticism."[104] The accomplishment of history written in this manner was, according to István Hont, to "integrate the fragmented aspects of Pufendorfian natural jurisprudence into a single theory of the history of civilization."[105] This approach to history traced the emerging progress from a savage condition—uniquely located in eighteenth-century Europe to the Scottish Highlands—with commercial society as its final stage.

Thus, in *Jurisprudence* (*LJ*), Smith offers a characteristic example of historical progress, emerging from the hunter-savage stage; to the first emergences of property (and as he does not hesitate to add, the first appearances of material inequality) among the shepherds; to the rise of agriculture, and the first inklings of commodity exchange; finally arriving to the age of commerce, where laws and regulations to protect against the hazards of poverty were needed more than ever. The starkest example of wealth inequality for Smith is slavery, which he opposes not for moral reasons but because of the "hazards of insurrection." In "the West Indian sugar islands," "a multitude of slaves . . . far exceed the number of freemen," which keeps overseers and owners "in continual dread . . . [of] the least appearance of insurrection" (*LJ* A, 184, 187). Smith is also clear that slavery presents "an immoderate cost of labor, [which] would soon fall" if the masters set their slaves free (*LJ* A, 189). He remarks, "a freeman who works for wages will work far more than a slave in proportion to the expense that is necessary for maintaining and bringing him up" (*LJ* B, 453). We shall see below that, though sublimated by the unitary *philosopheme* of human nature, the "permanence" of what Hume assigns to "popular prejudice," like Smith's "continual dread," persist in troubling history even under the conditions of wage labor.

Thus we should also note that Robertson's feint over contradictory historical evidence is bracketed in the paragraphs immediately before and after our epigram with what are two key terms that we have addressed with regard to popular Jacobitism: "multitude" and "accident." Robertson continues, "a small circumstance might abate that indignation with which the multitude were at present animated against the queen, and deprive them [the uncertain nobility] of that popular applause which was the chief foundation of their power" (*HS* I, 350). The multitude here is both the source and the target of sovereignty, and it is suspected of changing its allegiance to Mary according to conditions too fleeting or too minor to appear on historical record. In that zone of popular discontent, chance predominates Mary's fate: The condemning casket letters thus appear as "an unexpected accident, [which] put into the hands of Mary's enemies what they deemed the fullest evidence of her guilt" (*HS* I, 351).

This circumstance of multiplicity and therefore chance is fatal to Mary. Elizabeth's remarkable skill, by contrast, to reign effectively within the (to anti-Jacobites like Robertson, anyway) fickle condition of "popular applause" is the leitmotif that underwrites *The History of Scotland* throughout. Even as Mary escapes, she is betrayed back into captivity by "some unforeseen accident." She plagues her keeper's vigilance by nudging them toward "ambitious hopes" that reverse without warning, only to reveal a "doomed future." This problem of

slippage, of temporal unintelligibility within what should be a legible narrative of historical progress, is connected by Robertson to Mary's own misguided
temper, as the Scottish queen's "hopes were naturally sanguine" (*HS* I, 366).
Robertson concludes, "These revolutions in Mary's fortune [leading to Mary's
execution] had been no less rapid than singular. . . . Her fears impelled her to
an action [namely, retiring to England], the most unadvised, as well as the most
unfortunate, in her whole life."

Mary, in short, was "rash" (*HS* I, 371). The introduction of velocity in addition to sequential anomaly, as the word "rapid" suggests, adds another layer of
temporal complexity that is traceable directly to Locke, specifically in his *Essay
Concerning Human Understanding* (hereafter *EHU*):

> [T]here seem to be certain Bounds to the quickness and slowness of the Succes-
> sion of those Ideas one to another in our minds, beyond which they can neither
> delay nor hasten.
>
>   . . . The Reason I have for this odd conjecture is, from observing that in
> the Impressions made upon any of our Senses, we can but to a certain degree
> perceive any Succession; which if exceedingly quick, the Sense of Succession is
> lost.[106]

He adds, if succession "is exceedingly quick, . . . [it] is lost, even in Cases where
it is evident, that there is a real Succession" (*EHU* 184). The same problem of
our inability to recognize temporal sequence can occur if the rate of succession
is too slow, wherein "we perceive no succession at all," even though, as Locke
is careful to point out, the possibility of too slow or too fast an instance of succession might appear, though potentially imperceptible, is also entirely "real"
(*EHU* 185). What influences our experience of velocity for Locke is a spatial
matter, which is also how "the sense of Motion is lost." "The Body," he writes,
"though it really moves, yet not changing perceivable distance with some other
Bodies . . . the thing seems to stand still" (*EHU* 185).

The delicate gradualist premises found in Locke (one could trace this as
well to Leibniz and Newton) underwrite the project of stadial history root and
branch. We can think about historical method then as a problem of the proximity of objects, insofar as they must be positioned outside the subject and at
an appropriate distance—not too close, not too far—from a temporally intelligible relation to the present. Kames (in *Elements of Criticism*, *EC*) worries in a
way similar to Locke about the "rate" or "velocity" of succession," a problem he
attaches to the "false reckoning of time."[107] Whether the perception of succes-

sion is quick or slow, "it must evidently produce different computations *at the same time*" (emphasis ours, *EC* 121).

This is where we can connect Lockean notions of historical rate to points we made earlier with Hume regarding causality. As we established above, Hume rejects *a priori* notions of cause and effect and thereby introduces the recognition of multiple factors of causality among which philosophers (and we can now add historians) must choose in order to identify this or that effect. Recall, too, Hume's term for that principle of selection was the adverbial form of mediation, as in the *mediate* idea, versus the *immediate* sense. What Robertson, Locke, and Kames identify here is set of similar methodological difficulties that plagued historical writing in the same way the epigram from Robertson suggests Mary's jurors were plagued. "False time"—the nonsuccessive realities of historical experience when the evidence is mixed, vague, or contradictory—is based on three concomitant problems: (a) *immanence*, as in Locke's problem of the proximity between subject to object; (b) *absence*, as in Locke's theory of nondurable "sensation," as well Hume's reference to "latent" historical agency; and (c) *plurality*, as in Humean *mediation*, Fielding's problem of "numbers," and Kames's worry over *different* "computations [of temporal experience] at the *same* time."

We might say then about Mary's failed succession over Elizabeth that it was simply a matter of bad timing. But in a crucial sense, "bad" here becomes "false": Mary becomes for Robertson a figure who embodies all the aspects of what Kames calls "flying perception." This is evident both in what Mary does and what is done around her. In *The History of Scotland*, she appears as a more developed but similarly limited offshoot of Robertson's American Indians, who have the peculiar "inability to count beyond three," as he describes them in a later book, *The History of America*.[108] The savage is not exterior to the European here but is, as we have already seen, immanent—and antagonistically so—as the Highlands are proximate to British modernity. Hume spoke volumes when he remarked that the "Scots . . . [did not have] any real history worthy of the name" (*HE* II, 83). "The only part of their history which deserves any credit," he continues, is when "Scotland readily gave their assent to the English proposal" to assume a unified British crown (*HE* II, 84). The savage's "turbulent spirit" means an inability to comprehend time the way historians and other civilized people do: They lack history, and their unwillingness to think in properly historical terms is what makes them adverse to the current state of things.

Thus Robertson gives us a version of Mary handled roughly by those who were better equipped to exploit the vicissitudes of popular contention, of temporal breaks and uncertain futures, namely Elizabeth, who receives praise from both Robertson and Hume for precisely this reason. While Mary was prone to "excite commotions in England" and "perpetuate factions," she was also a victim of the need for historical reconciliation (*HS* II, 2). This was true well before eighteenth-century Scottish historians needed to take into account the "permanent minefield" of the people's rage, more specifically, of Stuart agitation, identified by Hume. Mary's story is one of success and failure in dealing with the twin difficulties—essential for the sovereign *as well as* the historian—of time and the multitude, managed or mismanaged by "computation" (Kames uses the word more than half a dozen times in *Elements of Criticism*). By such a term we mean to underscore a calculus of futurity joined with memory so as to deal effectively with "numbers," "noise," and "power." Such a calculus can be seen in the form of Elizabeth's opportunism, as well as her belief that "no future benefits could ever obliterate the memory of past injuries" (*HS* II, 10). Like Hume's Cromwell, Elizabeth can use both "delay" and "celerity" whenever necessary to achieve "popular" goals (*HE* V, 499). Robertson's Elizabeth is even able to manipulate Mary's understanding of the past, convincing her that "her own [Mary's] interest might soon efface the memory of her obligations [to Elizabeth]" (*HS* I, 374).

This is a useful way in which to recall once again Rogers's point about the official political calendar originating with the Tudor and early Stuart period. What Elizabeth does correctly in terms of the regularization of time—not only linking the calendar to the state, as we have seen, but also seizing chance in the art of popular government—Mary appears to do incorrectly. To use the term that Robertson does, Elizabeth is able to "conjecture" her way through the temporal minefields (*HS* II, 228). Her duplicitous tactics allow her to "amuse Mary's allies, and to gain time" (*HS* I, 10). And by gaining time, Elizabeth asserts the superiority of England over Scotland. She does so by "laying future schemes" and "by revolving all these expedients [of sovereign rights] in her mind, and keep[ing] them in reserve to be made use of as the occasion might require" (*HS* I, 378). The queen presents what Jacobite royalty sorely lacks: effective ways to manipulate temporal experience. This explains why Hume quotes Charles I, uttering his final words before the popular regicide, as "remember" (*HE* V, 542).

But Elizabeth too is eventually betrayed by time in the form of her painful, death-inducing grief about the past, as she approaches the end of her life. While "various conjectures were formed concerning the causes of a disorder" of "incurable" melancholy, the grief for the Earl of Essex could not be overcome. Like Mary, Elizabeth succumbs to "an accident" despite concentrated attempts by others to "conjecture" on her behalf. The unexpected encounter with places that she associates with her tragic love for Essex triggers unsettling memories and "reviv[ed] her affection with new tenderness, and embittered her sorrows" (*HS* II, 228–229).

It is revealing to contrast Robertson's rather more Whiggish account of the conflict between Mary, Elizabeth, and the ascension of James to Hume's. Indeed, though he claimed to be of no party, Hume was charged by the Bishop of Gloucester in private of being an "atheistical Jacobite, a monster as rare as a hippogriff" (*HE* I, xiv). (Hume's politics aside, "hippogriff" is an apposite description for a philosopher who is sensitive to the mixed nature of reality in spite of traditional categorical habits.) Hume openly asserts, "the Whig party, [which has] enjoyed the whole authority of government . . . for a course of near seventy years . . . has proved destructive to the truth of history." Of particular concern here was a sense that "a regard to liberty, though a laudable passion, ought commonly to be subordinate to a reverence for established government" (*HE* VI, 534).

The specific reason for Hume's complaint against the Whigs, in this instance, was their promotion of hack political journalism. And as we have already seen, for Hume the popular press is not an appropriate place to find properly measured forms of historical evaluation, which in *The History of England* clearly promotes the unity of England and Scotland. Elizabeth is a crucial figure for Hume because she enters the stage in 1558 at a moment when the nation is divided. With the appropriate "apprehensions entertained about futurity" (*HE* IV, 3), she is at first swept up into "tumults among the people" surrounding the original "pretender" (not Charles II or his son James, but in this instance, Mary), but eventually "proceeds by gradual and secure steps"—the very skill of the stadial historian—to secure the Tudor crown.

Hume's Elizabeth shows the unusual (because, for Hume, "masculine") virtue of being able to use time as a means for governmental ends. She is able to "remain long in suspense with regard to the party," which is exactly where her sense of gradualism comes in (*HE* IV, 7). While seeking out the "London crowd," she was not "actuated by faction" (*HE* IV, 4). Elizabeth was, according to Hume, capable of bringing "the great multitudes" to heel when "she entertained apprehensions of an insurrection." She did so, moreover, through the ultimate temporal mechanism of a contract, which "dissipated the people by a promise" (*HE* IV, 22). In this and other ways, the queen is depicted as remarkable not only for escaping the "ungoverned fury of the multitude" (*HE* IV, 40), which she ensured her rival Mary did not, but was able to engage in measures to prevent such "fury," even "converting" the "tumultuous spirit" of her subjects to "support" (*HE* IV, 31). In short, Elizabeth exhibited "frugality" and "judiciousness" almost beyond the expectations of mere mortals.

But mortal Elizabeth clearly was, in Hume's account, and his evaluation of the twists and turns of her reign show her in difficult situations, specifically temporal situations, over which she has little or no control. In her confrontation with Phillip II of Spain in 1562, Elizabeth's superior virtues as a sovereign to seize the consequences of actions she cannot foresee coincide with mere "fortune, [which] in this instance, concurred with policy and nature" (*HE* IV, 55). Indeed, Elizabeth is not only subject to chance but is also criticized by Hume for her duplicity. Elizabeth is remarkable for Hume, and is suspect, for her ability to "negotiate perpetually . . . [and then] throw the blame . . . [of arranging Mary's death] on unforeseen accidents" (*HE* IV, 117).

Hume's version of the queen offers a different emphasis than Robertson's in that her "conjectural" skills are often overshadowed by dumb luck. Unlike Robertson, her skills lie not simply in reducing the multiplicity of forces that surround her to some sort of stadial good order through "conjecture." Instead, Hume's Elizabeth at her most effective promotes multiplicity, especially in encouraging the "rebellion of the Scots," in order to capitalize on the accidents that follow. But this also makes England's "most popular sovereign" (*HE* IV, 145) the penultimate "umpire between the factions" (*HE* IV, 107) and, therefore, at least sometimes, morally suspect. She is depicted by Hume as an affected "hypocrite" (*HE* IV, 238), full of "duplicity and artifice" (*HE* IV, 70) and "incapable from receiving any satisfaction from . . . fortunate event[s]" (*HE* IV, 349). Here the "melancholy" highlighted by Robertson as so much human tragedy given her fondness for Essex is accepted by Hume, but he wishes in the end to "lay aside all these considerations, [and] consider her merely as a rational being . . . entrusted with the government of mankind" (*HE* IV, 353).

The reduction of Queen Elizabeth to "merely . . . rational" status underscores Hume's rejection of royal prerogative and divine authority as the residual barbarism of government pre-1688. It also sets the stage for his preoccupation with the "people's rage," starting with the Stuart ascension to the thrown in 1603. In that sense, the word "merely" comes into full force: What bothers Hume throughout *The History* is the power of the multitude to obstruct and obscure historical progress, the same force, at a social level, that moves him to skepticism regarding causality in his philosophical work.

In Dugald Stewart's biography of Adam Smith ("Account of the Life and Writings of Adam Smith," hereafter "AL"), which appeared in 1793, only three years after Smith's death, "theoretical or conjectural history" is defined as a way of supplying historical succession "in want of direct evidence . . . [by] considering the way they [men] are *likely* to proceed" (emphasis ours).[109] Highlighting the importance of probability, Stewart continues,

> [I]f the progress delineated in all of them [different theoretical histories] be plausible, it is possible at least, that they may all have been realized; for human affairs never exhibit, in any two instances, a perfect uniformity. . . . [T]he real progress is not always the most natural. ("AL" 296)

Consistent here are some of the concerns we have already seen in Locke, Hume, and Kames. Kames's "law of succession," of "probability" as Stewart puts it here, is supposed to make intelligible the "real" state of human affairs, which are full of nonsequential, nonuniform perception and experience, even though that "real" dimension of humanity must be left by the by.

Not surprisingly, based on what we have said about Hume so far, "conjecture" was not a term in which he placed a great deal of analytical stock. This is especially true of *immediate* sense experience, as he describes in *Enquiry Concerning Human Understanding*: "From the first appearance of an object, we can never conjecture what effect will result from it" (*ECH* 7, 46). Hume repeatedly uses the phrase "mere conjecture" (*ECH* 106, 108) and writes, "we can only indulge the license of conjecture, and arbitrarily suppose the existence of qualities and energies, without reason or authority" (*ECH* 99). In some instances, for example, in surmising the earliest periods of history, "conjecture . . . [is] hardly allowable" (*HE* I, 194); other times, for example, with the Magna Carta in hand, "we may conjecture what [the] laws [of King Edward] were" (*HE* I, 446).

Indeed, unlike Robertson, when Hume's royals "conjecture" (or do so badly), trouble ensues. King James's development of a "speculative system of absolute government" belied the Elizabethan virtues of "the prudence and spirit of monarchs" (*HE* IV, 19). He "conjectured that it [a letter alluding to the Gunpowder Plot] implied something dangerous and important" (*HE* IV, 29). But the *something* mentioned here remained invisible until after the event. Charles too fails to "conjecture the cause of so sudden an alteration" of his cabinet's opinions (*HE* IV, 161).

As we have established already, "the contingency of human actions . . . has been found . . . to exceed all the power of philosophy," which for Hume remains the preserve of "sublime mysteries." This contingency is often associated with the superstitious tendencies of the "gazing populace," or simply, the "vulgar" (*ECH* 74–75, 91), "who [contrary to the philosopher] take things according to their first appearance" (*ECH* 63), or worse, "propheyize" themselves into a revolutionary state. The populace here stands in as the social equivalent of sense experience before it is processed by philosophical refection. Hume has shown this contingency at work in both a philosophical and a historical way, but only to the extent that it can be *mediated*, respectively, by thoughtful and serious writing, or by the actions of reasonable monarchs.

Stewart pits the "real" contingency of progress that Hume proposes as multiple points of causal possibility *against* that which appears "most natural." To put a finer point on this encounter between the "conjectural" and the "real," Stewart offers further clarifications:

> Real progress . . . may have been determined by particular accidents, which are not likely again to occur, and which cannot be considered as forming any part of that general provision which nature has made for the improvement of the [human] race. ("AL" 296)

Thus the generic category of the human being, and more than that, its implicit tendency to move in the forward historical direction of what is supposed to be historical "improvement," works in retrospect as a sort of conjectural sorting device to suss out accidental conflict from what appears (theoretically, at least) a matter of linear cause and effect.

This is not to say that Stewart dismisses accident as irrelevant. In the same way that Smith values the pleasing wonder of ignorance brought about by surprise, as we addressed in Chapter 1, accident matters a great deal. And it does so in a way evoking not only the frisson of a temporal break (Smith's dreaded "gaps") but also as matter of finding too little—or more dangerously, *too much*—data, our ongoing problem of "numbers." For Stewart, like Smith, "an immense collection of facts, and . . . a combination of the accidental lights daily struck out in the *innumerable* walks of observation and experiment" afford great advancement in the production of knowledge, as in human life (emphasis ours, "AL" 310).

But also like Smith, "accident" and "immensity" are addressed in the first instance through the proper application of category. In addition to wanting to read back upon history a conjectural, that is, theoretically plausible narrative of human development, Stewart offers a second clarifying point, consistent with

Locke and Kames, that "such speculations" are important for narrating history because they "have no tendency to . . . inflame the passions of the multitude" ("AL" 311). The problem of "numbers" thus moves from an epistemic to a social problem. The "real" nature of historical change—which is accident prone, riddled with lacunae, and replete with unseen agencies—is subsumed by a more idealized, rational (indeed, *speculative* if not fictive) account of developmental progress. Stadial history, like the process of inference itself, allows for the imagination. Indeed, it requires fictional speculation in order to produce outcomes broad enough to include the British unity of Scotland and England, not to mention mankind on the whole.

This way of writing history is reflected by the way that historical objects are themselves supposed to behave: Subjects and objects are kept at an appropriate distance but are also contrived, at least provisionally, to align. History's players behave most effectively when they think in the way conjectural historians do. As we have seen, the historians themselves are writing according to a set of lessons that are already discovered in how the sovereign—Mary, badly; Elizabeth, more effectively—deals respectively with time. Epistemic multiplicity and the so-called multitude thus connote a common risk to historical method and to effective ways of governing, respectively. This is a risk not simply of insurgency within history, though it is surely that, but also of too much historical data.

The effectiveness of conjecture is to render a *quantitative* problem of history's overabundance into a *qualitative* one that allows for the subjective capacities of judgment and good taste, capacities that we only later come to regard as part of the literary rather than the historical or even scientific enterprise. To again recall Stewart, historical difference, whether data overflow or insurrectionary change, is effectively countered by keeping the "numbers" at bay: conjectural *praxis*, because it relies on our "imaginative" capacities, as Kames and Hume would no doubt agree, is best left according to Stewart in the more trustworthy hands of "the speculative few" ("AL" 311). Moreover, for Stewart, as with the critics we addressed in Chapter 1, "the invention of printing" is a source of concern not only because of its connection with "numbers"—*print* is responsible for his reference to "*innumerable*" observations above—but also because "communication afforded by the press" has "accelerated the progress of the human mind . . . beyond what the most sanguine hopes of our predecessors could have imagined" ("AL" 310). The problem with "numbers" is resolved by the twin solutions of category and appropriately *mediated* temporal experience. As we will show in our next section, the distinction between historians and novelists is wrought with similar difficulties, and along the same *numerical* lines.

Excursus: The Novel and Its Multitudes

> *There remains to be treated of, another species of composition in prose, which comprehends a very numerous, though, in general, a very insignificant class of writings, known by the name of Romances and Novels.*
>
> Hugh Blair, "On Fictitious History"[110]

If, on one hand, the sheer prodigiousness of the eighteenth-century novel was enough to make it an "insignificant" kind of writing, then, on the other hand, the scarcity of a few better texts among the larger numbers must be perceived to give the novel at least some—*albeit* qualified—sense of value. But to note this move in the epigram from Blair of preferring *qualitative* over *quantitative* ways of assigning literary value is only to begin to address the troubled status of this "class" of writing. Adjoined to the problem of its being too "numerous" is the solution, or would-be solution, of dividing those numbers in ways that made both categorical *and* historical sense, and did so in mutually reinforcing ways.

Christina Lupton reminds us of what by 1750 were the standard complaints of eighteenth-century critics to disparage the novel's *over*-production, though we see similar statements as early as Pope's well-known objection about poetry "swelling" into prose.[111] Drawing on the theoretical sources that we noted in Pittock's Jacobite materialism, Lupton means to emphasize less the way novels help readers order things than she is regarding the novel itself as a "thing," especially insofar as its "numerous[ness]" becomes something that is thereby—either affirmatively or dangerously—quantifiable. The novel in this sense is not reduced to the status of an object ideally aligned with the subject it is alleged to reflect. Thus a second caution is due in addition to the numeric and, we should also say, technical one of *over*-production: The formal coherence of what we now call the novel is possible only in a specifically modulated form of retrospect.

As J. Paul Hunter has famously pointed out in *Before Novels*, the novel, roughly defined as a "new textual species responsive to human concerns about the structuring of everyday life as well as . . . ordinary actions," would not have been self-evident to critics up to and even immediately following Blair.[112] Instead, most so-called novels would have been regarded, and problematically so, as a composite or combinatory genre, a form that is hardly *formal* at all in the sense that it was also perceived to be mixed and multiple, until the nineteenth-century at least, and somewhat categorically confused. Therefore critics like Jesse Molesworth (in *Chance and the Eighteenth-Century Novel*, hereafter *CEN*) have "given up trying to define precisely what is 'novel,'" an approach (or a refusal of approach) which is of a piece with a new wave of postformalist scholarship (*CEN* 15). The consequent affirmation of the novel's "numbers" belongs to Franco Moretti's reworking of the novel's history as—until now, anyway—supposedly "countless" (*CEN* 58).[113]

But before Moretti, William Warner and others stopped attempting to objectify the novel in generic terms, stating: "I do not assume the novel to be a type of literature."[114] In the same way that eighteenth-century critics worried over the novel's proliferation, Deidre Lynch and Warner have observed, there is "no end of definitions of the novel."[115] Likewise, Siskin escapes the problem of genre entrapment by offering the challenging term "novelism," which is used to interrogate the naturalization of print in the eighteenth century. Novelism encompasses novels and a great deal more of the writing, namely, the periodicals and criticism that were related to, and sometimes, for example in Fielding, directly embedded within them.[116]

Given the advance of new media technologies supplanting the old novelistic ones of print, all of this kind of work, under Siskin and Warner's key term "mediation," moves from the mere *what* of literary study to the conceptual interconnections of the *how*. We could almost say that the kind of counting that stems from here has more in common with the antiformalism of a different *pre-* or *post-*novelistic time or, at least, a time inspired by a rigorous remixing of what we only later recognize as the time of the modern disciplines: a sufficiently old and sufficiently new time and one no longer limited by the once-dominant technology of print.

The end of the novel, as we knew it, is now. And in the sense that other ways of producing knowledge are opening up, the *post*-formalist charge of Moretti's *pre*-literary move requires an attendant shift in our traditional analytical categories (e.g., of discipline, selfhood, nation). Such a shift makes the novel itself, its original opacity as well as its contested history, exactly the right beginning place for a new kind of "global anthropological" work.[117] Moreover, and especially relevant for our purposes, the first debates about genre as a popular cultural affair occurred under the heading of novel: It was not just *about* popular contention. The novel was itself writing experienced *as* popularly contentious.

It is now commonplace to push against the boundaries of the novel that for a long time divided it into appropriate genres and subgenres, either a romance *or* a novel; a fiction *or* a history—but certainly none of these things mixed together, even though their mixedness, as the most important symptom of their proliferation, was what all eighteenth-century *novelistic* writers struggled mightily to sort out. This is not to suggest that Enlightenment arbiters of taste wanted to dismiss the novel, exactly. Although James Beattie says that "romances are a dangerous recreation," he revealingly adds, "a *few*, no doubt, of the best may be friendly to good taste and to good morals; but far the *greater* part are unskillfully written" (emphasis ours). As Beattie continues, "a habit of reading them breeds a dislike to history, and all the substantial parts of knowledge."[118]

What makes the danger safe to encounter involves, first, a proper form of winnowing the "numbers." This is achieved by a second way of avoiding the danger: making a set of generic distinctions that also slide into hierarchical ones. This double move of division works to "part"-out the *most* popular but—at least initially—the *least* categorizable modes of eighteenth-century writing, and therefore make possible their rendering into stadial historical form: first tales, then romance, now novels. Such partitioning and subpartitioning of the novel itself, coupled with its historical serialization, eventually presumed a larger, overarching disciplinary division, driving the wedge between the "fictitious" and the "historical" modes of discourse that Blair and others found themselves, even in the second half of the eighteenth century, still needing to sort out: novels but *not* romance; history but *not* novels.

But there remains a close if occulted kinship between history and novels, which is easier to see if we sacrifice asking what they *are* for the question of how novels *work* (or, as Nancy Armstrong says, "how novels think"[119]). Evoking Baconian induction as Siskin and Warner do, John Bender alerts us to the common terrain between fiction and the discourses of probability by placing what he broadly calls "novelistic fictions" in proximity to "hypothesis- and knowledge-making."[120] He thus suggests that novels were both dangerous and attractive because they offered "sites of experiment issuing into surrogate experience." Bender continues,

> Perhaps they produced not too much knowledge about vice but too many thought experiments and, with them, too great an expansion of experience and, with it, a potentially dangerous capacity for independent judgment.[121]

Bender's point about the ubiquity of prose fiction bears out Blair's estimation that, unlike history, there was evidently far too much of it being read by too many of the wrong sorts of readers. At his own historical moment anyway, the first chair of English literature in the world (and the first to publish a sustained study of the characters of Shakespeare) could not simply ignore the proliferation of "dangerous" or otherwise unwanted imaginative writing in the way that the advance of modern literary canons have allowed us to do in the more recent past.

Thus Bender's keyword above, "judgment," belies the idea that novels arrived (and for that matter, remained) fully formed as novels without requiring the strenuous qualifying moves of literary good taste to placate the ongoing problem of too many. That this matter of taste depended on a specific aesthetics of probability is of course also crucial. To sum up this particular brand of good judgment, Bender reaches back to 1957, to the *locus classicus* on the realist novel, Ian Watt's *The Rise of the Novel*. Watt's notion of a "realism of assessment" is useful here, even if his formalism is less so, in that it puts the burden of the "real" not in reality per se, but in the fictive sources of reason in experiment and expectation, which for Watt are represented by the characters of the relatively few successful formal realist novels, sufficiently removed from contamination by the romance.[122]

This "realism of assessment" over what we might call instead the realism of the *real* (i.e., of the multiple and the mixed) is what links the novel with historical thought in the eighteenth century insofar as good (read "probabilistic") literary judgment helped guard both discourses in a qualitative way against a quantitative problem of "too many." The more curious matter is the way in which Watt's own history of the genre explicitly ignores the vast (and varied) majority of the novels written in the eighteenth century, thus providing a novelistic example of the "realism of assessment" at the level of his own writing. Homer Obed Brown calls Watt's commitment to this approach a matter of "generic cleansing."[123] What we want to explore is the fundamental importance of the novel to conjectural history and to the concurrent promotion of historical writing—not least, the novel's own—in a specifically stadial way.

In "Fictitious History" (hereafter "FH"), Blair is explicit about the urgency that the numbers of novels produce. This is unique to a time in which print production and distribution allowed for new kinds of writing to circulate in new ways, to new readers, and clearly at cross-purposes with the qualitative critical standards of the day: Because the novel "especially occupies the imagination of the youth of both sexes"—and we should add, occupied the middle and lower literate ranks to boot—so-called "fictitious history . . . must demand particular attention" ("FH" 417). "Its influence," Blair continues, "is likely to be considerable, both on the morals and the taste of the nation" ("FH" 417). He then reaches for the progressive *topoi* available in the kinds of history he prefers over the "fictitious" kind and offers a stadial account of "fictitious history" from the "fables of ancient Greece," to "the magnificence of the heroic romance," and finally, to the way romance was "dwindled down to the familiar novel" ("FH" 419).

In setting up his next move as to how novels might be "executed . . . for very useful purpose"—even while they must always risk "expos[ure] to . . . contempt"—Blair adds to the narrative of "dwindl[ing]" the other concern we have been tracing, which is as we have already seen is essential to conjecturally based evocations of the "nation." That third issue is the problem of time. That the novel is "likely" to either corrupt or correct the national ability to judge a work, and therefore also ensure that the nation itself may exhibit a *qualitatively* worthwhile body of writing, reveals Blair's adherence to the production of probable historical narratives over which the novel could either be valued or dismissed within the vast *quantity* of so much other prose.

While the 60,000 British novels that appeared in the nineteenth century have been unaccounted for by technological default, the move beyond print to digital forms of preservation, cross-searching, and distribution—Moretti's controversial pitch for "distance reading"—has put on the scholarly agenda a new set of problems and potential solutions.[124] The more enigmatic point, which we are not the first to make, is that the novel itself was partly responsible for the probabilistic standards by which its history would be written, its massive "numbers" judged. The novel itself was a problem of "numbers," that is, of wrong reading, which was, for the first time, a problem of popular contention. This poses a unique set of questions because, unlike history, pacifying the objections to its own hazardous ubiquity was the novel's first order of business.

One of the most common ways in which literary good taste was negotiated in reference to the novel's "numbers" was through an antithesis that Blair still elides, even as late as the 1760s, between itself and romance. Fielding's staunch defense of probability in the novel in the 1740s was itself a fairly late one. The association between improbability and the romance, as Michael McKeon has shown, was by that time "increasingly pejorative," conjuring associations with witchcraft, superstition, and reckless aristocratic torpor.[125] McKeon's more generally applicable point is that despite the novel's rising status as a new literary tradition, the standard worry by mid-century was that it might at any time devolve into its opposite.

Thus in the early 1700s, historical narratives about how the novel has risen are written in a more or less stadial fashion (as in Hutcheson's *Essay on the Nature and Conduct of the Passions and Affections*, hereafter *ENCP*), from "Epicks and Romance" to the "leading of . . . tempers into an imagined *series* of Adventures."[126] The emphasis (our own) on the word "series" should be taken to mean that the novel—later defined according to probable outcomes—is mimicked by the history it is also said to have. That early modern prose fiction began, to continue citing Hutcheson's example of novelistic history from the 1720s, with the preoccupation of "greatness of the Change of Fortune in the person, or the surprise with which it comes" (*ENCP* 61), belies the permanence of a later division that remained dotted within Blair's notion of "fictitious history." Writing before the surges and oscillations that accompanied the novel decades later, Hutcheson offered an example of progressive history that already embedded the novel so called—this popular, unfinished, and unstable fictional form—to debates over probability, causality, and the role of the imagination in determining useful historical knowledge. As another sign of Hutcheson's premonition, he would place unusually affirmative emphasis on the imagination to "the lower rank of Mankind, whose only revenue is their bodily labour" (*ENCP* 120). "They have more often," he continues, "more correct imaginations thro' Necessity and Experience, than others can acquire by philosophy." To assume otherwise, "is indeed a poor excuse for a base selfish Oppressor" (*ENCP* 120).

These lines should be contrasted to the predominance in later criticism of the novel, even of the affirmative kind, which painted the masses of lower-ranking readers with the same brush as the masses of lower-ranking literature, as a moral threat that did not exist as urgently for Hutcheson. As we have intimated, later critics—*as* critics—wanted to deliver moral rectitude from this problem of too many. They were game to pursue what Turnbull (in *Observations Upon Liberal Education*, hereafter *OU*) would call "the tutorage of fancy," but in a way that resonates with our references to Fielding early in this chapter. Turnbull, for example, wanted to square fiction with "reason's business to compute and balance pleasures and pains of all kinds," and to introduce to popular imagination the special "governing principle, [whereby] the mind hath acquired the habit of deliberating and computing *before* it chooses; and is qualified for computing readily as well as truly" (emphasis ours).[127] Note again here the implicit role that categorization—Turnbull's reference to "all kinds"—plays in reducing plurality according to genre; but also how this reduction, precisely as a "computing" problem, is experienced in a temporal way. In the Humean sense, "habit" works to adjudicate the effect of what Turnbull calls a "young mind's . . . itch for novelty," which runs counter to "taste" (*OU* 134). In this way, choice is limited (we are not saying "determined") even while it seems to be embraced. Judgment kicks in *before* "numbers" have time to become "dangerous."

Turnbull is not an obvious candidate for comparison with the most influential philosophers and tastemakers of the Scottish Enlightenment, like Blair, Kames, and Smith. But reference to him is relevant insofar as the history of the novel presents the same problems that preoccupied them: dealing with excessive "numbers" in morally "comput[able]"—albeit more affirmative—ways. Kames insisted, "the power of fiction to generate passion is an admirable contrivance" (*EC* 66). He adds, "fiction [contains] examples to improve us in virtue [that] may be multiplied without end" (*EC* 77). The trick of course is how to produce such "multiplication" in safety, how to adjudicate fiction's numbers in accordance with "the uniformity of taste" (*EC* 724). Rather than "the complete idea of memory," which would simply contain too much data to sort, Kames defines "past time [as] a circumstance" (*EC* 69) of—at least partly—the imagination. Memory is therefore defined as set of *incomplete* relations, drawing upon the same fictive modes of thinking that stem from Turnbull's "tutorage of fancy" in order to keep that incompletion from filling up in ways that attenuate individual moral danger as much as social unrest. Thus, according to Kames, memory itself is like criticism, and "as many rules of criticism depend on ideal presence," which memory clearly lacks, "the reader, it is hoped, will take some pains to form an exact notion of it" (*EC* 68). The specific memory in question here is of the Porteous Riots of 1737, which—as if to call forth Sir Walter Scott's later novel, *Heart of Midlothian*, on demand—joins the memory work that criticism does to the issue of popular contention and resolves the latter in a nationally coherent way.

The point is that the novel was in its own right contentious along exactly the same lines. Johnson, for example, equates "the works of fiction, with which the present generation seems more particularly delighted," with "the young, the ignorant, and the idle" according to an overarching concern about what he simply calls "masses."[128] He writes, "the chief advantage [of contemporary fiction], tho' not to invent, yet to select objects, and to cull from the mass of mankind, those individuals upon which the attention ought most to be employ'd."[129] Johnson goes on to offer the expected history of how novels must oppose the "fictions of the last age," which are "danger[ous]" insofar as they initiate imitation among the lower orders by a "wild strain of imagination."[130] He offers, that is, an expected history writ precisely as the history of expectation. The novel emerges from romance as a turn toward more probable events and more normative people. Johnson, too, does stadial history. But in a slight variation from his Scottish contemporaries—whose concern, traceable to Hutcheson, was to emphasize the role of imagination and affect in producing credible narratives—Johnson switches imperceptibly between "masses" of novels, readers, and objects in general. This is similar with the way Kames equates memory and criticism in that it calls for fictive modes of selection, limited by reason and probability, for remembering certain historical events, while forgetting so many others.

As James Raven points out, most early reviewers of the novel were relieved by their apparent transience.[131] The innumerable majority of them appeared only in a first edition, and with print runs of no more than 500 (though circulating libraries made them distributed widely enough to young boys and servant women, a cause of great concern). Such a figure compares in revealing ways with Fielding's bestseller, *Tom Jones*. Its first edition of 2,000 bound copies sold out before its publication date of February 10, 1749. An additional 1,500 copies of the novel appeared in March, then 3,000 copies in April, and 3,500 more books followed in September.[132]

The point of the comparison between the great success of *Tom Jones* and the still far-larger quantities of novels we have now forgotten shows how a *qualitatively* valuable piece of writing serves a problem of *quantitative* demand: "mass" distribution of tasteful writing narrowly defined, versus too many different definitions of the novel *en masse*. The value of the novel for Johnson, though he does not yet use the word "novel" itself, and of the novelistic criticism that accompanied it, work in common as "cull[ing]" devices. The goal is to determine morally acceptable ways to judge the "masses" of novels for the "masses" of readers and to rely on the majority of novels disappearing by default. This matter of "cull[ing]" worked partly through the contrivance of genre, but equally, if less obviously, by capitalizing on this mixed and ubiquitous genre's unsettled relation to time: its *immediacy* as well as its ubiquity, its newness as well as its "numbers." Johnson sought an easily reproducible means for sorting through the problem of overabundance wherever he found it—with readers, with objects, and ultimately with the novel as a problem of "masses" in its own right.

Like so many others, Smith singles out Samuel Richardson among what he still calls "romance writers" as being best able to "paint the refinements and delicacies of love and friendship."[133] And he too notes the preoccupation of romances to depict the "misfortunes" of "virtuous" people (*TMS* 226). But insofar as those people remain cast as "magnanimous princes"—which is to say, hardly a people problem in the modern, individualist sense, at all—the readers of romances are too often given over to "the most enthusiastic and even extravagant imagination" (*TMS* 226). Thus the categorical imperative that Smith helped invent throughout his philosophical writing (recall our history of the disciplines in Chapter 1) is evident in his commentary on the novel. In a nod of advance warning against the contemporary vogue of gothic taste, Smith mentions the "gloomy horror of the cavern . . . [of] nymphs, fawns, satyrs, [and] dryads," narratives that tend toward "prophetical inspirations" and "gloomy emotion."[134] Hume complains in similar fashion when he describes "a gothic building" as "distracted by the multiplicity of ornaments [such that it] loses the whole by its minute attention to the parts."[135] And Smith here exhibits Hume's sensitivity about the "prophetic" mode as being both disruptive of time and evidence of either past antisocial behavior or anxiety of it in the unknowable future.

Between Smith and Hume, the outcome of such vision produces two inverted forms of antisociability—what we might anachronistically call a pre-Romantic and a post-Romantic form. Hume (*Treatise of Human Nature*) expresses caution when "the imagination is not restrained," and subdivides our mental capacity to move beyond the immediate encounter with objects by fine-tuning it in the form of "memory" and "belief" (*THN* 1233–1246, 190). "Memory," at least, "fixes itself on a determinate object," even if it still takes imagination—the "fancy," the capacity for "the transference of past to future"— in order to become "belief." The danger Hume identifies is that such a "fiction" can also lead to "poetical enthusiasm . . . and even a kind of vision of his [in this case, the poet-storyteller's] objects" (*THN* 175). Here the subject at risk is the familiar one of the primitive, whose "real history . . . , corrupted by tradition, and elevated by the marvelous, became a plentiful source of fable." Beginning with fable, later hands "successively improved upon the wonder and astonishment of the multitude."[136]

But as we know from Hume's preoccupation with the English civil wars in his *History of England*, the violent past to which Hume alludes was never very far away from England's present. The "success[ion]" Hume had in mind was a slow one in Scotland, as he was anxiously aware. "Poetical enthusiasm" writ as "liberty of the imagination"—or otherwise, as the interruption of "the transference of past to future" that Hume called "vision"—spelled insurrection in thinly veiled terms (*THN* 173, 57). The part of this process that makes Hume unique, and sets the stage for his well-known skepticism as well as his preoccupation with insurrection in history, is that these "poetical" *qua* popular interruptions of stadial thinking are always vital and in play. "From law arises security," he writes, "from security, curiosity: And from curiosity, knowledge. The latter steps of this progress may be more *accidental*; but the former are altogether necessary."[137] And lest it be lost to the past, "accident," which is consistently for Hume both a "curiosity" *and* a matter of "security," can cut in more than one direction. "The ideas of chivalry . . . imported by the Normans . . . among the plain and rustic Saxons" share a clear lineage with romance, and both are a matter of dreaded French invasion. It is "fortunate for letters that . . . [the] tales, [and] fables" of "rude" ages are "buried in silence," which Hume assures us, we should "neglect."[138]

Indeed, Hume notes the practice of thirteenth-century Welsh kings to put their bards to death, "a barbarous, though not absurd policy" (*HE* II, 82). But there is no such luck for the writers of romance as they threaten to overwhelm eighteenth-century letters. "Fortune," in the form of the novel's own massiveness, has produced an event that, while not exactly articulate, is anything but "silent." When Hume impugns "the reign of Charles II . . . [for] retard[ing] the progress of polite literature in this island," his own "silence" on the advance of romance speaks volumes (*HE* VI, 543). The inauspicious year of the Stuart restoration is the same moment that literature "accidentally" begins to be corrupted by popular hands and therefore begins, like the inhabitants and governments of England and Scotland, to go horribly wrong.

The survival of the romance strain in later novels is also accounted for by Smith (*Lectures on Rhetoric and Belles Lettres,* hereafter *LRBL*), who presents similar, though as we have proposed, inverted kinds of risks than we see identified by Hume: Instead of initiating a security question as popular contention, Smith's evaluation tends to generate equally antisocial behavior at an opposite extreme, that is, of "solitude" and "invisibility" (*LRBL* 71). This state of retreat would appeal later to William Wordsworth and his literary kin, though Smith's philosophy itself certainly did not.

Smith insists upon distinguishing "modern historians" from romance. But he also says that "most modern historians, and all the romance writers . . . render their narration interesting . . . to keep their event in suspense" (*LRBL* 96). On one hand, of what use would conjecture be without the risk of falling off the temporal precipice, the all-important cliffhanger that threatens popular readership but also plays directly into what popular readership seems to want? On the other hand, what would a cliffhanger be without a probabilistically "comput[able]" rescue that remains within the boundaries of good taste? One of the most condemning things Smith can say about the novel is its tendency to offer sudden change without a reasonable explanation: "Newness is the only merit in the novel and curiosity the only motive which induces us to read them" (*LRBL* 97). At stake in this remark, which in itself is "curious," is the novel's remarkable capacity to *re*-new itself perpetually and safely in the form of its own history and concurrent reception.[139] This form of reproduction, where newness effectively means just the right variation on more of the same, is something that connects with the carefully measured and directed reproduction of consumer desire.[140]

The act of renewal Smith impugns is not an exact one because while history mirrors the novel as a stadial narrative, it also renders it an appropriate subject of *qualitative* judgment against the *quantitative* overproduction of romance. History becomes the sovereign discipline for Smith and his cohort, even though, as Blair's (to us) awkward use of the term "fictional history" betrays, history shares an inextricable lineage with the novel's division from romance. Insofar as the novel can be said to have left romance behind, it becomes categorically reducible to—that is, may stand out as guardedly worthwhile among—so many other "numbers" of less worthy narrative prose.

What Smith offers as a remedy against (novelistic) suspense without (historical) completion is telling. Even as the novel renews itself as history, history—because *less* popularly contentious as a genre in the *present* and *more* able to sort out popular contention in the *past*—is finally of greater value. If history produced "new[ness]" without "cause," Smith suggests, "we would count the pages we had to read to get to the event, as we generally do in a novel" (*LRBL* 97). And if we hold on to a notion of the "event" as Siskin and Warner do, as "taking a *quantitative* turn" (our emphasis), we can argue, in addition, that Smith's *qualitative* affirmation of *certain* novels is a fundamental part of the "security" questions that Siskin and Warner (*This Is Enlightenment*) leave for others to address (*TIE* 11). The move to hierarchy that Smith offers in his account of the novel as a discourse, "a proliferating [mode of] mediation," to use Siskin and Warner's term, is concurrent with new ways of rethinking sociability, and enforcing, upon the many by the few, specifically commercial forms of collective behavior.

To Ann Blair and Peter Stallybrass's interest in "the history of information management" as a problem of amassing printed knowledge specific to early modernity, we must add the concurrent problem of the management of masses of people.[141] The famous London bookseller and former cobbler, James Lackington, congratulated himself in the eighteenth century for being "highly instrumental in diffusing that general desire for reading." But he also comments that this "general desire" has been produced in a way that intimated social disruption, since reading is specifically remarkable for being "now so prevalent among the inferior orders of society."[142] The novel's would-be "masses" of readers—the subordinate ranks, the young, women, servants—are active in the eighteenth century in ways that are as dangerous as they are in need of literary supervision. What remains to be "calcul[ated]" for both the masses of readers and the masses of novels is what happens when "numbers" are given their due. Smith continues, "the more lively and shocking the impression in which any Phenomenon makes on the mind the greater curiosity does it excite to know its Causes" (*LRBL* 93). But he also insists,

> Historical writing is supposed to entertain and instruct. . . . In this, it differs from Romance, the sole view of which is to entertain. . . . The facts must be real, otherwise they will not assist us in our future conduct. (*LRBL* 91)

About the final distinction between history and romance, Smith hedges his bets on the qualitative side of judgment and good taste. His adherence simply to the facts would seem to contradict what we have gone to great lengths to show above and in Chapter 1: that Smith was extremely attentive to, and was forced to painfully admit, those "chasm[s] or gap[s] in the thread of the narration" that "we should never leave . . . even though there are no remarkable events to fill up that space" (*LRBL* 100). As we have seen, both philosophy and the later emerging specialty of history depended at their most crucial moments on fictive connectivity and the philosophical imagination in order to explicate change in a stadial way. Our point here is that at the time fiction and history became disconnected, the imagination was reconnected almost exclusively to the so-called fine arts.

We say history *at its most crucial moments* because, as we have also seen, conjecture is called upon especially when there is an overwhelming sense of connective discontinuity, experienced paradoxically as absence, which is generated by what we have been calling by shorthand a problem of "numbers." We have seen examples of this particular version of the "numbers" problem in the episodes of historical insurgency that we have detailed, and in the notion of the lower ranks running *quantitatively* at cross-purposes with the *qualitative* standards of taste. At a more abstract—but still "dangerous" level—there are also moments, best regarded as chance, where historical knowledge is overwhelmed by what appear to be unrelated objects. The point we are making now is to add the novel—an object connected to the problem of "too many" in all of these ways—to our account of popular contention.

Smith points out that "poets [were] the first historians," and that they "expressed themselves in the language of wonder . . . , amazement, and surprise" (*LRBL* 105). "In all countries," he continues, "poetry has been the first species of writing, as the marvelous is that which first draws the attention of unimproved men" (*LRBL* 104). Since Smith does not offer an account of what causes the movement from poetry to prose, and with it, the movement from "the barbarous" to the commercial nations (*LRBL* 105), we are left to assume a Jupiter-like connection of an invisible or accidental relation between temporality and form, which is to say, we are left unable to interrogate those instances of historical change. In Smith's rough formula, the greater distance that history progresses over time from stage to stage, the more distinct the categories, genres, and therefore the stages of history themselves become to the historian. Put reductively, history produces the knowledge we need to produce history with. There would be a tautological element to this, if it were not for the issue we have already discussed regarding Lockean notions of differential historical velocity: Different geographies of change occur at different rates. Therefore, to the extent that one place is proximate to another that exists at a different moment in stadial time, categorical distinction remains contestably open, and at risk of coming undone. This is precisely how Scotland is said to be situated with respect to England.

In the passage cited above from Lecture 18 on poetry-as-history, Smith's historical touchstones are "the oldest original writings in Latin, Italian, French, English, and Scots" (*LRBL* 104). The division in this list between England and Scotland is an interesting one, and not just for being historically accurate. It is interesting because the English/Scottish geographical division, supposed to have been removed by union, lingers on in a temporal way as Europe's savage remainder. As poetry gives over to prose, the wonder of "fables . . . most likely to please a rude and ignorant people" is replaced by more probable fictional narrative (*LRBL* 111). "We now see," Smith remarks, "that the stories of witches and fairies are swallowed greedily by the ignorant vulgar, which are despised by the more knowing" (*LRBL* 110). The vulgar are overwhelmed by a matter of volume that they cannot control, as the word "greedy" implies. Popular read-

ers of the kind Smith notes as being "despised" are not only subject to the risk
of fictional overproduction but are also sociological stand-ins for the literary
problem of romance.

Producing a stadial history of the novel by giving it a sequential narrative
of development such that the romance is left at an archaic stage behind the
modern one both limits eighteenth-century fiction and extends a certain version of it. As Siskin has argued, the earliest histories of the novel found ways
to encourage the genre to proliferate—the "numbers" to *amass*—but in a qualitatively restrictive way linked to taste and good judgment. By the time Anna
Laetitia Barbauld writes *The British Novelists* in the early nineteenth century,
the term "fictional history" had finally split. The two separate terms were then
retroactively solidified in the early nineteenth century such that "fiction" was
cordoned off within its proper literary boundaries. "Richardson, Fielding, and
Smollett" are thus said to have "appeared in quick succession."[143] Barbauld
merges these novelists, and ignores differences between them, so that one coherent object—the novel—can be seen to emerge, free from traces of earlier
genres. This allows further refinement of the novel in a later period as realist,
modern, and, above all, something said to have had a stadial—read *novelistic*—
past. This past results in identifying a set few novels, representative of a presumably dominant form, against the vast majority of others. In the sense
initiated by Smith and his cohort, the stadial narrative *is* as the stadial narrative
does: Fiction and history share similar rhetorical modes before they take on
different generic values.

Above we noted Hume's connection between fiction, tales, fables, and the like
to a state of savagery or "rudeness," which is also linked to premodern propensities for war. Not uncommonly, Blair links the time of "fables, parables, [and]
tales"—what he calls a "singular form" of composition—to "the martial spirit"
("FH" 344). We will have more to say about the crucially important way that the
"martial spirit" plays into the question of Scottish insurgency in the writing of
eighteenth-century stadial history in our final section of this chapter. Foreshad-
owing that, note here how the history of the novel as it progresses over time—
first from the fable or tale, then to romance, then finally to its realist form—is
itself a kind of narrative counterexample, pitted against the "singular" yet also
massive way in which rude ages mishandle their own challenges with time.

Romance has not yet "dwindled" to the novel, which takes place for Blair
"during the age of . . . King Charles the II" ("FH" 345). Note that this specifically
Jacobite way of mishandling time triggers the same warning given to popular

readers, as they are encouraged to seek probability among the different available fictional modes. What bothers Blair about the "gross ignorance of these ages" is a rejection of "the legends, and superstitious notions concerning magic and necromancy, which then prevailed" ("FH" 344). Here the romance stands in for false associations with the future, as sorcery, witchcraft, and necromantic communications with the dead; it is cordoned off from the developmental history of the realist novel by offering the same kind of narrative that novels produced.

To stay with the theme of fiction and the "martial spirit," Adam Ferguson linked "traditionary fables" to the "vulgar" but also insisted that it is "absurd to quote the fable of the *Iliad* . . . [to relate] to the history of mankind."[144] Smith gives a decidedly martial twist to his objection over reading popular romances by expounding on the term "the force of blood." "This force of blood," he writes, "exists nowhere but in tragedies and romances. . . . To imagine any such mysterious affection between . . . [members of a tribe] would be too ridiculous" (*TMS* 222). For Hume, such a "specious title as that of blood, which, with the multitude, is always the claim," signified illegitimate Jacobite objectives to "preserve succession" and therefore marked not only a bygone period of imperial tyranny, but its bedfellow, insurrection and riot.[145] Smith continues, "it is not many years ago that, in the Highlands of Scotland, the Chieftain used to consider the poorest man of his clan, as his cousin and relation" (*TMS* 223). This kind of affection is counter to modern advancements of reason in several ways. Here we could ask the same question Tony Jarrells does about the so-called Bloodless Revolution, which as we have seen above in our attention to Jacobite insurgency was attended by wide-ranging forms of popular contention, as well as outright military violence: How did the novel become bloodless?[146]

In the same way that romance must be generically cordoned off from the novel and then rendered into a stadial past, the presocial state of savagery begets a form of kinship that reaches out to the suffering in other than commercial, individualistic, or, most crucially, conjugal patriarchal ways. Indeed, as Ruth Perry has shown, the novel was the primary way in which new family connections were dramatized in the eighteenth century, with the ideals of filial love, which in turn enabled a form of kinship based on gendered familial reciprocity, community, and early modern capitalist society.[147] Habermas's foundational account of the public sphere, within which the novel's focus on personal intimacy plays a definitive role, is after all based on Richardson and Fielding's bloodless (and in the later case, anti-Jacobite) familial fictions of that sort. And Smith is clear about the civilizing effects of the family, where "the father is superior," and the child, like the spectator in general, must "bring down its passions and curb its desires" for eventual "peace and enjoyment within society" (*LJ* A, 164, 143).

Pro-marriage legislation at mid-century—like Lord Hardwicke's Marriage Act of 1753, better known as the Act for the Better Preventing of Clandestine Marriages—and various attempts at bachelor's taxes are further evidence that fictional treatments of private desires could be useful in a public way. As John Dwyer has shown, marriage represented "temporal happiness" to cite an often-used phrase from the *Scots* magazine.[148] It meant worldly satisfaction in the conjugal sense, depending upon reproduction in the form of children and their stadial growth.[149]

This is not to say that women were excluded from helping to form the standards of literary taste at this instance. To the contrary, Hume writes: "the fair sex [is the] sovereign Authority over the republic of letters."[150] The reading habits of women were of concern for Hume for the same reasons savages and Highlanders and the "ignorant multitude" must move ahead to the historical present. Women are, he writes, "most addicted to superstition" (*NHR* 35, 43). He continues (in *Essays Moral, Political, Literary*), "there is only one subject, on which I am to distrust the judgment of females, [and that is] concerning books of gallantry and emotion." This is because women are "easily affected" (*EMPL* 537). As a remedy, Hume recommends "to my female readers . . . the study of history" instead (*EMPL* 563).

In a manner similar to the slow history of Scotland—Highland kinship existing, as Smith says, "not that many [read "not enough"] years ago"—romances linger on dangerously as well. What it takes to remedy both problems is, first, to make a qualitative move that distinguishes between socially appropriate and otherwise dangerous fiction; and, second, to devise a sense of sequential logic that is fatal to the preservation of the latter. Thus Ian Duncan makes the important point regarding Sir Walter Scott that by assigning Scotland to antiquity, and therefore to "national obsolescence," the historical novel he invented produced "a transcendental national interest," a "subject-tempering activity" against histories and rivalries that were anything but bloodless. As Duncan also points out, Scott took his historical scheme from the conjectural historians, and particularly from Smith.[151] We might say, then, if Scott invented the historical novel, the novel's history or, better, the novel as manifest within history *invented* him. In the same way as Scott collated the local distinctiveness and violent history of Scottishness as Scotland's "national minstrel" (Duncan's term), what we have seen in earlier examples of novelistic writing is a similar dynamic of collation as the novel is said to achieve coherence against the romance.

In short, Scotland is to England as romance is to the realist novel. While both sets of pairs are in fact historically proximate to one another, and therefore mixed in their association, stadial history tells a different story that casts these pairings as a story, first, of separation and then eventually as progressive cooperation against the common problem of "too many."

The "Precarious Acquiescence of the People"

Each exertion of authority in the chieftain must have been particular, and called forth by the present exigencies of the case: The sensible utility, resulting from his interposition, made these exertions become daily more frequent; and their frequency gradually produced an habitual, and, if you please to call it so, a voluntary, and therefore precarious, acquiescence in the people.

David Hume, "Of the Original Contract"[152]

In this passage from Hume's essay ("OOC"), we can recognize certain philosophical preoccupations put to both historical and political use. Here the ultimate goal is to trace government "to its first origins in the woods and desarts [*sic*]" ("OOC" 468). At this point in time, before "the use of writing and all the other civilized arts," we find in the "nature of man . . . something approaching equality" ("OOC" 468). In Hobbesian fashion, such equality also means that "force" either belongs to the "people" or must be derived from a single authority. But—until the "profound tranquility" and "regular[ity]" of succession of William in 1688 (*HE* VI, 528)—the sovereign "could never subject multitudes to . . . *command*" ("OOC" 468). Instead, authority must become institutionalized in the form of "an established government" based on "their own [the multitude's] *consent*" (emphasis ours, "OOC" 468).

What Hume signals above is a philosophical process in ideal political form. Even in the early stages of history, the people "sense[d]" the regular outcomes of their obedience in the form of "frequen[cy]," rather than blind obedience to the chieftain's command. And on schedule, "habit" formed, which though the people may be almost blind to it, became a means of governing the population on its own terms. The eternal danger of the "people's rage" is here contained and canalized in the eventual form of private property laws, and one would hope by mid-century, the monopolization of violence by a centralized British state.

But the keyword above is "precarious," which is a term we should expect from Hume's mitigated skepticism toward habitual temporal experience wherever it may be found. Hume is extremely cautious about establishing government in the form of a contract between the "multitudes" and the sovereign, on the order of Hobbes. He writes,

> It happens unluckily for those who maintain an original contract between the magistrate and the people, that great revolutions of government . . . are commonly conducted with such violence, tumult, and disorder, that the public voice can scarcely ever be heard. (*HE* VI, 528)

Thus even in the "singular exception" that saw peaceable elections bring William to the throne, the division between a contentious "multitude" and a governable "people" is not an absolutely reliable one. In the same manner of breaking philosophical customs, less affirmatively, governmental "habit" is also liable to break forth in the same temporally disruptive way, writ here aptly by Hume as "unfortunate" encounters with popular discontent. Even the more sanguine Adam Smith was concerned that the rise and fall of government funds and its increased reliance on credit during the reign of George I would promulgate "some risk of revolution" (*LJ* B, 536). To think otherwise would have been to adopt a teleology of historical improvement underwritten by Whig history, which neither Smith nor the more skeptical Hume attempt to provide. As we shall see further below, for them there are no guarantees for the peaceable stability of commercial society given the inequalities it is bound to produce.

Colin Kidd calls Whig history "one of the central 'achievements' of the Scottish Enlightenment," in that it was used to "defuse the explosive potential lurking in the nation's powerful political and religious heritage."[153] William Robertson, Kidd goes on to remark, is "the central villain of this piece."[154] Pittock too has been strong on impeaching the claims of Whig history as nonpartisan on the grounds that such accounts are "linear . . . [and] progress-oriented, minimizing of difference in terms of which such history expresses itself."[155] Whig history depends upon the relatively (and falsely) conflict-free consolidation of British empire after 1688, as the adjective "bloodless" in the obfuscating phrase Bloodless Revolution belies.

By using 1688 as a premise for the history of England, and in the case of Robertson, of Scotland, the agency of non-jurors and dissenters (the force of popular Jacobitism we have outlined above) are "compressed by purposive hindsight."[156] In the same way as Kidd, Robertson features in Pittock's work as a key figure in the perpetuation of Whig historiography. The *History of Scotland* offers a narrative of unbroken progress between ancient Saxon liberties momentarily overturned by the Norman invasion, set back on track after correct opposition to the Stuart monarchs by William's arrival in 1688. In that way, the infamous Norman yoke of feudalism prefigures a backwards-looking Stuart dynasty, balefully associated with the French up to 1745. Pittock sees the "triumphant recovery of unassailable incrementality" in the visit of George IV to Edinburgh in 1822, which was orchestrated by Sir Walter Scott as a pageant of saccharine nostalgia and apolitical loyalty.[157] For moving the Jacobite risings of the "Fifteen" and the "Forty-Five" to the margins of our understanding of the past so that the historical lines between Scotland and England could appear unbroken by insurgency: "Whig history is to blame."[158]

The singling out of Robertson (and to some extent Kames) for conservative Whig principles begins to illuminate the opacity of political purpose embedded in conjectural history, even if those politics are occulted by appeals to certain forms of temporal intelligence. But there are additional points we need to adjoin to the insights of Pittock and Kidd, whose important contribution is to critique the linear narrative of Whig historiography as in need of revision, and as vulnerable to certain historical breaks. To develop insights not made fully explicit in existing critiques of conjectural thought, we would agree that the alternative forms of temporal complexity attached to insurrection cannot be based on a margin versus center paradigm, which is implied by reducing Scotland to England's periphery. As mentioned above, the dynamic we have in mind regarding popular Jacobitism is one of historical immanence: a complex *intra*-dependency among multiple political players, Robertson's "mixed multitudes," who are not subject to traditional ideological borders. Moreover, our rejection of Jacobitism as a reductively dyadic or polarized form of conflict means putting in place of the margin/center duality something more akin to popular disorder, or so-called riotous behavior. From that position, in addition to historical gaps that can be found within the developmental typology of Whig history, we have been exploring the ideal of alternative *linearities*, emphasizing the plurality of time and an affirmative approach to the phenomena of chance.

There is no doubt that Robertson's political allegiances were with the Hanoverian status quo that he helped create, even though Christopher Berry sees him as offering the most "conscientious and 'scientific' approach" to writing history.[159] One of the first professional historians, Robertson is in our view accurately regarded as "an establishment man."[160] He offers us an account of the "united two kingdoms, divided from the earliest accounts of time, but destined by their situation, to form one great monarchy." And he wishes to render the rise of "Great Britain [as] . . . the junction of its whole native force" (*HS* II, 235). George I founded chairs of modern history to achieve just the kind of public service of "conflict harmonization" that the *History of Scotland* (not to mention Robertson's later writing on America in 1777, and India in 1791) would provide.[161] Robertson, a founding member of the Select Society, received 600 pounds for this book, more than anybody had ever received for copy money, except Hume. Lord Bute managed to revive the Historiographer Royal of Scotland, attached to which was the substantial income of 200 pounds a year, and a private carriage, to boot.

Robertson did have groundbreaking achievements during his thirty years of presiding over Edinburgh University. But his biography, like his histories, is fundamentally intertwined with having to respond—and he did so badly—to popular disorder. As the leader of the Church of Scotland from 1762–1780, his concern was to preserve the unity of religious organization and its support of the state. As Stewart Brown has shown, Robertson was fundamentally against tendencies within the church to assert its independence from the patronage of the landed classes and tried to replace this arrangement with elections by members of the local parish communities.[162] Against Robertson, local Presbyteries meant to defy the Supreme Court. The attempt by the patronage system to maintain centralized control over a vast and complex network of local agencies—there were 970 parishes in the Church of Scotland alone—was matched at an earlier time by the forfeiture of Jacobite estates after 1745, making the Crown the largest patron in Scotland. As we have seen in earlier strains of popular Jacobitism, the patronage issue was founded in a confrontation between leading landowners and the fight of a majority of people without such influence. Patronage was in fact replaced by elections in the rural parishes in 1688. But after union, and in the heady period of Jacobite insurrection, the newly unified British parliament reimposed this system in 1712 as a mechanism of centralization against fierce local opposition.

Robertson thus complains of being personally "expose[d] to popular odium and personal danger."[163] The antipatronage group, known as the Popular Party, also supported the American colonialists, which Robertson expressly did not. Indeed, his entrenched response to popular resistance, which he continued to encounter firsthand, is alleged to have made the Popular Party that much more widespread. As Brown reveals, Robertson's unyielding commitment to patronage despite mass opposition inadvertently spurred its growth. In 1760, there were over 120 meetinghouses, serving more than 100,000 members.[164]

Robertson's encounters with the multitude showed the limits of patronized authority, the reverse of his official ministerial intentions to limit, not add, to the growing numbers of the popular discontented.

Like Robertson and Hume, Kames admits the fundamental importance of Scottish insurgency to British history. Though like Mansfield he had a Jacobite upbringing, Kames was keen to suss out the shared Anglo origins of English and Scots jurisprudence. In the *Essays upon Several Subjects Concerning British Antiquities* (hereafter *EBA*), Kames is especially explicit about the habitually linear—if also uneven—nature of rational thought. For him, the "proper Order and Situation . . . in the Contemplation of Objects" is achieved by the commitment to "never leap from one [object] to another which is distant, without running over, at least, in a cursory manner, all interposed Objects."[165] This "transition of ideas from one to the other" is based on a "law in our nature," also called "the universal rule of succession" (*EBA* 123), which is repeatedly linked by Kames to "probable conjectures" (*EBA* 4, 6, 9, etc.), more specifically, "conjectures by degrees" (*EBA* 24–25). Clearly the universality Kames has in mind by thinking in conjectural terms pertains to the Act of Union, which he means to reinforce against the rebellion of 1745. Thus the introductory paragraph to the *Essays* begins with the invocation of our "late troubles" (*EBA* i). Despite the "calamities of a Civil war," a certain "firmness in the Author" enabled him to refuse to "g[ive] over his country for loss" (*EBA* ii). The pitch here is for history—or, better, a specific kind of history Kames calls "Speculations . . . not realized but in Times of the greatest Tranquility" (*EBA* ii)—to "raise a Spirit among his [Kames's] Countrymen, by searching into their Antiquities, those especially which regard the law and Constitution" (*EBA* ii).

Consistent with Robertson, we see in the "search" that follows the development of common Anglo roots against Norman interruption, as well as the more immediately pressing concern of Jacobite opportunism. These narratives are then conjoined with the risks and resolutions of practicing conjectural history itself. Against the political capacity of Jacobite "hazard" (*EBA* 215), the historian who thinks in linear—if also "speculative"—terms is equipped with more effective ways of dealing with time. But crucially, this turn toward "speculation" is born out of an original condition of the object of history not to be identifiable in a univocal way but to exist as entirely mixed: Kames searched for so-called British antiquities and wrote the histories he did in order to "unit[e] numberless individuals into one complex object, [which] enlarges greatly the sphere of benevolence.

"By that faculty alone," he continues in *Sketches on the History of Man* (*SHM*), "our country, our government, our religion, become objects of public spirit. . . . The individuals that compose the group, considered apart, may be too minute, or too distant, for our benevolence."[166] The spatial references in the latter part of the citation are as important as Kames's notion that the historical object is in itself "numberless." The proper calibration of scale and distance (we have been calling it a problem of Scotland's immanence to England) is what manages the otherwise disruptive factors of "numbers" in time. Like Mary, Queen of Scots, for Robertson, contemporary Jacobitism for Kames points out the temporally disorienting and disoriented figure of the (Scottish) savage, who is insufficiently pacified from within a properly European (British) historical perspective of an otherwise inert and distant past: "[P]rospects of the future good or evil never have influence upon the savage," he writes (*SHM* I, 43). The savage "acts by sense, not foresight" (*SHM* I, 53). And like Fielding's lower orders, "savages are addicted to gaming" (*SHM* I, 213). This is one reason Kames insists upon the "immoral effects of public charity"—"I would not have the poor be pampered," he remarks (*SHM* II, 542)—and advocates the establishment of workhouses instead (*SHM* II, 530).

The speculative homologies established by Kames between the savage, the Jacobite, the poor, and, more generically, popular contention itself are described as variously out of sync with civilized temporal intelligibility. But each of these "complex object[s]" are in their own way corrected by the still unfulfilled promise of *peaceable* commercial exchange as facilitated by a unified British government. Though he staunchly opposed "admitting low people to vote for members of Parliament," and rallied, on the order of Robertson, against "admitting the popular to vote in the election of parish-minister, a frequent practice in Scotland" (*SHM* II, 534), Kames was committed to producing an original history of Scottish and English jurisprudence that develops in the same direction. His more complicated point is that historical development occurs in each region according to geographically specific speeds.

In the end, "the mildness with which the Highlanders have been treated of late and the pains that have been taken to introduce industry among them . . . [has] rendered them the most peaceable people in Scotland" (*SHM* II, 493). But before this, the Highland anomaly must fail as an aberration internal to English civility, stuck in a past stage that all the rest of Europe has already passed beyond. The "due subjection" of the last European savage does not arrive until "after the rebellion of 1745" (*SHM* II, 352). This "subjection" is said not only to enforce the state's "promot[ion of] industry" but also to "provide a sovereign remedy against mobs and riot, diseases of a free state" (*SHM* II, 504). From a savage state, "people improve by degrees" (*SHM* I, 74). Moreover, they do so by thinking on the order of barter precisely in the temporal terms suited to both capitalist markets and conjectural thought: by "promising an equivalent at a future time [according] to the standard for comparing goods . . . [or the] comparative value of commodities" (*SHM* I, 76); the founding of a "national character [means] . . . we reject with disdain the notion of chance, and perceive intuitively that effects so regular and permanent must be owing to a constant and invariable cause" (*SHM* I, 30). The specific version of probability being proposed mirrors the commitment of the conjectural historian tracing the "gradual progress of sense, from its infancy among . . . savage . . . degeneracy." This is put by Kames in commercial terms as the "probability of gain" (*SHM* I, 68–69).[167] But "gain" also designates a way to keep history moving forward along rational stadial lines.

In order to underscore a certain conflict between geography and historical progress, it is important to emphasize once again that Kames shares with other stadial historians the idea that Scotland arrives belatedly to the commercial stage of modern civilization. All of the historians we have been addressing are aware of this slippage of time. In that sense, to keep the commercial register at hand, Scotland must be coaxed forward into European modernity, in effect, toward the end of its own history. Seen as a historical remnant within Great Britain proper, it threatens to retain too much "complex[ity]" to pass the capitalist test of "comparative value." The unusual proximity of past and present in the case of the savage Highlands, Scotland's nonsynchronous identity with England after union, is manifest in geographically resistant terms. There is not—or not yet—in the middle part of the eighteenth century the shared commercial future Kames imagines of abstract equivalence where local customs are subsumed by so-called universal ones alleged to be arriving just around the historical bend. "One nation," Kames allows, "may have arrived at the supposed perfection of society, before another has advanced beyond the savage state" (*SHM* II, 366). Following Immanuel Wallerstein's account of uneven development, Cairns Craig in *Intending Scotland* (*IS*) refers to geographic variability as giving over instead to a new form of temporal heterogeneity. Craig calls this, "the subordination of geography to history," which seeks to "assimilate backward Scots to the culture of progressive England" (*IS* 208).

As we have been saying, northern Scotland was commonly regarded as containing the last of Europe's "savage and untamed" groups (*IS* 9). In the important sense that the Highlanders were the first—indeed, the only—*contemporary* Europeans to be regarded as savages, Scotland represents a temporal abnormality, a state of stadial retardation that threatens human progress with a peculiar sort (to recall Hume's word) of *durability*.[168] With Hume's "permanent minefield" of popular contention in mind, such an anomaly was capable of cropping up suddenly *within*, not simply *against*, the otherwise civilized condition of Great Britain proper. As Pocock (in *Barbarism and Religion*, hereafter *BR*) reminds us, "it is a paradox to meet 'primitive' peoples in modern history" (*BR* IV, 157). Indeed, the word "civilization" was not an analytically useful concept until the middle of the eighteenth century.[169] Pocock rightly surmises that stadial historians place the savage "outside history" (*BR* IV, 175). But he also notes within the Scottish school a "relative dynamism" between the stages of history, such that the "'barbarian' . . . ceased being an 'other' and became an outright origin of the self" (*BR* II, 263). We would develop this dynamism as internal to the emerging centralization of British national consciousness and give it a role that troubles conjectural history in a way that is connected to popular Jacobitism.

The final point we need to make is that the historical idea of multiple trajectories of development also allows for the prospect of insurgency as the revenge of geography—a reassertion of space over time—against so-called natural development put in stadial (if also carefully differentiated) terms.[170] Pocock notes that a key feature of the so-called barbarian as "unspecialized man" was his propensity to form militias (*BR* III, 399). As such, "clan spirit" was not only an ancient problem, brought up close in the form of Britain's perceived internal border, but it was also a perplexingly current one. Because it was still current, Highland valor did not fit retrospectively into a historical narrative based upon stadial change. To put Scotland on the developmental track at a speed appropriate for catching up to European modernity, Kames proposes a kinship for "our Highlanders" (whether the possession indicated by the word "our" is Scots or British is unclear) with the "Ancient Germans" (*SHM* II, 352). Notably, for the ancient Germans, wealth was commensurate with war booty.[171]

But there is a critical difference between Scots and German *ancientness*. The "clan-spirit" of the Highlanders, their propensity according to Kames for "open war," for meting out justice "privately by depredations and reprisals," in short, their "martial spirit," lingers in ambivalent ways as a contemporary communal force that raised as much anxiety as admiration among eighteenth-century conjectural historians. Displaced by southern landowners during the clearances that came after the "Forty-Five," Highlander emigration was made possible in large part as a result of their enlistment in the army, this time on the side of the British *imperium*.[172]

The association of war as replete with ancient virtue and, equally, as threatened by modern forms of luxury and the progress of stadial history as such was thus a complicated one. This was due precisely to the fact that the "martial spirit" of the Highlander was—in very recent memory—both connected to an expressly anti-British cause as well as capable of being put to good use in the expansion of empire. The curious transformation of the Highlander from a "savage," unpolished, and retrograde brute to an example of ancient virtue worth preserving depended on how past communal bonds and distant heroic actions could be accounted for in a historically useful way. It depended on whether or not the virtues of war could serve to transcend the ephemeral social relationships of commercial society without exactly rejecting them.

As James Macpherson's infamous *Poems of Ossian*, which were published between 1760 and 1763, would show, if the martial spirit could not be identified within the extant historical record, then conjectural history could serve well enough to entertain its mere invention. Here Ossian's near 10,000 lines on the supposed wars of Fingal in the third century served as both a chronicle and a celebration of old-fashioned martial valor against new-fangled British greed.[173] In reflecting on the ancient Scots and Picts, Smith notes that these "two nations, who as we see from the poems of Ossian, were much the same state as the Americas" (*LJ* A, 239). "What a perfect uniformity of character do we find in all the heroes described by Ossian," Smith declares in an early draft of *Wealth* ("EDWN" 573). Though at other times suspicious of their authenticity as was his general wont, Hume wrote a letter of introduction to the publisher Strahan on behalf of their publication. Johnson was quick to call Macpherson a "mountebank"; but the ideals of martial virtue were so fittingly conformed to the stadial models proposed by Ferguson and Kames that a certain nostalgic primitivism could well enough pass the test of historical logic. Though serious criticism of Ossian as "mere modern compositions" occurred among Scottish antiquaries as early as 1766, the Highland Society of Edinburgh did not declare Macpherson's so-called discovery a historical fraud until 1805.[174]

Kames can be noted as being particularly vocal in proclaiming Ossian "the most celebrated bard in Caledonia, as Homer was in Greece" (*SHM* I, 216). But, in fact, Kames was more than a little cagey as to whether or not Ossian was an imagined rather than an actual historical figure. He carefully preserves— albeit within the specific confines of probability—the role of imagination in how tradition ought to be remembered. "I willingly give all advantages to the unbeliever," he writes. But

> Supposing the author of Ossian to be a late writer, adorned with every refinement of modern education; yet, even upon that supposition, he is a miracle, far from being equaled by any other author ancient or modern. (*SHM* I, 216)

And since "miracles" are clearly not the stuff of the conjectural method,

> [T]he absurdity [of fraud] is so gross, that we are forced, however reluctantly, to believe, that these manners are not fictitious, but in reality the manners of his country, colored perhaps, or a little heightened, according to the privilege of the epic poet. And once admitting that fact, there can be no hesitation in ascribing the work to Ossian. (*SHM* I, 216)

The next move, as Kames struggles to make the myth of Ossian serviceable to eighteenth-century historical "belief," is the decisive one—a close reading—which evokes the *qualitative* measurements of literary judgment we described in reference to the novel's excessively *quantitative* "numbers": "What shall we conclude upon the whole? For the mind cannot forever remain in suspense. As dry reasoning has left us in a dilemma, taste perhaps and feeling may extricate us." He continues, "let a man choose either side" (*SHM* I, 217–218).

The point here is less whether or not Ossian is an actual historical figure than whether or not Macpherson's poems preserve the "martial spirit" for a specifically contemporary purpose. That contemporary purpose is to perpetuate memories that allow historians to view humanity "on the whole," and therefore not divided by a different history of "savage" Highland culture—never mind of Jacobitism—that would otherwise require a "man [to] choose either side." But before we use the word "history" here in a way too definitively divided from literary kinds of evaluation, a process of specialization that the Scottish historical school was only beginning to forge, we need to keep in mind Hugh Blair's endorsement of the Ossian poems as the dean of Scottish letters and doyen of good taste, chair of rhetoric and belles lettres at the University of Edinburgh from 1762–1783. Like Smith, Kames, and the rest of the Edinburgh literati, Blair was a member of the Poker Club, whose purpose among others was to stir up support for a Scottish militia. Blair's 1763 treatise, *A Critical Dissertation on the Poems of Ossian*, upheld the work's authenticity against Johnson's and other's dismissals. It was attached to every edition of Ossian published after 1765 in order to give the work credibility.

Kames makes a rhetorical shift in his own evaluation of Ossian that Blair would clearly appreciate, as he admits to a subjective understanding of the past according to the qualitative logic—fully embedded within conjectural history—of good literary taste. The "whole" to which Kames refers in *Sketches on the History of Man* is clearly a notional one of the history of "man," of modern, commercial, and in a more occulted way, of *British* "man," or of man so regarded as British by being compared the world over with the current state of things following the pacification of the Highlands. This is clearly not "man" riddled by the specifically martial complexities of British versus Scottish conflict—a too proximate and less usable past than what is presently offered with Ossian. This "wholeness" is achieved according to a temporal strategy, one that settles the agency of fortune and reversal attendant to war at the level of "feeling," of a more benign and appreciable ancientness, whose purpose is to ensure that the warrior spirit no longer goes wrong and delivers us from a specifically national form of anxiety, writ here as "suspense."

It is revealing that Kames supported the "subjugation" of the Highlanders for reasons of putting them to the task of "industry" while also lamenting the loss of Scotland's unique proficiencies in "the art of war" (*SHM* II, 501). In accordance with the Poker Club that we mentioned above regarding Hugh Blair, he and his cohort carried on the (unsuccessful) advocacy for a Scottish militia that was originally vetoed by the English parliament in 1708. Kames hoped that "in every shire a special commission [would] be given to certain landholders of rank and figure, to raise recruits out of the lower classes, selecting always those who are the least useful at home" (*SHM* II, 504). Commensurate with the "benevolence" Kames wished for as the basis for a unified national consciousness, he also hoped that the arts of war, patriotism, soldierly comradeship, and self-sacrifice would provide the necessary counterpoints to "the pernicious[ness] [of] a commercial state . . . , [where] every accident makes him totter" (*SHM* I, 333).

Let us recall Fielding here, too. As Tom Jones wanders toward Bristol from Somersetshire, his encounter with a military company heading southward after defeating "the rebels of the '45 rebellion" gives the eighteenth-century novel's arch-hero a chance to exhibit "some heroic ingredients in his composition."[175] Fielding is cited approvingly by Kames. And for both, the problem of luxury is written up as of special concern regarding the mobility and manners of "the lower ranks" (*SHM* II, 426), one that could be treated with a hardy dose of patriotism. Tom's warm embrace of—as well as his eventual service to—"the glorious cause of liberty, and the Protestant religion," is an appropriate case in point.[176]

Kames pondered the political consequences of how money disturbs older hierarchies. And like Johnson, he connected the good fortune of luxury to the appeal for popular rights expressed by the Wilkes Riots. Mere "private interest . . . [and] selfish gratification" is for Kames "the voice of the multitude" (*SHM* II, 426). He thus worried mightily about "overflowing riches unequally distributed," and how this form of inequality "multipl[ies] artificial wants beyond all bounds" (*SHM* III, 780). The inequities inherent to a market economy, which would have been especially apparent in Scotland in the years following 1688, as well as those immediately following union in 1707, concerned Kames as potentially corrupting on all fronts. The rise of the tobacco barons in Scottish ports after the lifting of the Navigation Act produced previously unseen disparities of wealth. Although Smith endorsed livable wages—"a gradual descent of fortunes betwixt these great ones and others of the least and lowest fortunes" (*LJ* A, 196)—he also insisted that it "would be detrimental to crush . . . overgrown fortunes" (*LJ* A, 197). Too much money concentrated in too few hands is thought by Kames to "foster luxury, sensuality, and selfishness, which are commonly gratified at the expense even of justice" (*SHM* III, 780), which should be held in check, as Smith would agree, by moral rather than material means. Moreover, too wide a gap between rich and poor threatened to "eradicate patriotism"; and Kames continues in no uncertain terms, remarking, "the decline of a nation prevails from the corruption of affluence" (*SHM* III, 780).

The paragraphs following this string of indictments against unfettered commercial society allow us to further develop the link between wealth's corruption of private morals and the related need for state security and property laws. Smith's stadial narrative bringing "mankind . . . before civil society" through the four stages of social and economic development in *Jurisprudence* is well known. What we want to emphasize in particular is that for Smith one of the ills of the natural state is that equality of property equals the prevalence, if not the permanence, of social (or pre-social) violence that he equates with "war" (*LJ* B, 397).

In "a barbarous state," which is the time of hunters where there is "properly no government at all . . . , there are perpetual wars" (*LJ* B, 522). Smith notes that in the second stage of development, which initiates the "appropriation of herds and flocks . . . [,] inequality of fortune" is also introduced. Moreover, episodes of indiscrete violence take on a particular form as a war against the inequities of property: "[T]il there be property there can be no government, the very end of which is the secure wealth, and defend the rich from the poor" (*LJ* B, 406). But Smith does not want to see war simply go away. "The bad effect of commerce," he writes, "sinks the courage of mankind and tends to extinguish the martial spirit." Given "the arts of luxury, [men] grow effeminate and dastardly" (*LJ* B, 540). Characteristically among the stadial historians, Smith chastises "the rich" for "not tak[ing] the field . . . [,] making it necessary to employ mercenaries and the dregs of people to serve in war" (*LJ* B, 412).

As we have said, the unique position of Scotland as lagging behind the contemporary historical stage of capitalist development means at the same time that some Scots have retained a right, however problematic Scottish historians found it, to popular resistance and extra-parliamentary forms of anti-governmental hostility. Hume sees this in 1549 as "the populace began to rise . . . against enclosures" (*HE* III, 371–373). And Hume's concern about Puritan leveling and popular Jacobitism run along the same lines. The sources of disorder under King James VI and I are based on his precarious "support [of] the martial spirit of the Scots" (*HE* III, 208). The "turbulent aristocracy" under James kept the Highlanders in particular "perpetually in a warlike posture" (*HE* III, 349).

Smith further codified the association of Scottish historical backwardness with violence by nonstate actors, suggesting, "if barbarous nations be in the neighborhood, they [the civilized states, England] can employ them as soldiers at an easier rate . . . as the Dutch did in Scotland" (*LJ* B, 415). He makes the statement in 1766, a time when Highland troops were being used to expand and secure the British colonies in exactly this way. Smith is clear that the sluggish improvement of "cultivation by tenants of steel bow . . . [,] still remains in some parts of the highlands of Scotland" (*LJ* B, 464).

That barbarous-ness was *still* "in the neighborhood" during Smith's time had two consequences that ran counter to each other. First, there was the recognition that commercial society may well create conditions where the security of property might be threatened by capitalism's very success. The rich were suffering from the corrupting influences of luxury, which made them incapacitated as warriors, leaving war to the vulgar, or worse, the mob. Second, even though the security of property was initiated in the second stage of social development, so-called war among the people remains a liability, directed in later historical states at the rich by the poor. Such violence must be civilized and channeled, as Hume and Smith hoped against hope it would be after 1688, on behalf of a commercially oriented, centralized state. Smith writes, "whenever commerce is introduced to any country, probity and punctuality always accompany it." In the same passage, he remarks that the English exhibit these traits "more so than the Scots" (*LJ* B, 539). On the historical stage, Scotland was any thing but *punctual*. Hume's remark about "popular rage" producing a "permanent minefield," which is either buried within history in some "latent" form or about to break out as "surprise," comes home in the depletion and ambivalent promotion of the "martial spirit."

This ambivalence can be seen in both Smith and Hume on the issue of the "right of resistance," which as Hume says, is "possessed by every subject" ("OOC" 469). Smith too is convinced that resistance to Charles I and James II was justified. He notes with some trepidation "during the Civil War and usurpation of Cromwell it became a question [of] how far it is lawful to resist the power of government [given] the popular doctrine that the king is only a steward" (*LJ* B, 429). Moreover, he is of the opinion that "at the revolution . . . the Stuart family was set aside, for excellent reasons," namely, because "the court party believed the king to be absolute" (*LJ* B, 429). As Hume remarks, "it became necessary to oppose them with some vehemence," though he also cautions that this must be "admitted [only] in extraordinary emergencies," and that "I [Hume] always incline on their [the government's] side."[177] In spite of the fact that "there is [still] some risk of revolution" after the so-called bloodless one of 1688, and even though "subjects must have a right of resistance," Smith insists that "it cannot *now* be so" (emphasis ours, *LJ* A, 316).

This argument against the *immediacy* of resistance is based on the latest advancement of jurisprudence precisely to curb the people's involvement with internal wars. By suturing "the principle of authority [with] the principle of common or general interest," a balance between "the government in general [and] the security and independence of each individual" was said to be established, even if that balance proved to be unsuccessful when individuals gathered in riotous ways. Moreover, there is a propriety in obeying and an unreasonableness in disobeying for Smith (*LJ* A, 318). Such is "the governableness of our nature," once made that way by the twin advances of civil society and a property-based development of the law (*LJ* B, 543). Hume similarly contrasts past infractions of tyranny with the immediate sense of government—or more precisely, against acting with a sense of *immediacy*—by insisting on the effective use of "habit" for obedience to the law. We might therefore simply call Hume and Smith's governmental subject, as they both argue against resistance "now," an appropriately *mediated* one, in the sense that resistance should not happen at the present time.

History itself plays a role in that mediation, and in the lessons it teaches both for and against past episodes of popular violence: "Republican writers," which both Hume and Smith abhor, are "not justified by history of experience, in any age or country in the world."[178] History has both a macro- and a microcosmic application, once we see its connection to Hume's philosophy of so-called *mediate* knowledge. On the topic of governments, it applies in the macrocosmic sense to the history of England, if not "the world," which as Hume has made clear, narrates the stages whereby the "fury of the multitude" is banished after William (or more specifically, with the Riot Act, by Queen Anne). And history applies in the microcosmic sense of the subject making itself governable on similarly temporal grounds by way of "habitual, and . . . voluntary, and therefore *precarious* acquiescence" (emphasis ours, "OOC" 469).

We emphasize the word "precarious" to indicate the way in which Hume and Smith had to admit while denuding the right of resistance from whatever applications it may have had (or better, *was* having) in their own day. This is why both of them go out of their way to take issue with Hobbes's idea of a people's contract with the sovereign, choosing to rely on subjectivized—and therefore, *mediated*—forms of "governability" (Smith's word), than merely juridical ones. To quote again from Hume on habit, "Obedience or subjection becomes so familiar, that most men never make any enquiry or origin about its cause." And, again with the emphasis on historical instruction, he writes, "as soon as they learn, that . . . their ancestors have, for several ages, or from time immemorial, been subject to a form of government . . . [,] they immediately acquiesce."[179] In this way, memory turns into governmental "habit," once the "learning" is appropriately done. Hume tells us that this is precisely what Hobbes leaves out by assuming the dangerous proposition that "the people . . . are the source of all power and jurisdiction" ("OOC" 468). If that was so, then they could take violence into their own hands against government at any given moment. Such a moment, where "a continued violence *was* committed in the crown" (emphasis ours), as is the Stuart case in point, may be finally put to rest as a part of a bygone past.

The "original contract" that Hume assigns to Hobbes "preceded the use of writing and all the other civilized arts of life" ("OOC" 468). It preceded, to use the term again, *mediation*, historiography, the more effective contributions to governability than mere laws can provide. "While the subjects have tacitly reserved the power of resisting their sovereign" ("OOC" 466), Hume prefers the philosopher's prerogative—we called this before, after Hume, the "indifference"—of "hesitation . . . [,] reserve," and "derision against the multitude . . . , [who] are altogether unfit as judges."[180] Regarding "the tragical death of Charles,"

Hume reluctantly confesses, "if ever, on any occasion, it were laudable to conceal the truth from the populace; it must be confessed, that the doctrine of resistance affords such an example" (*HE* V, 544).

Both Hume and Smith concede that such Hobbesian eruptions of the people's rage are never fully out of the question in the unknowable future, as important as it is for the lower orders to think otherwise. Hume remarks about "the claims of the banished [Stuart] family," that "I fear [they] are not yet antiquated: and who can foretell, that their future attempts will produce no greater disorder?"[181] And because social disorder is never fully pacified in the form of its becoming an "antique," it *may* also be here "now," if in ways philosophy cannot admit. If Hume's desire to "conceal the truth from the populace" is to be taken at all seriously, then clearly the vulgar must be prohibited from the history that Hume also admits they have made. He prefers that "the doctrine of obedience alone ought to be inculcated" over "the doctrine of resistance," and that "history supply examples . . . for the future . . . against resistance and dethroning" (*HE* V, 544).

Smith similarly remarks, "no government is quite perfect, but it is better to submit to some inconveniences than make attempts against it" (*LJ* B, 435). But as we have seen, Hume's primary philosophical point is that foreknowledge is never on firm ground. Thus too, for Smith, even in the epoch of civil society, or more accurately, because of it, "many more laws and regulations," and "punishment with the utmost rigor" are necessary. Only in this way can we be sure to "secure the property of the rich from the inroads of the poor," who would otherwise proceed "by open violence" (*LJ* A, 208, 210). The "inconveniences" remarked upon by Smith are liable to intensify given either tyranny or a persistent disparity of wealth. The resulting violence Smith identifies must find another channel of expression, one that supports commerce, secures property, and is monopolized by the state, while holding the spoiling effects of capitalist luxury in check. This explains the interest in recovering the lost virtues of the "martial spirit."

It is interesting to note the historical correspondence between antiluxury polemical literature and times of war and economic duress during the eighteenth-century. The War of the Spanish Succession, the South Sea Bubble, the War of Austrian Succession, the "Forty-Five," the Seven Year's War, the American Revolution, and the French Revolution were events concurrent with bursts of anxiety over the problem of commercial consumerism.[182] The antagonism between luxury and state security is implied above by Kames's use of the word "justice."

The problem is that Kames believed British state security and the preservation of the "arts of war" among Scotsmen could exist together as a patriotic form of restraint against the base self-interests of a market economy. He sees Jacobitism as objectionable in this context insofar as it became subordinate to the pursuit of career political advancement in its final—least insurgent—guise. A former Jacobite turned conservative Whig, Kames mourns the abandonment of patriotic honor, trumped as it appeared to him to have been by mere parliamentary politics after the defeat of the "Forty-Five." Having abandoned insurgency once and for all, "the Jacobites . . . had no view but to obtain justice [for] themselves. . . . [They] made no great difficulty," he scoffs, "to swallow oaths to the present government" (*SHM* III, 782). Ironically, what is being grieved for here—the abandonment of the "martial spirit" for shortsighted personal gain—has been lost because of the same advancement of commercialism that stadial history is otherwise written to support. But what was being supported instead of unrestricted commercialism—that is, martial virtue—is what stood in the way of modernity up to the Battle of Culloden in the first place.

Faced with the frustrating confrontation between riches and the "arts of war," Kames finally offers a Panglossian response to the open question of whether or not luxury can be checked by "martial spirit," and if not, whether a market-based society can continue to exist without inadvertently spawning violence from the majority of people either pushed to its margins or swept up by its greed. About a future state of what could not yet be called class war, Kames for once *refuses* to "indulge in conjecture" (*SHM* II, 556). Indeed, it is here that he insists upon the limits of linear temporal intelligence, and curbs the appeals of historical probability, by playing the trump card of self-imposed human ignorance: the providential plan of historical progress. Oddly, when it comes to thinking about the future of unrestrained commercialism, Kames refuses to think about whatever stage of apparent disaster might follow the insurrectionary one that he has written his history against.

Relying upon the "dispensations of Providence," Kames goes beyond epistemology and toward theodicy in order to find a way *not* to conjecture about a future stage of commercialization as it proceeds toward what he alludes may be its ultimately tragic course. "As men ripen in the knowledge of causes and effects," he writes, "the benevolence as well as wisdom of a superintending Being become more and more apparent. How pleasing is that operation! . . . How salutary is it for man, and how comfortable, to rest on the faith that whatever is, is best!" (*SHM* II, 370). Kames introduces here a weak theodicy, however "comfort[ing]," however emphasized by exclamatory punctuation, in place of conjectural history, once the stadial way of thinking comes up against a future that restores violence to the "people," once commercialism has run its course. In that sense, the reliance on providence becomes a way for this conjectural historian to refuse to do any thinking at all. Hume's suggestion that the "mine-field" of insurgency is "permanent" is perhaps truer than he or Kames could know. What Kames offers, as we will see later, quite differently from Hume, is his own version of Smith's invisible hand (about which, a good deal more in the following chapter). Against his own hopes for—and fears about—the fading "arts of war," a flicker of skepticism about society's commercial stage (critique is too strong a term) mutates into the providential "faith" in a market-based pre-carious present. Commercial outcomes are thus not only best left unplanned, left to Jupiter, to the secret machinations of the market, and to a silent God, but they must apparently also be left unattended by the hubris of human thought.

There is another aspect of Kames's ambivalent interest in the "martial spirit" that we should develop. This will underscore the permanence of war within stadial histories where the highest stage depicted is the commercial one. Earlier we noted that examples of Jacobite associations with ancient Israel are easily found in the eighteenth century, and that this was true for supporters of the exiled Stuarts, such as Lord Belhaven in the tearful melodrama performed dur-ing the dissolution of the Scottish parliament, as well as for anti-Jacobites like Fielding, Robertson, and now Kames, who all wrote in support of union. We also noted, following Pittock, the uniquely Scottish version of the Jewish pro-phetic tradition, focused on cataclysm, exile, and earthly struggle. "The per-verse Jews claimed God almighty as their tutelar deity," Kames concludes in his *History*, "in the vulgar acceptation of the term" (*SHM* III, 816). The word "tutelar" entered the English language in the early sixteenth century, and origi-nates from the Latin *tutela*, which literally means "keeping," as in holding onto something resistant to historical change. The word of course also has clear con-nections with "tutelage," a term connected to sovereignty, as in being protected under the king's (or thinking here of Mary and Elizabeth, the queen's) tutelage.

We see further in this passage from Kames that what is at stake in this term is the question about whose protector God is: the "vulgar," or as it turns out, the propertied classes. But at issue as well is not simply *who* can claim God's tutelage, but more importantly *when* and *where* such tutelage might go into effect. We see here the same combination of spatial problems with temporal solutions that we identified with regard to Scotland's savage immanence in relation to England.

Regarding *when* God's tutelage might be manifest, Kames puts the question in terms of who has the better—he calls it the most "pure" (*SHM* III, 816)—rendition of prophecy. The way in which Kames answers this question about *time*, or unknowable time, is to suppress certain *spatial* realities, and this is what we mean to propose by the idea of the revenge of geography mentioned above.

As revealed in the burning of a Jewish effigy in Southwark in 1749, the so-called Jew Bill, which received royal assent to naturalization in 1753, created extreme hostilities in the metropolitan commercial centers where Jewish hawkers appeared openly in the marketplace.[183] While he may have held the value of religious toleration, Kames rejected the Jewish notion of God's justice because it connected too concretely with worldly concerns. He dismisses their idea of salvation from exile—of being without land or property—because it is too literal, too much of this earth. "The Jews," Kames continues,

> "[in] their groveling and impure notion of a tutelar deity . . . believed there was
> a prophecy . . . that the Messiah would come among them in person to restore
> their kingdom. The Christians gave a different sense to the prophecy, namely,
> that the kingdom promised was *not of this world*." (emphasis ours, *SHM* III, 816)

As we mentioned, there will be more discussion about how such a commitment to the unearthly (and unknowable) plans of providential order is connected to political oeconomy by Smith in the following chapter. For now, our more limited point is to see how futurity, how the speculative mode of stadial history, is ambivalently connected to tension between commercial society and the arts of war.

Again from Kames, "that untractable race [the Jews; but the Greeks are similarly impugned] did not adhere to the purity of the institution [of worship]: they insensibly degenerated into the notion that their God was a *mercenary being*" (emphasis ours, *SHM* III, 843). So the "vulgar" prophetic tradition is linked to war, the more "pure" tradition is not. But this is too simple a way to read Kames: The God of providence is less a God of peace than one of silence, the God who does not take sides, especially about inequality on earth and in the *immediate* sense of the "now." Quite literally, as we have seen in Robertson and Kames's endorsement of the patronage system for the Scottish clergy, this too is the God of private property. The founding paradox in Kames is that the very system his God protects is the source of his original worry.

To sum up how the prophetic tradition is connected to war, especially as this exists within the Scottish school of conjectural history, Pocock's classic work, *The Machiavellian Moment* (hereafter *MM*), is useful. In the vein we have been following above, he compares how time was made intelligible according to the ways in which differing philosophies of *virtù* and *fortuna* produce specific versions of historical self-understanding.[184] The reason Machiavelli is key in Pocock's still-important argument is the unique way in which virtue and fortune confront one another as a political rather than a religious problem. In Boethius, for example, "knowledge of particulars was circumstantial, accidental, and temporal. It was based upon the sense perceptions of the knower's transitory body" (*MM* 4). Most importantly, this *body*-knowledge of fortune was "theodical rather than political," and "philosophical and contemplative rather than political and active" (*MM* 38). By contrast with theodical notions of temporality, Machiavelli's new Prince, like Hume's Elizabeth, is a political innovator: Virtue is defined as colluding with fortune and is therefore placed outside the norm.

Machiavelli's ruler-as-innovator cultivates the exposure to chance as a strategic enterprise entirely wrapped up with the security of—or insurgency against—the state. Such a unique collusion between virtue and fortune harkens back to an earlier (and Italian) meaning of the former term as having knowledge or expertise, and not simply having moral turpitude. This stands in sharp contrast to Kames's ambivalent stance on the relation between martial virtue and capitalist luxury. As Pocock argues, "the science of the behavior of actors" is defined, according to Machiavelli, "by the power they possess." The confrontation between virtue and fortune here becomes "a strategic problem" (*MM* 166), which Kames will render silent in name of a providential God. "Prophets," Pocock reminds us, "require swords because they are innovators" (*MM* 171). But as we have seen, Kames's God is not only armless but passive as well.

While he does not offer a reading of Kames, Pocock does mention the similar peculiar status of Ferguson's *History of Civil Society*. Ferguson, a Gaelic-speaking Highlander and chaplain to the Black Watch in 1745, though on the side of the British government, is rightly singled out as "the most Machiavellian of the Scottish disquisitions of this theme [of pessimism about commercial society]" (*MM* 499). Ferguson's stadial history argues for the "movement from a warrior society marked by primitive virtue [and] intense solidarity toward a state of commerce, refinement, and humanity" (*MM* 499). By alluding to the importance of martial virtue, an essential philosophical concern of stadial history, Pocock opens a way to reexamine the linear features of that kind of narrative: specifically, how conjectural thought may—or more likely, *may not*—be extended into the future.

Ferguson, too, anxiously contemplates the disparity of riches.[185] And like Kames and others, he offers in his *History of a Civil Society* (hereafter *HCS*) what we can now see are comments that are standard within stadial history regarding the savage and time: "The condition of the savage . . . is not any permanent station but a mere stage," he writes (*HCS* 14). "The Caribees . . . study no science, and go in pursuit of no general principles" (*HCS* 88). And characteristically, "the wild man caught in the woods . . . always lived apart from his species. . . . [He is] a singular instance, not a specimen of any general character" (*HCS* 9). The idea that savagery is part of a general human condition—both a part of the species past, and for the West Indies, North America, and more problematically within Great Britain, very much of the present—is a point we have already made. The more curious aspect of Ferguson's history is that the generalizing abilities the savage lacks are precisely the ones the historian must develop. In the paragraphs just preceding his pitch to solve a temporal anomaly of savage underdevelopment with a species solution of including the "wild man" within a category of "mankind," Ferguson offers certain caveats and qualifications about the writing of history itself.

The division of man into a universal species is as important as the eventual divisions established between novels and history, as Ferguson warns us not to "confound the provinces of imagination and reason, of poetry and science" (*HCS* 8). "The natural historian thinks himself obliged to collect facts, not to offer conjectures" (*HCS* 8), he continues; and elsewhere, when

> we have no record . . . [,] we are often tempted into these boundless regions of ignorance or conjecture. . . . We are the dupes of subtlety, which promises to supply every defect of our knowledge, and, by filling up blanks in the story of nature, pretend to conduct our apprehension nearer to the source of existence. (*HCS* 12)

What is curious about Ferguson's skepticism about "filling up blanks" with "mere conjectures" (*HCS* 76) is that the risks to adequate historical knowledge are the same for the historian as they are for humanity as it moves precariously through its historical stages. As we will see, unlike Kames, Ferguson is willing in spite of certain caveats about the imagination to take precisely those risks in surmising a future, however grim, for commercial society.

What is provocative in Ferguson's narrative is that the state of savagery in even the most advanced stages of social development is never completely relegated to the bygone past and may be nearer in the future than most conjectural historians would be willing to say. Ferguson's history is very much of the present.

And as we shall see, it opens up to the same catastrophic future against which Kames conjured providence to keep beyond our historical ken. Ferguson is explicit in emphasizing the martial characteristics of the savage, which he does not want to see diminished by the single-minded pursuit of luxury and wealth:

> If both the earliest *and* the latest accounts collected from every corner of the earth represent mankind as assembled in troops and companies . . . [and] employed in the exercise of recollection and foresight; . . . these facts must be admitted as the foundation of all our reasoning relative to man. (emphasis ours, *HCS* 9)

It is unclear whether or not the "affection" Ferguson finds in making "troops" a permanent feature of the human species is an evocation of the "martial spirit" in an exclusive sense. Indeed, Ferguson goes out of his way several paragraphs before to disagree with Hobbes, who "made the state of nature to consist in perpetual wars" (*HCS* 8). Ideally, and in keeping with the general tenets of Scottish moral philosophy that run from Hutcheson through Smith and Hume, mankind has a "mixed disposition [of] friendship or enmity" (*HCS* 9). His reason alone keeps him balanced toward the former and is the way in which the stages of human development move ahead through history from one stage to the next.

Still, regarding historical knowledge, and in particular, those risks we identified as implicit within conjectural reasoning, trouble for Kames emerges in precisely a Hobbesian way. This is so, in the first instance, in the case of Hobbes's key figure: the *multitudo*. The multitude for Hobbes (*On the Citizen*, hereafter *OC*), or what is sometimes translated as the "crowd," is a temporal problem in the literal sense. It connects past and future according to Hobbes's all-important emphasis on contractual obligations: "[A] crowd cannot make a promise or an agreement."[186] Moreover, and based on this notion of contract, state security based on private property is focused on a very *particular* danger in the so-called state of nature: "the danger [that] arises from equality" (*OC* 30). The connection between this danger is perpetual within the stadial context of emerging capitalist society insofar as poverty is perpetual: "Those who have no patrimony must not only labour to live but fight in order to labour" (*OC* 137).

Writing in the context of—and expressly against—the same Puritan civil war in England that so bothered later Scottish conjectural historians, Hobbes too sees state security against the leveling tendencies of the multitude as embedded in the issue of temporal intelligence. Indeed, Hobbes complains about being "hurried" given "the approaching war" in such a way as to disrupt the pace of his own writing (*OC* 13). Evoking the "crazy men, who got themselves a store of sacred words from reading scripture" (*OC* 136), Hobbes makes the powerful aphoristic point that "two things are necessary to a people's defense: to be *Forewarned* and to be *Forearmed*" (emphasis in original, *OC* 144). The enemy here is earthly prophecy, which we have mentioned before with Kames's remarks on ancient Jewish tradition. In the event of war, Hobbes reminds us, "military activity is like gambling" (*OC* 150). And, extending that association to the issue of stadial history, Smith uses the provocative phrase "gamesters and savages" (*LJ* B, 451). In *Leviathan* Hobbes is careful to state that "the time of Warre"—that is, of governmental risk, as well as historical underdevelopment—is significant in human relationships less for the simple fact of overt violence than for creating a situation where there is "no account of Time" (*Leviathan* 186). "Warre consiteth not in Battell only, or the act of Fighting," he continues, "the notion of Time is to be considered in the notion of Warre" (*Leviathan* 186), as well.

For Ferguson this crucial link between time and war is apparent in his discussions on historical method, and along the same lines, even approximating the vocabulary, of Hobbes. Here not only is the multitude an agent of chance but, connected to Hume, multiplicity also serves to derail the habits of linear thought: "[I]n collecting the materials of history . . . we are embarrassed with a multiplicity of particulars, and apparent inconsistencies" (*HCS* 21); and "it is the purpose of science . . . in the multiplicity and combinations of particulars . . . [to] save us from the embarrassment which the variety of singular cases might create" (*HCS* 21). The status of the "singular" case matches the "singularity" of the savage in that both need to be grouped within one or another generality, and can only be so grouped by working with time in a particular way. The anomalous historical case must be assimilated within a general linear pattern, or be rendered accidental, and ignored; the case of the savage, not yet within the fulcrum of human achievement, must be relegated to an unusable past on the same grounds of having no use for linear time.

However, for Ferguson, this loop between historical method and historical object gets broken because of his lingering interest in martial virtue and his willingness to posit an almost unthinkable *post*-commercial historical stage. This is a second instance of Hobbesian debt that we can add to the persistence of the *multitudo*. As we have seen with Smith, Hume, and Kames, the martial spirit is an archaism worth retaining because it serves a moral regulatory function where "the unequal division of wealth" and "the unequal distribution of property" is admitted, and where fortune is allowed to bestow "distinction and rank" (*HCS* 152). "Luxury," Ferguson adds in a Kamesian vein, "is ruinous to human character" (*HCS* 235). Ferguson conjoins this worry over the ruin of character, and by implication, the return of the savage warrior—Hobbes's "time of Warre"—to a projection of capitalist disaster. Unlike the other historians we have examined, "ruin" is precisely the direction Ferguson's history points his readers toward. Rather than settle on the comfort offered by Kames's faith in providence, he warns "the scenes of human life have been frequently shifted." He continues, "security and presumption forfeit the advantages of prosperity" (*HCS* 264), suggesting a future where war and the inequities of wealth are gearing up to collide.

Ironically, but appropriately given Hume's preoccupation with the prophetic thinking of the Puritans, Ferguson's history takes on a note of grim futurity. It also reasserts into immediate time a past stage of insurrection and imperial demise portended by the fall of Rome:

> When by the conquest and annexation of every rich and cultivated province, the measure of empire is full, two parties are sufficient to comprehend mankind; that of the pacific and wealthy, who dwell within the pale of empire; and that of the poor, the rapacious, and the fierce, who are inured to depredation and war. (*HCS* 262)

Ferguson thus alludes to a coming fifth stage of historical development in his stadial narrative where, following Smith's arrival at commercial civilization, civil society comes to an end: "[I]nstitutions of men . . . are, indeed, likely to have an end as well as a beginning" (*HCS* 264). There is an uncanny mixture in such a statement of past and present that responds to the precarious life of "the poor" who are, we could say, repositioned by history on the front lines. Ferguson's history presages, "no nation ever suffered internal decay but from the vice of its members" (*HCS* 264). And he leaves entirely open the question that follows: "Who was ever willing to acknowledge it in himself?" (*HCS* 264).

The blank implicit in that historical failure—it is a look back without an answer—is the space of the savage, the poor, and the insurgent—in short, a break in the history of civilization where a "time of Warre" breaks forth in the Hobbesian sense. It is also the space of imagination, which as we noted Ferguson promised to avoid as far as possible and stick to reason and science. That he could not keep that promise as indicated by the suggestion of a coming commercial apocalypse is a sign that the stadial history he proposed to write did not necessarily lead in a progressively forward direction.

In Hume's last book, he returns to the bugbear of religion, a topic that put him in trouble early in his career, bringing charges of heresy and atheism on account of his skeptical philosophical beliefs. In the last paragraph of this book, Hume shows characteristic determination to maintain his disconcerting stance. "The comfortable views exhibited by the belief of futurity," he writes, "are ravishing and delightful." But like Ferguson, Hume was not easily given to "comfort" and "delight." "But how quickly [it] vanish[es]," he continues, "on the appearance of its [futurity's] terrors, which keep a more firm and durable possession of the human mind?"

Like Ferguson, Hume leaves us with an open question, one of "doubt, uncertainty . . . [,] and the frailty of human reason" (*NHR* 87). But unlike Ferguson, the "durable" anxieties Hume mentions here—of which the "continual" "fury of the multitude" has been the most important—leave him finally in a Kamesian state of epistemic disavowal. Regarding the "irresistible contagion of opinion," regarding "fury and contention," in the last line of the final work published in his lifetime, Hume suggests that we "happily make our escape, into the calm, though obscure, regions of philosophy" (*NHR* 87). His appeal to Jupiter ought to be set alongside the more famous references (although there are only two) in Smith. Hume writes,

> The draughts of life, according to the poet's fiction, are always mixed from the vessels on each hand of Jupiter: Or if any cup be presented although pure, it is drawn only, as the same poet tells us, from the left-handed vessel. (*NHR* 85)

The reference here is to Homer, specifically, Book 24 of *The Iliad*, where Achilles continues mourning the loss of Patroclus, but finally gets control of his rage and accepts a ransom to return the defaced body of Hector, his adversary, to an equally agonized opponent Priam. Jupiter's (or here Zeus's) urns are depicted, as he "moves now in evil, [and] again in good fortune."[187]

The work of sorting through Jupiter's fortune, even if only in a mediated, contingent, or provisional way, is something philosophy, and to some degree history, is able to do well enough for Hume and his cohort. But in the final analysis, that sorting also comes up against limits in the form of everything else: those multitudes of causal factors, those multitudes that continue to "rage," those historical forces variously said to be invisible, inarticulable rendered "noise" or, simply, concealed. The further history of this concealment we leave to the following chapter.

4 "IMMUNITY, THE NECESSARY COMPLEMENT OF LIBERTY"
The Birth of Necro-Economics

Laisser Faire / Laisser Mourir I

We have already noted both the importance and the paradoxes of Smith's reading of Stoicism for his notion of self-interest. "Stoical doctrine," he wrote, was based on the notion that

> Every animal was by nature recommended to its own care, and was endowed with the principle of self-love, that it might endeavour to preserve, not only its existence, but all the different parts of its nature, in the best and most perfect state of which they were capable. (*TMS* 272)

Can Smith, then, be said to be a philosopher of the *conatus* (the endeavoring to preserve one's own existence), if not exactly in Spinoza's sense, then in Hobbes's, maintaining that individuals will always choose not only pleasure over pain, health over illness, but, above all, life over death? We have already seen that Smith, despite his praise for the pursuit of wealth and glory and his depreciation of those ascetic doctrines that demand a renunciation of the pleasures purchased by great fortunes, is no partisan of pleasure.

The passions that lead us in search of pleasure are not of a piece: Some, such as sexual desire, while contributing to the multiplication of the species, threaten to overpower and subjugate the rational passions that enjoin us to achieve the best and most perfect state possible. The virtues of self-command so important in *The Theory of Moral Sentiments* (hereafter *TMS*) ground Smith's condemnation of prodigality in *The Wealth of Nations* (hereafter *Wealth*) where the inability to govern one's tendency to seek the immediate gratification of pleasures leads to immoderate expenditure, which in turn prevents the accumulation of stock necessary to the progress of wealth. The prodigal man "perverts" capital, Smith tell us, squandering on his debauches the fund otherwise destined to employ productive labor and thus to add to the general wealth of his society (and it is here above all that Smith departs from Mandeville). Smith offers an analogy that we should take seriously: The prodigal is "like him who perverts the revenues of some pious foundation to profane purposes" (*Wealth* 339). To refuse the parsimony necessary to the accumulation of capital is to "diminish the real quantity of industry, the number of productive hands, and consequently the exchangeable value of the annual produce of the land and labor of the country, the real wealth and revenue of all its inhabitants" (*Wealth* 339).

Of course, the sacrifice that frugality demands, however disruptive of one's present pleasure, is only undertaken in order better to secure one's own existence and ensure comfort, if not pleasure, in the future, and thus whatever the degree to which it serves the interests of society as a whole, it is grounded in the individual's endeavor to preserve his own existence:

> The uniform, constant and uninterrupted effort of every man to better his condition, the principle from which public and national, as well as private, opulence is originally derived, is frequently powerful enough to maintain the natural progress of things towards toward improvement, in spite both of the extravagance of government and of the greatest errors of administration. (*Wealth* 343)

Smith repeats the phrase "natural progress" two pages later: What precisely is the meaning of "natural" here? Nothing other than the movement of capital itself, the growth of stock and savings, and the increase of its employment, arising from "the private frugality and good conduct of individuals, by their universal, continual and uninterrupted effort to better their own condition" (*Wealth* 345) separate from any government action (except that of protecting individuals in such efforts).

Although the rational form of self-betterment appears, at certain moments in *Wealth*, as quasi-universal, an impulse proper to humankind as such, it is more often in Smith's work as a whole shadowed by "perverted" or improvident forms of self-seeking in which future improvement is sacrificed to an intensity of present pleasure. Here, we refer not only to the prodigal landlord, but to that myriad of criminals who populate the pages of the *TMS*—the pickpockets, housebreakers, and horse thieves—who can hardly be restrained even by the near certainty of capital punishment. The pursuit of one's betterment then is not the outward expression of some primal drive (the reader will look in vain for the figure of *homo oeconomicus*); rather, it is the outcome of an internal struggle against the temptations of bodily pleasure, not only those usually associated with the "flesh" (which play so little role in Smith's philosophy), but those of mere comfort and ease, the pleasures of the palate and eye, or more commonly those of avoiding the exigencies of a life of hard labor.

Thus (and this too separates Smith from Mandeville), the centrality of the virtue of self-command is itself the precondition of the individual's pursuit of his own betterment in Smith's sense. For the problem is not simply the ability to command one's passions in view of a future goal, that is, of being able to imagine a future pleasure, greater than that possible in the present, which can only be achieved by deferring "immediate gratification." There is also the problem of the very limited possibility of self-betterment among the laboring poor, and the fact that their own individual actions may have little to do with determining whether or not they are employed at any given time—or a rise or fall in wages or the prices they must pay to secure their subsistence—factors that at various moments in eighteenth-century Britain could decide whether they or their family members lived or died.[1]

It is at this point that we can see another aspect of Stoicism whose importance for Smith is at least as great as that of the *conatus,* namely, the concept of providence. How can he address the fact that there is every chance that the most strenuous efforts at improvement will yield few palpable results for the laboring majority? That, for example, a modest rise in wages, which might otherwise be cause for celebration, could be rendered irrelevant by a rapid doubling of the cost of food, on which under typical conditions laborers spent half their weekly incomes?[2] It is as true of the market as of salvation: Many are called but few are chosen. To them Smith offers the following Stoic homily:

> If we ourselves, therefore, were in poverty, in sickness, or in any other calamity, we ought first of all to use our utmost endeavors, so far as justice and duty to others would allow, to rescue ourselves from this disagreeable circumstance. But if, after all we could do, we found this impossible, we ought to rest satisfied that the order and perfection of the universe required that we should in the mean time continue in this situation. . . . The prosperity of the whole should, even to us, appear preferable to so insignificant a part as ourselves. (*TMS* 274)

Further, when we adopt the point of view of the whole, we may come to understand not only the function of our life, however impoverished and painful, in its prosperity, but also that of our death:

> Assured of the wisdom which directs all the events of human life, whatever lot befalls him, he accepts it with joy, satisfied that, if he had known all the connections and dependencies of the different parts of the universe, it is the very lot which he himself would have wished for. If it is life, he is contented to live, and if it is death, as nature must have no further occasion for his presence here, he willingly goes where he is appointed. (*TMS* 276)

If he had known, he would have wished for nothing other than what has befallen him, however painful: But he, we, in fact do not and cannot know "all the connections and dependencies of the different parts of the universe." Here the austere virtue of self-command must come to the aid of knowledge to fortify our resolve and master our terror of the grave so that we may choose the prosperity of the whole over our own survival. What is particularly notable here is the immediate relation of death to the wisdom that directs all the events of human life—not the death that arrives to conclude the maturation of an organism, but "premature," unexpected death that befalls an individual not otherwise prepared to die, a death not required by the exhaustion of the body's forces, but arriving from outside, a death solicited by the very oeconomy of human events.

Those who govern or ought to govern the events of human life already directed by a wisdom upon which it is impossible to improve and who govern wisely precisely by acknowledging and refraining from interfering with this oeconomy, as well as those who are governed in a double sense, economically as well as politically, have been led by the problem of life to the question of death. Are we then to accept a certain death, a certain kind of death, our own death or the death of a certain number of others, as one of the dependencies Smith asserts above, the condition upon which the prosperity of the whole may at a given moment depend?

We will begin to address this question by turning to one of Smith's most perceptive readers: Hegel. We want to follow Hegel's reading of Smith not where he explicitly refers to Smith in the discussion of the system of needs in the *Philosophy of Right* but in the *Phenomenology of Spirit*, where Smith is invoked but not named; it is the point where reason understands that its essence cannot exist in observation alone and that it must actualize itself. Hegel argues that reason's actualization of itself necessarily takes the form of a community (*Gemeinschaft*), the universal community, not as an ideal or even in a formal, juridical sense, but as a reality produced by concrete individuals. He is careful to note, however, that the universal is produced by individuals who not only do not labor with the aim of producing the universal community, but who on the contrary seek only to satisfy their own needs, even at the expense of others. It is at this precise point that Hegel invokes Smith, specifically Smith's concept of the market, as the concrete form of the universal:

> The *labor* of the individual for his own needs is just as much a satisfaction of the needs of others as of his own, and the satisfaction of his own needs he obtains only through the labor of others. As the individual in his *individual* work already unconsciously performs a universal work, so he again also produces the universal as his conscious object; the whole becomes, as *a* whole, his own work, for which he sacrifices himself and precisely in doing so receives back from it his own self.[3] (emphasis in original)

The reference to Smith here is clear. As he argues in *Wealth*, an individual in "a civilized society . . . stands at all times in need of the co-operation and assistance of great multitudes" (*Wealth* 26). And despite the apparent qualification introduced by the phrase "in a civilized society," Smith a few lines later posits cooperation as the necessary condition of human existence per se, going so far as to ascribe it to the natural state of the species. The individual member of "almost every other race of animals" is "entirely independent and in its natural state has occasion for the assistance of no other living creature," while the human individual remains dependent and has, for mere survival, "almost constant occasion for the help of his brethren" (*Wealth* 25). Read from Hegel's perspective then, society or community is not simply necessary for humanity's development and progress; it is necessary from the point of view of human life itself. The species cannot reproduce or even survive in the absence of cooperation. The life of the individual, for Hegel, depends upon the "life of a people" (*dem Leben eines Volks*), which furnishes "the universal sustaining medium" necessary to human life. It is thus only the "power of the whole people" (*die Macht des ganzen Volks*)[4] that confers upon the individual sufficient power to exist. In the universal there is life; in the particular only death. The term "people" should be understood here as a biological entity, the concrete form of the universal that arises in the course of the natural history of humanity and the irreducible foundation of life, human life, itself.

But if the cooperation necessary to the sustaining of life itself characterizes the life and power of a people, this cooperation itself must be explained, and it was precisely in explaining this cooperation that seventeenth- and eighteenth-century European philosophy divided into two opposing camps. Smith alludes to this division as he develops his analysis of the optimal form of cooperation. In particular, he is compelled to confront the argument that there exists in the human individual a social instinct as powerful as self-interest that drives individuals to assist others in the satisfaction of their needs with the same urgency that impels them to satisfy their own. Here, Smith's discussion of Hutcheson's moral philosophy in the *TMS* is particularly interesting. Because Hutcheson, following Shaftesbury and Butler, postulates the existence of what Smith calls an "instinctive good-will," (*TMS* 301) he is led to devalue those actions that originate from other motives, especially self-interested motives, so that, regardless of the effects of such actions, their self-interested origins deprive them of any consideration of benevolence. The latter becomes, in effect, the principle in relation to which even the mere attempt to secure one's survival, that is, the principle of self-preservation, is subject to moral condemnation.

Significantly, Smith sees Mandeville, otherwise his predecessor in so many ways, as tending merely to invert the philosophy of benevolence. The "fellow-feeling" or benevolent inclination that ought to reign over our sentiments is redefined as a base, nearly animalistic passion that the most hardened criminal feels and, given its involuntary, instinctual character, can no more be described as virtuous than the supposedly selfish passions of greed and lust. Further, greed ought to be judged by its effects rather than by its motives, and when the mass of individuals acts at the behest of the passion of greed, the effects are far superior to those of the generalized self-denial that benevolence demands. Therefore, lust and greed, if not virtuous in themselves, lead to the production not only of a prosperous world but a world that can be regarded as virtuous insofar as it will relieve the sufferings of the poor more effectively and to a far greater degree than any system of charity based on self-denial or asceticism.

For Smith, the problem is that Mandeville refers to all self-interested actions as vices (even if "private vices are public benefits"), a reduction that prevents him from distinguishing between the rational and laudable self-interest of the corn merchant seeking to maximize the return on his investment and the vicious behavior of a common thief seeking to convey another's property into his own possession, or even between the sober pleasure of witnessing the

increase of one's own wealth and the improvident enjoyments procured by immediate expenditure. Smith does not regard the "popular ascetic doctrines"
(*TMS* 313) to which Mandeville's system, as he read it, constituted a response, as
a serious threat to the prosperity of society. The social passions that he groups
together under the label of benevolence nowhere possess sufficient force to interfere with the degree of self-interest necessary to progress. The cooperation
that constitutes the necessarily universal existence of human individuals cannot be a cooperation that anyone seeks or desires; this particular form of cooperation, the only form vital to the life of a society, derives from each seeking
his own betterment at the expense of others. Precisely when individuals believe
that their actions will lead to their advantage, they act in such a way that produces the very universality that they appear to deny.

For Smith, this "veil of ignorance" that prevents individuals from knowing
the benevolent consequences of their self-interested actions is necessary to the
design of the whole.[5] Thus, individuals are governed by self-interest that they
may better serve their fellows by producing and exchanging as much as they possibly can. In the famous passage from the *TMS* that we discussed earlier, Smith
remarks of "the rich" that

> In spite of their natural selfishness and rapacity, though they mean only their
> own conveniency, though the sole end which they propose from the labors of
> all the thousands whom they employ, be the gratification of their own vain and
> insatiable desires, they divide with the poor the produce of all their improve-
> ments. They are led by an invisible hand to make nearly the same distribution of
> the necessaries of life, which would have been made had the earth been divided
> into equal portions among all its inhabitants, and thus, without intending it,
> without knowing it, advance the interest of the society and afford means to the
> multiplication of the species. (*TMS* 184–185)[6]

It is here, in relation to a passage that certainly furnished one of the major
reference points for Hegel's reading of Smith in the *Phenomenology*, that the
precise effects of Hegel's reading become clear. First, in Smith's work, the discrepancy between the intentions, knowledge, and actions of individual actors, on the one hand, and the consequences of these actions, on the other,
is as we have seen a necessary and permanent feature of society. It is in fact,
as Smith himself clearly says in the lines following the passage from the *TMS*
cited above, a political oeconomy that is part of a greater "oeconomy of nature,"
that is, a continuation in the human world of the providence that governs all

things. That "the wisdom that directs all the events of human life" is immanent in them as the internal principle of their interrelated order rather than transcendent and working through final causes emanating from a divine will does not change the providential character of the oeconomy (*TMS* 276). On the contrary, an adequate knowledge of the market's natural order demands an exact accounting of the quantity of deprivation that must be allowed to secure the prosperity of the whole: In the same way, even God, who would never create evil in order to distill good from it, may nevertheless permit a particular evil to exist (in a theological form of *laisser faire*) if a greater good than would have occurred without its existence follows from it. Is it then necessary to understand Smith's theory as a secularized providence or theodicy or, as the necessary correlative to Schmitt's notion of political theology, an economic theology (to invoke a notion recently proposed by Giorgio Agamben)?[7]

Such a view might once have seemed shocking enough to provoke the defensive reactions of neoclassical economists, or at least those among them who had any interest in the historical development of their own theories. Jacob Viner, an important policymaker in the Roosevelt administration, devoted the last years of his life to a thorough examination of the role of religion in the development of economic thought and that of Adam Smith in particular. He was compelled to do so, he argued, because modern economic theories "have been secularized to the point where the religious elements and implications which were once an integral part of them have been painstakingly eliminated."[8] According to most historians of economic thought, Viner argued, Smith's economic theory marked a kind of scientific revolution precisely insofar as it deliberately eliminated the supernatural, "religious" concerns (including such extraneous notions as morality, justice, and charity—the last once an important principle in western European societies) from its study of the laws that governed the market.

For these historians, Smith had accomplished for economic life what Copernicus, Galileo, and Newton had for physical nature, and in doing so had stirred up similar anxieties and resentments: Man is no more the center of the economic than of the physical universe, both of which are governed by immutable laws, for example, of motion or supply and demand, indifferent to the claims of morality. Viner, in opposition to this understanding of Smith, insisted that such notions, however laudable in and of themselves, did not correspond to what Smith actually said or did in his work. His writing, read carefully, can only be considered partly "naturalistic," and thus only partly allied with a new scientific worldview (which as Agamben points out was itself hardly free from providentialist elements): "It is also providentialist and teleological and is so expressly, deliberately and repetitively."[9]

Viner, not content to denounce the dominant reading of Smith as false, seeks to account for how and why it operates as it does; that is, he goes on to produce a theory of the reading of Adam Smith as it had been practiced up to his time by those economists who recognized Smith as the patriarch of the discipline (but such a reading, it must be acknowledged, was by no means restricted to them):

> If perchance Adam Smith is a hero to them, they follow one or the other of two available methods of dealing with the religious ingredients of Smith's thought. They either put on mental blinders which hide from their sight, these aberrations of Smith's thought, or they treat them as merely traditional and in Smith's day fashionable ornaments to what is essentially naturalistic and rational analysis, especially where economic matters and *Wealth* is concerned.[10]

Viner's reading of the intellectual history of economics as a pattern of overlooking or marginalizing "the religious ingredients" that shaped its own development, up to and including its most "rigorous" concepts, such as that of general equilibrium, is a striking example of what Althusser, one year before Viner's lectures, and in reference to many of the same texts, would call a symptomatic reading. We must be careful, however, not to assume that we know why the systematic denial of the otherwise strikingly obvious theological concepts and operations in Smith (to cite only his example) was necessary to the constitution of modern economic theory. After all, Smith who did not hesitate to depreciate, and not always with great subtlety, the idea of charity, could openly and, as Viner notes, "repetitively" invoke the notion of providence in his analysis of society, even if his was a natural and immanent rather than supernatural and transcendent teleology and therefore susceptible to human knowledge rather than faith, as Agamben has maintained. It is very tempting indeed to argue that the more the notion of providence became necessary to and widespread in economic reasoning—that is, the more modern economic theory tended, most often unwittingly, of course, to draw upon various available models of providence and theodicy—the less visible it became in economic writing. The distinction between Walras (and the emergence of the idea of general equilibrium)[11] and Smith, an interval of about a century, is striking in this regard. It may be, however, that if, as Odo Marquard maintains,[12] theodicy remains one of the hallmarks of modernity, in no area of knowledge is it more important than in what is now known as economics.

Indeed, Agamben's recent work on the origins of "the economic" forces us to go still further. Many scholars have traced the origins of the idea of the economic (or oeconomic) back to the works of Aristotle and Xenophon in which the administration of the οἶκος (*oikos*—household or estate) is the object of a specific kind of knowledge called οἰκονομία (*oikonomia*). It would appear, and generations of historians of economic thought have assumed, that the lineage linking these concepts to Quesnay's notion of "*gouvernement économique*," according to which the state supervises or "governs" the productive and commercial activities of an entire nation, is direct.[13] Unfortunately this particular, unquestioned narrative of genealogical development turns out to be afflicted with a blindness perhaps more serious in its effects than even the rendering invisible of the role of providence in the conception of the market.

Agamben's great merit here is to have documented with precision that for a period of two thousand years—that is, between Aristotle and Xenophon and Quesnay and Smith—the concept of *oikonomia* was used and developed primarily in the context of Christian theology where it served to denote God's supervision of his creation, that is, of providence. Several recent studies have even demonstrated its importance in the New Testament;[14] Agamben focuses particularly on its role in the origins of Christianity in the period of late antiquity. Clearly, the notion of *oikonomia* in theology is neither simply a continuation of nor a break from the pre-Christian Greek usage; its deployment in "religious" discourse, however, certainly left its mark on the concept, not only broadening it from household to cosmos but developing its internal contradictions. Why has this long and complex history been almost completely suppressed in the history of economics until relatively recently?[15] More specifically, how has the reading of Smith been shaped by the relative absence of this history?

Before we attempt to address such problems, however, we must first consider the meaning of the very act of analysis by which "religious" or theological ideas, once concealed or simply overlooked, are made visible and their influence duly acknowledged. To put it in the most concrete terms, what does it mean to say that the structure and operation of the market for Smith and his heirs is that of a theodicy, or that it is not simply derived from the conception of providence (which might suggest that it had been emptied of its theological meaning), but can function only in a universe that is itself "one immense and connected system" (*TMS* 289) governed by a superintendent wisdom? Or that the knowledge necessary to the overseeing of this providential design other-wise known as the oeconomy bears a striking resemblance to the theological notion of *oikonomia*? Further, if indeed theological constructs were (and per-haps still are) hidden and in some sense deliberately or necessarily so, why was this the case and what, in turn, is the effect of, if not the intention behind, the act of uncovering or, more precisely, unmasking them?

No one has more painstakingly explored the network of problems of which those just mentioned represent a subset, a network usually designated by the term "secularization," than Hans Blumenberg, particularly in *The Legitimacy of the Modern Age*.[16] First, Blumenberg shows clearly that the rhetoric of the-ories of secularization in its most recent sense (the term once denoted the diminishing influence of religion in the social life of modernity) can be mo-bilized to support incompatible and competing historical views. Perhaps even more to the point, the idea that modern, "secular" thought remains in fact a disguised or unacknowledged form of earlier (the chronology is crucial here), explicitly theological notions could be and in fact was mobilized for absolutely opposing political or theological-political purposes. A reactionary (or perhaps better, a counterrevolutionary) like Carl Schmitt might speak of politics in the twentieth century as an unwitting secular theology in which the question of God's kingdom was transposed into that of the earthly sovereign. The impli-cation of such an analysis, for Schmitt, was not that modern theories of sov-ereignty are derivative and therefore degraded forms of originally theological concepts, but rather that the theological and the political are finally "indisso-ciable," and secularity is perhaps no more than the self-deception of theology, the moment of its unhappy consciousness. To thus assert the fundamental con-tinuity of medieval and modern is of course to deny the specific existence of modernity, except perhaps as a kind of false consciousness (the position, as well, of another of Blumenberg's targets: Karl Löwith). To go beyond and, in a way, against Blumenberg's critique of Schmitt, we might even say that for the latter the opposition between "decisionist" and "formalist" theories of law and sovereignty was finally nothing more than the millennial (perpetual?) struggle of Christian civilization against Jewish legalism.

There exists, however, another separate and perhaps opposed use of the secularization thesis. It is often associated with the Left, but perhaps is just as frequently deployed by the Right. To illustrate this other variant, we will cite two of Blumenberg's contemporaries who, as such, do not figure in his work but who serve to illustrate his point quite precisely: Louis Althusser and Jacques Derrida.

In his contribution to the collective work *Reading Capital* (1965), Althusser begins by noting that Marx, in his reading of Smith, had to

> break with the religious myth of reading . . . the complementary religious myths
> of the voice (the Logos) speaking in the sequences of a discourse; of the Truth
> that inhabits its Scripture;—and of the ear that hears or the eye that reads this
> discourse, in order to discover in it (if they are pure) the speech of the Truth
> which inhabits each of its words in person.[17]

Here, the persistence of theological motifs in an absolutely secular guise (or disguise)—in this case, the analysis of a text as a teleological—or functional—whole, had first to be exposed in order that a genuinely scientific and therefore nontheological theory of reading would even become possible. Theological concepts persist everywhere as counterfeit secular and scientific concepts (Althusser's analysis here is an indictment of the pretensions of structuralism, for him, too often theology by other means). Accordingly, theology becomes the ultimate theoretical obstacle, that from which one must break resolutely in order to think in a new way; it is a survival, and a pernicious one at that, which waxes and wanes through history like a virus thought to be extinct but which may flare up at any time to pose a serious threat to humanity.

Derrida's analysis in *Of Grammatology* (1967), in many ways similar to that of Althusser, is at least as concerned with the unmasking of theology in realms where its presence was least suspected, such as the study of language in the mid-twentieth century. "The age of the sign is essentially theological" is a gesture that reveals the agency of the metaphysics of presence and the degradation of the world, the body, and writing in relation to the spirit in modern linguistics.

Derrida is more cautious in his estimate of the chances of escaping theology than Althusser: The age of the sign, which has the same "place and time of birth" as "divinity," may "never *end*. Its historical *closure* is, however, outlined."[18] There is, despite everything, a certain Kantianism common to both philosophers: Modernity has not yet entered into its maturity; it remains dependent on theology that belongs by definition to an earlier, decidedly pre-modern age. Modernity will assume its proper identity only when it has become independent of what has preceded it.

Needless to say, the mode of criticism that operates by unmasking and denouncing theological residues in otherwise nominally secular texts is hardly restricted to the Left: Liberals and neoliberals for a century and a half have

denounced socialist and communist movements and Marxist theory as es-
chatological, messianic, and/or redemptive (and therefore irrational). They
did so in the belief that simply to bring to light the *pudenda origo* of theology in these discourses was enough to demonstrate their groundlessness.
None other than Jacob Viner himself would produce a highly critical review of
C. B. Macpherson's *Possessive Individualism*, the central thesis of which was that
Macpherson's text was organized around a disavowed concept of original sin.[19]

For Blumenberg, these uses of the concept of secularization merely show
its inadequacy. Not only is the thought of modernity irreducible to that of the
Christian Middle Ages, but theology cannot even be said to have gone un-
derground to wage a rear-guard action against the victor in the battle of the
books. In opposition to such notions, he proposes an austere historicism that
in many respects resembles that of Dilthey, with all the problems associated
with the latter's theory. For Blumenberg, because history consists of a succession of epochs—antiquity, the Middle Ages, and modernity—the most urgent
theoretical problem is that of periodization. Between epochs there is no meaningful continuity; each bequeaths to its successor nothing more than the empty
shell of its "forms": "positions" or "questions" that the new age fills with its own
contents as well as it can. Thus, despite the appearance of the secularization of
theological concepts in the modern epoch (beginning perhaps in the sixteenth
century), there exists for Blumenberg precisely the contrary: Theological concepts have been emptied of their theological content and filled with absolutely
"worldly" contents.

It is worth noting that in 600 pages of text, Spinoza (whose formula "Deus,
sive Natura" would appear to be the perfect illustration of Blumenberg's theses)
is mentioned only briefly on two occasions. There is perhaps no need to demonstrate that Spinoza merely manipulates theological terms for absolutely
worldly purposes. More surprising and revealing is Blumenberg's discussion
of Leibniz's *Theodicy*, which explicitly claims to demonstrate "the goodness of
God, the freedom of man and the origin of evil" in response to Bayle, Malebranche, and Arnauld (the latter two names do not appear in *The Legitimacy of
the Modern Age*). Blumenberg informs the reader:

> The *Theodicy* is anything but a theological work; it could not even be the secu-
> larization of such a work, for one unmistakable reason: The vindication of God
> is, for Leibniz, the means of securing the most radical principle of the autonomy
> of philosophy that could be conceived of, the principle of sufficient reason.[20]

The vehemence of the rhetoric here is revealing and possesses the value of a symptom: "The *Theodicy* is anything but a theological work."[21] Blumenberg chooses Leibniz to demonstrate his point, but he might just as well have chosen Arnauld or Malebranche whose debate on grace formed an important part of the background to Leibniz's text: Nowhere are the theoretical costs and risks of his historicism more apparent. The seventeenth century as a whole for him "is anything but theological." The invocation of the divinity of Jesus, the question of God's grace, or original sin, despite appearances, all lack the slightest theological import. Blumenberg's historicism demands of its epochs absolute homogeneity: The controversies exhibited in each period are family quarrels that never exceed the absolute horizon of the moment, and the elements that appear to have survived from another epoch are assigned new meanings and functions by the logic of the present. This theoretical "contemporaneity" (to borrow a term from Althusser), which functions to exclude any notion of unevenness and heterogeneity, in turn can be sustained only by instituting an absolute discontinuity between historical periods: Nothing survives the transition.

The choice here is stark: Either there is no history or historical transformation, because the present can only be a repetition of the past that does not know itself as such; or, between past and present epochs there can be no communication or connection: The present is as innocent of the past (and hence legitimate) as the past is of the present. The problem here, as Husserl pointed out in relation to Dilthey's historicism, is that the very possibility of one epoch understanding another is radically called into question. Blumenberg solves the problem of intelligibility, as it was called, by insisting on the absolute, "nonnegotiable" continuity of the questions (from antiquity to modernity), which each epoch will answer in its own, absolutely original, way. In fact, he suggests, a "universal human interest" may well underlie the succession of epochs and serves as the backdrop that allows the particularity of epochs to become visible through contrast.[22]

The theoretical homogeneity of each epoch, however, is not easily achieved. In Blumenberg as in Hegel, it requires a certain labor of the negative to render Leibniz and Spinoza functionally identical, while simultaneously severing their ties to the (irreducibly different) theological discourses and traditions from which they so freely and openly draw. The evacuation of all theological significance from Leibniz's *Theodicy* is, however, predicated upon a much more ambitious operation. After all, it would appear that the *Theodicy* is at least in part a continuation of the discussions of providence that occupied Christianity from the time of its origins (and indeed, Leibniz cites Origen, Justin Martyr, and Eusebius, as well as Augustine, Aquinas, and Molina), which is to say that it might well have a closer relation to certain thinkers from late antiquity or the Middle Ages than to such contemporaries as Hobbes. Indeed, can it not be argued that the concept of providence has a history with its thresholds and mutations (many of which occur synchronically, rather than diachronically), a history separate from that of the epochs imagined by Blumenberg?

Such a threat to his scheme can only be countered with the most audacious of moves: He points out that few theoreticians of secularization have advanced a notion of secularized providence. This hesitation derives from "a quite sound though unexpressed understanding of the criterion that an element must belong originally to Christianity if it is . . . possible to speak meaningfully of its later being secularized."[23] He does not mince words: Providence is "a concept of which there is no trace in the New Testament whatsoever."[24] Christianity, it appears, contains both "native" concepts (eschatology, despite its apparently Jewish origins, is one) and those, originally foreign (pagan or Jewish), which long ago migrated or were annexed to its rightful territory. Providence within Christianity, for Blumenberg, is like a stranger who long ago appeared from a distant land to occupy (or perhaps usurp) the place of a discredited eschatology (once it was generally accepted that the End of Days was not at hand) but who refused to assimilate to his new home. Providence was the ideology of the Church's secularization, and therefore not a theology at all, the correlative in thought of the Church's endowing itself with a worldly existence to endure the time that remained to humanity. Blumenberg has thus demonstrated in the most striking way not only the inadequacy of his chronological scheme, but more crucially that Christianity (and thus, for him, theology itself) is uneven, heterogeneous, and antagonistic at its origins, always already infiltrated with "foreign" elements. Has he not in this way called its essential identity into question?

Blumenberg is not unaware of this problem. He issues a warning: We must not think that because Christianity is made up of concepts originating elsewhere that it lacks a consistent identity of its own, as if it were a derivative and superficial version of elements more powerfully stated in their original (pagan and Jewish) forms. Instead, it becomes theoretically necessary to sort the concepts it "appropriated" from pagan and Jewish sources into the assimilable and inassimilable. He cites Augustine's imperial pronouncement that the jewels of pagan thought cannot be abandoned to the pagans, but must be carried away by those (that is, the Christians) who can best make use of them.

Christianity has shown itself capable of a total assimilation of worthy foreign elements, whose foreignness would thus be entirely overcome.[25] In opposition to Augustine, however, Blumenberg also identifies those originally foreign elements that, although appropriated by Christianity, resisted assimilation and thus retained an alterity that could not be overcome: Though they reside in Christianity, they do not truly belong to it. In this way it appears that the theological and the secular cannot be disentangled and separated into distinct epochs—that their opposition, like their coexistence, is perpetual and necessary, without beginning or end, insofar as Christianity itself is not only heterogeneous at its origins but has been so throughout its history, as the site of incessant schisms that were often understood as the irruption within of essentially external ideas.

Further, the theoretical challenges that confronted Christianity throughout its history forced it to borrow or appropriate concepts, models, and images from its adversaries. The extent of this appropriation, and indeed the very necessity that drives it, raises the permanent possibility that rather than using pagan and Jewish elements and adapting them to its own ends, Christianity might rather be used by them, subverted from within by "resident aliens" in the service of objectives inimical to it. Hence, to take only one example, there is the perpetual fear of the emergence of "Judaizing" tendencies in Christianity, from Arianism to Socianism, grounded in the quite remarkable anxiety about the very persistence of Jewish culture itself, despite its demographic insignificance and legally subaltern status.

It may now appear that the theoretical and historical costs of maintaining a distinction between the theological and the secular are too high; the notion that although all theological concepts are Christian, not all Christian concepts are theological entails highly questionable notions of original identity and belonging. But, more importantly, do the terms "theological" (or, for that matter, "religious") and "secular" adequately capture and summarize the antagonisms that traverse the thought (both theological and philosophical) of the last two thousand years—except perhaps from a perspective internal to Christianity itself (not, of course, the Christian view, but nevertheless a view made possible by the specific existence of Christianity itself)?

Herein lies the importance of Agamben's *The Kingdom and the Glory* in which he traces the genealogy of the concept of oeconomy (οἰκονομία or *oikonomia*) from the origins of Christianity to the work of the first economists, especially Quesnay, Turgot, and Smith, showing that the concept is intertwined from its emergence with that of providence (which, whether we choose to call it Christian or not, was a constant preoccupation of Christian thinkers). Together they form less a concept than a network of problems expressed in a set of Greek terms, allied but not synonymous: πρόνοια, πρόθεσις, and οἰκονομία (*pronoia, prosthesis,* and *oikonomia*). Agamben thus refuses a reduction to origins to declare "economics" a disguised theology. Rather, he understands the economic and the providential as mutually immanent and mutually constitutive. From the beginning, that is, despite Blumenberg's insistence, in the New Testament itself (see particularly Ephesians 1: 3–11) the terms seem logically to imply one another. If God is the sovereign, the creator of the world in a moment of decision, who from time to time is compelled to declare the state of exception to the laws of nature so as to restore order to a restive world, he is also an administrator (the οἰκονομος or *oikonomos*) who through the regular and predictable operation of his laws manages and governs the world in accordance with the purposes for which it was created. *Oikonomia,* as Agamben argues, is both the immanent order of the world, the orderly relation of the parts internal to it, and, simultaneously, the activity of maintaining that order.

Is Smith, then, the heir of a concept of (or set of concepts designated as) providence in which, from the beginning, pagan and Christian, secular and theological ideas are so thoroughly intermingled that it is impossible finally to separate them, a position that would allow us to set aside the theoretical zero-sum game in which Smith is either (secretly) religious or an exemplar of Enlightenment secularity?[26] We should be careful here to understand the theoretical conjuncture that determined Smith's use of the concepts of providence and oeconomy, as well as the precise forms in which they were available to be used. Smith's concept of providence, which he is usually quick to associate with the Stoics, in its explicit forms often appears quite crude, perilously close, in fact, to what Spinoza derisively called "superstition," the belief that everything happens for a reason, determined, as Smith put it, by the "wisdom that superintends all things." In fact, the concepts of providence and oeconomy function in a far more subtle and complex way in Smith's work.

This complexity is itself the effect of a century-long theoretical struggle in which providence was both the site and the stake, which in turn made possible its appropriation in the movement from the oeconomy of nature to the nature of the oeconomy. In the mid-seventeenth century, a most unlikely set of "objective allies," moved by diverse and incompatible objectives, launched perhaps the most ferocious attack on the idea of providence in its history, and among these allies were some of the most formidable thinkers in the history of philosophy: Hobbes, Pascal, Malebranche, and, above all, Spinoza. The first and last notoriously rejected the idea of a universe organized around ultimate ends and purposes, and Part I of Spinoza's *Ethics* very openly rejects the idea even of an immanent teleology and therefore any notion of an "oeconomy of nature."

Little more was expected from these philosophers, universally regarded as atheists who sought to cast the world into the disorder that they believed to be its essence. Less expected and perhaps subtler was the questioning of the dominant notions of providence by two otherwise antagonistic figures: Pascal and Malebranche.[27] For the former, common notions of providence were infected with neo-pelagianism—the most fundamental of heresies according to the latter-day followers of Augustine. For the idea of a universal harmony supervised by an omnipotent, omniscient, and benevolent being seemed to suggest that all had been given sufficient grace to be saved. Only those who willfully and perversely turned away—not only from the revealed truth of the scriptures but also from the very prompting of providence within—would suffer damnation. For Pascal and his fellow Jansenists, such notions, undoubtedly pagan in origin and inspiration, denied the consequences of the Fall, of the first sin. For, if "in the condition of innocence" (before the Fall, "God could not with justice damn a single man"), so "in the condition of corruption, God could, with justice, damn the entire mass."[28] Human action and thought are determined in such a way that few, very few, of "the mass" will receive the grace necessary for salvation.

If the intransigent Jansenists could find in the increasingly common notions of providence a denial of human corruption and the damnation that humanity both merited and was sure to receive, their adversary Malebranche found in it (perhaps drawing here from Spinoza) an irrationalist and childishly anthropocentric notion of God. Malebranche begins the *Treatise on Nature and Grace* (1680) with an image that captured the imagination of Louis Althusser at the end of his life and stimulated his theory of aleatory materialism: Rain falls just as regularly on the sea where it is not needed as on cultivated land (I: 14). Indeed, "rain falls on certain lands" and "the sun roasts others"; sometimes "weather favorable to crops is followed by hail that destroys them" (I: 18). Does this mean that God wanted the crops to fail in order to punish or to test the faith of his people?

For Malebranche, such notions diminish the very idea of God by assigning him a particular will that, instead of following the general order of his creation, would capriciously disrupt it. God in his infinite wisdom sees "all the possible ways of executing his plans" (I: 12). The means he chooses to do so must be preferable to all others. As the most excellent of workmen, "he does not accomplish by complex means that which he can execute by simpler ones, he does not act without an end and never makes useless efforts" (I: 13). Of the infinity of possible worlds, God "determines himself to create that world which could have been produced and preserved by the simplest laws" (I: 13). If rain falls uselessly into the sea, we are to conclude that to make the rain water the withering crops,

> It would have been necessary to have changed the simplicity of his ways and that he have multiplied the laws of the communication of motion, through which our world exists and then there would no longer be that proportion between the action of God and his work which is necessary in order to determine an infinitely wise being to act. (I: 14)

God has through his general will determined the law that governs the motion of colliding bodies; he does not by a particular will determine a given body to move in a given way. Thus, crops wither, people starve, and fortune, like rain, may fall indifferently upon the just and the unjust alike; such events serve no purpose, nor is the world in which they occur the best of all possible worlds except in the sense that it is produced by the most efficient and simple general laws, themselves expressions of God's general will.

The Jansenist Arnauld was scandalized by Malebranche's account of creation, particularly because God's grace itself fell as randomly as the rain, squandered on those whose hearts were hardened and denied those who were willing to seek salvation. Malebranche's God showed no anger at those he should in all justice damn for eternity; on the contrary, the attribution of anger to God was an anthropomorphic error, even a species of idolatry unworthy of the theologian. On the other side, God's perfection was manifest in his laws and not in their consequences; they might well produce monsters and create disorder. To stop such effects would have meant multiplying his wills and thus diminishing the simplicity and elegance of his reign. Malebranche's world is strangely filled with the byproducts and side effects of God's perfect wisdom. His contemporaries did not fail to grasp the significance of this work: as Fénelon put it, Malebranche's argument in the *Traité* "destroys providence."[29]

One might thus be tempted to say that Pascal and Malebranche despite their allegiances had thus joined Hobbes and Spinoza in "clearing the way to knowl-

edge" (to use Locke's figure) by removing whether intentionally or unintention-
ally the remnants of teleological thinking that impeded scientific progress. This
reassuring scheme of the linear development of history and knowledge, however, cannot be sustained. The emergence of political economy (especially in
France in the decades before Smith, where the early economists borrowed from
the notion of providence to resolve the theoretical and practical problems generated by unrestricted commerce) is not only not grounded in the "rationalist"
assault on providence; it was made possible only by the powerful counterattack
in defense of providence launched at the beginning of the eighteenth century
by another and opposing "objective alliance" of otherwise divergent thinkers
that included (to take those of particular importance for Smith's development)
Bossuet, Leibniz, Mandeville, and Pope. This counterattack produced a rein-
vigorated version of providence that was in no way secular or secularized but
that in fact effaced, or at least systematically diminished and called into question, the distinction between the theological and the secular, between worldly
and unworldly, and between nature and society.

It was Bossuet in his *Discourse on Universal History* (1681) who launched the
direct assault on the reemergence of the notions of chance and fortune in the
early modern period:

> Let us no longer speak of chance or fortune, or let us speak of them as a name
> we use to cover our ignorance. What is chance in relation to our uncertain
> counsels, is a design arrived at in a higher council, that is, in that eternal council
> that encloses all causes and all effects in the same order. In this way, everything
> moves toward the same end, and it is from a failure to understand the whole,
> that we find chance or irregularity in particular encounters.[30]

This failure is a failure to apprehend the will and providence of the one who

> Sees everything change without changing himself, and who makes all changes
> through an immutable counsel, who gives and who loans power, who transports
> it from one man to another, from one house to another, from one people to
> another, to show that all they have is borrowed and that it is in him alone that
> all resides naturally.[31]

Bossuet's text, written in 1681, for the instruction of the Dauphin in order that
the future ruler of France would learn "to relate human things to the orders of
eternal wisdom on which they depend," cautions that "God does not declare his
will every day through prophets addressing the kings and monarchies that he

raises up or destroys."[32] But by studying the history of the world's great empires, one can see how he, at whose pleasure alone they exist, has made them serve his designs.

It follows that the rulers of this world, whose power is not their own, fulfill a design of which they are ignorant: "They do more or less than they think and their decisions never fail to have unforeseen effects."[33] Every human intention "serves in spite of itself other intentions than its own. God alone knows how to reduce everything to his will."[34] So the Roman empire extended its rule without the slightest intention of laying the groundwork for Christian civilization, just as the barbarians who entered Rome for plunder left it carrying God's own word; this is indeed the cunning of history. The events of history become intelligible only when the observer moves from the intentions and knowledge of the actors to the design they unwittingly serve. They are blind and necessarily so to the end of the actions that have been diverted to good use. Thus, the disorders and catastrophes of human history are but means to the end of God's will, which even the most cruel and destructive human actions cannot fail to help bring about. Bossuet, of course, does not seek to justify the evil that has been done, although beyond its role in the realization of God's design, it works as a chastising reminder of the first sin.[35]

The last decade of Leibniz's life was spent preparing the definitive refutation of the critiques of providence described above. In a certain sense, providence or theodicy became for him the standard against which previous philosophies were measured and judged. Hobbes, for whom Leibniz had expressed admiration, not only, as noted previously, sought to deny any teleology in the physical world, but went on to deny the existence of any but a physical world. Hobbes's refusal to acknowledge the existence of "incorporeal substance" and thus anything other than body meant for Leibniz (*Theodicy*, hereafter *T*) that

> Mr. Hobbes refuses to listen to anything about a moral necessity . . . on the ground that everything really happens through physical causes. But one is nevertheless justified in making a great distinction between the necessity which constrains the wise to do good, and which is termed moral, existing even in relation to God, and that blind necessity, whereby according to Epicurus, Strato, Spinoza, and perhaps Mr. Hobbes, things exist without intelligence, and without choice, and consequently without God.[36]

Leibniz concludes that a "philosophy, which asserts that bodies alone are substances, hardly appears favorable to the providence of God" (*T* 394).

The case of Spinoza, as the passage above would suggest, is relatively clear (in spite of Leibniz's lifelong fascination with Spinoza): Spinoza too by confusing God and world excludes any conception of providence. Leibniz singles out Proposition 7 of Part II of *Ethics*: "The order and connection of ideas is the same thing as the order and connection of things," from which Spinoza concludes that "thinking substance and extended substance are one and the same thing." With these assertions, Leibniz tells us, he cannot agree. From such notions follows the idea that God's power has nothing to do with free will or decision. Here he cites the scholium to Proposition 17 of Part I of *Ethics*: "Things follow from God with the same necessity and in the same way that from the nature of a triangle, for all eternity it follows that its three angles will be equal to two right angles." And if God lacks free will, so too does man, created in his image. Spinoza argues that a man's power of thought increases as he understands the necessary determination not only of the things around him, but of his own mind and body, the very feelings or affects that he experiences. To this Leibniz responds:

> Spinoza thinks that as soon as a man understands that all events occur necessarily, his mind is wonderfully strengthened. But by this constraint he does not satisfy the mind of the sufferer, nor does the latter on that account suffer less acutely. Happy indeed would he be if he understood that good arises out of evil, and that whatever happens is best for us, if we consider it wisely.[37]

But perhaps it was in response to Malebranche that Leibniz most fully elaborated his notion of theodicy, or at least those elements most adaptable to the theorization of that second providence, the market. Malebranche's postulation of God's general will, the set of invariant laws of nature that God might overrule or supersede only at the expense of his perfection, determines that rain may, in accordance with these laws, fall uselessly on the sea, while crops, on which populations depend, wither and die. It determines that "monsters" with no place in the visible order of God's kingdom may be born.

The idea of a God who suspends his own laws, even to spare his children tragedy or suffering, to Malebranche, exalts his power at the expense of his wisdom. As we have noted, such arguments appeared to Malebranche's critics to undermine any notion of providence, by positing the operation of an order that ceaselessly and necessarily produced disorder as its "side effect." Leibniz, however, was far more sympathetic to Malebranche's attempts to "naturalize providence" than such figures as Bossuet or Fénelon and responded to Malebranche not by rejecting his project but by declaring it incomplete. Malebranche stopped too soon in his reasoning; he too easily accepted the suggestion that rain falling on the sea and drought ruining crops were in fact, as they appeared to the vulgar, counterprovidential, unfortunate byproducts of the operation of God's natural laws, providence's waste. It is here that Leibniz prompts him to continue rather than suspend his analysis. Resuming Bossuet's argument, Leibniz maintains that what Malebranche accepts as "irregularity" (T 277) in nature is no more than a failure of knowledge, a mistaking of appearance for reality. While Leibniz commends Malebranche for refusing to violate general laws in his discussion of the origins of monsters, the latter fails to see that "these very monstrosities are in the rules and are in conformity to the general acts of will, even if we are not capable of discerning this conformity" (T 276).

To illustrate his point, Leibniz turns to mathematics:

> It is just as sometimes there are appearances of irregularity in mathematics which issue finally in a great order when one has finally gotten to the bottom of them. . . . I endeavor to elucidate these things by comparisons taken from pure mathematics, where everything proceeds in order, and where it is possible to fathom them by a close contemplation which grants us an enjoyment, so to speak, of the vision of the ideas of God. One may propose a succession or series of numbers perfectly irregular to all appearance, where the numbers increase and diminish variably without the emergence of any order; and yet he who knows the key to the formula and who understands the origin and structure of this succession of numbers, will be able to give a rule which, being properly understood, will show that the series is perfectly regular and that it even has excellent properties. (T 277)

In this sense, every small disorder belongs to a larger order.

But Leibniz, not content to demonstrate that every apparent disorder, seen in the context of the totality of which it is a part, is a component of a greater, if often initially hidden, order, moves from the synchronic to the diachronic: The earth itself was the site of a gigantic upheaval, a general conflagration that raged unchecked, followed by equally destructive inundations and movements of the earth.

> But who does not see that these disorders have served to bring things to the point where they are now, that we owe to them our riches and comforts, and that through their agency this globe became fit for cultivation by us. These disorders passed into order. (T 278)

Further, Leibniz argues, we do not even see as disorder "the inequality of conditions" (*T* 278) in our societies, where the deprivation of servants and laborers relative to their masters is universally recognized as the necessary foundation of an orderly society. But surely, he argues, citing Bayle, there is a distinction to be made between disorder among inanimate things and the disorder among humans who feel and think and suffer. Is it not possible to imagine "worlds without sin and without unhappiness?" Of course it is, answers Leibniz,

> But the same worlds again would be very inferior to ours in goodness. I cannot show you this in detail. For can I know and can I present infinities to you and compare them together? But you must judge with me *ab effectu*, since God has chosen this world as it is. We know, moreover, that often an evil brings forth a good whereto one would not have attained without that evil. Often indeed two evils have made one great good. (*T* 129)

Here, Leibniz cautions us not to imagine that God would ever do evil that good may come, but rather that God derives "from the permitting of sins greater goods than such as occurred before the sins" (*T* 129). So intricate are the connections that compose this world that, "if the smallest evil that comes to pass in the world were missing in it, it would no longer be this world; which, with nothing omitted and all allowance made, was found the best by the creator who chose it" (*T* 128–129).

What Leibniz has done for the concept of providence or what we must now call, following Smith, the oeconomy of nature, Bernard Mandeville does for the nature of the oeconomy, that is, he, in an operation startlingly similar in its strategy and tactics to that of Leibniz's theodicy, produces a vindication of the justice of the political oeconomy. In a key passage in the "Vindication of God's Justice" a Latin summary of the arguments of the *Theodicy* (which was originally written in French), Leibniz reminds the reader that

> The divine wisdom directs the divine goodness which extends to the totality of created things. Therefore the divine providence manifests itself in the total series of the universe. It follows that among the infinite number of possible series God has selected the best, and that consequently this best universe is that which actually exists. For all things in the universe are in mutual harmony and the truly wise never decide without taking the whole into consideration.[38]

Were they given access to knowledge of the totality "even innocents would not wish not to have suffered."[39]

It is to the "truly wise" in Leibniz's sense that Mandeville's account of social providence is directed. In "the Grumbling Hive" first published anonymously in 1705 (and thus five years before Leibniz's *Theodicy*), he attempts to demonstrate that what makes man

> a Sociable Animal, consists not in his desire of company, good nature, pity, affability and other graces of a fair outside, but that his vilest and most hateful qualities are the most necessary accomplishments to fit him for the largest and, according to the world, the happiest and most flourishing societies.[40]

Mandeville's choice of the animal fable allows him to imagine with Leibniz how "if the smallest evil that comes to pass in the world were missing in it, it would no longer be this world" (*T* 128–129). Through a kind of thought experiment, he demonstrates that the extirpation of vice from society (without, it should be noted, either denying that it is vice or exempting it from punishment) will merely render it inferior to what it was before, unable finally even to provide for its own population. In Mandeville's society it is not simply that individuals pursue their own interests without regard to their neighbor, but that they will lie, cheat, and, finally, steal in their pursuit.

Moreover, they are puffed up with pride and vanity, engaged in a perpetual quest to elevate themselves above their fellows, devoting themselves to ever-changing fashion at the expense of that wisdom and morality whose objects remain unchanged. If "every part" of society was "full of vice, / Yet the whole mass a paradise," it was because such "jarrings" in the sense of "musical harmony" were together made to agree.[41] To use Leibniz's language, the vices that appeared to afflict the civil state were nothing more than the evils "necessary" to produce the best of all possible societies. It is what prompts individuals to engage in the degree and form of cooperation required by a flourishing economy: Despite the vicious intentions of each member of society, all unwittingly "assist each other as 'twere for spite" and even "The worst of all the multitude / Did something for the common good."[42] It is crucial for any understanding of Mandeville to note this last phrase: the common good, as important a concept for him as it is for Smith. The economy, allowed to operate free of interference, would improve the lot of the poor to the greatest possible extent, something charity could not do. And as wealth flourished, so too would arts, letters, law, and learning.

It is precisely in the context of the natural and political oeconomies or rather in the space between them that Smith's account of the invisible hand takes on its full significance: "Providence," which in his words "divided the earth among a few lordly masters . . . neither forgot nor abandoned those who seemed to have been left out in the partition" (*TMS* 185). "Seemed" is crucial here: In appearance a few enjoy abundance, while the majority suffer deprivation. This apparent evil, however, is an illusion; in reality, the rich consume "little more than the poor" because the capacity of the proud and unfeeling landlord's "stomach bears no proportion to the immensity of his desires and will receive no more than that of the meanest peasant" (*TMS* 185). "In ease of body and peace of mind, all the different ranks of life are nearly upon a level."

Other evils, however, are undeniably real. The rich, as imagined by Smith, neither love their neighbor as themselves nor are they prompted by duty to attempt in however minimal a way to aid their fellow man. They are moved only by "natural selfishness and rapacity"; they seek "only their own conveniency" and "the gratification of their own vain and insatiable desires" (*TMS* 184). Smith's text literally says that "in spite" of their selfishness and rapacity "they divide with the poor the produce of all their improvements," but he has in fact shown, in a muted version of Mandeville's argument, that it is because of their devotion to vain grandeur and the "oeconomy of greatness" that arises from their very vices that others receive their share of the fruits of the earth. It is from the "luxury and caprice" of the proud and unfeeling landlord that the laboring poor who make up society's majority "derive . . . that share of the necessaries of life, that they would have in vain expected from his humanity or his justice" (*TMS* 184). The invisible hand that distributes the necessaries of life is then nothing other than the very concatenation of the vices and evils of the rich into a design that compels them "without intending it, without knowing it" to "advance the interest of the society and afford means to the multiplication of the species" (*TMS* 185).

It is on this precise point that Hegel's commentary on Smith is particularly illuminating. What was Hegel's attitude toward the concepts of providence and theodicy? As we have already noted, he was extremely critical of Stoicism, and this attitude extended to their notion of providence (he employs the Greek πρόνοια) as the site of conceptual confusion in which God, fate, necessity, nature, and reason become indistinguishable: "Thus in the Stoics all the superstitions of Rome had their strongest supporters; all external teleological superstition is taken under their protection and justified."[43] Stoicism, Hegel argues, is "a system of reasoning in which the entirely particular ends of individuals also form the interests of the gods."[44] His attitude toward Leibniz's *Theodicy* was if anything even more critical: In what might be regarded as the cunning demonstration of the intricate interweaving of good and evil necessary to the design of the best of all possible worlds (and here we are coming very close to Smith's account of the invisible hand), Hegel parodies as "this and that are stated to be necessary . . . God is therefore . . . the waste channel into which all contradictions flow."[45]

Precisely because Hegel dismisses Leibniz's *Theodicy* as a popular summary of superstitious ideas, it is all the more interesting that Smith is spared this criticism. Of course, Hegel did not simply reject providential thinking, but rather by historicizing it ends up positing an end that can only be perpetually deferred. He thus cannot allow the dislocations between consciousness and action, between intention and consequence, to become functions of a stable system, the very principles of a social equilibrium. For him, at least in the *Phenomenology*, this dislocation marks the site of a contradiction that propels Smith's system beyond itself, namely into the becoming conscious of universality, in which reason, having undertaken the work of its own rational actualization, must also know and appropriate to itself the universality it had initially produced "without knowing it." By historicizing the theodicy proper to Smith's theory, Hegel allows us to see the essential role of the concept of providence understood both as a natural and human system for Smith, whose concern is finally with the oeconomy of life and its administration. We must now understand the emergence of another notion that otherwise would appear absent in Smith's works: that of life itself.

The importance of life as a political concept has been underscored in recent years, in particular with Foucault's reflections on the notion of the biopolitical in the *History of Sexuality* (1975), which he defines as "that which brings life and its mechanisms into the domain of an explicit calculus and which makes the power-knowledge complex an agent of the transformation of human life."[46] According to his analysis, with the emergence of absolutist states in Europe, there arose the model of sovereign power, a model organized around rights and obligations in which the exercise of power operated according to the prescriptions of the law: a right over life and death.

The sovereign could by right "*faire mourir*," literally, "make die" (as distinct from the verb "*tuer*," to kill) those who violated his laws, and he could indirectly but nevertheless legitimately "expose" the lives of his subjects to the risk of death in war. His relation to life, however, was a passive one: The sovereign governed through the decision not to act, the decision to allow or permit life to continue, "*laisser vivre*." In contrast, the model of biopower that emerged in the eighteenth century substituted for these rights "a power to make live (*faire vivre*) and to abandon to death (*rejeter dans la mort*)."[47] Although the objective of a biopolitics was undoubtedly the management of that biological and political entity, the population, depending on circumstances, in order to promote or limit its growth and hence preserve its health and well-being (paradoxically in doing so, Foucault argues), increasingly exposed humanity to death, a death required in defense of life itself in wars that became "vital."

Agamben's *Homo Sacer*, published nearly twenty years after the *History of Sexuality* (but ten years before the posthumous publication of Foucault's lectures on economics and biopolitics from the late seventies), was not only a critical response to Foucault's theorization of sovereign power and biopower as historically separate modes of government (in which the first yielded to the modernity of the second) but was also an active recollection of what Foucault himself had said but was in danger of forgetting: the way in which the protection of the life of a population might require genocide, the extermination of another people, who pose a vital—or today, existential—threat. For Agamben, the extent of violence in the twentieth century, violence on a scale unknown to previous ages, was a testimony not simply to the persistence of sovereign power, but to the primacy of normless decision over rational administration and the state of exception over the legal order.

The active relation to life was less *faire vivre*, a fostering of life, than an abandonment of the living to a *violence* unrestrained by law, their rejection from the realm of law in order to leave them exposed to death, as if a certain violence were necessary to the fostering of life. Biopolitics, the government of life, was thus accompanied by what Achille Mbembe—following, but critical of, Foucault and Agamben—called necro-politics: both mass killing through a militarization of politics, as well as a controlled permitting of death through famine and epidemic.[48]

The publication of Foucault's subsequent lectures— "Society Must Be Defended" (1976–77), "Security, Territory, Population" (1977–78), and "The Birth of Biopolitics" (1978–79)—showed that he had added to the notion of a microphysics of power: the idea of a subtle coercion of corporeal forces not merely by the state, but by apparatuses both private and public in the disciplinary regime, the concept of the government of populations (according to which the act of governing that was not identifiable with the state alone). This latter insight led him to the study of the French economists of the eighteenth century, including the physiocrats, and finally Smith himself.

It was through this body of work that the outline of a new concept of government took shape, governing populations not through an expansion of the role of the state, but precisely through its strategic contraction and the abandonment of some of its traditional functions—that is, a concept of government whose strategic repertoire included controlled exposure to want, dearth, and deprivation to determine conduct far more efficiently and predictably than mere legality, and allowing the market to administer life though a rationality that, though of human origin, surpassed human design. It was to these texts by Foucault (published only in the first decade of the twenty-first century) that Agamben's *The Kingdom and the Glory* offered a response, deepening and historicizing the notion of economy far beyond what Foucault had set out to do.

To continue this work, it is perhaps time to shift our attention to the place of death in the government of life; perhaps we should ask whether the "marketplace of life," as it has recently been called,[49] is not also the place of death that would no longer simply be outside life or its limit, but rather a necessary moment in its growth and function: functionally identical to the sin that makes possible the greater good, the negative whose dissolution of the present makes the future possible. To pose this question is to confront the existence of a kind of necro-economics, another way of thinking about the relation of death to the government of life as it emerged as much in practice as in theory in eighteenth-century Europe.

Necro-economics might be understood as the corollary of the indirect sovereign violence that does not take life but requires that life be exposed to the risk of death. The innovation proper to the emergence of political economy in the eighteenth century, in this sense, would lie not simply in the discovery of the immutable and immanent order of what would come to be called the market, but also in the advocacy of a broadening of the sovereign power of "exposure" from the mere right to expose subjects or citizens to death in battle at the hands of an enemy to the legitimate power to expose them to death through hunger, as if individuals, in the name of the laws of the natural order, could (or should) no more be protected from possibility of death by starvation than from the possibility of death on the battlefield. The very notion of necro-economics allows us to understand the emergence (violently contested in both theory and practice) of a notion, never directly stated as such, of "letting die" (*laisser mourir*) that is consubstantial with the science of governing through "*laisser faire*," that is, through action that consists of a deliberate refraining or withdrawal from action—not simply the inertia of non-action, but a strategically conceived retreat, a leaving alone or an abandonment, often in the face of powerful counterforces, whose effects could be far more devastating than any advance of government controls. *Homo sacer*, an obscure and little-studied category of Roman law denoting the man who could be killed with impunity, increasingly governed, despite or perhaps because of its very obscurity or invisibility, states' use of violence in the twentieth century, as if remaining unidentified and therefore outside the sphere of deliberation or contestation allowed this category to achieve a near universality in practice. In a similar way, the notion of *laisser mourir*, letting die, itself based on the quasi-legal principle that no one alive has a (human or civil) right to the means of subsistence, governs us by virtue of having been forgotten and banished beyond theoretical memory, its nonexistence as a matter of deliberation the surest sign of its continuing domination of a certain way of thinking about such notions as "the economy" or "the market."

To proceed, we will resume our reading of Hegel reading Smith. For Hegel, Smith's rejection of any pre-social human existence, his declaration, as necessary to life itself, cooperation and therefore not simply the labor of dissociated individuals perhaps exchanging after the fact, but a certain minimal form of society and therefore politics, renders him a thinker of the immanence of the universal in human life by virtue of the necessarily collective labor that makes human life possible. He is therefore for Hegel the thinker of universality not in a juridical or moral sense but insofar as it is realized in the production of life. The question we must now pose is whether Hegel's reading of Smith is a tenable one. To put it in another way, is the market, understood globally, if not universally, that natural–human sphere of the production and reproduction of life, the life of a people, the life of people? Can human life be conceived as a market?

As we argued earlier, Hegel could make Smith the thinker of the universal and of life only by depriving his system of its providential character, turning the unconsciousness of Smith's producers into a temporary failure of knowledge that could only destabilize and call into question their relation to the world of their making, setting it on the course to that becoming—other characteristic of the moments of spirit's long return to itself. If, to part company with Hegel, we allow Smith to think the market as part of a larger natural teleology that exceeds the grasp of the human intellect, what is the relation of the market to life (and, correlatively, to death)?

Here it is useful to recall Smith's own rather pronounced and pervasive necro-politics: his interest in death and the infliction of death not only by the state, but by the individual himself, as if he were appointed to carry out the dictates of justice at the moment he understands he "is the just and proper object of the hatred and contempt of his fellow creatures" (*TMS* 84). For Smith, if society is necessary to the sustaining of human life, "the dread of death, the great poison to the happiness, but the great restraint upon the injustice of mankind, which while it afflicts and mortifies the individual, guards and protects the society." Every man "in the race for wealth, and honors and preferments . . . may run as hard as he can and strain every nerve and muscle, in order to outstrip all his competitors"; if he were, however, to "jostle or throw down any of them," he would become the object of "hatred and indignation" and as such liable to punishment (*TMS* 83). A necessary part, then, of the collective production of life, a process here driven by self-interest, is an awareness of the ever-present force of justice that takes, or ought to take, life with a machinelike regularity that will immediately attend to the excess of self-interest that leads an individual to step outside the realm of fair competition and engage in theft or fraud to acquire the possessions he desires. In fact, the sociability necessary to human existence is itself only possible through the constant example of the taking of the life of the individual judged guilty.

What is significant here is not the justice of capital punishment, whether one who unjustly kills another (or for that matter takes a handkerchief out of another's pocket) can himself justly be put to death, but rather the sense of the utility of the death, neither natural nor accidental, which is inflicted by the state. Without the example of the state's willingness actively to take the lives of wrongdoers before them, people "feel so little for another with whom they have no particular connection in comparison with what they feel for themselves" that, in the absence of a terror of merited punishment, they would, "like wild beasts, be at all times ready to fly upon him; and a man would enter an assembly of men as he enters a den of lions" (*TMS* 86).

Further, the desire to inflict capital punishment is simultaneously rational and rooted in the human passion for vengeance, a simultaneity that again expresses the working of providence: The production of life both requires and induces the exercise of the right to kill. Thus, "a man of humanity . . . applauds with ardor, and even with transport, the just retaliation which seems due" to crimes against the lives and properties of others (*TMS* 90). And if the transport that the man of humanity feels at an execution appears itself ignoble, we must understand that, like the passionate pursuit of self-interest, capital punishment understood as the expression of the instinct of self-preservation, is the actually existing (as opposed to ideal) means nature has provided to achieve "the end which she proposes." This arrangement of means and ends is the surest sign that the "oeconomy of nature is in this respect exactly of a piece with what it is upon many other occasions" (*TMS* 77).

The taking of life for "crimes against the lives," but also and far more frequently in Smith's time, "the properties of others" is necessary to society's very existence, perhaps the most passionate form of the social bond according to which one loves one's neighbor by hating the criminal who has despoiled him and by rejoicing in the latter's execution.[50] But is there not, precisely to protect and defend the properties of others, a correlative action by which the state, instead of taking life, allows death, permitting it to come to those who can have no claims to that which they do not own and cannot legitimately acquire?

The phrase "oeconomy of nature," which here marks the junction of the political and economic,[51] allows us to make the transition from Smith's necro-politics, his founding of life on death, of the maintenance of life on the production of death, to the necro-economics he appropriated from the French economists whose work was so critical to his development.[52] The permitting of such deaths, or rather the refraining from preventing them out of deference to an immanent order that would bear no interference, it was argued, would lead to an opulence and thus an ever-increasing supply of food that could not come into existence without this restraint: What appeared at that moment in history to some observers as an intolerable and moreover dangerous abandonment of the people at their moment of need was defended by its proponents as the tincture of evil in reaction to which good would grow more powerful, the lack or dearth for which prosperity would arise as compensation.

Insofar as the proponents of unrestricted commerce argued more or less explicitly that the effective government of men could best be achieved through a contraction of the activity of government rather than its expansion, which would thereby permit the operation of an intricate harmony that any intervention but the intervention to prevent intervention could only diminish, the state appeared to have implicitly annulled the individual's customary right to exist and the correlative right to expect from the government a guarantee of the means to do so (above all, food). Thus, around the middle of the eighteenth century, the question of the poor, which had often focused on the problems of vagrancy and mendicancy, shifted to the issue of hunger and in turn the notion of a right to survive, not merely the right not to be killed unjustly, but the right not to be allowed to starve to death—the assurance of which was one of the primary justifications both of the state's very existence and of the individual's subjection to it.

It was certainly not the case that because the operation of the market was declared the only rational and effective means of distributing subsistence, any action by the state to procure food for a section of the population during times of scarcity and famine was simply foresworn. On the contrary, the assertion of the market's natural/social order in the quarter century before the French Revolution granted a formal, even quasi-legal, existence to the assumption (grounded as much in custom and mores as in Christian theology) that the state was responsible for assuring that living individuals were able to persist in their existence, transforming it into a question of the individual's legal right, which in a sense codified what had remained more or less assumed (and often, as in the case of the English Poor Laws, not very clearly).

But this codification initially took the form of a right that appeared to be identified so that it could be denied and ruled out, as if it were an implicit demand that could be refused only when it was explicitly articulated by those with the power to determine its legitimacy. Moreover, the right to existence or subsistence (or rather, to distinguish it clearly from Locke's notion of the individual's right to the life of which he or she is sole proprietor, the right to be assured of the means of subsistence) emerged as such not in the great texts of eighteenth-century political philosophy but in the works of economists, especially in France, who with admirable honesty confronted some of the more troubling aspects of "*la liberté indéfinie du commerce*," particularly commerce in what was then called "*subsistances.*" One question in particular emerged as a kind of battlefield—especially in the face of the repeated subsistence crises between the years 1754 when the *Arrêt* liberalizing the grain trade was issued and 1774–75 when the threat of ungovernable protest (*la Guerre des Farines*) forced a return to price and supply regulations—on which the exponents of the unrestricted market determined to oppose any obstacle to its operation clashed spectacularly with those who sought precisely to impose life, human life, as its necessary foundation but also its limit. For the former, the discovery of the market's natural order, that is, an order necessarily independent of any political intervention except that of preventing interference, compelled them to confront the following question: If, as custom seemed to dictate, the state could not legitimately permit even the slow starvation and decline of a part of the population (understood as possessors of a legal right to their existence), how could it assure their subsistence without damaging (through an artificial lowering of prices, raising of wages, or even requisitions of grain that could only ruin merchants and drive them from the trade) the very system of production and distribution that alone could guarantee subsistence to the population? Would not any governmental measure designed to provide sustenance to the starving—other than allowing the market to do so according to the means and at the pace proper to its mechanisms—simply postpone and, in postponing, aggravate the subsistence crisis such measures were intended to alleviate (as Smith himself argued)?

These and other related questions compelled both the proponents of free commerce in food and their opponents to stake out a position relative to the idea of a legal right to existence. Their positions were often expressed with great subtlety; rather than offer a direct critique or defense of this right, they often reformulated it in a way that either broadened its claims upon the sovereign power or, in opposition, emptied it of any but a formal or abstract significance, subordinating, whether explicitly or implicitly, the individual's right to exist to the ability of the market to produce a supply sufficient to meet the needs of the population (as long as it could pay market prices).

These questions, which emerged in their modern form for perhaps the first time in France over the twenty-year period that preceded the publication of *Wealth*, were no more at the center of the discussion of freedom of commerce and the sanctity of private property then than now. In fact, it took the opponents of this freedom to show that the partisans of the unrestricted market had already proposed an answer to a question only their critics would or could directly pose. To impose the rigors of a free market in grains that would not bear artificial intrusion into the concatenation of intricate, but necessary, mechanisms of its growth meant confronting not simply a state accustomed to regulating significant aspects of economic life, but even more importantly a people always ready to revolt and whose uprisings the state traditionally would take any measures to avoid.

The importance of these debates for Smith's work is incontestable: He refers to them directly, and much of his argumentation, especially in the "Digression Concerning the Corn Trade and Corn Laws" in *Wealth*, on which we will focus, is taken directly from the tracts of the advocates of the unregulated commerce in grains. Some of these were physiocrats; others, like Smith himself, did not share the physiocratic positions on a number of other issues—from the primacy of agriculture over manufacturing to the single tax—but were allied with them around the defense of the natural order even of the grain market, whose volatility was matched only by its importance for the survival of populations, against attempts to interfere in and thus subvert its design. And whatever Smith's reservations concerning "imperfections" of the physiocratic system, he regarded it as "perhaps the nearest approximation to the truth that has yet been published upon the subject of political oeconomy," above all, for representing "perfect liberty as the only effectual expedient" for a constant increase in the production of consumable goods (*Wealth* 642). It is perhaps worth inquiring more closely into the real theoretical complexity of this "perfect liberty" of commerce, less a concept than a constellation of theoretical and political positions that took shape through the French debates that preceded *Wealth* and determined both what it says and what it does not and cannot say.

To what extent does the question of the individual's right to subsistence as it took shape in these debates, if injected into our reading of Smith, function as a kind of contrast medium that will make visible not simply the structure of his argument but its idiosyncratic features, its gaps and fissures? To undertake this experiment we must begin not with the more well-known figures such as Quesnay or Turgot, but instead with the "elegant" but less familiar figure of Claude-Jacques Herbert whose *Essai sur la police générale des grains* (1755) Smith cites directly.

Writing in support of the *Arrêt* of 1754, which liberalized commerce in grain and allowed its export through Languedoc, a policy many viewed as "dangerous" in the face of rising prices, Herbert seeks to show the advantages that "may result from more extensive commerce."[53] He cautions the reader to keep in mind that "sometimes the suffering of the people is needed to achieve the common good" and that freedom of commerce precisely because it does require suffering (the nature and degree of which is never specified) "works more easily, if it is better understood."[54] Is this an economist's version, fifty years later, of Leibniz's declaration, echoed in Smith's account of the Stoics cited above, that even the innocent would not wish not to have suffered if they could only see the necessity of the evil done to them in the design of the whole? Perhaps, but Herbert will tell us later, "the multitude is always unreasonable"[55] and thus perennially prone to murmurs and revolt: They almost certainly lack the capacity to understand the place of their suffering in the progress toward the common interest.

It is far more likely that Herbert addresses those whose task it is to care for the people by preventing them from harming themselves, especially when they are carried away by the passions of fear and anger, by acts of violence and rapine that are apparently aimed at others but in fact affect the people themselves far more severely. But, as an admittedly small number of his contemporaries asked, what exactly is the meaning of "suffering" in the passage cited above? If it is hunger (given that this is a tract on the grain trade), how long and to what degree must (or indeed can) the people suffer, and what negative effects both for and from the people will this suffering provoke? These questions were not only posed by those, motivated by morality or religion, to whom it had never occurred that a government would simply allow such suffering; they were also asked by those who thought Herbert naive and foolish. How long will the people endure this suffering before they revolt?

Anticipating such responses, Herbert argues that his goal is to assure the means of subsistence to the entire population of France, but that for the last two centuries at least the measures taken to ensure food for the people have instead worked to bring about the very crises they were intended to prevent. Price controls designed to make food available at below-market prices produced losses and eventually ruin for the merchants, while public granaries where emergency supplies could be stored in case of a particularly bad harvest are attended with "numberless inconveniencies. It is from the freedom of commerce alone that one can expect the storage of grain at the least cost and of the greatest utility to the peoples' subsistence."[56]

At the center of the argument then is the question of "*disette*," that is, food shortage or scarcity, which Smith translates as "dearth." It is a term whose exact meaning is seldom clear: It may refer to a shortage of food that will result in no more than a reduction in consumption without noticeably affecting the health and activity of a given population (which may nevertheless suffer hunger pangs and a sense of want). But *disette* may also signify a reduction in food consumption that, if left unchecked, would lead to the death of a politically meaningful number of people after a period of weeks and to a noticeable decrease in the level of activity of the remainder of the affected population. Sometimes, it appears indistinguishable from famine (certain writers, for example, speak of the *disette* of 1709–10 in which as many as a million people died), except perhaps that it is limited to a certain province or region.[57] Suffice it to say that the ambiguity of the term serves to blur these distinctions, and the uses of *disette* tend to abstract it from the concrete conditions upon which its precise meaning depends, a fact of which many of the polemics will take full rhetorical advantage.

Further complicating the semantically unsettled status of *disette* was the insistence on the part of the economists, of whom Herbert is an example, that what is taken for a *disette* is almost always only apparently so, an illusion created by a combination of ignorance and fear among the peasantry and a desire on the part of the state both to control France's economic life and to appear bountiful and solicitous of its people. The slightest fluctuation in the price of grain is enough to set off a panic: The most fleeting effects of supply and demand immediately produce an unholy alliance of the people and their governors for whom any rise in the price of grain can only be the consequence of monopoly and hoarding. Similarly, when merchants, in response to higher prices for grain abroad, export their goods, they are accused of allowing France to starve for their own gain. In opposition, Herbert, together with the other *"partisans de la liberté,"* as they liked to call themselves, argued that absolute freedom of commerce, including the freedom to import and export at will, was the sole guarantee of the people's subsistence. Just as high prices in, say, Holland, will attract French grain, so high prices in France will attract "a crowd" of foreign merchants seeking a profit whose competition will only succeed, over time, in lowering prices to levels affordable even to the people.

Louis Paul Abeille took the argument further in both *Réflexion sur la police des grains* (1764) and the longer *Principes sur la liberté du commerce des grains* (1768). In a nation capable of feeding itself and one that often produces a surplus, "how are *real disettes* even possible,"[58] except perhaps in the rare case of a catastrophically bad (as opposed to a merely "disappointing") harvest? The increasingly frequent phenomenon mistakenly referred to as *disette* is in fact merely an "apparent" or "artificial" *disette*, caused not by any genuine shortage of grain, but by the irrational passions of the "multitude," encouraged, if not created, by the philosophy underlying state regulations.[59] Abeille insists that it is no more reasonable to complain that grain is too expensive than that it is too cheap. The very notion of "too expensive" (meaning, Abeille repeats, nothing more than that the price is more than the people *"want* to pay"[60]) inevitably gives rise to demands for state intervention, thus creating an obstacle to free commerce. A significant increase in price causes a general alarm and, among *"le petit peuple,"* panic: "Fear so contagious by itself, becomes still more so when it is expressed in shouts."[61] The contagion spreads, and the state, out of fear of peasant revolt and urban riot, initiates artificial measures to lower the price of grain without regard to market conditions or proprietary right: "Those to whom the grain does not belong propose to force the proprietors to sell it at the same price as during times of abundance."[62] If the proprietors refuse to allow this violation of their property rights and "take precautions to protect their grain from the invasion with which they are threatened" (that is, by concealing their stores of grain or understating the quantity they actually possess), they are denounced as criminals by a rapidly mobilizing population whose outrage both frightens the state and determines its policy. Such merchants are regarded as little more than thieves who have stolen grain that the people are convinced somehow belongs to them. Thus, "violence is converted into right, and need takes precedence over property."[63]

The result, familiar to Smith's readers, is that the lowering of prices by the decree of a government, itself acting at the behest of an indignant multitude, allows an amount of grain that at a high price would suffice for three months to be purchased and consumed within a month, causing a general calamity. This is the reality concealed by the chimera of "fair price" or "just price," as if price is determined by the people's need (real or imagined) rather than the relation of supply and demand. The people cry "the government is responsible for (*s'est chargé de*) guaranteeing me bread at a cheap rate," arrogating to themselves the right to legal protection from an increase in the price of grain.[64] Even if we grant that the demand for bread is motivated by actual need rather than mere preference and that a rise in price might place it beyond the reach of a part of the population,

> Can one imagine without terror where one would quickly and immediately have placed oneself if it were admitted that need has a title superior to that of property? What then would be the meaning in our language of the words *right, property* and *security*, and even the words *authority* and *administration*?[65]

Abeille insists that the government must recognize that although it is true that the people cannot always afford the price of grain, to respond to this need by attacking the right of property and undermining the security necessary to the operation of the market will only aggravate an already desperate situation. The proper action of government in such cases, Abeille argues, is a deliberate refraining from action: Even in the face of violent protest it must "*laisser agir*,"[66] that is, allow the action of causes and effects that, independently of human need or desire, sets the appropriate price of grain at any given moment.

Foucault remarks in his commentary on Abeille that by letting prices rise as they will, there will no longer be

> scarcity in general, on the condition that for a whole series of people in a whole series of markets that there was some scarcity, some dearness [*cherté*], some difficulty in buying wheat, and consequently some hunger, and it may well be that some people die of hunger after all. But by letting these people die of hunger [*en*

laissant ces gens-là mourir de faim], one will be able to make scarcity a chimera and prevent it from occurring in this massive form of scourge [*fleau*—catastrophe] typical of the previous systems. Thus the scarcity-event is split. Scarcity-scourge disappears, but the scarcity that causes the death of individuals not only does not disappear, it must not disappear.[67]

Foucault suggests here that death by starvation must not be allowed to disappear, must not be prevented if it is a function of market price, but should be permitted to perform its function in the sequence of causes that will determine that no shortage ever becomes famine. In the silences and ellipses of these urgent declarations of faith by the partisans of liberty who feared that the very conditions under which unlimited freedom of commerce were perhaps most necessary were those that would create the greatest resistance to their proposals (both from above and below), a certain question took shape to which understandably few of these otherwise intrepid authors would respond directly: If a government must act by refraining from action in order precisely to allow food supplies to increase, must the imperative "*laisser agir*" also mean that a government can or even must "*laisser mourir*," that is, allow those who without state intervention will starve to do so?

It would be a mistake to think that such positions went unchallenged, or were challenged only by state functionaries who, whether motivated by self-interest or a commitment to mercantilism, could only respond by defending the existing policies. There were also those who, even before the prolonged subsistence crisis of 1767–70 called into question the experiments in the grain market, heard the unasked question resonating in the hollow spaces of the discourses on the freedom of the grain trade. No response was more effective than that of Abbé Galiani whose *Dialogues sur le commerce des blés* (1770) provoked a furious reaction from the advocates of the unregulated market.[68]

Although often dismissed even today as a text of wit and refinement whose qualities are literary rather than scientific and as such lacks the rigor that characterizes the works of the physiocrats, as well as thinkers such as Herbert and Abeille, Galiani's *Dialogues* succeeds both in bringing to light some of the guiding but unstated assumptions of the liberals and in demonstrating the concrete and quite predictable effects of the proposed reforms omitted from their texts. Referring to doctrines and ideas rather than particular authors or texts, Galiani confronts the position articulated by Abeille, among others, that "need" (*besoin*) cannot be allowed to take legal precedence over property right, even if the need in question is the need for food, itself necessary to mere survival.

The position in question is not a Lockean defense of a natural right donated to each individual by God and indivisible from his own person, the property that even the poor man must own, and that, existing prior to any joining together with others, remains outside the reach of any human law or government. Instead, it is a defense according to which private property distinct from the proprietor's own person, but legally at the disposal of and directed by the individual will of the proprietor alone, is necessary to the operation of the market, which is itself the only rational means by which even, or perhaps especially, a commodity like food can be effectively distributed. Thus, despite the economists' expressions of concern for the injustices suffered by grain merchants during times of hunger and scarcity, it increasingly appears that the right of property is less a matter of what *should be* than of what *must necessarily be* if societies are to endure, let alone prosper.

Turgot noted the difficulty of responding to Galiani's *Dialogues*, not so much because its arguments were not arranged in a demonstrative order but because he posed the problem of commerce in grain differently than the economists (and "seductively," in a way that would not be easy to counter),[69] undercutting their scheme not by moral argumentation that could be easily answered but by arguing that economic considerations must begin with two principles: "What is man?" and "What is the relation of bread [*pain*] to man?" Responding to the charge that the people's obsession with bread (or even grains in a broader sense) obscures the fact that they probably could subsist on such foods as chestnuts and cabbage, as Turgot himself suggested, Galiani rejects an anthropology that would provide a norm by which the people's needs would be denounced as excessive or superfluous. Instead, he, represented in the *Dialogues* by the Chevalier Zanobi, insists on the historical and even geographical variability of these needs, without thereby rejecting their irreducible reality. His interlocutor, le Marquis, responds to the Chevalier's insistence on the nutritional requirements of the human body, which, whatever the historically specific forms through which these requirements are met, cannot be abolished or denied by decree, by calling him "a delicate anatomist of man."

But it is precisely this delicate anatomy, the stubborn and untimely reminder that behind supply and demand (the latter understood not simply as preference but more importantly as the ability to pay for what one wants) is the irreducible physical need for nourishment, a need all the more pressing when it cannot take the form of market demand, that is, when the human individual cannot afford to exist, that allows the Chevalier to begin his interrogation of the doctrine of free commerce in grain. Even as grain is a product sold on the market, it is also, unlike nearly all other such crops produced in Europe, a matter of physical necessity and therefore the central concern of any civil order: "To eat or not to eat bread is not a matter of taste, caprice or luxury" (Dialogue IV). As such, unlike other commodities, grain is a political matter before it is an economic matter and "once provisioning becomes a matter of politics, it ceases to be an object of commerce" (Dialogue II). Political acts, legislation such as the Edict of 1764 deregulating the grain trade, Galiani argues, must be judged by their effects. Against the notion that there is an irreversible march (natural progress) toward allowing the market to set prices and thereby determine the availability of food, le Chevalier asks, "Do you believe that eating bread at an affordable price is something that may go out of fashion?" (Dialogue IV). The true philosopher is a "physician of the state" who in this case must warn against the patient destroying himself through repeated and ever-more radical attempts at a cure, the political equivalents of bleeding and purging more likely to kill than to heal the patient.

It is in Dialogue VI that Galiani takes up the question of commerce in grain in its specificity and most openly confronts the stated and unstated assumptions guiding the partisans of liberty. He begins by defining commerce in a general sense as "the exchange of the superfluous for the necessary," thereby substituting the term "superfluous" for "supply" and "necessary" for "demand." In this way commerce, above all commerce in grain, cannot be separated from the question of the needs of the population: A commodity is never simply a supply, a given quantity without reference to the population that produces and consumes it. On the contrary, it exists as a supply only to the extent that it exceeds not the demand of a population able to purchase what it requires, but rather the physical need of that population, a need that high price, for example, may make it impossible for the people to meet. Grain or wheat (*le blé*) can in fact never be superfluous: It "is after the elements the greatest, most pressing and most continuous of man's needs" (Dialogue VI). Just as elements like water, equally necessary to human life, can never be the object of commerce (as if a nation could trade away its water supply), stores of wheat cannot be allowed to be sold abroad, leaving a population vulnerable to the slightest vicissitudes of climate. It can be considered superfluous only from the point of view of an individual proprietor or producer, but never from the perspective of "the entire French empire. All the subjects of the same master, all the children of this good father have an equal right to be guaranteed food [*un droit égal à être assuré de leur nourriture*]" (Dialogue VI).

It is this necessary right to food, a right coextensive with existence itself, which accordingly must be understood as the actual capacity to obtain and consume food, and not simply the right to a supply of food theoretically but not in fact available to the people, that distinguishes food from other commodities such as shoes. One can go without shoes, can repair them, make crude sandals or sabots out of wood, but one cannot go more than a few days without being severely weakened by the absence of nourishment: "Can you make a pound of bread last twenty days in your house?"(Dialogue VI). Further, from the perspective of human anatomy, Galiani begins to interrogate the theory of free commerce—not so much to reject its postulates as to read the necessary actions of the market in relation to the body. He does not dispute, for example, that the high price of food during a *disette* will likely attract grain merchants from other provinces and even other nations seeking gain and that, after an interval, "equilibrium" will be restored. But what if this interval is too long and "equilibrium arrives too late, when people have already died of hunger?" (Dialogue VI). By insisting on the existence of an interval that is not that which changes the relation of supply to demand, but rather that which separates food from those who cannot afford to purchase the quantity necessary to their existence (those whose need, however urgent, does not qualify as demand), Galiani makes visible what would otherwise be outside of and invisible to the market.

And it is here, in this interval or opening, that we can begin to see the relation of the unrestricted market in grain to life and to death. At this point, his interlocutor responds to the significance, the life or death significance, that the Chevalier assigns to the interval by complaining that he "cannot understand how such a small thing as the absence of a few hundred sacks of wheat can be regarded as so great an evil?"(Dialogue VI). Le Marquis here introduces his own "anatomical" argument (which is, we should note, similar to those of the physiocrats or Smith himself, but if anything more understated than theirs): Surely the people can get along on less food than they normally consume, perhaps even significantly less and for an indeterminate period of time. The Chevalier responds with a description of "some particulars" of famine, confronting the imaginary body, so wonderfully malleable that it can be made to adjust to nearly any condition, necessary to the arguments of the economists, with the anatomy of starvation. Hunger in this sense is not "a universal affliction"; the rich do not suffer from it, and farmers and merchants may profit greatly from the opportunities it affords. But while doing so, perhaps in order to do so, they refrain from looking upon the others,

> The people dying of hunger who can be seen wandering in the streets, specters, hideous skeletons whose skin is burned red, with bleary eyes and limp hair, covered with sores and vermin; you see them approach you with a shuffling gait, asking in a hoarse whisper and with trembling hand for a piece of bread. And sometimes at the moment you try to help them, you see them fall at your feet and die in the dirt.

But perhaps only 5 percent of the population is reduced to such a condition, that is, only one in twenty will die of hunger: The Chevalier responds by forcing the reader to imagine the effects of even "a single person dying of hunger in the street" (Dialogue VI). It is, he tells us, enough to bring horror and desolation to an entire city.

But Galiani does not insist on the extreme case of famine: He is one of the few, perhaps the only one in this entire debate, to ask what it means for a family to go days without food while waiting for the equilibrium of the market to be restored, or to make a week's provisions last for two in the face of high prices. He is one of the first to use the term "malnourished" and to point out the greater susceptibility to disease that prolonged malnutrition inevitably produces. Absolute freedom of commerce in grain without the public granaries so costly to taxpayers and so injurious to the operation of the market can assure nothing more than that sooner or later, after an interval whose duration cannot be determined in advance, grain will arrive where it is not to be found or that prices will fall over time where it exists, but in short supply and priced out of reach.

To establish by law a commerce without restriction of any kind what is necessary to the people's survival, that is, through legal action to place it beyond the reach of law and of political decision making even in the name of the abundance to come, is to renounce any guarantee of the subsistence of the population, especially insofar as such a guarantee could only interfere with the only means of preventing future famine, if not *disette*. It is precisely in order to make death and malnourishment visible that Galiani insists on a right proper to the individual considered as a subject of subsistence as well as the form of the subject's subsistence, as if the subject were the living substrate on the basis of which alone something like subjection to a sovereign is possible. Obedience to the sovereign authority is predicated on that authority's ability to guarantee existence; the reformers have proposed to annul any

such guarantee. In this sense, to abandon price controls, regulation, and public granaries is to abandon the subjects themselves to whatever provision the
market makes—with its intervals, its interstices, its bottlenecks, and its crises
of over- and underproduction. It is to call upon these subjects to accept (or be
compelled by force to accept) their own deprivation as the necessary means
to the market's equilibrium.

Galiani makes visible the contradiction that haunts this doctrine: The right
to be guaranteed subsistence—that is, to be able to continue to live, is different from other rights; it is the very possibility that there exists someone to be
endowed with rights and is therefore the foundation even of the right to subject
oneself to the sovereign. If the sovereign not only refuses any such guarantee by
allowing the market to act upon her subjects without restriction of any kind—
and if they are not killed as punishment for a criminal act but abandoned by
legal decision and allowed to die; or even merely exposed to the threat of death
by hunger and malnutrition not only without any guarantee of aid, but on the
contrary, guaranteed that no such aid will be provided by the government—
and her subjects are told that they must wait for the invisible hand to provide
for them as it will, is not the tie of subjection broken? And if this is the case,
if the people have been abandoned by law, by what right does the government
command their obedience? Even more seriously, on what legal and political
grounds can it condemn those whose uprisings, riots, and seditious assemblies
demand nothing more than the people's subsistence, itself the ground of any
conceivable political or legal existence?

Galiani's questions and arguments, his insistence on the political priority of
the anatomical facts of the human body over mathematical calculations or even
questions of legality, which made the question of subsistence a political rather
than an economic matter (precisely the fundamental political matter: the basis
of law in life), posed enormous challenges to his critics. And of the challenges,
none was more vexing than the assertion of an equal right to be guaranteed
food, a right as seemingly incontrovertible as it was ruinous to the very idea of
the market's natural order. Perhaps only a "conservative" like Galiani could risk
proposing a right that by definition could not be confined to a merely formal
existence guaranteed in law, while material conditions prevented many from
exercising it, as in the case of the famous freedoms enshrined in the great constitutions of the late eighteenth century. The right to be guaranteed food, on
the contrary, was a right whose fulfillment lay in its realization: It exists as a
right only if people have food. Even more, the demand for equal provisioning

is only in part aimed at the state; it is also a demand to reject and overcome the unequal distribution of food according to price by the market itself, whose partisans could no longer invoke the adequate supply it has provided without concerning themselves with the question of whether or not the people actually have enough to eat. According to Galiani's formulation, if the people do not in fact consume sufficient food, what is theirs by right has been denied them, and the legitimacy of the political order, upon whose use of force the operation of the market and the very existence of the private property that is its necessary foundation relies, is called into question.

Two of the most notable responses to *Dialogues*, both by physiocrats who otherwise collaborated quite closely, addressed the question of a right to be guaranteed subsistence in distinct and even opposing ways. Le Mercier de la Rivière, in *L'intérêt general de l'État et la liberté de la commerce des blés* (1770), far from rejecting the guarantee of food as an obstacle to the market, sought to argue, or to appear to argue, for freedom of commerce in grain on the basis of the right Galiani had proposed. In promoting what he called "a right to existence," however, he provided what Galiani's argument, at least in any explicit sense, lacked: a theory of society in which alone the right to subsistence could assume its full significance. There could be no society without a general interest, "the natural and constant counter-force" that prevents particular interests and wills from dissolving society:

> It is obviously impossible that a multitude of men, a multitude of sensible and intelligent beings made to determine themselves and to act only according to the motives that operate within them, could form one and the same political body, except if the unification of their particular interests produced the unification of their particular wills and forces to give them one and the same direction; unity of interest is therefore the very essence of this body.[70]

This unity of interest must not be confused with the interest of the majority in a given society, nor with that of a specific class, no matter how numerous. In fact, the very existence of something like a general interest will "only be publically recognized to the extent that the essential and fundamental objects to which it is confined, are obviously fixed and obviously determinate."[71] In this way, it may be understood by the public at large that the general interest is itself founded on an invariant, law-governed, and therefore natural order. In the case of the provisioning of society, the order that forms the basis of the general interest is that of the market itself, based not on arbitrary and artificial laws themselves determined by particular interests, but by the immutable and impersonal laws of supply and demand.

Thus, Mercier de la Rivière has supplied a new foundation for a right, if not identical to that formulated by Galiani, at least close enough to appear to endorse its motives. He has subtly shifted the argument from the life of the individual in its particularity, which now appears as nothing more than an expression of that individual's will, to the general interest and therefore the life that is the object of this interest of society as a whole. It is this general life, if we may call it that, founded not on particular (individual or collective) interests but on reason itself, concerned only with the unvarying and inalterable laws that govern natural beings, that makes the particular life possible. Thus, "among men united in society, the primary root of the common interest is to assure, as much as is possible, the means of existence."[72]

That this right is not identical in substance or form to that proposed by Galiani is clear enough. Mercier de la Rivière's introduction of "as far as is possible" (*autant qu'il est possible*) as a qualification of this right that he will later call absolutely necessary to society raises the question of the nature of the possibility or impossibility of assuring individuals the means of existence. This right or law, as he will go on to explain, both makes necessary but is itself dependent on other fundamental laws, namely "the laws concerning the reproduction and distribution of necessities [*subsistances*]."

In order to give substance to the primary law of existence, secondary laws must provide for the "multiplication of those goods necessary to our existence."[73] Among them, the right to or law of property in land, the means by which the particular interest of the owner or cultivator leads him to produce as much as possible to earn a profit and thus unites him with others in a general interest in the subsistence of the general life: "The more he seeks to increase his production in order to increase his pleasures, the more he serves the common interest of society."[74] For such service to occur, the proprietor must have exclusive right to his harvest and the freedom to distribute it as he wishes. To complain about the proprietor's freedom is not only to call into question one's own freedom to dispose of one's own person as one sees fit, but more importantly to oppose the necessary order on which the production of abundance is founded and thereby endanger the very distribution of life's necessities that human existence demands.

In this way, Galiani's right must be understood as a paradox: The very quantity of food to which everyone is guaranteed equal access is endangered by the guarantee itself, which, despite appearances, discourages production and thereby opposes the common interest, undermining the freedom of proprietors and calling into question the natural right of property. In this sense, the market's distribution of food, no matter how unequal and how intensive and extensive the deprivation it imposes on the majority of the people, can be considered just, the sole way to the abundance that alone can guarantee a right to existence.

In contrast, Abbé Roubaud's *Récréations économiques* (1770) draws from Abeille's comments to launch an assault on the very notion of a right to be guaranteed food. His tone is one of outrage: The mere fact that people need food does not give them a right to it. Is not all food already the legitimate possession of proprietors whose right would be violated if they were compelled to surrender it to others who merely require it but who have no legal title to it? The erroneous association of subsistence needs with the right to the means of subsistence without any regard to proprietary status has in fact brought about a general inflation of the very notion of right, expanding its realm by multiplying individual rights without regard to consistency. There now exists an incoherent "excess of rights," which functions as a "prohibition" on the right of property.[75]

Property, if it is to be more than merely what happens to be in a person's possession and that, if it is more necessary to another, may legitimately be transferred to that other with or without the holder's agreement, cannot simply be the object of one right among so many others. It must carry with it "immunity, the necessary complement of liberty,"[76] above all the liberty to dispose of one's property as one sees fit. Merchants, for example, are often the object of popular opprobrium, as if by merely owning the nation's grain supply and by rightfully keeping it in their possession, distributing it when they alone see fit, irrespective of the "needs," real or imagined, of those around them, they were guilty of a crime, theft or extortion, or even at the extreme, should some unfortunate happen to die of starvation, murder:

> The merchant does not steal, he buys, and what he has paid for belongs to him. . . . To the extent that he sells, he feeds men and murders no one. To the extent that he buys, he collects food for the places where it is needed, and he is the happy supplier of those who would otherwise die of hunger without his aid and service. He is neither thief nor murderer and is in a sense the savior and nourisher of peoples. If it should come to pass that there are unfortunates unable to buy their food, it is nevertheless not permitted to take food from him or even

to force him to sell it at a certain price. For it is his possession, he owes it to no one, and if he is not the master who decides what is to be done with it, he will abandon a business so useful to others but so onerous to him.[77]

Let us leave to the side for the moment the now-familiar argument that without absolute property there can be no (motive for) commerce, no competition to lower prices and improve both quality and quantity, and therefore no progressive enlargement of society's wealth. What is striking in this passage is the legal and political admonition: If it comes to pass, as it may, as it will, that there are persons (whose number as a percentage of the population is irrelevant to the argument at hand) who for whatever reason are unable to buy the food that the merchant owns, it is not his duty or responsibility to provide them with what is nevertheless necessary to their existence, and no third party, not even the state (which on the contrary must indemnify him), can in justice ask him to do so.

Roubaud calls such persons "*les malheureux*," and while they are indeed unfortunate, given that they are starving, their very inability to pay for their subsistence is construed in this passage as a demand. The mere presence of many who cannot buy what they must have to live is experienced as a kind of threat to the merchants and their property: "*Il ne faut pas pour cela la lui enlever ou le forcer à la donner à tel prix*."[78] Their hunger, the immediate threat to their life, otherwise so compelling, is explicitly ruled out as a justification for requisitioning the food that belongs to the merchants or even of forcing them to sell their stock at a price low enough to allow the malnourished and starving to purchase the nourishment they require. Merchants, grain merchants, precisely in order to fulfill their function as provisioners of the nation must enjoy a freedom that takes the form of immunity from any obligation to recognize or respect a general right to existence.[79] Those who oppose this "freedom, or immunity," whether out of fear of the multitude or pity for the hungry are in fact "enemies of the public good,"[80] preventing the amassing of wealth necessary to increase the cultivation and therefore supply of food, the only effective means to lower prices and feed the people as a whole.

Others, especially in this time of *disette*—that Roubaud admits is an unfortunate but necessary consequence of the lifting of restrictions on the grain trade in 1764, which included measures designed to guarantee food to the population ("there is no revolution without crisis; the current crisis has already arrived, and it must be suffered because it is necessary to the well-being of the people and the restoration of the State"[81])—have proposed a temporary regime of shared and proportional sacrifice simply in order to supply the necessities of life to the poor, a sacrifice that falls particularly on those who alone own and control the nation's food supply. But, he asks,

> Can the Authorities order *sacrifices*? Sacrifice is voluntary; it is a relinquishing of right derived from the freedom to use one's property as one will for the advantage of another. It is an act of generosity and generosity is not commanded. Forced sacrifice is therefore a chimerical idea, the force which constrains it being the work of tyranny. When you deprive yourself of the right over legitimately acquired goods, the enjoyment of which is both useful and agreeable in favor of another person, this is a sacrifice. If Judges issue an order for you to deprive yourself of such goods for the benefit of another who has no legal title to them and under the pretext that the other needs them, this would be an injustice. The Authorities cannot through regulations order the proprietor of food to sacrifice any of his rights over this food to satisfy the interests and needs of a third party who has no such rights.[82]

The nation's food supply is thus in the hands of those who are precisely exempted from any responsibility for the life and death of their fellows, and so it must be if its benefits are to reach "those who have not yet felt its advantages."[83]

Because we are not speaking here of something as vague and indeterminate as mere poverty or penury, but of the need for that which, like water, is necessary to human survival, the immunity that food merchants enjoy, while not a nullification of the right to exist (indeed, Roubaud argues that the right of property is coextensive with the right to exist in so far as proprietary rights over food constitute the necessary foundation of unrestricted commerce and competition), exempts the merchant from any claims, legal or customary, based on the right to existence and extends protection precisely to the merchant's goods that alone can give reality to others' right to live. The grain merchant owes nothing to anyone else and by his immunity is absolved of any responsibility for their survival.

The obligation, service, or sacrifice unjustly demanded of the merchant for the benefit of "*l'autrui*" is, as Roberto Esposito reminds us (*munus* and *cum* or *communitas*—community), precisely "the totality of persons united not by a 'property,' but by an obligation or a debt."[84] The legitimate proprietor (in this case, the proprietor of grain) must be in advance immunized against the very possibility of an expropriation by means of an imposed sacrifice and exempted from the burden of the bonds of community, an exemption that leaves those who cannot augment his property abandoned to a death by starvation for which he no longer bears any responsibility. Through a kind of homeopathy, the proprietors of grain described by Roubaud paradoxically provide for the lives of their fellows only in so far as they are released from any responsibility for the welfare of others. The universality or (to cite Hegel again) *Gemeinheit* actualized in the material form of the market has thus abolished community or *Gemeinschaft*, replacing it with an immunitary regime in which the *res proprium* precedes and makes possible the *res publica*, as if a perpetually reasserted absence of, or indeed an increasingly violent protection from, the responsibilities of fellowship is all that can determine the individual—unwittingly—to aid his fellows.

And, in a way, this very freedom, the freedom that Roubaud imagines, is coextensive with the proprietor's immunity and is extended to those against whose claims he is immunized, as if there occurs a kind of reciprocal exclusion or the realization of a mutual independency (that is, a non-dependence) in which the unfortunate individual abandons his claim on the proprietor who has abandoned him. The social relation henceforth is understood as a subtraction, even a despoliation, from which individuals must be protected by the state. The effects of this protection, however, are far from equal: While the proprietor flourishes and affirms his being by extending the realm of the proprium as far as possible, the non-proprietor of food is protected from himself, from the dependency he would demand that both the state and the proprietor recognize, and is by that fact restored to himself and abandoned to death.

If the immunity proper to free commerce protects the grain merchant from the expropriative violence of the people, the contagion of whose fear and hatred may spread to the officers of the government during a *disette*, requiring a generalized surveillance (as Turgot in his capacity as Intendant of the province of Limousin argued in his "Lettre aux Officiers de Police des villes de sa Généralité où il y a des Marchés de Grains" in 1765), it does so only through a violent rejection of any attempt on the merchant's liberty to enjoy his right over his property as he sees fit. The granting of immunity to those apparently most able to fulfill the right to existence who, because they seem the most powerful to the multitude are in fact most at risk of plunder, theft, and violence, implies that they, as much as or more than the starving, merit the state's protection and require it to assure the security of their property. In fact, the state's withdrawal, however partial and intermittent, from the economic sphere in both Britain and France was more than matched by the militarization of its response to food protests and the increasing repression employed to protect the merchant's immunity.[85] But we should be clear: Economists might dream of neutralizing claims based on a right to subsistence through an immunization of the proprietors of the nation's grain supply, but such dreams or projects inevitably foundered against the realities of resistance that prevented the absolutization of property right, especially insofar as the property in question was food. Indeed, as E. P. Thompson has shown,[86] the mere threat of disorder was often sufficient to exact concessions from even the most ardent defenders of the unrestricted market.

Thus, Turgot, faced with the reality of a relation of social forces that could at any moment, through a crystallization of otherwise disparate and dispersed movements and protests, overwhelm the meager resources of a provincial government, could not afford, if only for strategic reasons, merely to abandon the hungry and the panic stricken. As is well known, despite his unwavering support for the unrestricted market in grains and in food more generally, coupled with his opposition to traditional forms of charity that he regarded as obstacles to their industry, Turgot moved decisively and above all quickly to allay both hunger and panic among the people.[87]

But even his relief measures worked tactically to weaken popular resistance. Feeding the hungry in their homes, he argued, would prevent them from congregating together in a common space where rumors could spread and agitators could incite riot and revolt. By dividing them into those who had to work (in public works projects of his creation) and those who didn't, those who were trusted with money wages and those who weren't, Turgot effectively established a hierarchical separation of the poor that diminished the possibility of collective action. Because he feared that local administrators might sympathize with the hungry, he sent each of them a copy of Le Trosne's *La liberté du commerce des grains toujours utile et jamais nuisible* (1765) to persuade them that free commerce in grain was the only effective means of increasing the food supply and lowering prices. If the authorities encourage "the people's prejudice against commerce," through "indiscreet searches" of warehouses and shops where large stores of grain were rumored to be hidden, and failed to assure merchants of profit on their investments, the latter will abandon the grain trade to the detriment of the nation's food supplies.

According to Turgot, the people in their "blind rage" either want the merchants to sell grain at a low price or simply have it taken from them. They must be made to understand that whatever the inconveniences and deprivation, commerce in grains must be left to act according to its own rationality, which may mean that for a time their needs will not be met. But the measures of "enlightened prudence" may not entirely succeed in "calming emotions" or preventing the spread of alarm among the people. In such cases,

> Too much indulgence would have much greater effects for the people who, abandoned to itself, would grow increasingly passionate and, knowing no restraint, would proceed to the most deadly excesses against the objects of its absurd imputations and, even more, against itself. The Government is obliged, despite itself, to arm the just severity of the laws and the guilty to expiate on the scaffold the crime to which their blind impetuosity had led them before it could be repressed.[88]

In its choice of measures, the government must at all cost avoid those "that might tend to stir up the populace, to gratify it, to allow it to believe that its fears, its false imputations against the proprietors of grain, the supposed monopolists, are shared."[89] Despite itself: Turgot fears that the power of the seditious assemblies (*les attroupements seditieux*), the roving packs (*pelotons*) of rioters and looters, may be converted into a right and divert the food from the ends determined by the free will of its proprietors to the people's consumption, with the connivance, if not the legal cooperation, of the government.

And his fears were well-founded: In the struggle against death by starvation, that is, in the struggle for life against death, few possessed the requisite faith in the opulence to come. The immunity of the proprietors of food to the claims of those who otherwise could not pay for their subsistence was accordingly perpetually in question. Even Turgot himself recognized that the people's mobilization, which repression alone might not dissipate, could overturn the social order beyond the possibility of any restoration and was forced to demand of the rich that they surrender a portion of their wealth to avoid such an eventuality, as if in a paradoxical turn of events, their very immunity threatened their own existence.

The right, as formulated by Galiani, of every individual to be guaranteed subsistence, and thus a right irreducible to a merely formal existence, emerged in reaction to the assertion of the merchants' absolute proprietorship of grains, itself understood as the necessary foundation of market order. It appeared to the partisans of liberty not only as a defense of a bad cause, but as a failure to recognize that just as God, according to Leibniz, by the "permitting of sins," brings about "greater good than such as occurred before the sins," so the market by being permitted (*laisser*) to deprive some of subsistence will bring about greater opulence than existed before the deprivation. The question of "an enforceable right to existence," by its stubborn persistence not only in the discourses of political economy but in the slogans and demands of popular resistance, demonstrates that the very notion of the unrestricted market has the structure of a theodicy that by compensating every evil by a greater good immunizes itself against intervention or critique, and in which imperceptibly what was once evil has become good, and what was good has become evil, so that life itself threatens to become nothing more than a means to the end of an inhuman order.

In fact, the inquiry into the order and dependencies of the different parts of the system of commerce will reveal still greater goods to be achieved by the apparent evil of refusing any guarantee of subsistence. By abandoning individuals to death by starvation through the act of refraining from taking any action, the state again, by letting the market act as it does, fosters that very "dread of death . . . that guards and protects the society": Not the dread of death by hanging, but the dread of death by exposure, hunger, disease, the fear of dying in the street or on the road—all the more distressing in that one cannot help but imagine oneself an object of contempt and disgust to those who pass by. It is as if the invisible hand works not by providing for all, but by *not* providing for all, or as if through a kind of monstrous and parodic doubling, a second invisible hand arrives immediately after the first, placing what has been distributed by it just out of reach of a certain number of the earth's inhabitants.

No one, of course, knows or intends that these particular individuals be deprived of the "necessaries of life" ("Let not your left hand know what your right hand is doing," Matthew 6: 3): Just as the rain that could have watered withering crops fell instead on the ocean, so the food that could have fed the indigent went to satisfy market demand elsewhere, the unavoidable effect of the design of the whole. Further, the knowledge that what has been given may be taken away without warning creates the sense of insecurity (not in relation to property of course, but in relation to life) necessary to a prosperous society. Thus, it is not simply the illusion that hard work will make one rich that leads the mass of people to spend their lives in hard labor; they are goaded into work and kept there as much by the ever-present specter of deprivation, the sense that at any time and through no fault of their own they could be deprived of the means of subsistence and left to starve.

Smith's response to these debates is to change terrain entirely. He carefully avoids the question of a legal right to subsistence by abandoning questions of legality and right altogether, while nevertheless responding in other terms to the argument that free commerce requires that populations from time to time be exposed (with all that this interesting term implies) to starvation (if it is to remain free and not governed directly or indirectly by the irrational multitude). It is commonly argued today that Smith was not the proponent of the free market that he was understood to be for two centuries; if that is true, his attitude to the market in grains, which, unlike the market in pins, is necessary to the people's subsistence, is an exception. "The unlimited, unrestrained freedom of the corn trade" (*Wealth* 527) is the only way to prevent famine and to manage dearth. In opposition, famine has never been caused by merchants' hoarding or by excessive market prices: It "has never arisen from any other cause but the violence of government attempting, by improper means, to remedy the inconveniencies of a dearth" (*Wealth* 526). As Thompson has pointed out,

> Smith was not "the only standard-bearer for 'natural liberty' in grain," but he was one of the more extreme standard-bearers for this liberty to remain uncontrolled even in times of great scarcity. And he must have known very well that it was exactly this point of emergency measures in time of dearth that was most controversial. His notable forerunner in developing *Political Oeconomy*, Sir James Steuart, had refused this fence, and was an advocate of the stockpiling of grain in public granaries for sale in time of dearth.[90]

Similarly, as we have noted, Turgot, a figure for whom Smith had the highest regard, proposes very elaborate measures for a non-market response to famine. In this context, Smith's avoidance of the problem of emergency or short-term measures during times of dearth or famine— which in turn implied the question of whether such measures, insofar as they constitute artificial intrusions into the market, should be carried out at all, and if so, under what conditions— is all the more striking.[91] We want now to explore the precise form this avoidance takes and how it shapes both Smith's argument and his rhetoric.

In the passage on the invisible hand invoked above, the world's rich, very much against their intentions, are led to distribute to the rest of the earth's inhabitants the "necessaries of life." Apart from the small sum that the world's beggars succeed in "extorting" (Smith's term) from them, this distribution takes the form of the payment of wages. Here, and we refer to Chapter 8 of Book I of *Wealth*, we no longer confront a world of autonomous individuals led by self-interest to truck, barter, and exchange for their advantage, a theoretical framework that could easily accommodate the labor contract, understood as an exchange between individuals. Instead, as noted previously, Smith explains the antagonism that, in part, determines the rate of wages, that is, the extent of the distributions made by the world's rich, as collective in nature:

> What are the common wages of labor, depends everywhere on the contract made between those two parties, whose interests are by no means the same. The workmen desire to get as much as possible, the masters to give as little as possible. The former are disposed to combine in order to raise, the latter in order to lower the wages of labor. (*Wealth* 83)

We will leave to the side the fact that the very notion of collective action invoked here poses a series of questions and problems that Smith does not, and perhaps cannot, address given the constraints of his theory. Suffice it to say, though, that the competing "parties," a term that allows him to move freely between the individual and the collective, function exactly as individuals whose competition and opposition produces, without their knowledge or consent, a "nearly" equal distribution of life's necessities.

Appearances are indeed deceiving: The nature of the market is, of course, such that all the advantage in this contest between workmen and their masters lies with the latter. The workmen cannot quit, nor can they refrain from work in protest over wages for more than a few days. Their ability to maintain themselves, their very subsistence, depends on their earning a wage: They are thus constrained by a dread of destitution every bit as effective as the dread of execution in a world without any guarantee of subsistence.

The masters, in contrast, have sufficient stock, in most cases, to "live a year or two" without employing labor. This advantage allows them "to force" the workmen "into a compliance with their terms" (*Wealth* 83). And their terms are often not very favorable: Smith's masters "are always and everywhere in a sort of tacit, but constant and uniform combination, not to raise the wages of labor above their actual rate" (*Wealth* 84). Further, they will "sometimes enter into particular combinations to sink the wages of labor even below this rate" (*Wealth* 84). The market appears to have placed few, if any, limits on the ability of the masters to increase their profit simply by lowering the amount they expend on wages.

Does this then mean that at the whim of the employers, wages, barring interference from the state, may fall below what is necessary to the laborer's mere survival (and not even that of his family)? It is at this point that Smith inserts a floor that has nothing to do with law or the state. The limit on the lowering of wages is the limit of the market itself: It is none other than the bare life of the workman, whose "wages must at least be sufficient to maintain him . . . at a rate consistent with common humanity" and even "somewhat more; otherwise it would be impossible for him to bring up a family, and the race of such workmen could not last beyond the first generation" (*Wealth* 85).

How could the market permit the destruction of the labor force from which its existence derives? In this way, Smith (with Turgot) offers an alternative to the artificial declaration of a right to be guaranteed subsistence based on a legality or even morality external to the market's design. Instead of denouncing or redefining such a right, as the notoriously imprudent physiocrats did, Smith insists that subsistence is necessary to the system of commerce itself, one of the heretofore invisible intricacies of its order, as if the physical existence of the worker were simultaneously the logical and biological foundation of the market itself. Thus, there is no more need to regulate wages than prices: It is impossible for them to fall below the rate at which the laborer can purchase the means of subsistence. State intervention through wage laws cannot possibly keep pace with the constantly fluctuating ratio of wage to price, and any such action will subvert with perhaps grave results the rationality that realizes itself in each of the market's movements.

While such a postulate might seem to offer the great majority in any society nothing more than an assurance of a life of hard labor for their mere subsistence, in fact it is the foundation for the only rational means to increase the rate of wages and thus improve their lives. A reduction of wages to the level of subsistence paradoxically (dialectically?) allows the fund available for the payment of wages to accumulate to such an extent that the only outcome can be the employment of more hands:

> When in any country the demand for those who live by wages, laborers, journeymen, servants of every kind is continually increasing, when every year furnishes employment for a greater number than had been employed the year before, the workmen have no occasion to combine in order to raise their wages. (*Wealth* 86)

If government could simply see that by "leaving things at perfect liberty," unbridled competition between both workers (to which every form of labor organizations—whether guilds or the incipient forms of trade unions—pose a grave threat) and masters will naturally produce a continual increase in demand for wage labor arising from the continual expansion of a market: This is the answer to deprivation and hunger, as well as to the shocking violence of workers protesting wage reductions. Full employment and rising wages will render such disasters relics of the superseded past. And just as the poor today live better than the rich of several centuries ago, so too will tomorrow's poor enjoy what is today unimaginable opulence.

Does this mean then that Smith's sympathies lie with the masters rather than the workmen, or that even if he can complain, for example, about the quality of persons who today elect to become corn merchants, he nevertheless must take their side in the struggle against labor, since it is their accumulation of capital that guarantees progress? This is clearly not the case. As numerous recent commentators have pointed out, he appears more sympathetic to the laboring classes in *Wealth* than in the *TMS*—as if the idealization of suffering and of the capacity to endure it had faded in the face of the realities of poverty, starvation, and disease (perhaps, above all, the great hunger that afflicted both France and Britain in the fall and winter of 1766–67).

For just as masters seek the highest prices the market will bear for their products, so they will seek to pay the lowest wages they can convince, compel, or coerce their laborers to accept, even or especially if these are below the "prevailing rate." Sometimes these actions, while understandably irksome to the laborer, are no more than expressions of a change in the ratio of supply to demand and thus of the wisdom of an unhampered market. At other times, though, Smith suggests that masters can through collective action (that is, monopoly) artificially lower wages below their market rate and thus interfere with the operation of its immutable laws in a way that will ultimately disturb their own trade. Further, when legislatures in the past have regulated wages, they have done so to set an upper, not a lower, limit on wages, and their "counselors are always the masters" (*Wealth* 142). If they have occasionally passed laws "in favor of the workmen," such laws are "always just and equitable" (*Wealth* 142).

Since any law interfering with the operation of the market (e.g., a minimum wage law or laws restricting the employers' right to dismiss their laborers at will) cannot genuinely be in favor of the workers, it is clear that Smith here refers to the "sacred right" of the laborer's property in his or her own person. Just as there can be no restriction on the master's right to adjust wages as his interest compels him to do given the labor market or to increase or decrease the number he employs at will, so nothing can legitimately restrict the worker's direction of his own person: He has the sacred right to change his employment or his place of residence as he sees fit, and the repeal of laws that have historically hindered this right is perhaps the most important action that legislatures can take in favor of labor.

In fact, there should be, Smith argues, a legal equality between masters and workers in the matter of combination: Why is the conspiracy of masters any less harmful to the competition necessary to an increase in general wealth than that of the workers? Why shouldn't their freedom to cooperate for mutual gain be as limited as that of the workers when it is clear that it disrupts the chain of necessity by which the market governs itself? It is worth noting here that while movements of workers to raise or masters to lower the price of labor appear to take place within the system of commerce, they are in fact extrinsic and inimical to it: Laws limiting these movements therefore not only do not constitute interference in its operations, but they are necessary precisely to protect them.

The market, which the state both leaves to itself and makes sure through the threat of punishment that others leave to itself, thus insures that the laborer's deprivation can never fall below the level of basic subsistence into starvation; however, the precise nature of this wage floor—which by virtue of arising spontaneously from the market itself rather than from legislative action is imposed with the force of a law of nature—remains to be explained. This renders the deprivation tolerable and survivable so that like the small evil the innocent suffer so that a greater good may follow, the worker's deprivation is the evil permitted to exist, left alone without any ill-advised attempt to "remedy" what is not a disorder but part of the very mechanism of order, because it is the sole means to the end of the perpetual expansion that alone guarantees the improvement of the laborer's lot.

Whatever the incommodities of such an order—and, here Smith is disarmingly honest, they are considerable, especially for the workers who spend most of their waking hours in mind-numbing labor for little more than subsistence wages—the alternatives can only be worse: There exist certain societies, and Smith adduces examples only from the non-European world, a fact that undoubtedly merits attention and cannot be simply attributed to a generalized Orientalism, where the nature of the "laws and institutions" (of which there is no further specification here) does not permit them to acquire greater wealth, societies he deems "stationary" and incapable of growth, in which the downward limit on wages appears far more variable that the phrase "consistent with common humanity" would appear to suggest. The vagueness of the formulation allows us to imagine that the laws and institutions referred to are those that countenance or mandate interference in the immutable order of economic life and in doing so inhibit its functioning.

By attempting to aid the people, such laws and institutions only hurt them, just as every attempt to alleviate a subsistence crisis by attempting to overrule the natural laws of supply and demand only aggravates it. The only genuine guarantee of subsistence lies in the abandonment of any merely legal guarantee that will inevitably be invoked when it is not needed—that is, when the people fear crisis and the government fears the people, disrupting commerce and finally bringing about the famine that such laws seek to prevent. For in China, understood as the nation whose governments have for centuries attempted to impose human laws on the oeconomy's natural order and thus represents an experiment in the effects of a quasi-permanent market regulation, not even a high rate of infant mortality such as is consequent to the poverty of the Scottish Highlanders—where, he tells us, perhaps only two out of twenty children survive (*Wealth* 133)—will suffice to allocate wages to the degree necessary to maintain the laborer: Only the market freed from legal guarantees of subsistence can offer an effective guarantee that can no more be violated than the law of gravity.

Instead, even in the face of high infant mortality (which according to his narrative is not simply endured, but permitted and even facilitated), the fact that many thousands of families subsist on such scant resources as "the carcass of a dead dog or cat, for example, though half putrid and stinking" and is "as welcome to them as the most wholesome food is to the people of other countries," means that in order for the laborer to subsist, his children must be destroyed, that is, if not killed, abandoned, "exposed in the street or drowned like puppies in the water" (*Wealth* 90). The rhetorical force of these lines is striking: Smith could have conveyed his point simply by noting a diet that consists of carcasses of dead animals considered inedible by Europeans, a formulation that is by itself strongly hyperbolic. Too add the qualifier "though half putrid and stinking," which emphasizes the olfactory experience of such food through repetition ("putrid" itself already signifies the odor emitted by rotting matter) is to attempt to create a sense of disgust in the reader at a scene of rotting carcasses in which the living must feed off the dead. While Smith in all probability could not have known that food consumption in eighteenth-century China was perhaps equal to if not greater than that in most of Europe in the same period,[92] and can be excused for deriving his information from the available sources, it is surely worth considering more carefully than has been done the nature and function of the passages and images he extracts from the four volumes and nearly three thousand pages of Du Halde's portrait of China in his text.[93]

To begin with, the images cited above are typical of the scenes of famine reported in many European languages throughout the eighteenth century. Moreover, food crisis, as it is now called, was neither unusual nor unacknowledged throughout Europe: Indeed, far from being the result of clumsy state intervention, it appeared, with varying degrees of severity of course, to be a regular feature of life in the West and probably, as is now recognized, more so than in China.[94] For a catalogue of disgusting and disturbing images, Smith needed go no further than the eyewitness accounts of Ireland, provided by Anglican clergymen and gentleman farmers, where a major famine occurred once a generation throughout the eighteenth century and significant food shortages at least once a decade. The famine of 1740–41, occasioned by the last and perhaps worst winter of the so-called little ice age that affected most of northern Europe, including parts of England and Scotland, killed between 300,000 and 400,000 in Ireland alone, possibly a greater percentage of the population than the Great Famine of the mid-nineteenth century.[95] Eyewitness accounts, including by philosopher George Berkeley, offered images strikingly similar to those Smith extracted from Du Halde. One Protestant clergyman noted that

> Whole parishes in some places were almost desolate; the dead have been eaten in the fields by dogs for want of people to bury them. Whole thousands in a barony have perished, some of hunger and others of disorders occasioned by unnatural, unwholesome, and putrid diet.[96]

Another wrote: "I have seen the helpless orphan exposed on the dunghill and none to take him in."[97]

Thus, Smith's portrait of the lives and deaths of China's laboring poor—consuming for purposes of nutrition carcasses of dead animals that in fact were more likely to sicken than to nourish them—reproduces and recalls to the reader accounts of European famines. China, far from representing Europe's other, the ideal type of Oriental despotism as understood by Montesquieu, appears instead to embody an only half-delineated fantasy of what might be called a permanent economic state of exception—that is, a perpetual suspension of the natural laws of free commerce through political interference—that in turn produces low-level famine, not simply, as in Europe, a recurring or even common feature of Chinese life, but as its normal state. Such a condition would prefigure the fate of any European society unwillingly to set aside customary rights and established institutions and abandon itself to the immanent rationality of the market.

Perhaps even more significant to the demonstration is Smith's evocation of the exposure of infants, a practice usually associated with Greco-Roman antiquity (although it was at least as common in the Medieval period),[98] a method of population control thus associated with Europe's superseded past. The term "exposure," as used by Smith, was derived from the Latin *expositio* (from the verb *expono*, to express or to put out, to place outside), and signified the relatively common practice in Rome of removing unwanted children from the family and relinquishing responsibility for them; as such, it could just as easily refer to selling the children as slaves as to leaving them by the side of the road. In fact, the Latin term does not suggest that the action involves subjecting the exposed individual to risk, as if placing the baby outside the family removes her from the protection it offered. Exposure, used in this sense in English, is a stronger term, understood as the equivalent of abandonment, the act of illegitimately divesting oneself of an obligation to one's child, particularly the obligation to protect it from harm.

Exposure of children or of others, the elderly, for example, considered incapable of caring for themselves and hence of requiring the care and protection of those who through ties of blood are responsible for them, was characteristic, as noted above, of severe famine when even the natural ties of mutual obligation that once bound the family together disintegrate, and each and every one is closed upon himself, literally self-consumed and consuming. In a sense, famine offers a spectacle of universal or quasi-universal exposure in which no individual can provide or care for himself but none can expect the protection or support that alone would allow survival. It is also the nightmare that haunts the proponent of unrestricted commerce in food who has urged the liquidation of emergency grain supplies and has exposed an entire population to the wisdom that surely directs all human events: the image of a people too weakened to rebel and thus unable to force the aid that would otherwise be denied them. If this is Europe's past and China's present, perhaps these few images—the family feeding with relish on the rotting carcass of a cat, the infant deprived of the protection due to it by nature and left in the street to die without food or water—are images of a possible future; this is a future no providence can avoid because it would represent a failure of providence, an unthinkable exposure of providential order to that which cannot be provided for, the irruption of chance where event should follow event according to the decrees of destiny (Lucretius),[99] an interval or syncope that widens without warning into general death.

Among the readers captivated by this passage, one in particular found its power in a truth—an axiom, in fact—that had escaped Smith himself. To Robert Malthus there appeared in the description of China precisely a theory of the market as a mechanism that, far from expanding without limit if allowed to operate according to its own rationality without external, political interference, would infallibly adjust the proportion of laborers to the fund available for wages by withholding food from the social ranks whose numbers exceed their ability to obtain subsistence. By "destroying a great part of the children," without any agent "intending it or knowing it" (even if Smith suggested that market rationality had, in this case at least, to be supplemented by direct human agency), the market will restore the equilibrium between food supplies and population. Malthus, writing a generation after Smith (*An Essay on the Principle of Population*, hereafter *EPP*, 1798), when war and revolution had made famine commonplace in Europe again, was moved by the brief discussion of China to articulate his critique of Smith (*EPP* chap. IV). Smith failed to recognize, according to Malthus, that malnutrition and infanticide were not the results of governments meddling with the immanent order of the market, but were the direct consequences of "the different ratios in which population and food increase" (*EPP* chap. II), an absolutely necessary and natural disproportion that persists to the extent that the passion between the sexes prevails over reason and concupiscence triumphs over the individual's capacity to consider whether or not he can provide sustenance for his offspring (*EPP* chap. II). Smith's failure to grasp the disproportionality (and therefore disorder) that prosperity itself introduces by encouraging a population growth that is determined with mathematical certainty to outstrip even the maximum supply of food the world is capable of producing in a very short time makes him, in Malthus's eyes, dangerously close to those "optimists," Godwin and Condorcet, who are the primary targets of *An Essay on the Principle of Population*.

Although Smith makes scant use of the notions of natural goodness and the perfectibility of man, by postulating that the stationary condition of Chinese society, a condition that imposes a level of suffering and violence shocking to the European reader, is a consequence of "its laws and institutions," Smith appeared to suggest that with different laws and institutions, particularly those relating to property and commerce, China might realize its enormous commercial potential and feed its population. From Malthus's perspective, Smith seems like a dangerous visionary who denies not only the inescapable fact that population will outstrip food sources, but also that the very increase of manufacturing will draw both capital and labor away from agriculture at the very moment its growth is imperative. Smith writes as if, once a society possesses sufficient natural resources and geographical features, with a large and growing population and a market protected by laws and encouraged to operate according to the rationality immanent in it, the kind of demographic apocalypse imagined by Malthus becomes an impossibility.

Accordingly, nowhere is the distinction between Smith and Malthus more apparent than in their treatment of famine per se, as a phenomenon distinct from the chronic food shortage—determined, according to Smith, by a dangerous combination of low wages and insufficient supply—characteristic of China. In his discussion of famine in the chapter on wages, Smith's focus is eighteenth-century Bengal rather than any one of a number of eighteenth-century European examples:[100] "In a country where the funds destined for the maintenance of labor were sensibly decaying," wages would be reduced "to the most miserable and scanty subsistence of the laborer" (*Wealth* 90–91).

It becomes clear at this point that the term "subsistence," denoting the "rate below which it seems impossible to reduce" wages, has no fixed social or biological limit: The development of Smith's own argument, its examples and images, suggests that the downward limit on wages that the market imposes on the English laborer in order to preserve the mere life of "labor" is a theoretical expedient designed to ward off the very real possibility that the fluctuation of the price of labor in the marketplace—or, more menacingly, the struggle of the masters unchecked by resistance—could and in all probability will push wages below subsistence in a way that is itself both improvident and counterprovidential. In a case like that of India, a decaying wage fund so far lowers the demand for labor that the subsistence of the individual worker is no longer necessary, given the vast numbers of unemployed prepared to take the place of those fortunate enough to have found employment. The rest

> would either starve or be driven to seek a subsistence either by begging or by the perpetration perhaps of the greatest enormities. Want, famine, and mortality would immediately prevail in that class, and from thence extend themselves to all the superior classes, till the number of inhabitants in the country was reduced to what could easily be maintained by the revenue and stock which remained in it. (*Wealth* 91)

While here Smith appears to gesture at a kind of infallible rationality immanent in nature itself that restores even by means of mortality an equilibrium between workers and the wage fund sufficient to guarantee their survival—prefiguring, even if in an aside, some of the arguments Malthus would develop into his theory of population—Smith is quite clear elsewhere that there is nothing natural about such a crisis and even less about the mortal "solution" that arises to resolve it. On the contrary, only the unwillingness of governments to permit and, perhaps even more importantly, protect the freedom of the market to be "governed by the laws proper to its own existence," as Mercier de la Rivière argued, rather than those imposed by men, immanent laws that alone will permit it to realize its full complement of riches, can produce such calamities.

Smith's theory of dearth and famine as articulated in the "Digression Concerning the Corn Trade and Corn Laws" constitutes one of the most contested and debated sections of *Wealth*, cited frequently by Amartya Sen[101] among others for its empirical and theoretical failings, even as its epigrammatic phrases continue to serve a liturgical function, intoned more or less as written, in the rites and ceremonies of such institutions as the International Monetary Fund and the World Bank. While it is undoubtedly true that, as Thompson has argued (and as our reading of the French sources alone confirms), *Wealth* "may be seen not only as a point of departure but also as a grand central terminus"[102] for a number of lines of eighteenth-century argumentation, it has historically served as the primary reference for doctrine of the free market, both because it offers a succinct but coherent summary of the positions of Smith's predecessors and because it does so with force and clarity.

Our aim here, however, is to understand his discussion of famine, and hence mortality, in relation to free commerce in grain as symptomatic of the conflicts that animate his work as a whole, conflicts inherited from the French debates we have explored but shaped by Smith into an original, singular form. In particular, it is here that the assertion that wages can never fall below the level of subsistence in an unrestricted market takes on its full significance and by that fact is pushed to the limit of sense. Behind it, as if it were written on a palimpsest, is the description of China, in turn written over descriptions of Ireland and India, of infants exposed on dunghills, of the living feeding on the dead, animal and human indistinguishable, and the dead filling the streets, the fields, and the forests, too many to bury, from the cities of Bengal or the counties of Ireland, tables, figures, and lists, calculations of the dead from famines near and far, so densely written around and within the declaration of the market's protection of life, filling the spaces between its words and crowding its letters, that it is nearly illegible.

He begins with a refrain familiar to readers of the physiocrats: Dearth, clearly understood here as a scarcity of food, is sometimes the result of war and the destruction of agriculture, but is most often a result of a poor harvest occasioned by the changes in weather, higher or lower than normal temperatures, precipitation, and so forth that might in turn bring plant disease or infestation. Such harvests, properly managed and distributed, can nevertheless be stretched to feed the nation's population and meet the nutritional requirements of its people.

But proper management and distribution can be carried out effectively only by those whose interest, self-interest, as we would say, enlists the aid of the knowledge of supply and demand that they alone possess, in the attempt to better themselves apparently (but not really—the apparent world is not the real world, as every philosopher knows) at the expense of those who must buy their goods merely to survive: The interest of the merchant and that "of the great body of the people, how opposite soever they may at first sight appear, are, even in years of the greatest scarcity, exactly the same" (*Wealth* 490). The merchant will be "necessarily led by a regard to his own interest" (and therefore by the most powerful of motives), a rational passion as distinct from avarice as it is from benevolence, to serve "the interest of the people," and to do so more dependably and efficiently precisely because he does not intend or even desire such an outcome:

> It is his interest to raise the price of corn as high as the real scarcity of the season requires, and it can never be his interest to raise it higher. By raising the price he discourages the consumption, and puts everybody, more or less, but particularly the inferior ranks of people, upon thrift and good management. (*Wealth* 524)

His interest dictates that if he sells his stores of grain too soon, he will fail to take advantage of the higher prices that come with declining supplies at the end of the season, and that if he waits too long, he will be left with an unsold surplus. For him to increase his profit, he must distribute grain exactly as it is needed by the people, whose "daily, weekly, and monthly consumption should be proportioned as exactly as possible to the supply of the season" (*Wealth* 525).

The merchant's regard to his interest compels him, despite himself, to treat the people as

> the prudent master of a vessel is sometimes obliged to treat his crew. When he foresees that provisions are likely to run short, he puts them upon short al-

lowance. Though from excess of caution he should sometimes do this without any real necessity, yet all the inconveniencies which his crew can thereby suffer are inconsiderable, in comparison of the danger, misery and ruin to which they might sometimes be exposed by a less provident conduct. (*Wealth* 525)

The master and his crew: on the one side, corn dealers, although competitors and rivals each seeking to get the better of the other, are "led" (Smith's verb of choice in such matters) to cooperate and to such an extent that their combined activity can be described as belonging to a single supra-individual; the dealer, the master of the ship, endowed with an intelligence and prudence greater than that of any of its members acting singly. As such, the dealer/master, whose mastery here precisely consists less in his possession of the ship's provisions than in his authority over their distribution, undertakes to ration the remaining supply of food so that the crew will have a daily supply until the ship is able to take on new provisions.

What is notable here is Smith's attribution of a collective intention, a collective intelligence, and a collective action to grain merchants that necessarily escapes their awareness: They are instruments of an order of which they remain ignorant and that perhaps can only be appreciated from without. They are also the bearers of a collective responsibility to feed the nation with the supplies that belong neither to the people nor to the state but to them alone. Individually, of course, they are perhaps unworthy of such authority; collectively, however, they, irrespective of their individual wills, infallibly carry out this responsibility.

The ship analogy is significant in another way: The prudent master, precisely because of his prudence, must put the crew on "short rations," even half rations, to get them to the next port. However necessary such an action may be, it may arouse the ire of the crew who will resist the "inconveniencies" of hunger, even when the reduction in food consumption is necessary to their survival. It is now the master who, in this quasi-state of nature, a ship in the middle of the ocean, far from any port and therefore from the protection of the force of law, is exposed to the danger of mutiny and the improvident rage of the crew; however, the crew, should they succeed in plundering the ship's stores, will only in turn hasten their own starvation.

We are thus led to Smith's response to the question of a right to subsistence, or rather the indirect way in which he denies the validity of the question: There is no need to grant a right to that which must necessarily occur if, that is, the distribution of subsistence is left to the direction of the natural and essential order of free commerce. The physiocrats had already advanced the argument: It is absurd to grant individuals a right to breathe, for example, when breathing is a matter of necessity. Smith, however, does not even trouble himself with questions of right or obligation; he leaves the terrain of law, morality, and politics altogether. Instead, if we examine "with attention the history of the dearths and famines which have afflicted any part of Europe during either the course of the present or that of the two preceding centuries, of several of which we have pretty exact accounts," we learn that

> In an extensive corn country, between all the different parts of which there is a free commerce and communication, the scarcity occasioned by the most unfavorable seasons can never be so great as to produce a famine; and the scantiest crop, if managed with frugality and oeconomy, will maintain, through the year, the same number of people that are commonly fed in a more affluent manner by one of moderate plenty. (*Wealth* 493)

We now understand that it is nothing other than the immanent order arising from merchants' regard to their interest, an order that certainly surpasses their understanding, that manages the crop with frugality and oeconomy, and coincides perfectly with the interest of the people, although perhaps not their desire. The mechanism of rationing here is not governmental decree, a more or less arbitrary decision by the political authorities; it is the effect of the price of food itself determined by the immutable laws of supply and demand. If food supplies are placed under the impersonal and anonymous direction of the supra-individual rationality of the market, there can be no need to declare or even discuss a right to subsistence. By yielding to this order, by giving up the production and distribution of the necessaries of life to its direction, there can be no increase in mortality.

Indeed, Smith to all appearances has announced a miracle, a version in fact of the miracle by which Jesus fed the five thousand who had followed him into the desert with five loaves of bread and two fish. But this is not a miracle if by miracle we understand a suspension of nature's laws; on the contrary, nature's laws, the natural laws according to which the social order must operate if it is to flourish, have been repeatedly disregarded and violated. The good that it will necessarily produce, the feeding of the hungry, if allowed to operate according to its immanent order, will arise only if and when we are collectively submitted to its reign. Then, the scantiest crop can maintain the same number of people as a much larger supply of food. This is indeed a bold move on Smith's part: Even Turgot, ever mindful of the people's tendency to revolt, warned Hume, some ten years before the publication of *Wealth*, not to entertain hope concerning the possibilities of

> reduced consumption. Needs are always the same. That kind of superfluity, which one can if need be reduce, is still a necessary element in the normal subsistence of artisans and their families. Molière's miser said that when there is enough dinner for five, a sixth can always find something to eat, but to take this reasoning even a bit further would be to fall immediately into absurdity.[103]

Has Smith, who has just argued that a much smaller supply of food than is common will "maintain the same number of people," arrived at absurdity?

Indeed, if "we examine with attention" the dearth or famine that occurred in Britain in 1766, in which much of southern and western England experienced a significant increase in mortality, and in which there occurred perhaps 150 major disturbances or "price riots" protesting the cost rather than the raw supply of food,[104] it appears that Smith's argument is nothing more than a declaration of faith in the divine government of providence in the face of a reality his philosophical positions do not allow him to acknowledge. But he is adamant that this is not the case: Every famine that has occurred in the last two centuries has been the consequence of an unwillingness or inability on the part of those who govern to abandon the administration of the production and distribution of food to the order that free commerce imposes on itself and on those who depend upon it. Dearth becomes deadly famine only through "the violence of government, attempting by improper means, to remedy" what are merely its "inconveniencies." Smith repeats the word "inconveniencies" four times within the space of a page to describe what people suffer during what he continues to call dearth, the condition perhaps of being "half-starved" but still alive. Governments have failed to recognize and allow the small evils necessary to the production of the greater good, the inconvenient but survivable deprivation required to produce and reproduce human life itself and in doing so "disorder and discompose the whole machine of the world" (*TMS* 289). In part, the violence Smith refers to is the violence by which governments' attempts to make food available to the people "break that great chain of succession, by the progress of which that system can alone be continued and preserved" (*TMS* 289).

But this perpetually repeated violence by the state against the natural order of the market raises another question: If every man's natural effort to better his condition leads to "the natural progress of a nation towards wealth and prosperity," if every party's regard for its own self-interest leads it to satisfy the interests of every other party in society more effectively than if it intended to do so, and the growth of opulence is everywhere to be seen, what would cause a government to interfere in the sequence of causes and effects that gives rise to such a system? The answer lies in the phrase, "it is the merchant's regard to his own interest" that leads him to satisfy that of the people. Although it would appear that the nominally conflicting interests of merchant and people in fact coincide precisely through the form of their opposition, as if they served each other through spite, as Mandeville suggested, there remains an evil from which no good will follow in this otherwise providential scheme.

As Turgot wrote in the letter to Hume cited above, "in every complicated machine there is friction which slows up the effects which are theoretically demonstrated to be the most infallible."[105] While the corn merchant always "regards" and "consults" his interest and, by the nature of his occupation, possesses the knowledge that, while perhaps imperfect, is always sufficient to allow him to do so, the people, in contrast, just as consistently resent that which they should approve and accept, as if they are incapable of discerning, let alone acting upon, their own interest. Although their consumption of the existing supply of food is limited and managed as it must be for the supply to cover the entire season by high, even exorbitantly high, prices, the people regard the merchant's extraordinary gain during times of dearth neither as necessary to his remaining in business nor as a means of rationing provisions without which they would likely run out of food. Deprived of the merchant's familiarity with the state of the annual grain supply, the people (which as Thompson points out includes those who actually harvested, gathered, transported, and stored the grain) can only assume that merchants have engaged in hoarding in order to enrich themselves and that the scarcity is more apparent than real: "In years of scarcity, the inferior ranks of people impute their distress to the avarice of the corn merchant, who becomes the object of their hatred and indignation" (*Wealth* 493).

They are the friction that not only slows the great machine of providence but may bring it to a halt. Thus, while the merchant needs the "extraordinary profit" he derives from years of scarcity to "compensate the many losses which he sustains upon other occasions," given the very nature of the commodity in question, he is instead "often in danger of being utterly ruined, and of having his magazines plundered and destroyed by" the people's "violence" (*Wealth* 494). The government's violence against the unlimited, unrestricted freedom of the corn trade is the delayed effect of the originary violence of the people that, even when not exercised, operates as an implicit threat. By ordering "all the dealers to sell their corn at what it supposes a reasonable price" to appease the popular fury, the government has allowed the people's need for food (for Smith, an inconvenience rather than a mortal threat) to take precedence both over the merchants' right of property in their own goods, in this case, the nation's food, and over the market's superior ability to set price in relation to supply and demand, which can only precipitate famine. This is only the legal and political form of the mob's plunder.

If the friction of the people's struggle against starvation (real or imagined) impedes the economic machine, then the state must intervene, according to Smith, not on behalf of the hungry, but against them. It can effectually address their misery not by helping them acquire food when the market withholds it from them by virtue of price, but by protecting the merchants from the people and in doing so, as Turgot suggested, the people from themselves. To allow an attack on the proprietorship of grain would be to call into question the life of a society; it would be the political equivalent of eating the seed-corn, that is, of destroying the foundations of the "free commerce and communication" that alone guarantee that "the scarcity occasioned by the most unfavorable seasons can never be so great as to produce a famine" (*Wealth* 527). To keep the people from the food they think they need but cannot yet afford (the surest sign that their need is imaginary) thus becomes imperative, a matter of life and death.

But if price often places food out of reach, cannot a rise in wages (which if determined by supply and demand alone must procure the laborer's subsistence, as we have just heard) make it affordable? Smith's apparent commitment to high wages as a necessary sign of progress in general cannot apply in the case of dearth for the very reasons he has outlined. If the rationality of the high price of grain during a time a scarcity lies in the reduced consumption such prices impose on the hungry, a corresponding rise in wages—whether through government interference, mass pressure, or even the conditions of the labor market itself—would end rationing by price and lead precisely to the immoderate consumption that would exhaust food stores before the next harvest.

Thus, the periodic combination of high prices and (relatively) low wages, however difficult for the worker, is the very form of the market's management of life. Smith offers an example of a reduction in the workers' wages (and therefore a reduction in their subsistence), which although initiated by the masters might just as well be natural as artificial, an expression of modification in the relation of supply and demand or an irrational attempt on the part of the masters to disrupt the market's equilibrium. Smith does not say and in fact it does not matter: Whatever the origin, a reduction in wages of a certain magnitude will be "severely felt" by wage earners whose ability to purchase "provisions" is significantly compromised and whose subsistence is thereby rendered precarious. For Smith, these workers are like the crew on the underprovisioned vessel who must (and can) bear their hunger until they reach port; the workers must wait until a decline in the supply of labor raises wages.

But absent Smith's version of the miracle of the loaves and the fishes, they have every reason to fear the future: Their lower wages make them even more dangerously vulnerable to the sudden increases in the price of food so common in the latter half of the eighteenth century. Charles Smith, for example, whose advocacy of the unrestricted market in grains in *Three Tracts on the Corn-Trade and Corn-Laws* (1766), influenced Smith's own positions, noting that in the hunger/dearth/famine of 1740–42 (and he is speaking only of England, not Ireland) the price of grain doubled at a time when common laborers spent half their weekly wages on food.[106] Frederic Eden in *The State of the Poor* (with the telling subtitle "An History of the Labouring Classes in England"), published twenty years after *Wealth*, examined England parish by parish, but found himself on occasion unable to explain how the typical wages of an agricultural laborer could purchase sufficient food to feed the laborer and his family, let alone pay rent. In one case, for a gardener in his midthirties from Surrey, married with eight children, a "remarkably sober, hard-working, and inoffensive man," the annual cost of food alone exceeded the laborer's income.[107]

Smith has thus responded to the assertion of a right to subsistence with an assertion of guarantees apparently far more effective than that of legal or moral right. Guarantee 1: The price of food no matter how high, no matter how extensive the reduction in food consumption such price increases bring about, by means of the rationing produced by these high prices, if they are set by the laws of supply and demand independent of any interference by the people or the state, will sustain the "same number of people" as during times of lower prices and greater consumption of food. The market, free of government meddling, that is, allowed or left alone to operate according to the imperatives proper to it, renders death by starvation an impossibility. Guarantee 2: Among those things whose price must rise and fall with the modification of supply and demand is labor; unlike the case of any other commodity, however, it is impossible for the price of labor to fall below a level that allows the laborer to purchase the means of subsistence for him and his family.

Thus, two guarantees, two impossibilities. In the face of these axioms, the belief of a section of the lower orders that they are, or perhaps are only in danger of, starving is purely imaginary. Smith's argument that their rage against merchants in such circumstances is similar to the popular outcry against witchcraft a century earlier is based not only on the evil they impute to grain merchants, but on the notion that the evil of starvation exists at all. They imagine they are starving as their ancestors imagined they were victims of spells and curses. In the same way, workers fear that their wage reductions, severely felt, call their very subsistence into question and act like men who must fight or starve, that is, with outrage and shocking violence. In both cases, the people fail to see that the market left to its own immanent rationality will safeguard their existence and that the only relative deprivation they suffer is both its necessary effect and the cause of its future expansion.

We have noted that Agamben argued that among the political concepts that govern our world, with or without our knowledge or consent, one of the most important is a nearly forgotten category of Roman law: the paradoxical and horrifying figure of *homo sacer*, the sacred man who cannot be sacrificed but who can be killed with impunity. He is abandoned by law, excluded and exposed to anyone's violence, but especially the violence of the state itself once the individual is placed outside the law. He can be killed but not murdered; his is the life unworthy of being lived, or, worse, his very existence is a mortal threat to society, like a plague or epidemic personified. Have we not traced the emergence of a right, the very right to exist, but a right declared explicitly only at the moment it was called into question, a right extracted from the assumptions of custom, implied but not stated explicitly in the Poor Laws, and therefore a right not asserted until it was endangered, a right against which the physiocrats must direct their argumentation and which by its very absence determines Smith's account of the market's relation to dearth and the relation of dearth to mortality?

Alongside the figure of *homo sacer*, the one who may be killed with impunity, is another figure, one whose death is no doubt less spectacular than the first and is the object of no memorial or commemoration: Let us call him, after Roubaud, *le malheureux*, the one who cannot afford the available food, whose need for sustenance is not only not a right, it is not even a demand that will attract supply. He is outside the artificial order of law, as well as the natural order of the market. If in resistance to these orders is life, the *malheureux* has ceased to resist: He is the one, the many, who may, with impunity and without consequences, be exposed to starvation and allowed to die, slowly or quickly, in the name of the rationality and equilibrium of the market.

Chasing his contradictions before him, the contradictions that erupt within and against providence, images persist of the starvation that cannot happen— images that arise from within *Wealth* itself, the death of those precisely exposed and abandoned to the market in the food without which they cannot survive, a market whose immanent order, itself based on the private ownership of the means of subsistence, is not only allowed by the state but is protected with armed force from those who mistake their need for sustenance for a right to it. That these images are attributed only to the unfortunates outside of Europe, outside the rationality of unrestricted commerce, is the necessary consequence of the imaginary guarantees Smith offers those who accept its immutable order as they accept divine providence, without question.

But, as Turgot remarked to Hume, there is no machine no matter how perfectly designed without friction, that is, without resistance. The movements of the people unwilling or unable to grasp the necessity of their deprivation discompose the machine and endanger the system. And it is here that the proper relation of state and market exits: If the latter is prevented from below from regulating itself by an unruly and irrational but no less powerful multitude, the former, which might appear to have no other relation to the market than one of a contemplative acquiescence, is called into action. Those who refuse to allow themselves or their children to starve must be compelled by force to do so; the warehouses containing what is necessary to subsistence must be protected from the hungry, and the prices set by supply and demand preserved and enforced through what Turgot with disarming honesty called "repression."

That this ideal could never be fully realized and popular resistance to the market rationing of life never reduced to zero was and is lived by the partisans of the free market as tragedy; it also, however, discomposes Smith's own text, allowing the disavowed right to the means of subsistence to elude the conceptual order he attempts to impose, an order in which it would have no place, to resurface within a very few years as Article 21 of the "Déclaration des Droits de l'Homme et du Citoyen" of 1793: "Public aid is a sacred duty. Society owes subsistence to its unfortunate citizens [*citoyens malheureux*] either by procuring work for them or by assuring the means of subsistence to those without work."

"There Can Be No Enforceable Right to Subsistence":
Laisser Faire / Laisser Mourir II

Smith thus pursued a line of inquiry without thinking it through to its conclusions, as if he himself hesitated before the threshold he had discovered (perhaps another way of conceptualizing the terminus to which Thompson refers), beyond which it became axiomatic that the market, the means of supplying life's wants, could operate rationally only in an unprecedented realm of freedom: (1) freedom for the market to act without interference no matter what the consequences for a given population—not out of indifference to this population but precisely because these consequences, even those deemed inconvenient, were necessary to an increase in the market's ability to provide for it; and (2) the correlative freeing of individuals from any right or claim to subsistence for which they cannot pay or the market cannot at a given moment furnish.

It was left to Smith's successors—who although (or because) they often disagreed with such aspects of his theory as the perpetual expansion of the system of wealth capable of, under the appropriate laws and institutions, providing increasing wages and a gradually rising standard of living—to cross that threshold explicitly to propose a political economy of abandonment or a necroeconomics. In contrast to Smith's hesitation, they set out with great ardor to establish as axiomatic the idea that the free market could exist only on the basis of a refusal to guarantee subsistence to the very individuals whose needs it was supposed to satisfy and whose activity combined to form it.

Of course, they could not have done otherwise given the prominence that the right to subsistence had acquired in popular politics from the time of the French Revolution both as a formal, legal right, and, perhaps more importantly, as a norm, more vital than moral, against which the immanent rationality of the market was judged and found wanting. As Marx and Engels proclaimed in the *Communist Manifesto* (1848), a ruling class that cannot assure the means of subsistence to its labor force is unfit to rule. They declared capitalism the site of a fatal contradiction: It was a system of production whose unprecedented power could be realized only to the extent that it was freed from any obligation to or indeed expectation of guaranteeing subsistence to those on whose labor it depends. The fact that the proponents of the unrestricted market held that such legal guarantees were now impediments to the very development that would render them superfluous and that these proponents were as, if not more, devoted to the well-being of the people than critics of private property and the market did nothing to prevent the question of a right to subsistence from assuming a central place in the programs and propaganda of the emergent labor movements.

The idea of rescinding, de jure as well as de facto, in both positive law and mere custom, the centuries-old prohibition (which as the case of the English Poor Laws shows clearly was as motivated as much by the fear of disorder as by the love of one's neighbor) against allowing individuals to perish for want of food began by the latter half of the eighteenth century to appear to its champions not simply as an economic measure but as a means of social discipline as well, a way far more effective than mere law of determining the conduct of individuals. We have seen that for Smith the orderly state must govern through fear: A dread of death alone keeps people from falling on each other like beasts of prey (this is one of Smith's rare Hobbesian moments and flagrantly contradicts much of what he argues elsewhere). In turn, the threat upon which this dread is based must be credible (Hobbes: law without force is mere words). Criminals, such as those who remove a handkerchief from a man's pocket, must be made to understand from constant example that capital punishment is the reasonably predictable consequence of such actions.

We have also seen that laborers, who are for Smith not criminals, even if their combinations violate the law, are also motivated by the dread of death, not the spectacular public death on the scaffold, but the slow decline of a man and his family who pass their lives and deaths in obscurity. This is not a death carried out by the public authorities nor is it inflicted as punishment for the violation of an existing law. But the dread of this death works at least as effectively, in fact, more effectively than any law, to discipline and determine the conduct of those who experience it. Despite the best intentions of government, a thief may not be caught and if caught may not be convicted of the crime with which he was charged. In contrast, the men who abandon work to protest the master's reduction of their wages immediately and automatically cease to receive any income. Within a few days, according to Smith's computations, they can no longer buy food, pay rent, and so on, and are faced with a stark choice: submit or starve. The agricultural laborer is not compelled by any law or decree to move to the city where the demand for labor is greater. His own "free will"—that is, falling wages, scant employment, and finally the pressure of want, of hunger and cold, together with the fear of starvation—sends him where he is needed. To interfere with the subtle harmony between pain of body and mind on the one side and economic rationality on the other by attempting precisely to relieve the sufferings of the poor is to prevent the allocation of resources necessary to economic growth and therefore the only sustainable means of improving the lives of the laboring majority.

Drawing on Smith's suggestion, Malthus, above all in the controversial second edition of the *Essay,* sought to articulate the principle of government or the regulation of conduct that would be accomplished not through an expansion of the role of the state, but by its withdrawal, a mode of governing, therefore, not only outside the law, but government through a contraction of law that "frees" the individual once held within it, expelling him outside its limits without either obligations or rights. Thus, Malthus declares that the best means of population control is not through legislation, for example, that would deny the right of reproduction to any but those with sufficient funds to support both themselves and their offspring, or to order all those with families to support them (through wages and therefore by means of employment), but rather to abolish the laws that require each parish to support the indigent within their jurisdiction. For the poor man to marry and to have children is, Malthus argues,

> clearly an immoral act, yet it is not one which society can justly take upon itself to prevent or punish; because the punishment provided for it by the laws of nature falls directly and most severely upon the individual who commits the act, and through him, only more remotely and feebly, on the society. When nature will govern and punish for us, it is a very miserable ambition to wish to snatch the rod from her hands and draw upon ourselves the odium of executioner. To the punishment therefore of nature he should be left, the punishment of want. (*EPP* chap. III)

To be left to nature in this context very precisely means to be abandoned by society: "All parish assistance should be denied him," and he will be taught by nature that he has "no claim of *right* on society for the smallest portion of food, beyond that which his labor would fairly purchase." There is a sense here that abandonment to want, to starvation that may or may not be relieved by private charity, or more precisely incitement of the fear that such abandonment would be the outcome of one's failure to moderate one's passions, is a more effective way of actually governing the conduct of the individuals than any law. Despite appearances, it is not cruel: Such a position is based on the certainty that individuals will weigh the consequences of their actions and choose to avoid rather than suffer nature's punishment. To ensure such an outcome, Malthus is forced to warn his readers of the dangers even of private benevolence. For his proposal to work, it will be necessary "to restrain the hand of benevolence from assisting those in distress in so indiscriminate a manner as to encourage indolence and want of foresight in others."

It might be thought that such radical and unprecedented measures, contrary to both custom and religion, were the logical conclusion of his iron law of population and desperate attempts to restrain the birthrate though a set of deterrents. But at issue is not simply the reproduction of the poor, but their very existence. Poor relief, and not simply the Poor Laws in force at the beginning of the nineteenth century, but aid of any kind, above all that provided by the government to those without food or shelter, was precisely counterprovidential, an attempt every bit as intrusive as interference in the market, to correct the natural order as if it were somehow flawed. It was to this order that the poor must be left: "We are bound in justice and honor formally to disclaim the *right* of the poor to support." Here, as the physiocrats had argued, the need of the poor for assistance not only does not confer upon them any right to such assistance (given that all available food supplies are in fact the legitimate property of merchants), but even more, the mere fact of their destitution marks it as their legitimate condition, the condition in which as Smith put it, providence has placed them: All that is real is rational, and all that is rational is real.

Generations of socialists pointed to Malthus's statement, which appeared only in the second edition of the *Essay* (he apparently regarded it as too imprudent to be retained in the third edition),[108] as the underlying principle of capitalist society that only Malthus was naive enough to repeat out loud:

> A man who is born in a world already possessed, if he cannot get subsistence from his parents on whom he has a just demand, and if the society do not want his labor, has no claim of right to the smallest portion of food, and in fact has no business to be where he is. At Nature's mighty feast, there is no vacant cover for him. She tells him to be gone and will quickly execute her own orders. (EPP chap. III)

The many who have no business being where they are because they have nothing in a world already possessed are, like Smith's Chinese infants, exposed and left to "Nature's" capable hands. It is not simply that they might claim a legal right to the most minimal necessities of life and thereby endanger the accumulation necessary to the system of commerce; their very survival is an offense and is incompatible with the existence of private property on which this system depends. They must either take what does not and cannot belong to them by right or cease to exist in what is indeed a world possessed.

The economists of the nineteenth and twentieth centuries might have been expected to emulate Malthus's prudent omission and to adopt Smith's "solution" to the problem of a right to subsistence rather than engage in polemics against this right that might, if only in appearance, call into question the very legitimacy and efficiency of the market as a system of rational provisioning. But the concept of such a right had become, far beyond the labor movement, an accepted civil right in much of Europe by the end of the nineteenth century.

It was left to those who, in certain respects wrongly, are most often considered to be Smith's most direct descendants to demonstrate in the period following the first World War the fundamental irrationality of such a right, its incompatibility with the sole form of efficient social organization: the founders of the doctrine of what is now called neoliberalism, Ludwig von Mises and Friedrich Hayek. For it is they more than any other school of economic and political thought who developed the legacy of a necro-economics inherited from Smith and from Malthus's reading of Smith, both critical and appreciative. While their works enjoyed a particular prominence after the fall of the Soviet Union, an event they never ceased to argue was inevitable, we should recall that their doctrine precisely took shape in capitalism's darkest hour. It was born in the Viennese Chamber of Commerce as socialist revolution spread through Russia, Germany, Hungary, and into the Hapsburg capital itself where workers' and soldiers' councils blossomed throughout the city.

Von Mises and Hayek felt themselves not merely besieged but the last witnesses to the destruction of Western civilization at the hands of modern barbarians.[109] Eclipsed not simply by communism and social democracy, but even more by the general acceptance of Keynesian analyses of and solutions to the economic crisis (except, of course, for the few whose faith in the immanent wisdom of the unhampered market allowed them to see even the evil of the Great Depression as the cause of a greater good: notably the group at the University of Chicago, from Henry Calvert Simons to the young Milton Friedman), they continued to labor against the current, laying the theoretical groundwork for a return to the sole rational form of human social organization, the unrestricted market. Their fidelity was unshakeable: In the face of an international depression that Simons himself could describe as a near total economic collapse,[110] a crisis hailed as the definitive proof of the inadequacy of capitalism, if not its demise—that is, a time of mass unemployment, homelessness, and hunger when there appeared no alternative to starvation or revolution than massive state intervention—they argued for a shrinking of the state and a withholding of aid to the hungry and the homeless, for lower, not higher, wages and therefore for less rather than more consumption. Who but a von Mises would have the temerity in such a historical conjuncture to declare that no living individual has a legal, binding right to continue to exist? Their proposals appeared to contemporaries as inhuman and cruel, if not absurd. In a few decades, their axioms would determine the lives and deaths of tens of millions.

It will be said, of course, and with some justification, that the theoretical cycle that turns ceaselessly between market and antimarket theories and has done so since 1847–48 is itself a product of the business cycle in which prosperity and crisis alternate with predictable regularity. In part, however, the repetition of theoretical alternatives suggests the persistence of ideas and concepts beneath the threshold of visibility, which, having remained unanalyzed, condition and delimit the very debates about the market. Can we not say, at least as an initial hypothesis, that the neoliberals, while often critical of such aspects of Smith's theory as value and price, have adopted from him a notion of the market that includes the concept of life itself and more precisely the exposing of life to death—life, that is, as understood by Foucault, as the object of government?

It goes without saying that this object, both necessary and inconvenient to neoliberal theory, is disavowed at the moment of its utterance insofar as it is uttered to be disavowed, engaging neoliberal theory in a paradoxical movement from which it cannot escape: the enterprise of producing a category necessary to any notion of the market as the sole rational form of human cooperation— that of *laisser mourir* or letting die. Even Foucault, whose studies of economic theory from the physiocrats to the Chicago School are extraordinarily suggestive, did not entirely grasp the centrality of the juridico-economic category of those who, while they cannot be killed by the state, may be allowed by it to die, even if it is his theoretical contribution, above all, that allows us to identify and describe such a concept. His denunciation not only of the politics of what he called "state-phobia" (*la phobie d'état*) but even more of its theoretical effects enabled him to describe the ways that states govern populations not simply by expansion but also by contraction, by refraining from action at certain key moments, such as famine, epidemic, or natural disasters, taking advantage of such opportunities to discipline restive inhabitants or crush insurgent movements.[111] This should not be surprising: The concept of letting die forms the un-thought of neoliberalism, surfacing intermittently but never openly avowed and integrated into its theoretical apparatus. It is this as much as the concept of the market itself that determines von Mises and Hayek as Smith's heirs.

For Smith, writing in the last quarter of the eighteenth century, the market could appear as a promise, an ideal whose realization would demonstrably bring about the greatest possible prosperity. He might assert with all the confidence of a scientist who had discovered an immutable natural law that the market, allowed to function without interference, would render famine impossible and could only produce an ever-expanding system of wealth. The proponents of perfect liberty of commerce in the troubled decades of the 1920s and 30s faced the far greater difficulty of explaining how and why what was generally agreed to be the inability of the market left to its own immutable laws to provide subsistence without periodic crises of ever-increasing depth and breadth was the mere appearance of failure. They argued in turn that the market had never been allowed to act in its pure form, a fact that was itself the cause of the increasingly severe crises to which the world was subject, and simultaneously that "crises" of a certain magnitude (when they were not the results of governments attempting to rig or circumvent markets in order to feed their populations) were simply adjustments in the relation of supply and demand that were natural and unavoidable and that whatever the human burden of such apparent disorders they were the necessary costs of economic progress—an argument whose theoretical dependence on a notion of providence was functionally identical to those of Bossuet or Leibniz.

Unlike their forebears, however, the neoliberals had to confront constant attempts to interfere with the evils that had to be allowed for the market's greater good to be realized. Even war and imperialism were not, as so many thought, the inevitable consequence of competition, but the tragic outcome of state interference, not only by means of protectionism, but by states actively taking sides with "their" capitalists and settling through the use of arms that which ought to be left to the market to decide. Similarly, these indefatigable thinkers argued, the generally tolerable inconveniences of the normal business cycle easily weathered by those fortunate enough to enjoy a free market became by virtue of well- (and perhaps not so well) intentioned civil servants full-blown crises as every attempt to alleviate suffering only aggravated it.

And if this burden were not heavy enough, there was the additional problem of the labor movement (far better positioned to do battle with both employers and the state than during Smith's time) and the socialist and communist currents that emerged from it. When von Mises published the first edition of his antisocialist manifesto in 1922, the Soviet Union, just emerging from civil war and foreign military intervention, hardly offered a model to criticize. The

Hungarian Soviet Republic lasted only a few months, not the victim of the impossibility of socialist planning, but of counterrevolutionary violence.

His real adversary was the Social Democratic Party of Austria of Otto Bauer and Max Adler (whose allies included such formidable intellectuals as the legal philosopher Hans Kelsen), which had used the power of its mass organizations to extract wage increases and taxes from Austrian capital, producing improvements in public health, housing, education, and culture that made *Das Rote Wien* or "Red Vienna," to the great dismay of both von Mises and Hayek, the object of admiration in much of the rest of Europe.[112] Its vision of socialism was not the command economy of a bureaucratic dictatorship but that of an extension of democracy to producers and consumers: precisely the "direct democracy" that von Mises so reviled:

> Democracy is self-government of the people; it is autonomy. But this does not mean that all must collaborate equally in legislation and administration. Direct democracy can only be realized on the smallest scale. . . . Democracy does not demand either that parliament shall be a copy, on a reduced scale, of the social stratification of the country, consisting, where peasant and industrial laborers form the bulk of the population, mainly of peasants and industrial laborers.[113]

These developments both presented neoliberal theories with a challenge and furnished them with an alibi. It became not only rhetorically convenient but theoretically imperative to claim that no state had really refrained from some form of intervention in the market, and thus that contrary to all appearances, a truly free market had not yet been allowed to exist.

And yet if the famines, wars, and crises of the past could be explained away by the neoliberals as products of interventionism, their work as analysts of their own time presented them with the dilemma of having to confront the immediate effects of mass unemployment, of wage cuts, and of drastic reductions in social services. Smith might in all sincerity argue that famine could only arise from government interference in market rationality; von Mises knew better. He well knew what it would mean for a state at certain key moments deliberately to refrain from interfering in the market through price controls or, at the extreme, the mass distribution of food. In fact, the knowledge that the ideal of a market utterly free of state interference requires, if only periodically and never in relation to the majority of the world's inhabitants, the exposure of life to death and the courage to turn away from the imploring hand of famine or to strike it down if it should violate the laws of property and the rationality of the market drives the great works of neoliberalism as they strive simultaneously to suggest, deny, and justify what they deny. It explains the prolixity of works like von Mises's *Human Action*[114] (hereafter *HA*) and *Socialism* (hereafter *S*) or Hayek's *Constitution of Liberty*[115] (hereafter *CL*) with their repetitive and desultory texture, the shrill propagandism that resembles nothing so much as the inverted image of the hyperbolic Communist Party propaganda (circa 1930) they often ridicule.

To a great degree, however, this is all a feint, a diversion, a kind of camouflage. These texts work to exclude the question of life but can do so only at great cost. Everything that concerns them leads to a consideration of what makes life possible or impossible, and they must constantly strive to avoid the point to which their own argument leads. The very activity of avoidance and denial, of course, cannot help but to indicate to the reader that which must not be said in order for their texts to continue to say what they do. Such an operation is doomed at some point to failure, not only in the form of symptomatic repetition and disorganization, but also insofar as the question of life itself must finally, at certain points, be posed. It is the question necessarily posed with the emergence of the notion of an economic order that must be left or allowed to act according to the rationality immanent in it as if food were a commodity just like shoes (to use Galiani's example) and a temporary shortage of the one no more significant than a shortage of the other—all the more given that shortage is a signal, a call for the supply that will surely come, as if need is always demand.

But we are no longer in the eighteenth century: Laborers, peasants, and their allies are no longer regarded as mute supports for arguments among elites, paternalists against liberals. From the time of the French Revolution, they wrested this question away from their betters as a counterpoint to the sacred right of property, the right of the living to continue to live, which must itself be the basis of all other rights, including that of property. To respond to such a position was undoubtedly a delicate matter (as even Turgot, far less committed in practice to the model he embraced in theory, had said in relation to Galiani); it had to be approached with great caution and surrounded with reassurances, separated from the main lines of the argument so as not to introduce distractions or create moralistic resistances in the reader. There is no question of devoting a section of a book to it; it must always be raised in context, at the culmination of a specific argument or demonstration, but as a subsidiary conclusion.

For the market to work, for it to convey accurate information about consumer preferences to guide future investment, preserve the productive and destroy the unproductive enterprises free of the meddling of what von Mises calls the interventionist or destructionist state—that is, to put it more profoundly, for human society to be organized in the only way that will guarantee not merely progress but the avoidance of total social collapse (in this sense there is no real alternative to the market)—there cannot be "an enforceable human right to subsistence" (*HA* 839). Those who lack food or water or medicine cannot legitimately be killed by the state or by private individuals. But it is not only legitimate (according to both law and reason) to refuse them the sustenance they cannot afford to buy but nevertheless demand or simply require in order to continue living; it is also legitimate to resist by force, preferably the armed force of the state, their attempts to take that to which they have no claim. Marx's naive declaration that the capitalist class was unfit to rule because it could not assure the existence of its own laborers must now, in the context of the insurgency of those who fail to recognize that their needs are not rights, be reversed: For von Mises, a state is fit to govern only if it knows enough to refuse any such assurance on principle.

For these thinkers, classical political economy extended into the sphere of "social cooperation" the same search for laws that early philosophers had discovered in the workings of physical nature. Just as ancient peoples and modern primitives believed that a god (or gods) directed nature according to his will and pleasure, and in this way not only remained ignorant of the true causes of things but regarded any inquiry into natural as opposed to supernatural causes as a sign of atheism or heresy, so philosophers and political theoreticians well into the twentieth century believed that human society was directed according to human will and design:

> All were fully convinced that there was in the course of social events no such regularity and invariance of phenomena as had already been found in the operation of human reasoning and in the sequence of natural phenomena. They did not search for the laws of social cooperation because they thought that man could organize society as he pleased. (*HA* 2)

Following Spinoza, whom von Mises cites (with and without attribution) fairly frequently, he argues that we must cease to apply judgments of right or wrong to society, declaring it good or bad according to the degree of its conformity with norms extrinsic to it. The decision to "study the laws of human action and social cooperation as the physicist studies the laws of nature" and cease to regard these spheres as constituting objects of "a normative discipline . . . was a revolution of tremendous consequences for knowledge and philosophy as well as for social action" (*HA* 2). The science of economics thus presents a permanent "challenge to the conceit of those in power" (*HA* 67). Just as the Church continued to reject any diminution of God's role in directing nature long after the discoveries of Galileo, so vested interests reject the idea of immutable economic laws: "Despots and democratic majorities are drunk with power. They must reluctantly admit that they are subject to the laws of nature. But they reject the very notion of economic law. Are they not the supreme legislators?" (*HA* 67).

An anthropological superstition has replaced the theological superstition of old. Human beings believe themselves masters of the social world, a world that they are free to construct in accordance with their designs. They suffer

> from the inability to conceive of an effective co-ordination of human activities without deliberate organization by a commanding intelligence. One of the achievements of economic theory has been to explain how such a mutual adjustment of the spontaneous activities of individuals is brought about by the market. (*CL* 159)

In fact, this order, ever more complex and extensive, has to a great degree come to occupy what was formerly the domain of law. "Primitive man," Hayek informs us, was governed by elaborate rituals and innumerable taboos, by explicit rules, often enumerated in sacred texts and later codes (*CL* 65). These explicit injunctions and prohibitions, consciously known and adhered to by all but a few heretics, have been increasingly supplanted by an order that is produced as the unintended consequence of human activity. Individuals tend to "cooperate" with this order without knowing it or intending to do so.

Thus, the distinction between free and unfree societies does not derive from the degree of regimentation and discipline characteristic of a given society, the extent to which individuals are integrated into, their lives determined by, an order, or, in contrast, the proportion of work to leisure time that a society exhibits. Von Mises admits that unhampered labor markets "submit the individual to a harsh social pressure" and "indirectly limit the individual's freedom to choose his occupation" (*HA* 599). In fact, free societies may well exhibit a higher degree of discipline than unfree societies, but, Hayek reminds us, it is "the impersonal discipline of the market,"[116] as opposed to that imposed by a tyrant or a tyrannical majority. The distinction between free and unfree societies thus lies solely in their origin: Is their organization the realization of a human plan or design, or the result of a decision to suspend such efforts and to abandon oneself and one's fellows to the higher rationality that only a "spontaneous," unintended order may incarnate?

Smith, writing in the latter half of the eighteenth century, could describe the "perfection of so beautiful and grand a system" that the ever-expanding sphere of trade and manufacturing seemed to constitute as necessarily inspiring pleasure in those fortunate enough to be its spectators, a pleasure distinct from the end that this system serves: that of human happiness. The fact that this system makes "nearly the same distribution of the necessaries of life, which would have been made had the earth been divided into equal portions among all its inhabitants" (*TMS* 185) merely adds a moral purpose to a beauty that is its own end. Smith does not doubt for an instant that this order is apparent to everyone (except, of course, in the case of the corn trade, the object of the irrational beliefs that for some reason arise in relation to questions of subsistence as frequently as to questions of religion); his task is merely to explain how it is produced and maintained.

As we have noted, for those writing in the twentieth century the burden is immeasurably greater: There is a general sense in the 1920s and 1930s that no such order exists or ever has existed. In the face of this generalized skepticism, the task is twofold. First, they must demonstrate that the economic crisis that admittedly exists has arisen and persists precisely because of governments' refusal to respect the spontaneous workings of the market. Inspired either by grandiosity or a well-intentioned but misguided attempt to skip over necessary historical stages of development or to avoid the indispensable rigors proper to capital accumulation, states have through their interventions "obstructed" the regular movements of markets and worsened what they hoped to improve. Second, they must show that the interventionist error is itself predicated on an inability to see that what are popularly understood as failures or social problems to be solved are necessary functions of the market's causal order. Thus, for example, inequality and unemployment, whose necessary magnitude cannot be determined in advance, are elements essential to the expansion of the system as a whole. They are not in themselves problems or evils; at most they are, like Smith's dearth, inconveniences more or less easily tolerated by those who experience them. The moralists and misguided humanitarians see as failures phenomena that insure the capital accumulation necessary to growth and fail to see how transitory inconveniences form the condition of still greater convenience and ease in the structure of the whole.

Thus, von Mises is reduced—more than a century after the great works of political economy (Smith, Ricardo, and Bentham) and a half century after the attempts to refute the very possibility of economic calculation in a socialist economy by Bohm-Bawerk[117] and Carl Menger[118]—to having to restate the theory of the market economy, a theory all but obscured by the reigning doxa of Marxian theory. Von Mises is compelled to refute in painstaking detail the socialist charge that the capitalist market is characterized by anarchy and periodic, ever-worsening crisis:

> The market directs the individual's activities into those channels in which he best serves the wants of his fellow men. There is in the operation of the market no compulsion or coercion. The state, the social apparatus of coercion and compulsion, does not interfere with the market and with the citizens' activities directed by the market. It employs its power to beat people into submission solely for the prevention of actions destructive to the preservation and the smooth operation of the market economy. (HA 157)

The last sentence will prove troubling (the state exists to "beat people into submission" to ensure the "smooth functioning of the market") only to those ignorant of the fact that "the market alone puts the whole social system in order and provides it with sense and meaning" (HA 257).

It is at this point and with good reason that von Mises must remind the reader and perhaps himself that the market, which, in his words, not only "directs" and "steers" social existence, but "reveals" to the individuals that comprise it its truth, "is not a place, a thing, or a collective entity" (HA 257). The market is nothing more than the interaction of individuals in a form of cooperation that they neither see nor intend. "The state of the market at any instant is the price structure, i.e., the totality of exchange ratios as established by the interaction of those eager to buy and those eager to sell" (HA 258). Its rationality and design, indeed, something like a spontaneous plan, emerge in the sphere of price: "[P]rices tell the producers what to produce, how to produce, and in what quantity" (HA 258).

And of all the commodities bought and sold on the market, none is more generally misunderstood and its price irrationally contested than labor. For von Mises, the market alone determines wage rates (HA 593):

> Each entrepreneur is eager to buy all the kinds of specific labor he needs for the realization of his plans at the cheapest price. But the wages he offers must be high enough to take the workers away from competing entrepreneurs. The upper limit of his bidding is determined by anticipation of the price he can ob-

tain for the increment in salable goods he expects from the employment of the worker concerned. The lower limit is determined by the bids of competing entrepreneurs who themselves are guided by analogous considerations. (*HA* 594)

From the personification of the preceding explanation in which "entrepreneurs" and "workers" confront each other in that peculiar sphere of cooperation known as the labor market, he moves to the anonymity of a ratio: "Wage rates are determined by the supply of labor and of the material factors of production on the one hand and by the anticipated future prices of the consumers' goods" (*HA* 591).

The depersonalization and formalization of von Mises's argument are necessary at this point: It is here, around the issue of the determination of wage rates, that he must confront Smith himself, whose discussion of the rise and fall of wages in Chapter 8 of *Wealth* is so incommensurate with the logic of the market system Smith otherwise establishes that von Mises insists that he "seems to have unconsciously given up the idea" (*HA* 594, note). For, in a passage we have already examined in some detail, Smith, as read by von Mises, has explained a fall in the rate of wages not by recourse to the ratio of supply and demand but by a "'tacit but constant and uniform combination' among employers to keep wages down" (*HA* 594). Despite the fact that these "incidental remarks," as von Mises call them, amount to nothing more than "garbled ideas," they have succeeded in furnishing the "main ideological foundation of labor unionism" and thus must be analyzed "with the utmost care" (*HA* 594).

The problem is simple: In an unhampered market no group of employers, no matter how well organized, can successfully push wages below their market rate without attracting by their very action new entrepreneurs "eager to take advantage of the margin between the prevailing wage rate and the marginal productivity of labor" (*HA* 595). Smith's scenario could only take place under monopoly conditions in which "entrance into the ranks of entrepreneurship is blocked through institutional barriers" (*HA* 594). Further, employers in other sectors of the economy might offer higher wages to purchase the labor they need. There, finally, could be no successful lowering of wages except at the level of the market as a whole, an impossibility given its tendency to expand beyond its present limits through constant entrepreneurial activity and the search for new areas of investment.

> The characteristic mark of production activities in the past and in the foreseeable future is that the scarcity of labor exceeds the scarcity of most of the primary, nature-given material factors of production. (HA 593)

In general, as is the case for any commodity, it is relation of the supply of labor to demand that will determine whether wages rise or fall. Smith, however, argues that the masters may collectively act to push wages below their market rate, but that far more typically they simply lower them. Nothing suggests that the masters are not simply adjusting their wage rates to a changing market that has, for example, by virtue of supply, lowered the cost of labor below what the prevailing wage in a given industry has been.

In fact, von Mises himself in 1943 recommended exactly such wage reductions to Mexican elites who either because of a misplaced sense of sympathy or out of fear of powerful trade unions had allowed wage rates to rise above the level dictated by the market. In exacting significant cuts in wages and benefits, cuts likely to be as "severely felt" as those suffered by Smith's hypothetical workers in *Wealth*, Mexican entrepreneurs would be guilty of nothing more than adjusting to the rationality of the market, the sole road to economic development for Mexico. Nothing in the simultaneous actions of the nation's businessmen constitutes a conspiracy. They are simply acting as they must in order to remain in business: Acting in response to market signals, they neither intend nor undertake to combine against their workers, even if the unintended consequence of their actions is that collective action that Smith calls tacit. This indeed is what Hayek calls "order without command." Rather than speak of employers' actions, given that they only administer the directions of the market in cutting wages, von Mises prefers the impersonal and anonymous language of "wage rate fluctuations," which are "the measure adopted for the allocation of labor to the various branches of production" pushing workers from the "overmanned branches" and pulling them to the "undermanned branches" (*HA* 598).

Similarly, von Mises regards as absurd Smith's contention that a basic inequality of power gives the advantage in such "negotiations" to the employer. Why, asks von Mises, is a laborer "compelled" to accept a wage reduction, a notion that implies that the market is the site of compulsion or coercion rather than the place of freedom he knows it to be? The idea that the only alternative to the employer's dictates is unemployment and thus starvation and homelessness in no way corresponds to reality:

> It is not true that the job-seekers cannot wait and are therefore under the necessity of accepting any wage rates, however low, offered to them by the employers. It is not true that every unemployed worker is faced with starvation; the workers too have reserves and can wait; the proof is that they really do wait. (*HA* 596)

Moreover, unemployment is a choice:

> A job-seeker who does not want to wait will always get a job in the unhampered
> market economy in which there is always unused capacity of natural resources
> and very often also unused capacity of produced factors of production. It is only
> necessary from him either to reduce the amount of pay he is asking for or to
> alter his occupation or his place of work. (*HA* 598)

The unemployed have often allowed a sense of status or an attachment to a
community (or nation or hemisphere) to restrain them for obtaining employment: "The unemployed worker refuses to change his occupation or his residence or to content himself with lower pay because he hopes to obtain at a later
date a job with higher pay in the place of his residence and in the branch of
industry he likes best" (*HA* 579). However difficult it is for the worker to understand, the lowering of his standard of living, the restriction of his consumption,
the fact that he will have to migrate halfway around the world to endure long
hours of work and poor housing are all his contributions to the accumulation
of capital necessary to economic progress.

   Thus the unhampered market can reach its perfection only on a global
scale, and it is not only the labor market that demands a world without borders
in which workers would be free to leave family, culture, and nation to heed
the call of the market. Economic nationalism in the form not only of immi-
gration control or protectionism but even the attempt to exercise sovereignty
over natural resources necessarily and irresistibly leads to war with the predict-
ability of a natural law. There is something manifestly absurd and harmful in
the fiction of national sovereignty that renders any nation, however small and
weak, the equal of the richest and most powerful nations and endowed with
the same rights. This is, of course, the fallacy that underlies organizations like
the United Nations:

> Let us assume that the United Nations had been established in the year 1600 and
> that the Indian tribes of North America had been admitted as members of this
> organization. Then the sovereignty of these Indians would have been recognized
> as inviolable. They would have been given the right to exclude all aliens from
> entering their territory and from exploiting its natural resources which they
> themselves did not know how to utilize. (*HA* 686)

The point here for von Mises is not that such rights—however harmful to the
interests of humanity as a whole, which stands to benefit from the development

of this savage land—are illegitimate according to some juridical or moral norm, but that in relation to the economic necessity to which they stand opposed they are both meaningless and utterly without force or effect: Von Mises asks, "Does anybody really believe that any international covenant or charter could have prevented the Europeans from invading these countries?" (*HA* 686).

This was not mere indulgence in historical speculation; rather, it served to underscore the market's irresistible universal destiny. As countries such as Mexico under Cardenas or Iran under Mossadeq moved to wrest control of their nations' oil production from foreign firms, von Mises issued the following warning:

> It is illusory to assume that the advanced nations will acquiesce in such a state of affairs. They will resort to the only method which gives them access to badly needed raw materials; they will resort to conquest. War is the alternative to freedom of foreign investment as realized by the international capital market. (*HA* 502)

The *Lebensraum*, which von Mises rejected in its nationalist form, returns here as the universal imperative of the market: The underdevelopment of the world outside of western Europe and North America and "the eminence of the Western nations" which cannot be accounted for by biological theories of racial difference (which von Mises regards as groundless) cannot at the same time simply be explained by a "time-preference theory" according to which the superiority of the latter "consists merely in their having started earlier in endeavors to save and to accumulate capital goods" (*HA* 500). The rest of the world lacked and, for the most part continues to lack,

> institutions of safeguarding the individual's rights. The arbitrary administration of pashas, kadis, rajahs, mandarins, and daimios was not conducive to large-scale accumulation of capital. The legal guarantees effectively protecting the individual against expropriation and confiscation were the foundations upon which the unprecedented progress of the West came into flower. (*HA* 500)

Lacking these foundations, the African and the Asiatic cannot develop their natural resources and have no right to expect that those who have such a capacity will fail to do so.

The critics of the market demand justice without ever thinking to inquire whether their conception of justice is compatible with the laws that govern social reality and that are indifferent to human values. To denounce the inequality necessary to the capitalist order as unfair, to judge unemployment and poverty

as signs of failure, is tantamount to denouncing sexual urges, themselves necessary to the propagation of the species, as sinful. To condemn the expansion
of the market, even when it is achieved through armed invasion, into "areas
whose inhabitants are too ignorant, too inert, or too dull to take advantage of
the riches nature has bestowed upon them" (*HA* 686) is to denounce a falling
stone for obeying the law of gravity. One might as well, to invoke Spinoza's
image, pass laws forbidding the big fish to eat the little fish.

Sometimes the moralism that rejects the necessary character of economic
relations is theological in character: Profit, interest, wealth, even selfishness are
denounced as sinful. Other forms of moralism are perfectly secular but no less
mischievous in their effects than those derived from religion. Marxism, which
claims to seek a social order that will meet the needs of the toiling masses and
create real as opposed to formal equality, is nothing more than mass envy ma-
terialized in a political movement:

> The incomparable success of Marxism is due to the prospect it offers of fulfilling
> those dream aspirations and dreams of vengeance which have been so deeply
> embedded in the human soul from time immemorial. It promises a Paradise on
> earth, a land of heart's desire full of happiness and enjoyment and—sweeter still
> to the losers in life's game—humiliation of all who are stronger and better than
> the multitude. (*S* 7)

More common if less threatening is the moralism of those in government
and even business who have neither the courage nor the foresight to endure
for as long as is necessary (or, rather, to witness their populations endure)
the deprivation and sacrifice that alone will eventually bring prosperity. Even
Adam Smith—who, as we have seen, could not help yielding to a kind of sympathy for the laborer, allowing himself to imagine and to register in his discourse how severely felt a reduction of wages simply to market levels might
well be—assigned an ultimately moral purpose to wages, which insofar as they
coincided with the imperatives of life, furnished the foundation and limit of
wage reductions. A worker faced with the wage reductions that markets use to
reallocate labor according to need naturally resorts to protest, as we have seen.
Such protest, however, cannot be effectual: At the limit, the state will intervene
before the protest can affect the enterprise or industry in question. And however much von Mises would deny it, there may be great difficulties in moving
oneself (with or without one's family) halfway across the world in search of a
more taxing and lower paying job. Workers who must stay in their present job

and accept a severe wage reduction can, according to Smith, remain confident that wages can never go below a certain level—namely, that necessary to maintain the laborers themselves.

Although von Mises, following Smith, argues that a society in which even the lowest wages do not secure the worker's "bare subsistence" (*HA* 603) will likely disintegrate, he also maintains that any attempt to compute wage rates by reference to the cost of subsistence is meaningless. In fact, when examined with any care the very notion of "bare" subsistence is revealed to be nothing more than an elusive, ever-receding chimera. Any attempt to impute certain nutritional requirements to the human species is necessarily to mistake "historical tradition" and "customs and habits" for mere nature (*HA* 605). To attempt to penetrate beyond these cultural constructs is to discover behind them earlier cultural constructs *ad infinitum*, or at least to arrive at the very limit at which the human becomes indistinguishable from the animal:

> Furthermore, the notion of a physiological minimum of subsistence lacks that precision and rigor which people have ascribed to it. Primitive man, adjusted to a more animal-like than human existence, could keep himself alive under conditions which are literally unbearable to his dainty scions pampered by capitalism. There is no such thing as a physiologically and biologically determined minimum of subsistence, valid for every specimen of the zoological species *homo sapiens*. No more tenable is the idea that a definite quantity of calories is needed to keep a man healthy and progenitive, and a further definite quantity to replace the energy expended in working. The appeal to such notions of cattle breeding and the vivisection of guinea pigs does not aid the economist in his endeavors to comprehend the problems of purposive human action. (*HA* 604)

To argue that a human being as such requires a certain number of calories to engage in a certain quantity of labor, or even simply to survive under certain specified conditions, is impossible. In any case, the pampered laborers of today can certainly live and labor on much less than what they are accustomed to: Did not "primitive man" do so?

Nobody knows yet what a body can do and accomplish even when subjected to the rigors of market rationing that reduces their intake of food by half or more. It is clear that the very research into nutritional requirements is politically motivated, nothing more than an attempt to use pseudo-science to justify interference in the market by raising wages or lower prices: It is *a priori* impossible to define what is biologically necessary to subsistence. Even worse, since man does not live by bread alone, the attempt to set nutritional standards of caloric values and protein intake is to rob human beings, or at least those who labor, of their dignity and reduce them to the status of domestic animals. It is as if one sees

> in the wage earner merely a chattel and believes that he plays no other role in society, if one assumes that he aims at no other satisfaction than feeding and proliferation and does not know of any employment for his earnings other than the procurement of those animal satisfactions. (*HA* 604)

Such zoological/anthropological observations serve to ground what constitutes perhaps the most important theoretical intervention in the entire of von Mises's *Human Action*. He has taken the unstated conclusions of the eighteenth-century economists and drawn a line of demarcation within contemporary economic discourse that will make visible a distinction between science and morality, between natural necessity and human desire. Human subsistence (a term he has demonstrated to be without scientific validity) or even mere existence (life, survival, the condition that humans share with all other animals and that is therefore of no interest to economics, or the study of purposive human action) has no place in any understanding of the market. Worse, if such notions are allowed to survive, they will not only contaminate the theory of the market, they will threaten the functioning of the market as it exists, erecting in the guise of scientific data what is in fact a moral obstacle to the only rational form of social cooperation. Thus, von Mises will set aside all sentimental posturing and say it directly: There can be no "legally enforceable right to subsistence."

While the phrase is borrowed nearly verbatim from Malthus, despite von Mises's appreciation of Malthus's theory of population his argument is closer to that of the French economists of the eighteenth century and to Smith who held no such theories of population: It is the function of the market that is at issue here, not the ratio of population to food production. Further, Malthus evinced far less skepticism than von Mises about the notion of subsistence; indeed, his theory presupposes that a certain minimum is necessary for human existence. The very insistence that there be no legal claim to subsistence was based on the expectation that in the absence of such a right, any surplus in the population would be immediately reduced by the lack of food or at least a nutritional insufficiency to the level of mortality necessary to restore the natural equilibrium between food supply and population. This equilibrium, however, would be restored only on the condition that populations were deprived of the legal right heretofore possessed by them and thereby exposed to nature's action.

For von Mises, the very content of the right is a fiction: Subsistence can never be defined and thus can never be the object of a right. But beyond the critique of the concept of subsistence, he questions the very notion of right as it emerged in the constitutional documents of the eighteenth-century revolutions. It is striking that for him socialism is primarily a theory of fundamental rights (*S* 47), and its primary exponent the nearly (but undeservedly) forgotten Austrian legal scholar Anton Menger, whose *Right to the Whole Produce of Labour* (1886) was the great statement of what Engels critically referred to as "juridical socialism." In fact, certain of von Mises's critiques of the socialist theory of right coincide closely with those Lenin argued in a document adopted by the Third International in 1919 (three years before the publication of the first edition of *Socialism*), as if he had borrowed from the repertoire of the communist critique of "bourgeois democracy," even as he vehemently rejected the communist antidote, the direct democracy of the producers.

His emphasis on Menger (whose brother was Carl Menger, an antisocialist von Mises admired) is to a great extent archaeological: The question of the right of subsistence, its problematization under capitalist property relations as well as its (re)assertion, lay at the origin of European socialism, but it had been subject to a generalized forgetting, assumed or presupposed without reflection and hidden, as it were, under the strategic and organizational questions with which the Communist and Left-Socialist Parties were occupied in what appeared to be their moment of triumph. Von Mises seeks to confront what he regards as this decisive question in the form it took at its source, a form whose "legalism" and continuity with the liberal tradition would undoubtedly prove embarrassing to the adherents of the Third International. At the same time, his critique is perhaps aimed at the specificity of Austrian socialism noted above and its less apocalyptic view of law and of the question of right (let us recall that it was in the context of a "pure theory of law" that Kelsen articulated a critique of the privileged place of property right in European law since the seventeenth century).

Anton Menger argued that private law (primarily concerned with property) not only did not originate in considerations of economic necessity (being simply the translation into law of possession acquired by mere force), but that in a fundamental sense it did not seek to determine the very basis of any economy, the life of the individual: "Our codes of private law [*Privatrecht*] do not even contain a single clause which assigns to the individual even such goods and services as are indispensable to his existence."[119] While the great revolutions of the seventeenth and eighteenth century resulted in the codification of fundamental political rights whose legitimacy was independent of both particular laws and customs, socialism sought not only to complete this set of rights, but more importantly to provide them with their necessary foundation. The great political freedoms are infringed not simply by laws that can be and are frequently circumvented but by the inescapable and far more effective tyranny of want and insecurity; they will not be exercised until the subsistence of the individual is itself recognized as one of the primary obligations of the state: The right to subsistence, to continue to exist, is, Menger holds, the *Urrecht*, the originary right that is the condition of all other rights.

A right to have rights separate from and even exclusive of the right to all that makes it possible for the individual to go on means that life is subordinate to appropriation (the individual only has a right, irrespective of his need, to that which he himself owns) and that the preservation of private property takes precedence over the preservation of individual life. Thus, the right to life and liberty cannot logically consist merely of protection against the threat of violence against one's person, but must, if it is to be more than an empty phrase, embody a guarantee of subsistence, given that "life cannot be maintained for any length of time without food, clothing and shelter."[120] The right to subsistence, in turn, necessarily implies a right to the natural resources and material means of existence, which cannot be limited to those who are the legal proprietors of the resources.

> In the opposition to the abstract capacity according to property right to purchase or acquire and the concrete right to a common use [*Mitbenützung*] of the surrounding nature is contained the whole of the social question.[121]

Socialism, for Menger, is based on the proposition that every member of society has a claim to the commodities and services necessary to support existence that takes precedence over the satisfaction of the less pressing needs of others.[122] In a socialist society the right to subsistence would replace the right of property, although such a right might be possible in a society organized around private property if the meeting of the subsistence needs of the population were regarded as a kind of "mortgage on the national income as having a first claim before the unearned income of favored individuals."[123] For Menger, subsistence should itself be derived not from a system of relief but from the right to work—not an abstract freedom to look for work, but the right to have employment:

Every individual who cannot find work with a private employer will be provided common day labor by the state at customary wages.[124] In the end, he admits that such rights will absorb such a proportion of society's unearned income that private ownership of the means of production would prove impossible.

Von Mises begins examining Menger's account of the fundamental rights advanced by socialism by referring to demands concerning the natural rights of man and citizen advanced in the "programme of the liberal philosophy of the state" in the seventeenth and eighteenth century with which he in the main agrees. While he admires these "demands," however, he notes that they were often formulated as legal principles and enshrined in constitutional law, when they should have been understood as nothing more than guidelines "whose spirit must permeate the whole state" (S 47). Their existence as laws must not be confused with actuality; the effectivity of the law itself depends upon determinations external to it, which it is powerless to create. Thus, Austria, which legally grants the freedom of expression, sees far less exercise of this "right" than England, which endows its citizens with no such legal right.

The statement on bourgeois and proletarian democracy adopted at the first congress of the Third International in 1919 (written by Lenin) makes a similar argument: The formal rights and freedoms enshrined in law and in constitutions may in fact function not only as promises of a power to act that cannot be exercised in reality, but also as means of concealing the real limitations that prevent the actual performance of these rights.[125] For Lenin, however, legal right was prevented from becoming real power, by the world of discipline, constraint, and want (forms of class coercion not exercised by the state through legal means, but through the life of "civil society") that characterized the material existence of the masses. Von Mises, in contrast, for whom the world of coercion beyond the state was very real, but absolutely necessary to social existence, nevertheless explains the discrepancy between formal and real rights by the presence or absence of that "spirit," the spirit of liberal philosophy that permeates a society to give reality to the liberal program, with or without the corresponding laws. This idealism of a "spirit of the laws," however, quickly gives way to the materialism we have come to expect of von Mises, even if his variant is not that of Lenin.

After what he calls "the wars of liberation" in the eighteenth and nineteenth century, "anti-liberal writers" (a phrase that suggests the Right even as it refers primarily to the Left) tried to imitate the great declarations of "political rights" by attempting to establish "basic economic rights" (S 47). They did so precisely because, and here von Mises himself sounds quite anti-liberal, the current social order could not guarantee "these alleged natural rights of Man" without the corresponding economic rights that would allow them to be exercised. But the economic rights that appeared or were made to appear to fulfill or complete the great liberal revolutions were, as these anti-liberal writers well knew, nothing more than what the Communist Parties were beginning to call "transitional demands." These were calls not for socialism but demands, with a high degree of support among workers, that were not compatible with the operation of the market on the basis of capitalist property relations, that is, demands that were regarded by the masses as legitimate but that could only be realized through the socialization of the means of production.

What is extraordinary about von Mises's argument here is that he does not attempt either to argue that political rights, for example equality, are possible on the basis of great economic inequality or, in contrast, that the merely formal nature of political rights is the only way such rights are compatible with a regime of private property. Instead, he is led in a striking way to denigrate these "alleged natural rights" themselves, especially if they are "guaranteed" by law, as if they too are determined by forces beyond human control. Even more surprisingly, it is as if he believes in his own way that they are, if not incompatible with the market and the regime of property (a right, it should be noted, that is not and cannot be questioned, precisely because it is not truly a right but a necessary element of market society), at least in constant tension with them and as such perfectly expendable.

Of the basic economic rights that socialists have tried to introduce in imitation of the "alleged" natural rights of man and citizen, none is more dangerous to property and the market according to von Mises than the right of existence or subsistence as it is defined by Menger (whose definition is virtually identical to that of Galiani). First, it confuses moral and legal obligation and fails to specify precisely to whom such a right would belong. Most societies today, having precisely achieved by virtue of the market a level of wealth far exceeding that of previous times, can afford to recognize the claims "of those without means and unfit for work, with no relation to provide for them" (S 48), but the obligation to heed these claims is purely moral: "It gives to the necessitous no title recoverable by law" (S 49). The socialists, however, do not refer to such a limited case, von Mises cautions. By a right to existence, they mean that every member of society may claim the things and services necessary "to the maintenance [or preservation] of his existence" (*zur Erhaltung seiner Existenz*—here he cites Menger in translation) and that the right of subsistence must take precedence over "the satisfaction of the less urgent [*dringende*, also desperate or vital] needs of others" (*S* 9–10). While he begins by questioning the meaning of "urgent" (*dringende*) and "maintenance" (*Erhaltung*) (when is something really urgent to someone's existence and how can we adequately determine what is necessary to "maintain" a person, given all the difficulties associated with "subsistence"?), von Mises finally leaves no doubt as to the meaning of this phrase, even as he offers this meaning as one possible reading of it: "The form which this concept sometimes takes is that no one should starve while others have more than enough" (*S* 49).

Such a notion, he tells us, is both absurd and dangerous: There can be no natural or imprescriptible right to existence because "God or nature did not create men equal since many are born hale and hearty while others are crippled and deformed" (*HA* 175). Those unable to exist have no natural right to do so. As Malthus has shown, "nature in limiting the means of subsistence does not accord to any living being a right of existence" (*HA* 175). The scarcity of what is necessary to human survival deprives a great number of their lives to preserve the equilibrium between population and resources: Death here is necessary to nature's order and prevents the extinction of the human species, which, if allowed to proliferate (and neither regard to self-interest nor the development of birth control technology can be counted on to stop this proliferation) would face universal starvation. But the Malthusian and Darwinian (or perhaps social Darwinist) critique of a natural right to existence, a critique that von Mises repeatedly connects to Spinoza (one might as well attempt to establish a right of the little fish not to be eaten by the bigger fish), occupies a subordinate role in the economy of his argument.

For even as he argues that the world does not (and presumably cannot ever) produce even enough to feed its population at any given time and that therefore the equilibrium of nature will continue to maintain itself, a claim without evidence of any kind, von Mises resumes the argument whose development in the latter half of the eighteenth century we have already traced. From this perspective, it is no longer a question of absolute scarcity, a claim that Smith himself rejects at least for England and France, but rather of the disposition of what is variously called profit, surplus, or unearned income. Providing subsistence for an entire population "could be achieved only by the socialization of the means of production" (*S* 49). Were a right to existence established as an enforceable legal right, it would "absorb such an important part of the unearned income and strip so much benefit from private ownership" (*S* 50) that the very notion of private property would be called into question. Thus, to extend to "the individual poor a legally enforceable claim to support or sustenance" would pose "great social dangers" (*S* 430).

The granting of priority to the right of property over the right to subsistence, however, as von Mises never ceases to remind the reader, is not grounded in some "alleged 'natural' right of individuals to own property" (*HA* 285) but in the necessity that governs the system of human cooperation. Without absolute property there can be no market; without a market, human cooperation will be supplanted by force, violence, and the disintegration of society itself. A right to existence—enforced by the state through price and wage controls, housing subsidies, or, at the extreme, the distribution of the necessaries of life—will undermine private property, inhibit the accumulation of capital necessary for investment, and distort market mechanisms to such a degree that the continuation of society itself is endangered. This does not mean that societies should not care for the poor, although they must be careful that whatever relief they provide does not weaken the individual's resolve to work by "promising that if the individual's work is hindered by illness or the effects of a trauma, he shall live without work or with little work and suffer no very noticeable reduction in his income" (*S* 432). In this way, private charity (precisely by virtue of its essential unreliability) or penury (and the stigma attached to it) is far more effective in helping the poor, not by providing sustenance, but in forcing them to accept the most difficult and degrading labor as a means of improving their lot. It is a

> biological fact that the fear of penury and of the degrading consequences of being supported by charity are important factors in the preservation of man's physiological equilibrium. They impel a man to keep fit, to avoid sickness and accident, and to recover as soon as possible from injuries suffered. (*HA* 839)

These "incentives" are critical to the economic growth capable perhaps of satisfying the needs of even the poorest; to remove or diminish them is to produce "undesirable effects" (*HA* 839). Von Mises hastens to assure us that he is not a cruel man; the "incapacitated" have not been and should not be allowed simply to perish:

> But the substitution of a legally enforceable claim to support or sustenance for charitable relief does not seem to agree with human nature as it is. Not metaphysical prepossessions, but considerations of practical expediency make it inadvisable to promulgate an actionable right to sustenance. (*HA* 839)

The logic is clear: For the unhampered market operating according to a necessity as implacable as that of nature, "there is no interference of factors foreign to the market, with prices, wage rates, and interest rates" (*HA* 238). Wages must be allowed to fall and prices to rise as the market determines. For the state to intervene either through wage and price controls or by taxation would simply impede the process of capital accumulation necessary to restore the equilibrium of wages and prices. The pampered scions of capitalism can subsist on far less than they now have and mistake the prosperous life to which they have become habituated for some biological minimum: Do not peasants all over the world survive on less than is thrown away by the average North American or European worker? "The consumption of the American masses will be judged wasteful by the Egyptian fellaheen or the Chinese coolie" (*CL* 129).

And for those, less pampered, elsewhere, the market, no less merciful than "God or nature," must also limit the means of subsistence and therefore also the right of any individual to exist; those who cannot secure their own subsistence (or that of their children) have no enforceable claim on those who can, even if the latter have a surplus beyond what is "necessary" to their existence.[126] Further, the absence of guarantees of any kind—of employment, medical care, or even food and shelter—is necessary to the system of production, forcing individuals to do whatever will produce a profit for the proprietor and to go wherever the market, like providence, calls him or her to go. The individual thus conceived is truly, absolutely free, *vogelfrei* in the modern German sense: free as a bird, bound to no one, just as no one is liable for the harm that may befall the individual.[127]

A doctrine that relieves the state of any "enforceable" responsibility for the lives of its citizens and actually requires that it refrain from any form of social aid that could conceivably disturb the equilibrium of the market might appear, as its proponents often imply, to require a very minimal and passive state. Such, however, cannot be the case. It requires a firm and unerring hand to submit every member of society to the hazards of the unhampered market. A government that rejects the totalitarian measures that can only set it on the road to serfdom must at times seek to persuade the majority of its population that the reductions in their standard of living, reductions that in much of the world mean malnutrition and disease, are not only right (from a moral and juridical point of view) but necessary, the only means by which the capital accumulation necessary to economic progress can occur.

It is precisely the responsibility of those "in power" to explain that the emergence of greater inequality in their society is, despite appearances, a positive development that heralds the investment to come, together with the jobs and rising wages it is sure to bring. Leaders must resist the impulse (or, more commonly, the pressure) to aid those, again, apparently in distress, by interfering with or distorting pure market mechanisms of supply and demand. They regard the deprivation of the majority as a temporary but necessary sacrifice that alone will bring about the improvement that all desire. Such a government must be able to tolerate the sight of poverty and hunger, of communities broken up and destroyed forever, its inhabitants scattered across the globe, and it must have the power of will not to intervene. Underlying its policies is therefore anything but passivity: It is the most resolute decision. A government decides not to act, or rather it acts by refraining from action, by the "letting be" and at certain moments by the "letting die," even in the face of the popular indignation that the market requires in order to flourish.

It is precisely in relation to the indignation of the governed—the masses who in the best of times feel nothing but envy for those who appear to have won life's game and who in times of crisis are led not only to make claims upon the legitimate property and wealth of others but, worse, to seek, through legal or, too often, extralegal means to appropriate for themselves a share of that wealth—that the state must intervene. It must be acknowledged that many of those destined to learn in person the inaccuracy of inflated nutritional standards, who will come to know that what they have regarded as necessary to life consisted of nothing more than a set of preferences, may not easily be persuaded of the necessity of their deprivation. What can be expected from those, a majority in any given society, who, having seen better times, must learn to disaggregate comfort and survival?

This presents an extremely difficult problem for neoliberalism: Can the masses ever be persuaded to accept their deprivation, as they do wind and rain, as inconvenient but necessary? Hayek, for one, fears not:

> The changes to which such people must submit are part of the cost of progress, an illustration of the fact that not only the mass of men but, strictly speaking, every human being is led by the growth of civilization into a path that is not of his own choosing. If the majority were asked their opinion of all the changes involved in progress, they would probably want to prevent many of its necessary conditions and consequences and thus ultimately stop progress itself. And I have yet to learn of an instance when the deliberate vote of the majority (as distinguished from the decision of some governing elite) has decided on such sacrifices in the interest of a better future as is made by a free-market society. (CL 50–51)

Further, the "Western world today" has witnessed

> the growth of a majority of employed who in many respects are alien and often inimical to much that constitutes the driving force of a free society. . . .
>
> Freedom is thus seriously threatened today by the tendency of the employed majority to impose upon the rest their standards and views of life. It may indeed prove to be the most difficult task of all to persuade the employed masses that in the general interest of their society, and therefore in their own long-term interest, they should preserve such conditions as to enable a few to reach positions which to them appear unattainable or not worth the effort and risk. (*CL* 119–120)

This is, of course, not a theory of class struggle that implies an essential conflict of interest between worker and employer. After all, there is a spontaneous order and harmony that renders capitalism, the system of the unhampered market, the highest form of human social cooperation. And yet, for both von Mises and Hayek, the high levels of inequality during the best of times and the sacrifices demanded of "employees" during hard times will constantly and inescapably produce among the multitude "the temptation to strive for an ephemeral advantage by actions detrimental to the smooth functioning of the social system" (*HA* 148). It is to this temptation that socialism appeals: It "works on the emotions, tries to violate logical considerations by rousing a sense of personal interest and to stifle the voice of reason by awakening primitive instincts" (*S* 460). When the "passions of the masses" are inflamed and the primitive instincts that urge them to forgo deprivation and sacrifice the market rationality dictates, awakening their desire to seek their well-being, the "great masses who are unable to think," most of the time, become dangerous: "The mass psyche has never produced anything but mass crime, devastation, and destruction" (*S* 460).

It is precisely in relation to the masses from whom so little is to be hoped and so much is to be feared that the state is called into action. The state exists to ensure and enforce the rule of law, the subject of much of Hayek's writing, but no less important to von Mises. We should be very clear, however, that the phrase "rule of law" for von Mises and Hayek has nothing to do with juridical formalism, with the idea of law as a coherent, self-referential order. On the contrary, von Mises, who like Husserl insists on confronting positivism with the truth of its origins, declares that law "could not have arisen legally. Law cannot have begot itself of itself. Its origin lies beyond the legal sphere" (*S* 46). Other theories have located this origin in a founding contract or in reason, but for von Mises it lies solely in the fact that the economic action necessary to human existence "demands stable conditions," particularly an end to violence: "Violence and Law, War and Peace, are the two poles of social life; but its content is economic action" (*S* 44).

The violence against which the operation of law is required is not that directed against persons—such acts are "exceptional occurrences." Instead the violence that law exists to prevent is that "aimed at the property of others. The person— life and health—is the object of attack only insofar as it hinders the acquisition of property" (*S* 34). The liberty and freedom that law protects is that of a market economy itself founded on absolute private property. The "essential function" of government is that of "protecting the smooth operation of the market economy against aggression, whether on the part of domestic or foreign disturbers" (*HA* 282). In describing the exercise of this "essential function," von Mises, as we have seen, renounces any euphemism: The state "employs its power to beat people into submission solely for the prevention of actions destructive to the preservation and the smooth operation of the market economy" (*HA* 257). Such a state "must be prepared to crush the onslaughts of peace-breakers" (*HA* 149).

The concept of the democratic regime thus poses a serious dilemma: To the extent that an electoral majority represents the numerical majority of a given society, that is, the laboring population that may elect to forgo the "sacrifices" and "costs" Hayek deems necessary to progress, if it by virtue of representing "those that are less successful" acts on the basis of what is often called "social justice" but which is nothing more than "envy" (*CL* 93), such a majority may seek to interfere with the market through shortsighted attempts to relieve what it regards as destitution. For this reason, Hayek warns that "the current undiscriminating use of the word 'democratic' as a general term of praise is not without danger. It suggests that, because democracy is a good thing, it is always a gain for mankind" (*CL* 104). The danger inherent in majority rule is that a democratic majority might become, as von Mises put it, "drunk with power," and ignore the "limits to the range of questions which should be thus decided" (*CL* 106).

But the question of limits is more complex than might at first be thought. Just as states fail by extending the limit of interference in the market, they may just as harmfully restrict intervention in defense of private property and the market from the actions of their enemies. Thus, while modern states have squandered much energy (and tax dollars) in their misguided efforts to bring about that chimerical condition known as "social justice," imposing wage and rent controls, providing health care, and destroying workers' incentive to labor with unemployment insurance, they have failed to "crush" and "beat into submission" those whose actions threaten property and the market economy. The generation of the 1920s and 30s had all but destroyed the rule of law, argued Hayek, in that they were "unwilling to accept any limitation on collective action" (*CL* 247). Von Mises's "domestic disturbers" of the market economy constituted for Hayek "the totalitarians in our midst."[128]

The synecdochic figure of the mass violence of collective action against the market in the works of both thinkers is the labor union, the organization of workers in the workplace. As Hayek put it, "the whole basis of our free society is gravely threatened by the powers arrogated by the unions" (*CL* 269). To the extent that unions have succeeded in their struggle to extort through violence and intimidation higher wages and improved working conditions from the employers, they have used "their power in a manner which tends to make the market system ineffective" while giving them a dangerous degree of "control of the direction of economic activity," exerting a "constant upward pressure on the level of money wages" (*CL* 272). In addition to raising wages above the market level, they have succeeded in "confiscating the specific revenue of the capitalists and entrepreneurs partially or altogether" (*HA* 773).

The political effects of the mass unionism of the 1930s have been just as destructive to the social order as its economic effects. Unions have brought about a feudalization of society, effectively ending the state's monopoly on force.

> The labor unions are practically free to prevent by force anybody from defying their orders concerning wage rates and other labor conditions. They are free to inflict with impunity bodily evils upon strikebreakers and upon entrepreneurs and mandataries of entrepreneurs who employ strikebreakers. (*HA* 777–778)

Collective bargaining "is not a market transaction. It is a dictate forced upon the employer" (*HA* 779). Of course, unions powerful enough to issue dictates to employers and that have mastered the techniques of "strike, violence, and sabotage" in order to secure "ephemeral improvements" for workers wield a tyrannical power "before which the world now trembles" (*S* 437). Citing the case of the Kapp Putsch of 1920 in which a strike involving 12 million workers from a variety of parties and unions stopped an attempt by army officers to overthrow the Weimar Republic and impose a military dictatorship, von Mises warns

> Whether one finds the political attitude of organized labor sympathetic or not, is of no consequence. The fact is that in a country where trade unionism is strong enough to set into motion a general strike, the supreme power is in the hands of trade unions and not in the hands of parliament and the government dependent on it. (*S* 433)

The laboring masses so organized can truly be said to comprise the totalitarians in our midst:

> We have shown that the solidarity of the members of the trade union can be founded only on the idea of a war to destroy the social order based on private ownership in the means of production. The basic idea and not merely the practice of the trades unions is destructionist. (*S* 435)

Neither the problem of mass unionism nor its solution lies in the law: "Of course, the laws which make it a criminal offense for any citizen to resort—except in case of self-defense—to violent action have not been formally repealed or amended" (*HA* 777). Instead governments have decided to suspend the enforcement of such laws: "The police do not stop such offenders, the state attorneys do not arraign them, and no opportunity is offered to the penal courts to pass judgment on their actions" (*HA* 778). The neoliberals' despair in the face of collective action without limits leads them to conclusions so uncomfortable that Hayek will acknowledge them only at the end of his life, contemplating the "Chilean miracle" made possible by General Pinochet's "crushing" of the totalitarians in his midst. In the case that democracy degenerates into mob rule and a totalitarianism of the majority, a dictatorship in defense of basic freedoms may become necessary.[129]

It is around this point that Hayek comes very close to the pre-1933 positions of Carl Schmitt.[130] While Hayek very ostentatiously condemns "Professor Carl Schmitt, the leading Nazi theoretician of totalitarianism," in the *Road to Serfdom*, in the later *Constitution of Liberty* his attitude is far more positive. In the middle of a very long note on recent scholarship on the concept of the rule of law, he argues: "The conduct of Carl Schmitt under the Hitler regime does not alter the fact that, of the modern German writings on the subject, his are still among the most learned and perceptive" (*CL* 485). In particular, Hayek refers to Schmitt's 1931, *Der Hüter der Verfassung* (the guardian of the constitution) where Schmitt expands his notion of the commissarial dictatorship that exists solely in order to defend the constitution and the rule of law from those forces both internal and external that either paralyze the social order or actively subvert it. Unlike a sovereign dictatorship that seeks to destroy the old constitution and impose a new order, the commissarial dictatorship exists only to restore an order that has been disturbed; it is always temporary.

In a similar way, Hayek, just as he distinguishes between liberal and totalitarian democracy, distinguishes between liberal and totalitarian dictatorships. The

legislative action of a parliamentary majority may undermine the basis of a free
society and in that sense, irrespective of the fact that it represents the will of the
majority, loses its legitimacy. But just as threatening is the inaction of the execu-
tive in the face of mass violence that renders the law meaningless, "mere words"
as Hobbes put it. The spontaneous order of the market requires more than simply the rule of law to safeguard property and defend the market from those who
would disturb it. In order to be effective, the order and its laws must necessarily be
grounded in a relation of forces: Market equilibrium can only be achieved on the
foundation of an equilibrium of social forces that alone will ensure its operation.

The work of von Mises and Hayek testifies to their expectation of a collective, permanent revolt of wage earners against the market's present and future
demand for sacrifice—the sacrifice of strength, pleasure, fellowship, and possibly
life itself. It is this revolt that constitutes the permanent totalitarian menace to
the liberty of property and exchange that no constitutional order can in itself
prevent or guard against. The state, or those who constitute the guardians of the
legal order, must constantly work to compel people to accept the guidance and
direction of the market and to confront the resistances that such direction may
provoke. Depending upon the power of this resistance, democracy, to be sure the
preferred form of government, must sometimes give way to a dictatorship that is
able to step outside the law and use whatever force is necessary to restore its rule.

The impersonal discipline of the market itself often suffices to secure a sufficient degree of compliance even to its harshest and deadliest decrees. Only when
those affected organize to reject the demand to reduce their consumption and to
accept the consequences, however dire, of such a reduction does the supplement
of force become necessary: The greater their level of organization and combativ-
ity, the greater the corresponding force required to crush it and restore the spontaneous order of human cooperation. But if the works we have examined testify
to anything, it is to the fact that such resistance, however sporadic and lacking in
coordination, has never been reduced to zero. It is for this reason, rather than the
timidity and ignorance of governments, that the pure market has never existed.

It is at this point that we can appreciate what separates Adam Smith from
those who claim his legacy. We refer not to the common humanity, the advocacy of the generous wages that the unrestricted market is sure to bring, and
certain public services that set him apart from his twentieth-century descendants, although this is surely significant. Nor is it this quality that disrupts his
necro-economics and sets his theory against itself. No, something emerges at
the very outset of his argument, if only at its margins, irreducibly present, but

overlooked, something perhaps glimpsed if at all only in the form of certain images. We will therefore conclude with a few observations about an image from the opening of *Wealth*, specifically from the discussion of the second of the three major advantages of the division of labor according to Smith:

> A man commonly saunters a little in turning his hand from one sort of employ-
> ment to another. When he first begins the new work he is seldom very keen
> and hearty; his mind, as they say, does not go to it, and for some time he rather
> trifles than applies to good purpose. The habit of sauntering and of indolent
> careless application, which is naturally, or rather necessarily acquired by every
> country workman who is obliged to change his work and his tools every half
> hour, and to apply his hand in twenty different ways almost every day of his life,
> renders him almost always slothful and lazy, and incapable of any vigorous ap-
> plication even on the most pressing occasions. (*Wealth* 19)

What could be the theoretical interest, let alone importance, of this very concrete narrative designed to illustrate the way in which the division of labor will eliminate the waste of time and thereby increase productivity immeasur- ably? To begin with, no comparably detailed and vivid narrative of labor is to be found in all the thousands of pages written by von Mises and Hayek, although they are at least as concerned as Smith with the discipline of those "shirkers" who slow the speed of production. But is this Smith's concern in the passage cited above? In the context of the chapter as a whole, it would appear that Smith seeks merely to illustrate the loss of time when a workman must change places and tools, a loss that, when multiplied to the level of an industry as a whole, becomes immense.

What complicates Smith's illustration, even to the point of becoming infe- licitous, is the attribution of certain sentiments to the man whose movements Smith describes. This begins with the use of the term "saunter," which refers not simply to the slowness of the man's movement, but to the feeling that accompa- nies this slow movement, a deliberate lessening of his pace. The reference to the internal state of the workman continues as Smith notes his "indolent careless application" and the way that the labor process "renders him" not simply slower than he would be if he enjoyed the benefits of the division of labor, but "almost always slothful and lazy," terms that suggest a deliberate refusal to work as hard as he might, and finally, "incapable of any vigorous application even on the most pressing occasions." Such attitudes, together with their bodily manifesta- tions, become codified into customs or "habits," which are "naturally, or rather, necessarily acquired by every country workman" who labors under such conditions. Nor can they be understood as forms of adaptation to relatively primitive conditions of production: These attitudes persist even beyond their objective conditions to hinder, if not prevent, an increase in the speed of production, for example, "on the most pressing occasions."

Again, what is striking here is the accumulation of terms whose function is less description than denunciation (indolent, slothful, lazy, careless), signs of an excess or remainder beyond the operation of the argument. Each one of these terms marks a form of resistance, simultaneously in body and mind, to the demands of the master concealed in the phrase "pressing occasions." Thus, it is not simply or primarily as consumers of necessary provisions whose price demands certain wage levels that workers come into conflict with their employers. Rather, Smith conducts us into the workplace itself to show us the political economy of the body, the way in which its economic use is contingent upon its subjection in the most physical sense, as Foucault put it, "pitting force against force." His object is to submit the body, its forces and its movements, to the greatest possible degree of control, to minimize those determinations that might interfere with the pace of production, and hence the process of capital accumulation, and maximize those determinations that increase the body's productive or useful movements.

Of course, this can be understood as the image of the violence of appropriation: That which belongs to the workman—his time, his labor—is demanded of him, and he is denounced for not offering it up with sufficient rapidity and willingness. But this image can also, and perhaps better, be understood as the irreducibility of resistance in the most physical and corporeal sense. For the ultimate subjection of the body is the limit of life itself: We may think of those, both slave and "free"—from Jamaica to the Belgian Congo to Auschwitz—for whom mass production and mass extermination were not antithetical processes but one and the same thing. That which resists, that which appears at the opening of *Wealth* as the almost indecipherable intractability of the workman under pressure, is perhaps nothing other than life itself, not as a substratum or essence, but existing only *in actu*, in the act of resistance to that which endeavors to diminish or destroy it. It is this struggle that imprints the right to subsistence in indelible letters of flesh and blood in the people's book of life; each page written defers catastrophe, claims existence, and holds the dark night of silence and nothingness at bay.

NOTES

Introduction

1. U.S. House of Representatives, Committee on Oversight and Government Reform, *The Financial Crisis and the Role of Federal Regulators*, 110th Cong., 2nd sess. (October 23, 2008), http://oversight-archive.waxman.house.gov/documents/20081023100359.pdf Links to specific testimony at the hearings are included at this site.

2. Statistics on world wealth distribution are as appalling as they are easy to find. According to a UN study, significant because it is the largest such study yet conducted, the richest 1 percent of adults in the world own 40 percent of the planet's wealth. See James Randerson, "World's Richest 1% Own 40% of All Wealth, UN Report Discovers," *The Guardian* (December 6, 2006), http://www.guardian.co.uk/money/2006/dec/06/business.internationalnews (accessed March 11, 2014).

3. Scholars have made much ado about Smith's notion of the invisible hand, which is mentioned in only three places in his work. There is no consensus on the significance of this concept. For a long list of secondary literature devoted to it, see Peter Harrison, "Adam Smith and the History of the Invisible Hand," *Journal of the History of Ideas* 72, no. 1 (January 2011): 29–49. Harrison's essay is excellent for tracing contemporary usage of the term, which during Smith's time was firmly connected to the providential tradition. We will elaborate on Smith and providence in Chapter 4.

4. Giovanni Arrighi, *Adam Smith in Beijing: Lineages of the Twenty-First Century* (London: Verso, 2007).

5. Charles Griswold, for example, insists that he will ignore the rhetoric lectures altogether. Charles L. Griswold, *Adam Smith and the Virtues of the Enlightenment* (Cambridge, UK: Cambridge University Press, 1998), 29. Like Griswold, Stephen J. McKenna sets up Smith as a palliative against postmodern pluralism in *Adam Smith: The Rhetoric of Propriety* (Albany: SUNY Press, 2006). Similarly, T. D. Campbell chooses to give minimal attention to Smith's lesser-read works, citing a preference for "Enlightened interpretation, [where] the systemic unity of [Smith's] work will be assumed." See T. D. Campbell, *Adam Smith's Science of Morals* (London: Allen & Unwin, 1971), 15, 19. V. M. Hope takes Campbell's approach at face value, positing with Smith a consensus-minded intersubjectivist understanding of moral virtue. See Hope, *Virtue by Consensus: The Moral Philosophy of Hutcheson, Hume, and Adam Smith* (Oxford: Clarendon, 1989), 8. A rare essay that pays attention to the omissions and "silences"—not just around Smith but

also within the *Theory of Moral Sentiments* and *Wealth of Nations*—is Robert Urquhart, "Adam Smith's Problems: Individuality and the Paradox of Sympathy," in *The Philosophy of Adam Smith: Essays Commemorating the 250th Anniversary of "Theory of Moral Sentiments,"* eds. Vivienne Brown and Samuel Fleischacker (New York: Routledge, 2010), 181–197.

6. In a similar vein, Michael Hardt and Antonio Negri enjoin Leftist thinkers to seek a transcendent form of Smithian subjectivism uniquely charged with affective good will. See Hardt and Negri, *Multitude: War and Democracy in the Age of Empire* (New York: Penguin, 2004), 144–145. Other recent writers have stressed egalitarian themes in Smith's writing as well. See Spencer J. Pack, *Capitalism as a Moral System: Adam Smith's Critique of the Free Market Economy* (Cheltenham, UK: Edward Elgar, 2010); Stephen Darwall, *The Second-Person Standpoint: Morality, Respect, and Accountability* (Cambridge, MA: Harvard University Press, 2006); Emma Rothschild, *Economic Sentiments: Adam Smith, Condorcet, and the Enlightenment* (Cambridge, MA: Harvard University Press, 2002); and Samuel Fleischacker, *A Short History of Distributive Justice* (Cambridge, MA: Harvard University Press, 2005). For an early example of scholarship focused on radical writing in the latter eighteenth century, see Matthew Hodgart, "Radical Prose in the Late Eighteenth Century," in *The English Mind*, eds. Hugh Skyes Davies and George Watson (Cambridge, UK: Cambridge University Press, 1964), 156–152.

7. The following texts find within Smith's ethical work the promotion of frugality and impartiality that keep capitalism properly restrained: Donald Winch, *Adam Smith's Politics: An Essay in Historiography Revision* (Cambridge, UK: Cambridge University Press, 1978), especially chaps. 5, 6, and 7; Winch, "Science and the Legislator: Adam Smith and After," *Economic Journal* 93 (1983): 501–520; and Jerry Z. Muller, *Adam Smith in His Time and Ours* (Princeton, NJ: Princeton University Press, 1993). See also Andrew S. Skinner, *Adam Smith and the Role of the State* (Glasgow: University of Glasgow Press, 1974); Joseph Cropsey, *Polity and Economy: An Interpretation of the Principles of Adam Smith* (The Hague: Martinus Nijhoff, 1957); and Duncan Forbes, "Skeptical Whiggism, Commerce, and Liberty," in *Essays on Adam Smith*, eds. Andrew S. Skinner and Thomas Wilson (Oxford: Clarendon, 1976). For Smith, the anti-imperialist, see Jennifer Pitts, *A Turn to Empire: The Risk of Imperial Liberalism in Britain and France* (Princeton, NJ: Princeton University Press, 2005).

8. See August Oncken, "The Consistency of Adam Smith," *Economic Journal* (1897): 444. For an overview of "The Adam Smith Problem," see Keith Tribe, "'Das Adam Smith Problem' and the Origins of Modern Smith Scholarship," *History of European Ideas* 24 (2008): 514–525; David Wilson and William Dixon, "Das Adam Smith Problem: A Critical Realist Perspective," *Journal of Critical Realism* 5, no. 2 (2006): 252–272; and Laurence Dickey, "Historicizing the 'Adam Smith Problem': Conceptual, Historiographical, and Textual Issues," *Journal of Modern History* 58 (September 1986): 579–609.

9. See Jacob Viner, *The Long View and the Short: Studies in Economic Theory and Policy* (Glencoe, IL: Free Press, [1927] 1958), 216. Glenn Morrow finds the same discrepancy and explains this by way of Smith's visit to France in 1764–66, which included his encounter with Quesnay and his disciples in the physiocratic school. See Morrow, *The*

Ethical and Economic Theories of Adam Smith: A Study in the Social Philosophy of the Eighteenth Century (Cranbury, NJ: Scholar's Bookshelf, 1969), 4.

10. In addition to Morrow, see a succinct version of Jacob Viner's same position, "Adam Smith and Laissez Faire," *Journal of Political Economy* 35 (April 1927): 228–230. Wilson and Dixon argue that there is still no widely agreed version of what links Smith's two major published works. See their essay, "Das Adam Smith Problem," cited above. For an excellent overview of the issue of a divided Smith, see Tribe, "'Das Adam Smith Problem' and Modern Smith Scholarship."

11. It is not only the so-called minor works that have been under-read. A *New York Times Book Review* piece that examines P. J. O'Rourke's expressly conservative book, *On "The Wealth of Nations"* (Boston: Atlantic Monthly Press, 2006), raises the question of sheer unmanageable heft in reading Smith's original two-volume, 900-plus pages of text. O'Rourke's book is written as part of a series called "Books that Changed the World." But the reviewer proposes to amend a further title that he calls "Works Which Let's Admit You'll Never Read the Whole Of." See Allan Sloan, "Capitalist Punishment," *New York Times Book Review* (January 7, 2007), 12. We would like to thank Donald Charles Mendelson for this reference. Robert Heilbroner remarks provocatively that among the master economists of the past, Smith is "one of the most widely referred to and most rarely read." See Robert Heilbroner, "Economic Predictions," *The New Yorker* (July 8, 1991), 73.

12. Adam Ferguson, *An Essay on the History of Civil Society,* ed. Fania Oz-Salzberger (Cambridge, UK: Cambridge University Press, 1999), 175.

13. It was none other than Joseph A. Schumpeter (1883–1950), an early exemplar of sociological interests over strictly mathematical economics, who called Smith's 1746–48 astronomy essay the "the pearl" of his philosophical writing. See Schumpeter, *History of Economic Analysis* (New York: Oxford University Press, 1954), 182.

14. On this theme of what we might call generative absence, see Maureen Harkin, "Adam Smith's Missing History: Primitives, Progress, and the Problems of Genre," *ELH: English Literary History* 72, no. 2 (Summer 2005): 429–451.

15. See Ronald L. Meek, *Economics and Ideology and Other Essays: Studies in the Development of Economic Thought* (London: Chapman and Hall, 1967).

16. Cited by D. D. Raphael, "Adam Smith," in *A Hotbed of Genius: The Scottish Enlightenment, 1730–1790,* eds. David Daiches, Peter Jones, and Jean Jones (Edinburgh: Edinburgh University Press, 1986), 69.

17. On the various editions of *Wealth,* see Fred Glahe, "Introduction," in *Adam Smith and "The Wealth of Nations": 1776–1976, Bicentennial Essays,* ed. Fred Glahe (Boulder: University of Colorado Press, 1978), 1.

18. We will elaborate on this term "mediation" further below, where we discuss the pluralities of different Enlightenments. We use it in a similar way as Clifford Siskin and William Warner, with differences we will explain, in the introduction to their volume, *This Is Enlightenment* (Chicago: University of Chicago Press, 2010), 1–33.

19. Smith, for example, never used the word "capitalism," and though pronounced sometimes a Whig and sometimes a new Tory, he was regarded by his contemporaries

as notoriously illusive both in manner and explicit political commitment. See Nicholas Phillipson's intellectual biography, *Adam Smith: An Enlightened Life* (New Haven, CT: Yale University Press, 2010).

20. As reported in the November 1 and 2 edition of *The Scotsman* newspaper, in 1961 John M. Lothian, a reader in English at the University of Aberdeen, discovered and purchased a manuscript entitled *Notes on Doctor Smith's Rhetoric Lectures*. Lothian published these notes, with the exception of the still-missing Lecture One, in 1963 after a well-rewarded search of an Aberdeen junkshop. We accept now that Smith's own manuscripts for the *Lectures on Rhetoric and Belles Lettres* were destroyed as directed (as later were most of the essays published in *Essays on Philosophical Subjects*) upon his death. On the call for a Smith "renaissance" given the new material, see István Hont and Michael Ignatieff, eds., *Wealth and Virtue: The Shaping of Political Economy in the Scottish Enlightenment* (Cambridge, UK: Cambridge University Press, 1983), vii.

21. In the 1970s, the label "Scottish Renaissance" was applied to the period of the middle eighteenth century itself, later, to the scholarship on that topic. See chap. 2, "When Was the Scottish Enlightenment?" in Cairns Craig, *Intending Scotland: Scottish Intellectual Culture Since the Enlightenment* (Edinburgh: Edinburgh University Press, 2009), 80ff.

22. John Dwyer, "Virtue and Improvement: The Civic World of Adam Smith," in *Adam Smith Reviewed*, eds. Peter Jones and Andrew S. Skinner (Edinburgh: Edinburgh University Press, 1992), 190.

23. The books in question are Andrew S. Skinner and Thomas Wilson, eds., *Essays on Adam Smith* (Oxford: Clarendon, 1975) and Thomas Wilson and Andrew S. Skinner, eds., *Market and the State: Essays in Honour of Adam Smith* (Oxford: Clarendon, 1976). The four-volume work on Smith is *Adam Smith: Critical Assessments* (4 vols.), ed. John Cunningham Wood (London: Croom Helm, 1984). An exception to these books, which does discuss Adam's Smith's interest—if not his fear—of the poor, is chap. 4 of Richard F. Teichgraeber III's, *"Free Trade" and Moral Philosophy* (Durham, NC: Duke University Press, 1986). We are grateful to Mitchell Dean in tallying up these curious omissions. See Dean, *The Constitution of Poverty: Toward a Genealogy of Liberal Governance* (New York: Routledge, 1991), particularly chap. 7.

24. By pointing out the omission of poverty in predominant Smith scholarship, we are not suggesting that his ideals of moral prudence and sympathetic spectatorship have gone wholly unchallenged. Those who have taken issue with Smith's persistent idealization of social peace and disciplined personal conduct include: Sheldon S. Wolin, *Politics and Vision: Continuity and Innovation in Western Political Thought* (Princeton, NJ: Princeton University Press, [1960] 2004); John Durham Peters, "Publicity and Pain: Self-Abstraction in Adam Smith's *Theory of Moral Sentiments*," *Public Culture* 7 (1995): 657–675; Ronald L. Meek, *Smith, Marx, and After: Ten Essays in the Development of Economic Thought* (London: Chapman and Hall, 1977); Jacob Viner (who came down on the divided-Smith side of the famous Adam Smith problem), *The Long View and the Short*. On Smith's pessimism about historical progress in *Wealth of Nations*, see: James E. Alvey, *Adam Smith: Optimist or Pessimist? A New Problem Concerning the Teleological*

Basis of Commercial Society (London: Ashgate, 2003); Robert Heilbroner, "The Paradox of Progress: Decline and Decay in *The Wealth of Nations*," *Journal of the History of Ideas* 34, no. 2 (April–June, 1973): 243–262; Willie Henderson, "A Very Cautious or a Very Polite Dr. Smith?" *The Adam Smith Review* 1 (2004): 60–81; and Nathan Rosenberg, "Adam Smith on the Division of Labor: Two Views or One?" *Economica* 32, no. 1 (May 1965): 127–139.

25. In Chapter 1, we will be studying at greater length the importance of reading in the eighteenth century and what it meant for Smith and his cohort. On this topic, see Mark R. M. Towsey, *Reading the Scottish Enlightenment: Books and Their Readers in Provincial Scotland, 1750–1820* (Leiden: Brill, 2010).

26. For information on *The Adam Smith Review*, see http://www.adamsmithreview .org/index.html. See also Sankar Muthu, *Enlightenment Against Empire* (Princeton, NJ: Princeton University Press, 2003). Muthu seeks to "diversify our understanding of Enlightenment thought" (p. 2). He finds within a pluralized Enlightenment (about which more below) strong support commitments to the diversity issue, here in the form of eighteenth-century anti-imperialist British and French philosophy.

27. *The Cambridge Companion to Adam Smith*, ed. Knud Haakonssen (Cambridge, UK: Cambridge University Press, 2006).

28. See Eric Schliesser's review of the *Companion* in *Notre Dame Philosophical Reviews* 8 (2007), http://ndpr.nd.edu/news/23101/?id=10823 (accessed March 29, 2014).

29. The insistence on searching for wholeness as both the method and the goal of reading Adam Smith is echoed in Leonidas Montes, *Adam Smith in Context: A Critical Reassessment of Some Central Components of His Thought* (London: Palgrave Macmillan, 2004), 2, 5. Montes also insists upon what is for literary scholars, at least since T. S. Eliot, rather an insufficient way to access stable and authentic meaning by referring to the author's "intention reflected in the act of writing" (p. 7). Smith's lifelong preoccupation with revising his work would seem to suggest that his intentions, like his reception, continued to change. See W. K. Wimsatt and Monroe C. Beardsley, "The Intentional Fallacy," *Sewanee Review* 54 (1946): 468–488; revised and republished in *The Verbal Icon: Studies in the Meaning of Poetry* (Lexington: University of Kentucky Press: 1954), 3–18.

30. See Schliesser's blog, "On the Positivist Dogma of Historical Scholarship, or Adam Smith as Reader of Spinoza" (July 3, 2012) at *New APPS: Art, Politics, Philosophy, Science*, http://www.newappsblog.com/2012/07/on-the-positivist-dogmas-of-scholar-ship-or-adam-smith-as-reader-of-spinoza.html (accessed March 12, 2014).

31. Leonidas Montes and Eric Schliesser, eds., *New Voices on Adam Smith* (New York: Routledge, 2006).

32. Richard B. Sher, *The Enlightenment and the Book: Scottish Authors and Their Publishers in Eighteenth-Century Britain, Ireland, and America* (Chicago: University of Chicago Press, 2006), 1.

33. Books on the history of eighteenth-century print are too numerous to list here. For a recent assessment and overview, which includes essays by key figures in this area, see Sabrina Alcorn Baron, Eric N. Lindquist, and Eleanor F. Shevlin, eds., *Agent of Change: Print Culture Studies after Elizabeth L. Eisenstein* (Amherst: University of

Massachusetts Press, 2007). On the eighteenth century particularly, see Alvin B. Kernan, *Samuel Johnson and the Impact of Print* (Princeton, NJ: Princeton University Press, 1989). On the significance of the date 1774 and the (Scottish) enforcement of (English) copyright law, see William St. Clair, *The Reading Nation in the Romantic Period* (Cambridge, UK: Cambridge University Press, 2007), 31.

34. Alexander Pope, *The Dunciad,* Book I, lines 273–274.

35. Michael J. Shapiro, *Reading "Adam Smith": Desire, History, and Value* (New York: Rowman & Littlefield, 2002).

36. John Guillory's work on cultural capital evokes Smith's attempt to reconcile the principle of order in early modern society with individual self-interest under the heading of moral philosophy, also from an aesthetic perspective. In this sense, Guillory arrives from an alternate disciplinary viewpoint than Shapiro's at conclusions that would match the socially minded Adam Smith recently minted from within economics and the study of natural law already cited. See Guillory, *Cultural Capital: The Problem of Literary Canon Formation* (Chicago: University of Chicago Press, 1993), 321. Peggy Kamuf makes the provocative argument that literature designates that division of knowledge that "continues to divide." However, the history of the literary itself is missing in this argument. See Kamuf, *The Division of Literature: Or the University in Deconstruction* (Chicago: University of Chicago Press, 1997), 6. Alexander Dick and Christina Lupton's edited volume, *Theory and Practice in the Eighteenth Century: Writing Between Philosophy and Literature* (London: Pickering & Chatto, 2008), represents another example of new work on disciplinary redivision, but to the exclusion of political economy.

37. One thinks of Gunnar Myrdal's work in the late 1920s to reintroduce political issues to economics. See Gunnar Myrdal, *The Political Element in the Development of Economic Theory* (Cambridge, MA: Harvard University Press, [1925] 1965). More recently, see Gary Becker and Kevin Murphy's, *Social Economics: Market Behavior in a Social Environment* (Cambridge, MA: Belknap of Harvard University Press, 2000), 1, 5. Deirdre McCloskey has rightly achieved recognition and praise for critiquing the "sad parody" of mainstream economic science in its ignorance of "the intellectual and moral virtues of . . . Adam Smith." See McCloskey, *The Vices of Economists—The Virtues of the Bourgeoisie* (Amsterdam: Amsterdam University Press, 1996), 130; and *The Bourgeois Virtues: Ethics for an Age of Commerce* (Chicago: University of Chicago Press, 2006), 1. Our point is that, with few exceptions, interdisciplinary studies itself too often works in such a way that one discipline returns from its limited foray abroad with renewed self-satisfaction. On the problem more generally of the still discipline-bound nature of interdisciplinary work, see James Chandler, "Introduction: Doctrines, Disciplines, Discourses, Departments," *Critical Inquiry* 35 (Summer 2009): 739; and Clifford Siskin and William Warner, "Stopping Cultural Studies," *Profession* (2008): 94–107. On the relation between so-called interdisciplinary excellence and the decline of the public research university, see Bill Readings, *The University in Ruins* (Cambridge, MA: Harvard University Press, 1996); and Mike Hill, "Cultural Studies by Default," in *Class Issues*, ed. Amitava Kumar (New York: Routledge, 1997), 48–62.

38. In a unique early example of the problem of modern specialization and its effect

on Smith scholarship, A. L. Macfie remarks "today we are all so specialized that when we stray from our own disciplines the sense that we may be talking weak superficialities is an inadequacy that we must accept and face" (p. 34). See Macfie, *The Individual in Society: Papers on Adam Smith* (London: Allen & Unwin, 1967).

39. One underappreciated exception is David M. Levy, who insists that the "partial spectator" is key to Smith's economic system and not Smith's notion of the impartial ideal. Further, Levy claims that the problem of interpretation is central to the ways in which Smith imagines community. See Levy, *How the Dismal Science Got Its Name: Classical Economics and the Ur-Text of Racial Politics* (Ann Arbor: University of Michigan Press, 2001).

40. We could create here a very long list comprising what we might call the moral restraint school of pro-capitalist Adam Smith scholars. More selectively, see Jerry Evensky, *Adam Smith's Moral Philosophy: A Historical and Contemporary Perspective on Markets, Law, Ethics, and Culture* (Cambridge, UK: Cambridge University Press, 2005); Patricia H. Werhane, *Adam Smith and His Legacy for Modern Capitalism* (Oxford: Oxford University Press, 1991); Peter J. Dougherty, *Who's Afraid of Adam Smith? How the Market Got Its Soul* (New York: Wiley, 2002), 44; John A. Dwyer, *Virtuous Discourse: Sensibility and Community in Late Eighteenth-Century Scotland* (Edinburgh: John Donald, 1987); Athol Fitzgibbons, *Adam Smith's System of Liberty, Wealth, and Virtue: The Moral and Political Foundations of "The Wealth of Nations"* (Oxford: Clarendon, 1995); *Intersubjectivity in Economics: Agents and Structures,* ed. Edward Fullbrook (New York: Routledge, 2002); James R. Otteson, *Adam Smith's Marketplace of Life* (Cambridge, UK: Cambridge University Press, 2002); and Pierre Force, *Self-Interest Before Adam Smith: A Genealogy of Economic Science* (Cambridge, UK: Cambridge University Press, 2003). Philosophical appropriations of moral philosophy are also found in John Rawls, *Lectures on the History of Moral Philosophy,* ed. Samuel Freeman (Cambridge, MA: Harvard University Press, 2000). For a predominately liberal notion of Smith as a source of ethical inspiration, see Amartya Sen, "Capitalism Beyond the Crisis," *The New York Review of Books* (March 26, 2009), http://www.nybooks.com/articles/22490 (accessed March 13, 2014). For more on Sen's appreciation of Smith's ideals of moral prudence, see "Adam Smith's Prudence," in *Theory and Reality in Development: Essays in Honour of Paul Streeten,* eds. Sanjaya Lall and Frances Stewart (New York: Macmillan, 1986), 28ff.; also see Sen, *On Ethics and Economics* (London: Blackwell, 1987); and Sen, "Moral Codes and Economic Success," in *Market Capitalism and Moral Values: Proceedings . . . British Association for the Advancement of Science,* eds. Samuel Brittan and Alan Hamlin (Cheltenham, UK: Edward Elgar, 1994), 23–33.

41. Eighteenth-century moral philosophy initially came to Smith in the form of his teacher, Francis Hutcheson, and consumed Smith's as well as Hume's early intellectual preoccupations. Of course, both were well versed in the lineages of moral philosophy, within Protestantism, that extended from Grotius and the other natural philosophers. For more on the natural philosophy connection, see Knud Haakonssen, *Natural Law and Moral Philosophy: From Grotius to the Scottish Enlightenment* (Cambridge, UK: Cambridge University Press, 1996), especially chap. 1.

42. On the relation between Habermas's notion of communicative justice and popular contention outside the public sphere, see Mike Hill and Warren Montag, "What Is, What Was, the Public Sphere? Post-Cold War Reflections," in *Masses, Classes, and the Public Sphere*, eds. Mike Hill and Warren Montag (London: Verso, 2000), 1–12.

43. Francis Hutcheson, *An Essay on the Nature and Conduct of the Passions and Affections, with Illustrations on the Moral Sense,* ed. Aaron Garrett (Indianapolis: Liberty Fund, [1728] 2002), 94.

44. Sandra J. Peart and David M. Levy explain the term "analytical egalitarianism" in their introduction to *The Street Porter and the Philosopher* (Ann Arbor: University of Michigan Press, 2008), 1–14. In his use of "Christian virtue," Ryan Patrick Hanley places too little emphasis on the volatile political battles among Anglicans, Presbyterians, and Catholics facing Smith and his cohort in the eighteenth century. See Hanley, *Adam Smith and the Character of Virtue* (New York: Cambridge University Press, 2011), 9.

45. Neil Davidson, "The Scottish Path to Capitalist Agriculture 3: The Enlightenment as the Theory and Practice of Improvement," *Journal of Agrarian Change* 5, no. 1 (January 2005): 1–72. Davidson cites later developments by Duncan Forbes at Cambridge University in the 1960s and 70s. See Forbes, *Hume's Philosophical Politics* (Cambridge, UK: Cambridge University Press, 1975), xi. Davidson summarizes opposing viewpoints of subsequent debates in the essay listed above. For material in addition to other books we will cite below on the *specifically* Scottish aspects of the Enlightenment, see Christopher Berry, *Social Theory of the Scottish Enlightenment* (Edinburgh: Edinburgh University Press, 1997), 185–194.

46. See Joyce Oldham Appleby, *Economic Thought and Ideology in Seventeenth-Century England* (Princeton, NJ: Princeton University Press, 1978). Smith's comprehensive rejection of the earlier commercial norms of mercantilism, bullionism, and physiocracy is also ground well covered. See Roy Porter, *Flesh in the Age of Reason* (New York: Norton, 2004). For more on Smith's economic precursors, see Terence Hutchison, *Before Adam Smith: The Emergence of Political Economy, 1662–1776* (London: Blackwell, 1993); and Hannah R. Sewall, *Theory of Value Before Adam Smith* (New York: A. M. Kelly, [1901] 1968).

47. As Christopher Berry points out in *Social Theory of the Scottish Enlightenment,* the influence of Smith on Rousseau, or Hume on Kant, marks a flow of authority from the supposed province toward continental metropolis that is not widely recognized in subsequent histories of the period.

48. For the SSPCK's current mission, see http://www.spck.org.uk/. On the SSPCK's policy toward the Highlanders, see Charles W. J. Withers, "Education and Anglicization: The Policy of the SSPCK Toward the Education of the Highlander, 1709–1825," *Scottish Studies* 26 (1982): 37–56; and Geoffrey Plank, *Rebellion and Savagery: The Jacobite Rising of 1745 and the British Empire* (Philadelphia: University of Pennsylvania Press, 2005).

49. On Scottish literary societies, see J. G. A. Pocock, "Cambridge Paradigms and Scotch Philosophers," in *Wealth and Virtue,* 242.

50. See Thomas P. Miller, *The Formation of College English: Rhetoric and Belles Lettres in the British Cultural Provinces* (Pittsburgh: University of Pittsburgh Press, 1997).

51. See Daiches et al., *Hotbed*, 34. Of the many other books tracing the centrality of Scotland in the formation of Western modernity, see James Buchan, *Crowded with Genius: The Scottish Enlightenment, Edinburgh's Moment of the Mind* (New York: HarperCollins, 2003).

52. See Isabel Henderson, *The Picts* (London: Thames & Hudson, 1967).

53. Walter Bagehot, quoted by John R. R. Christie, "Adam Smith's Metaphysics of Language," in *The Figural and the Literal: Problems of Language in the History of Science and Philosophy, 1630–1800,* eds. Andrew E. Benjamin, Geoffrey N. Cantor, and John R. R. Christie (Manchester: Manchester University Press, 1997), 203.

54. Plank, *Rebellion and Savagery*, 9.

55. Anthony Jarrells has shown that the myth of bloodless-ness as a uniquely peaceable feature at the origins of modernity was established by imagining history not only in a particular way—for Jarrells a Romantically anesthetized way—but also at a particular distance from the history of writing itself. See Anthony Jarrells, *Britain's Bloodless Revolutions: 1688 and the Romantic Reform of Literature* (London: Palgrave Macmillan, 2005).

56. On Glencoe, see John L. Roberts, *Clan, King and Covenant: History of the Highland Clans from the Civil War to the Glencoe Massacre* (Edinburgh: Edinburgh University Press, 2000).

57. Tobias Smollett, *The History of England from the Revolution in 1688, to the Death of King George the Second; Designed as a Continuation of Hume* (Philadelphia: Thomas Davis, 1844), 15.

58. Of course, England was not only at war with itself. Serious financial woes came between 1688 and the union of 1707. Of the nineteen years between the revolution and incorporation of Scotland, there were only five years of peace. See P. W. J. Riley, *The Union of England and Scotland: A Study in Anglo-Scottish Politics of the Eighteenth Century* (London: Rowman & Littlefield, 1978), 198ff.

59. Sir William Hamilton, ed., *The Works of Thomas Reid* (Edinburgh: Edinburgh University Press, 1846), 773–774.

60. See Benedict Anderson, *Imagined Communities* (London: Verso, 2006). For a treatment of Anderson in the context of Scottish nationalism, see Craig, *Intending Scotland*, 41–52.

61. Riley, *Union of England and Scotland*, 283.

62. As we shall examine in Chapter 3, plebian aspects of Jacobite insurrection were thought of as specifically remarkable and threatening to moderate Enlightenment thinkers of the day; see George Rudé's classic *Wilkes and Liberty: A Social Study of 1763 to 1774* (London: Clarendon, 1962), 13ff.

63. Dugald Stewart, "Account of the Life and Writings of Adam Smith, LL.D.," in *Adam Smith, Essays on Philosophical Subjects*, eds. W. P. D. Wightman, J. C. Bryce, and I. S. Ross (Indianapolis: Liberty Fund, [1793] 1982), 331.

64. Stewart's letter of 1797 is cited in Wightman et al., *Essays on Philosophical Subjects*, 305.

65. The story of a boy Smith being captured by "vagrants" is repeated next in John Rae's *Life of Adam Smith: With an Introduction by Jacob Viner* (New York: A. M. Kelly,

[1895] 1965), and again in E. G. West's *Adam Smith: The Man and His Works* (Indianapolis: Liberty Fund, 1976), 28.

66. Carlyle is cited in Arthur Herman, *How the Scots Invented the Modern World* (New York: Three Rivers Press, 2001), 196.

Chapter 1

1. Adam Smith, "Of the Nature of That Imitation Which Takes Place in What Are Called the Imitative Arts," in *Adam Smith: Essays on Philosophical Subjects*, eds. W. P. D. Wightman, J. C. Bryce, and I. S. Ross (Indianapolis: Liberty Fund, 1982), 185.

2. Dugald Stewart, "Account of the Life and Writings of Adam Smith, LL.D.," in *Essays on Philosophical Subjects*, 305.

3. Adam Smith, *An Inquiry into the Nature and Causes of the Wealth of Nations*, eds. R. H. Campbell, A. S. Skinner, and W. B. Todd (Indianapolis: Liberty Fund, 1981); and Smith, *The Theory of Moral Sentiments*, eds. D. D. Raphael and A. L. Macfie (Indianapolis: Liberty Fund, 1984).

4. Eric Schliesser, "Some Principles of Adam Smith's Newtonian Methods in *The Wealth of Nations*," in *Research in the History of Economic Thought and Methodology* (vol. 23), eds. Warren J. Samuels, Jeff E. Biddle, and Ross B. Emmett (Emerald Group, 2005), 33–74; at 59.

5. Ibid., 37.

6. In "Wonder in the Face of Scientific Revolutions," Schliesser writes, Smith "does have an idealized picture of what motivates philosophers" (p. 711). See this article in *British Journal for the History of Philosophy* 13, no. 4 (2005): 697–732.

7. Ibid., 697–698, 726.

8. See Hume, *Enquiry Concerning Human Understanding* (Oxford: Oxford University Press, [1748] 2007), 28.

9. Schliesser, "Wonder in the Face of Scientific Revolutions," 701.

10. For a fuller assessment of "Romantic ideology" along these lines, see Clifford Siskin, *The Historicity of Romantic Discourse* (Oxford: Oxford University Press, 1988); and Martha Woodmansee, *The Author, Art, and the Market: Rereading the History of Aesthetics* (New York: Columbia University Press, 1994).

11. On the difference between Hume's notion of revolutionary change as a discontinuous break with normative values versus Smith's understanding of change as more happily taking place as an extension or peaceable adjustment of them, see Eric Schliesser, "Copernican Revolutions Revisited in Adam Smith by Way of David Hume," *Revista Empresa y Humanismo* 13, no. 1 (2010): 213–248.

12. See Wordsworth's "Essay Supplementary to Preface [1815]," *Harvard Classics*, http://bartleby.com/39/39.html#txt3

13. As Susan Manning reminds us, "philosophy did not become an irreversibly specialist profession until the publication of Kant's *Critique of Pure Reason* in 1781." See Manning, "Literature and Philosophy," in *The Cambridge History of Literary Criticism* (vol. IV), eds. H. B. Nisbet and Claude Rawson (Cambridge, UK: Cambridge University Press, 1997), 587.

See also Leonidas Montes, *Adam Smith in Context: A Critical Reassessment of Some Central Components of His Thought* (London: Palgrave Macmillan, 2004). In tracing Smith's debt to Newton, Montes writes: "With no barriers between the different branches of knowledge, the problem was not whether Newtonian method could be transferred to the social realm but how this new generation of 'social scientists' would attain this goal" (p. 142). On the history of political economy in the context of other disciplines, see Deborah H. Redman, *The Rise of Political Economy as a Science: Methodology and the Classical Economists* (Cambridge, MA: MIT Press, 1997); and Redman, *Economics and the Philosophy of Science* (Oxford: Oxford University Press, 1993).

14. Neil De Marchi, "Smith on Ingenuity, Pleasure, and the Imitative Arts," in *The Cambridge Companion to Adam Smith,* ed. Knud Haakonssen (Cambridge, UK: Cambridge University Press, 2006), 136–157; at 139.

15. Ibid., 154. For early recognition of Smith's interest in aesthetics, which does not comment on the eighteenth-century division between aesthetics and philosophy, see James S. Malek, "Adam Smith's Contribution to Eighteenth-Century British Aesthetics," *Journal of Aesthetics and Art Criticism* 31 (1972–73): 49–54.

16. Andrew E. Benjamin, Geoffrey N. Cantor, and John R. R. Christie's volume, *The Figural and the Literal: Problems of Language in the History of Science and Philosophy, 1630–1800* (Manchester: University of Manchester Press, 1997), should be singled out for the space it provides contributors who are interested in interrogating certain disciplinary impasses between literal and figural discourse. The editors see precursors to the problem of disciplinary division before it became a concern for the Scottish universities in, for example, Thomas Sprat and the Royal Society of London (p. 6). Though eschewing a historical take on the problem, Christie's essay provides a Derridean reading of Smith the rhetorician, "who was unable to integrate this [grammatological] perception structurally within his philosophical historiography, where it remained as a latent troubling of the text." See Christie's essay "Adam Smith's Metaphysics of Language" in *Figural and Literal,* 224, 227.

17. Schliesser is right to argue that the origins of the imagination is ground covered by Smith. In "Wonder in the Face of Scientific Revolutions," he writes, "there is . . . no evidence that Smith believes he could give a satisfactory account of the mind's creativity," and that imagination remains "one of the most vexing issues in Smith's philosophy" (p. 716).

18. Richard Terry, "The Invention of Eighteenth-Century Literature: A Truism Revisited," *British Journal for Eighteenth Century Studies* 19 (1996): 47–62. Other influential references for the history of the English discipline should include: Terry Eagleton, *Literary Theory: An Introduction* (Minneapolis: University of Minnesota Press, [1983] 2008); Raymond Williams, *Marxism and Literature* (Oxford: Oxford University Press, 1977); Alvin Kernan, *Samuel Johnson and the Impact of Print* (Princeton, NJ: Princeton University Press, 1989); Lawrence Lipking, *The Ordering of the Arts in Eighteenth-Century England* (Princeton, NJ: Princeton University Press, 1972).

19. On the importance of technology for thinking not only about the history of eighteenth-century writing but also for the Enlightenment in general, see Clifford Sis-

kin and William Warner, *This Is Enlightenment* (Chicago: University of Chicago Press, 2010), especially the volume's introduction.

20. Terry, "Invention of Eighteenth-Century Literature," 60.

21. Ibid., 57.

22. See Nicholas Phillipson, "Adam Smith as Civic Moralist," in *Wealth and Virtue: The Shaping of Political Economy in the Scottish Enlightenment*, eds. István Hont and Michael Ignatieff (Cambridge, UK: Cambridge University Press, 1983), 192.

23. Nicholas Phillipson, *Adam Smith: An Enlightened Life* (New Haven, CT: Yale University Press, 2012), 86.

24. On the invention of literature by eighteenth-century criticism, see Clifford Siskin, *The Work of Writing: Literature and Social Change in Britain, 1700–1830* (Baltimore: Johns Hopkins University Press, 1999), 30.

25. George Turnbull, *Observations Upon Liberal Education, in All Its Branches,* ed. Terrance O. Moore (Indianapolis: Liberty Fund, 2003), 31, 120.

26. Hugh Blair, *A Critical Dissertation on the Poems of Ossian* [1763] (vol. 1), ed. Harold F. Harding (Carbondale: Southern Illinois University: 1965), 36.

27. Sir Joshua Reynolds, *Discourses on Art* (1769–1790), ed. Robert R. Wark (New Haven, CT: Yale University Press, 1975), 15–16. For more on the generality and particularity issue in the eighteenth century, see Leo Damrosch, "Generality and Particularity," in *The Cambridge History of Literary Criticism* (vol. IV), eds. H. B. Nisbet and Claude Rawson (Cambridge, UK: Cambridge University Press, 1997), 381–393. On Reynolds specifically, see John Barrell's influential *The Political Theory of Painting from Reynolds to Hazlitt* (New Haven, CT: Yale University Press, 1986).

28. For further discussion of the reshaping of reading practices in the eighteenth century, see Mark Towsey, *Reading the Scottish Enlightenment: Books and Their Readers in Provincial Scotland, 1750–1820* (Leiden: Brill, 2010); and John Brewer, *The Pleasures of the Imagination: English Culture in the Eighteenth Century* (Chicago: University of Chicago Press, 2000). On the influence of the market on the circulation of literature, see George Justice, *The Manufacturers of Literature: Writing and the Literary Marketplace in Eighteenth-Century England* (Newark: University of Delaware Press, 2002).

29. See J. G. A. Pocock, *Virtue, Commerce, and History: Essays on Political Thought and History Chiefly in the Eighteenth Century* (Cambridge, UK: Cambridge University Press, 1985). This is not, however, to argue that Smith was a civic humanist.

30. Adam Smith, "'Early Draft' of Part of *The Wealth of Nations*," in *Lectures on Jurisprudence,* eds. R. L. Meek, D. D. Raphael, and P. G. Stein (Indianapolis: Liberty Fund, 1982), manuscript B: 570.

31. For reasons made clear in the Introduction and below, our focus on surprise in this chapter is on distinctly Scottish voices. There is a rich connection between Smith and other pan-European thinkers, especially Rousseau, traced by many works that already exist. For a compelling book contrasting "the spectacle of accident" in the two writers, see David Marshall, *The Surprising Effects of Sympathy: Marivaux, Diderot, Rousseau, and Mary Shelley* (Chicago: University of Chicago Press, 1998), 1. Robert Mitchell comments on "the tendency of the collective imagination to produce rivalry and violence" in

Rousseau, whereas "Smith sought to contain the projective capacities of this faculty by tying sympathy to the past and the dead" (p. 22). Rousseau *contra* Smith, Mitchell argues, "pushed the conflict . . . to its breaking point" (p. 62). See Mitchell, *Sympathy and the State in the Romantic Era: Systems, State Finance, and the Shadows of Futurity* (New York Routledge, 2007). Eric Schliesser notes that Smith argued against Rousseau's "speculation that language has its origin in a poetic and emotive language." This accords well with our account of Smith's and his cohorts singling out poetry for special danger to the eighteenth-century public. See Eric Schliesser, "Reading Adam Smith After Darwin: On the Evolution of Propensities, Institutions, and Sentiments," *Journal of Economic Behaviour and Organization* 77 (2011): 18. In addition to these references, see: Ronald Beiner, *Civil Religion: A Dialogue in the History of Political Philosophy* (Cambridge, UK: Cambridge University Press, 2011), especially chaps. 18 and 19; Spencer J. Pack, *Capitalism as a Moral System: Adam Smith's Critique of the Free Market Economy* (Northampton, MA: Edward Elgar, 2010); Samuel Fleischacker, *A Short History of Distributive Justice* (Cambridge, MA: Harvard University Press, 2004); Pierre Force, *Self-Interest Before Adam Smith: A Genealogy of Economic Science* (Cambridge, UK: Cambridge University Press, 2003); Étienne Balibar, "What Makes a People a People? Rousseau and Kant," in *Masses, Classes, and the Public Sphere,* eds. Mike Hill and Warren Montag (London: Verso, 2000), 105–131; and E. G. West, "Adam Smith and Rousseau's Discourse on Inequality: Inspiration or Provocation?" *Journal of Economic Issues* 5, no. 2 (June 1971): 56–70.

32. On the "newly disturbing technology of writing," see especially, Siskin, *The Work of Writing,* 26.

33. The relationship between proliferation and uniformity in the rise of eighteenth-century print culture is no less salient when it comes to the material production of books. As David McKitterick reminds us, between the fifteenth and late seventeenth centuries, "the distinctions between manuscript and print might be ignored." (p. 50). From a bibliographic point of view, "Texts are not fixed. They are always mobile" (p. 4). "Volumes bound originally at the end of the fifteenth century were dismembered" (p. 50), and "the practice of binding up manuscripts . . . according to individual need or taste . . . [was] well-established in the fifteenth century" (p. 51). The strive for uniformity in production is concurrent with the explosion of printed material available in the UK after 1770. See McKitterick, *Print, Manuscript, and the Search for Order, 1450–1830* (Cambridge, UK: Cambridge University Press, 2003).

34. Henry Home, Lord Kames, *Elements of Criticism* (vol. 1), ed. Peter Jones (Indianapolis: Liberty Fund, 2005), 3.

35. The *Oxford English Dictionary* traces the relationship between taste and writing to Joseph Addison's *Spectator* in the first decades of the eighteenth century. Sheldon Rothblatt refers to a 1725 pamphlet that speaks of the civility of Europe as a matter of "Refining the *modern* taste" (emphasis in original). See Rothblatt, *Tradition and Change in English Liberal Education* (London: Faber and Faber, 1976), 19. The Edinburgh Society announced a prize in 1755 for the best essay on taste; Hume's "Essay on Taste" appeared in 1757, which is near contemporary with Smith's commentary on the topic in the 1759 edition of *The Theory of Moral Sentiments.*

36. Voltaire, cited in James Buchan, *Crowded with Genius: The Scottish Enlightenment, Edinburgh's Moment of the Mind* (New York: HarperCollins, 2003), 2.

37. On Kames, Ian Hunter goes as far as to argue that between the publication of *Elements of Criticism* (1762) and Schiller's essay "On the Sublime" (1801), a fundamental transformation in the notion of criticism occurred that "abolished [the] idea of a universal faculty of taste rooted in human nature, [or] a divinely ordained universal order of nature" (p. 197). The point is well taken, but should not shade the significant role of literary standardization in its capacity to construct the question of taste as *both* of the narrowing of specific texts and effects, *and* the broadening of literary education. See Hunter, *Culture and Government: The Emergence of Literary Education* (London: Macmillan, 1988). It should also be noted, as we have in our Introduction, that we do not wish to diminish the important differences between different Scottish Enlightenments. Turnbull, unlike Smith, taught moral philosophy at Aberdeen and influenced the Common Sense philosophy of Thomas Reid.

38. See Richard Sher, *Church and University in the Scottish Enlightenment: The Moderate Literati of Edinburgh* (Edinburgh: Edinburgh University Press, 1985).

39. On literary education in India, see Gauri Viswanathan, *Masks of Conquest: Literary Study and British Rule in India* (New York: Columbia University Press, 1989).

40. For a classic account of the strong role "print [had] in unifying Great Britain and in shaping its inhabitants' view of themselves," see Linda Colley, *Britons: Forging the Nation, 1707–1837* (New Haven, CT: Yale University Press, 1992), 20. As we will detail in Chapter 3, this shaping of national self-understanding was anything but easy. Print both mediated that uneasiness and, because print was itself seen to be a mixed and massive blessing, produced much of it.

41. The term "imagined community" belongs to Benedict Anderson. See *Imagined Communities* (London: Verso, [1983] 2008).

42. The Reverend Mr. Knox, *Essays, Moral and Literary* (London: 1779), 375.

43. Smith's editors approximate the date for this essay on the senses as having been written before 1752.

44. Adam Smith, "Of the External Senses," in *Essays on Philosophical Subjects*, 155.

45. We are not therefore imposing on Smith a simple real versus imaginary concept, where one stands in for truth, the other, for falseness. While we appreciate Andy Denis's thesis that Smith prefers "reconciliation over investigation," we would hesitate over his use of the term "illusion," which is placed by Denis in an undertheorized opposition to "material causes." For Hume and Smith, materiality is often regarded as a problem of multitudes. And printed ideas themselves, as we are arguing, had to be *de*-corporealized by Scottish copyright laws but did not necessarily start that way. Therefore the idea of a division between real and imagined opposites does not work. Certainly, the imagination has material effects in Smith's account, which is why we prefer to stay with his word "corporeal" as way of designating different kinds of labor. See Denis, "The Invisible Hand of God in Adam Smith," in *Research in the History of Economic Thought and Methodology*, 23–A: 1–32; at 13.

46. This line from Boswell is cited in Martin Bell's "Introduction" to the Penguin

edition of Hume's 1779 publication of *Dialogues Concerning Natural Religion* (New York: Penguin, 1990), 1.

47. Smith, *Wealth of Nations*, 27.

48. See Athol Fitzgibbons, *Adam Smith's System of Liberty, Wealth, and Virtue: The Moral and Political Foundations of "The Wealth of Nations"* (Oxford: Clarendon, 1995).

49. Daniel Defoe, *The Poor Man's Plea . . .* (London: 1698), 19.

50. Thomas Malthus, *Essay on the Principle of Population* (New York: Penguin, [1798] 1970), 144. On the historicity of "class" as both heuristic and social category, see Peter Calvert, *The Concept of Class: An Historical Introduction* (New York: St. Martin's, 1982).

51. Henry Fielding, *The Works of Henry Fielding: Amelia Part III and Jonathan Wild* (vol. 5)(Philadelphia: John D. Morris, 1902), 67.

52. On Pitt (and Shelburne) as disciples of Smith, see E. G. West, *Adam Smith: The Man and His Works* (Indianapolis: Liberty Fund, 1976), 12ff.

53. For fuller elaboration on the connection between Smith and the later economic transformation of the nineteenth century, see C. P. Kindleberger, "The Historical Background: Adam Smith and the Industrial Revolution," in *Essays on Adam Smith*, eds. Andrew S. Skinner and Thomas Wilson (Oxford: Clarendon, 1975).

54. The explicitly political role of the term "middle-class," which as Dror Wharman notes enters the historical scene when "scores of observers of British Society [were] eagerly hailing [it], just as others were denying its existence," is typically placed within a chronological framework between the French Revolution and the Reform Act of 1832. See Dror Wharman, *Imagining the Middle Class: The Political Representation of Class in Britain, c. 1780–1840* (Cambridge, UK: Cambridge University Press, 1995), 8. For a valuable study of the British middle class as coterminous with the nineteenth-century industrial bourgeoisie, see Theodore Koditschek, *Class Formation and Urban-Industrial Society: Bradford, 1750–1850* (Cambridge, UK: Cambridge University Press, 1990).

55. In her extensive work on class in eighteenth-century Britain, Penelope J. Corfield remarks:

> By the 1740s, and certainly the 1750s, specific references to social structure were couched in the new terms [of classes]. Nelson's five classes of people appeared in 1753; . . . [And] in 1749 Joisa Tucker wrote of "classes of society," and identified the lower class of people. (p. 113)

But, she continues, the notion of class to denote particular occupational identities was "still in minority usage." See Corfield, "Class by Name and Number in Eighteenth-Century Britain," in *Language, History, and Class*, ed. Penelope J. Corfield (London: Basil Blackwell, 1991).

56. On class and the classroom system, see David Hamilton, "Adam Smith and the Moral Economy of the Classroom System" *Journal of Curriculum Studies* 12, no. 4 (1980): 281–298.

57. On the uses of class in its nineteenth-century sense of the industrial working class, as compared with class in the more general classificatory sense, see Michael McKeon, *The Origins of the English Novel, 1600–1740* (Baltimore: Johns Hopkins University Press, 1987); and for an account for the synchronicity of the two senses of class, see

E. P. Thompson, "Eighteenth-Century English Society: Class Struggle Without Class?" *Social History* 3, no. 2 (1978): 147–150.

58. Michel Foucault makes the argument that nineteenth-century notions of social class are predicated on previous conceptions of race, such that communist dictatorships can be regarded, in his terms, as state racism. See Foucault, *"Society Must Be Defended": Lectures at the Collège de France, 1975–1976* (New York: Picador, 2003), 189–214.

59. See Michel Foucault, *Discipline and Punish: The Birth of the Prison* (New York: Vintage, 1979).

60. See Jürgen Habermas, *The Structural Transformation of the Public Sphere: An Inquiry into a Category of Bourgeois Society* (Cambridge, MA: MIT Press, 1991).

61. After the Act of Union with Scotland in 1707, Edinburgh saw a proliferation of spectatorial clubs and societies. See J. G. A. Pocock, "Cambridge Paradigms and Scotch Philosophers," *Wealth and Virtue: The Shaping of Political Economy in the Scottish Enlightenment*, eds. István Hont and Michael Ignatieff (London: Cambridge University Press, 1983), 242. Before assuming his post as professor and chair of moral philosophy in 1752 at Glasgow, Smith began as a lecturer in rhetoric and *belles lettres* at Edinburgh 1748. Direct references to Addison are found in several places in *The Theory of Moral Sentiments* as well.

62. See Roger L. Emerson, "The Social Composition of Enlightened Scotland: The Select Society of Edinburgh, 1754–1764," *Studies on Voltaire and the Eighteenth Century* 114 (1973): 291–329.

63. The function of virtue in Adam Smith as a humanizing quality and as the foundation for social harmony is what adjoins *The Theory of Moral Sentiments* and *Wealth of Nations* as mutually supportive texts for most contemporary critics. See, characteristically, Fitzgibbons, *Adam Smith's System*.

64. Adam Smith, "History of the Ancient Physics," in *Essays on Philosophical Subjects,* 106. The word "embarrassment" is used a second time in this essay, also as an effect of being confronted by infinite variety.

65. On Plato and Smith regarding wonder, see Roy Porter, *Flesh in the Age of Reason* (New York: Norton, 2004), 350. The citation is from Adam Smith, "History of Astronomy," in *Essays on Philosophical Subjects*, 33. The "History of Astronomy" was published posthumously in 1795.

66. John Barrell, "The Public Prospect and the Private View: The Politics of Taste in Eighteenth-Century Britain," in *Reading Landscape: Country-City-Capital*, ed. Simon Pugh (Manchester: Manchester University Press, 1990), 19–40.

67. George Drummond, "The Rules of Conversation [1740]," cited in Thomas P. Miller, *The Formation of College English: Rhetoric and Belles Lettres in the British Cultural Provinces* (Pittsburgh: University of Pittsburgh Press, 1997), 167.

68. Following a Cartesian notion of invisible effluvia, Smith too must overcome the idea of empty space in the universe, and he uses the imagination as the philosophical bridging mechanism. See Smith, "History of Astronomy," 42.

69. Adam Smith, "Review of Johnson's *Dictionary*," in *Essays on Philosophical Subjects,* 232.

70. For earlier British influence on Smith's theory of interpretation, see Joel C. Weinsheimer, *Eighteenth-Century Hermeneutics: Philosophy of Interpretation in England from Locke to Burke* (New Haven, CT: Yale University Press, 1993).

71. On the figure of the savage in Scottish conjectural history, the "law of succession," we refer you to our third chapter.

72. John Barrell, *The Birth of Pandora and the Division of Knowledge* (Pittsburgh: University of Pennsylvania Press, 1992), 90.

73. John Locke, *An Essay Concerning Human Understanding* (New York: Dover, 1959), 23, 31.

74. This use of the word "economy" is consistent with the French use of the term cited by Robert Darnton in his history of the Encyclopédists' tree of knowledge. A citation from Ephraim Chambers *Cyclopedia*, the source for Diderot and d'Alembert's efforts, is particularly apt: "The difficulty," Chambers writes, "lay in the form and economy of it, so to dispose such a multitude of materials [into] one consistent whole." See Darnton, *The Great Cat Massacre and Other Episodes in French Cultural History* (New York: Basic Books, 1999), 196). For an account of the Marxist meaning of "economy" as applied to print culture, see Alexandra Halasz, *The Marketplace of Print: Pamphlets and the Public Sphere in Early Modern England* (Cambridge, UK: Cambridge University Press, 1995). See also Mary Poovey, *A History of the Modern Fact: Problems of Knowledge in the Sciences of Wealth and Society* (Chicago: University of Chicago Press, 1998), 147–149.

75. Mary Poovey, "The Social Constitution of 'Class': Toward a History of Classificatory Thinking," in *Rethinking Class: Literary Studies and Social Formations,* eds. Wai Chee Dimock and Michael T. Gilmore (New York: Columbia University Press, 1994), 15–69; at 43.

76. Sandra J. Peart and David Levy, eds., *The Street Porter and the Philosopher: Conversations on Analytical Egalitarianism* (Ann Arbor: University of Michigan Press, 2008).

77. On the poetry/philosophy distinction and overlap, see also Hume's *Treatise of Human Nature* (Oxford: Oxford University Press, [1739–40] 2000), 156.

78. To this point about the unique dangers of poetry, John R. R. Christie writes in the Introduction to *Figural and Literal*, "the scientific or philosophical text is expected to employ language facilitating the unmediated expression of literal truth" (p. 3). This is not exactly correct since the impartial spectator provides internal mediation, as does the written word. But his comment about Smith's special concern over the literary texts is well taken: "[T]he literary text [is in Smith supposed to] cajole the imagination into pleasure . . . in a field of indeterminate reference" (p. 3). What is missing here is further analysis of this indeterminacy, which for Smith and his cohort is often writ as popular contention. See Benjamin et al., *Figural and Literal*, 3.

79. Christopher Berry, *The Idea of a Democratic Community* (New York: St. Martin's, 1989), x.

80. *The British Tocsin; or, Proofs of National Ruin* (London: Daniel Isaac Eaton, 1795), 8.

81. James Lackington, quoted in William St. Clair, *The Reading Nation in the Ro-*

mantic Period (Cambridge, UK: Cambridge University Press), 118. We might also note that by 1760, Strahan, publisher of both Smith and Hume, was netting almost a thousand pounds a year.

82. Hannah Moore, quoted in St. Clair, *Reading Nation*, 352.

83. Soame Jenyns, quoted in St. Clair, *Reading Nation*, 109.

84. Recognition of this revolution goes at least as far back as Q. D. Leavis, *Fiction and the Reading Public* (New York: Russell and Russell, 1965).

85. The idea that the leisure for imaginative work enjoyed by the few depended on the work of the many has been noted before, especially regarding Hume. See, for example, Stephen Copely, "Polite Culture in Commercial Society," in *Figural and Literal*, 177–201; particularly, 185–186 and 190.

86. Smith, *Lectures on Jurisprudence*, manuscript B, 539.

87. For further discussion of SSPCK, see Colin Kidd, who describes the organization's curricula as designed to promote "the principles of religion," which we do not see recommended by Smith (unlike Kames); and "reading English, writing, [and arithmetic]," which we do. Kidd also notes the promotion of Church music in SSPCK schools, which brings up interesting questions in terms of Smith's insistence that music did not require interpretation so was among the safest of the arts for popular consumption. See Colin Kidd, *British Identities Before Nationalism: Ethnicity and Nationhood in the Atlantic World, 1600–1800* (Cambridge, UK: Cambridge University Press, 1999), 138.

88. See Geoffrey Plank, *Rebellion and Savagery: The Jacobite Rising of 1745 and the British Empire* (Philadelphia: University of Pennsylvania Press, 2005).

89. See Joseph Cropsey, *Polity and Economy: With Further Thoughts on the Principles of Adam Smith* (Southbend, IN: St. Augustine's, [1957] 2001), 149. For more on the stultification of the poor apropos Marx, see Nathan Rosenberg, "Adam Smith on the Division of Labor: Two Views or One," *Economica* 32, no. 126 (May 1965): 127–139. A more generous reading of Smith's compromise of state-assisted education is provided by E. G. West, "The Political Economy of Alienation: Karl Marx and Adam Smith," *Oxford Economic Papers* 21 (1969): 1–23. Jerry Z. Muller applauds Smith for promoting an impartial and disinterested view of public education, which should render revolts against the government less likely among the poor. See Muller, *Adam Smith in His Time and Ours* (Princeton, NJ: Princeton University Press, 1993), 151.

90. It is interesting to note that increased literacy among the laboring poor did not precede the industrial revolution of the nineteenth century, but as R. S. Schofield argues, compared to eighteenth-century literacy rates, was produced in part by it. And reading was taught before writing, which is again consistent with our argument concerning the standardization of taste. Even in the late and early nineteenth centuries, "the prospect of upward mobility for their children did not lead many working class parents to invest heavily in education" (p. 451). See Schofield, "Dimensions of Literacy, 1750–1850," *Explorations in Economic History* 10 (1973): 437–454.

91. In this sense, we agree with Joseph Cropsey who challenged those scholars who inferred that "political order [is] unambiguously of secondary importance in Smith. See Cropsey, *Polity and Economy*, 59.

92. For more on the unique geopolitical situation of Scotland and its contribution to the Enlightenment, see David Daiches, Peter Jones, and Jean Jones, eds., *A Hotbed of Genius: The Scottish Enlightenment* (Edinburgh: Edinburgh University Press, 1986); and Siskin, *Work of Writing*, 79–99.

93. In addition to those secondary sources cited above, see another *locus classicus*: Elizabeth L. Eisenstein's *The Printing Press as an Agent of Change: Communications and Cultural Transformation in Early Modern Europe* (2 vols.) (Cambridge, UK: Cambridge University Press, 1979); before this text, see Lucien Febvre and Henri-Jean Martin, *The Coming of the Book: The Impact of Printing, 1450–1800,* trans. David Gerard, Geoffrey Nowell-Smith, and David Wootton, eds. (London: New Left Books, [1958] 1976). See also St. Clair, *Reading Nation,* and Siskin, *Work of Writing.*

94. See Greg Laugero, "Infrastructures of Enlightenment: Road-Making, the Public Sphere, and the Emergence of Literature," *Eighteenth-Century Studies* 29, no. 1 (Fall 1995): 45–67.

95. St. Clair notes that there were about a thousand circulating libraries in Great Britain by 1801. See *Reading Nation,* 237.

96. William Wordsworth, "The Solitary Reaper" (1805), http://allpoetry.com/poem/8452821–The_Solitary_Reaper-by-William_Wordsworth (accessed March 26, 2014).

97. Quoted in Miller, *Formation of College English,* 1.

98. The statistics are from Miller, *Formation of College English,* 30.

99. Thomas Laqueur writes that the lower ranks "became powerfully attached to bourgeois forms of reason and reasonableness; they fundamentally accepted bourgeois definitions of improvement and of the parameters of political action." Cited in Miller, *Formation of College English,* 59.

100. For additional discussion of the Statute of Anne, which as England's first copyright law was designed to elevate authorial over stationers' rights, see Lyman Ray Patterson, *Copyright in Historical Perspective* (Nashville: Vanderbilt University Press, 1968); and Mark Rose, *Authors and Owners: The Invention of Copyright* (Cambridge, MA: Harvard University Press, 1993).

101. See White, *Formation of College English*, 35, 37. Anthology making would of course be consistent with the proliferation of writing and the narrowing of taste. For more on anthologies, see Jonathan Brody Kramnick, *Making the English Canon: Print-Capitalism and the Cultural Past, 1700–1770* (Cambridge, UK: Cambridge University Press, 1998).

102. William St. Clair calls the Edinburgh hearing, which began in July of 1773, "the most decisive event in the history of reading in England since the arrival of printing 300 years before," *Reading Nation*, 109.

103. Henry Home, Lord Kames, *Sketches on the History of Man* (3 vols.), ed. James A. Harris (Indianapolis: Liberty Fund, 2007), I: 159.

104. *Hinton v. Donaldson*, et. al., *The Decision of the Court Session, Upon the Question of Literary Property* (London: 1774), 19.

105. David Hume, "Of the Delicacy of Taste and Passion," in *Essays Moral, Political, Literary*, ed. Eugene F. Miller (Indianapolis: Liberty Fund, 1985), 7.

106. Regarding the socially benevolent function of vanity, see Eric Schliesser, "The Obituary of a Vain Philosopher: Adam Smith's Reflections on Hume's Life," *Hume Studies* 29, no. 2 (2003): 327–362. Christopher Berry calls Hume's social and political thought intrinsically conservative in his book, *Hume, Hegel, and Human Nature* (The Hague: Martinus Nijhoff Publishers, 1982), 80.

107. Schliesser, "Copernican Revolutions," 237.

108. Eric Schliesser, "Adam Smith's Benevolent and Self-Interested Conception of Philosophy," in *New Voices on Adam Smith*, eds. Leonidas Montes and Eric Schliesser (New York: Routledge, 2006), 342.

109. Lauren Brubaker, "Does the 'Wisdom of Nature' Need Help?" in *New Voices on Adam Smith*, 168–192.

110. Ibid., 187.

111. Schliesser, "Obituary of a Vain Philosopher," 332.

112. See Francis Hutcheson, *An Essay on the Nature and Conduct of the Passions and Affections, with Illustrations on the Moral Sense*, ed. Aaron Garrett (Indianapolis: Liberty Fund, [1728] 2002), 120.

113. See David M. Levy and Sandra J. Peart, *The "Vanity of the Philosopher": From Equality to Hierarchy in Post-Classical Economics* (Ann Arbor: University of Michigan Press, 2005).

114. As Smith's teacher, Hutcheson had great influence on Smith, as did Hume vis-à-vis Hutcheson, especially on the issue of moral sympathy. For discussion of this influence, see Fitzgibbons, *Adam Smith's System*, 13ff.

115. Wakefield as quoted by Lawrence Stone, "Social Control and Intellectual Excellence: Oxbridge and Edinburgh, 1560–1983," in *Universities, Society, and the Future*, ed. Nicholas Phillipson (Edinburgh: Edinburgh University Press, 1983), 17.

116. Ibid., 18.

117. Miller, *Formation of College English*, 84.

118. On scholasticism versus eighteenth-century liberal education, see Rothblatt, *Tradition and Change*.

119. As part of the reform of Scottish universities, the practice of regenting, where a single instructor followed the student for an academic lifetime, also ended. Regenting was abolished in Edinburgh in 1708, and at Glasgow in 1727. This change, combined with the establishment of new chairs in the humanities between 1690 and 1720, is the context within which Smith was to navigate the pressures of disciplinary specialization. See Roger Emerson, "The Contexts of the Scottish Enlightenment," in *The Cambridge Companion to the Scottish Enlightenment*, ed. Alexander Broadie (Cambridge, UK: Cambridge University Press, 2003), 19.

120. *London Times* (1790), cited in E. J. Hundert, *The Enlightenment's Fable: Bernard Mandeville and the Discovery of Society* (Cambridge, UK: Cambridge University Press, 1994), 234.

121. While Blair held the first professorship given over exclusively to English literature, the first university professor to lecture on English literature was John Stevenson, professor of logic and metaphysics at the University of Edinburgh, 1730–1777 (see

Miller, *Formation of College English*, 166). Thus, literary studies were exported to the farther-reaching colonies of, for example, India, only after being invented from within provincial Britain. See Robert Crawford, ed., *The Scottish Invention of English Literature* (Cambridge, UK: Cambridge University Press, 1998).

122. Miller, *Formation of College English*, 168.

123. Hugh Blair, *Lectures on Rhetoric and Belles Lettres*, eds. Linda Ferreira-Buckley and S. Michael Halloran (Carbondale: Southern Illinois University Press, 2005), 240.

124. Quoted in Miller, *Formation of College English*, 154. Kames traces the opening of coffeehouses in London to a statute of 1633. Tellingly, he connects this "great invention" to the introduction of pocket watches in 1577. See Kames, *Sketches on History of Man* I, 98.

125. Cited in Schliesser, "Obituary of a Vain Philosopher," 177.

Chapter 2

1. For an excellent overview of the "problem," see Leonidas Montes *Adam Smith in Context: A Critical Reassessment of Some Central Components of His Thought* (London: Palgrave Macmillan, 2004).

2. Maria Pia Paganelli, "The Adam Smith Problem in Reverse: Self-Interest in *The Wealth of Nations* and *The Theory of Moral Sentiments*," *History of Political Economy* 40, no. 2 (2008): 365–382.

3. The exceptions: Lee Rice, Douglas Den Uyl, and Steven Barbone.

4. David Hume, *A Treatise of Human Nature* (Oxford: Oxford University Press, 2000), Book II, Pt. 1, Sect. 11.

5. Alexandre Matheron, *Individu et communauté chez Spinoza* (Paris: Minuit, 1969), 150–210. Étienne Balibar, "Individualité et transindividualité chez Spinoza," in *Architectures de la raison: Mélanges offerts à Alexandre Matheron*, ed. Pierre-François Moreau (Fontenay/Saint-Cloud: ENS Éditions, 1996).

6. Warren Montag, "Who's Afraid of the Multitude: Between the Individual and the State," *South Atlantic Quarterly* 104, no. 4 (Fall 2005): 655–673.

7. See Jonathan I. Israel, *Radical Enlightenment: Philosophy and the Making of Modernity 1650–1750* (Oxford: Oxford University Press, 2001). Israel establishes the centrality of Spinoza to the Enlightenment as a figure whose thought was often both reproduced and attacked without attribution. While Israel focuses on Spinoza's critique of supernaturalism in the interpretation of scripture as well as nature, what follows may be seen as an extension of his argument to the question of affects/passions and the boundary of the individual.

8. All translations are our own and are based on the Latin edition of Spinoza's works, *Opera*, ed. Carl Gebhardt (Heidelberg: Carl Winter, 1924). Bernard Mandeville, "The Grumbling Hive: Or, Knaves Turned Honest," in *The Fable of the Bees* (2 vols.), ed. F. B. Kaye (Indianapolis: Liberty Fund, 1988), I: 24.

9. Anthony Ashley Cooper, Third Earl of Shaftesbury, *Characteristics of Men, Manners, Opinions, Times* (New York: Bobbs-Merrill, 1964), 282.

10. Louis Althusser and Étienne Balibar, *Reading Capital* (London: Verso, 1969), 63.

11. Ibid., 31.

12. Hobbes initially defines glory as "joy, arising from imagination of a man's own power and ability," Thomas Hobbes, *Leviathan* (London: Pelican, 1968), 124–125. In chap. 13, however, he will define glory as every man's desire "that his companion should value him, at the same rate he sets upon himself" (p. 185), a desire that may lead individuals when disappointed to attempt to "extort" (p. 185) such value from others, even through violence.

13. See Bert Kerkhof, "A Fatal Attraction? Smith's *Theory of Moral Sentiments* and Mandeville's *Fable*," *History of Political Thought* 16, no. 2 (Summer 1995): 219–233; and Pierre Force, *Self-Interest Before Adam Smith* (Cambridge, UK: Cambridge University Press, 2003).

14. André Tosel, *Spinoza ou la crépuscule de la servitude* (Paris: Aubier, 1984), 55.

15. See Étienne Balibar, "Potentia multitudinis quae una veluti mente duciter," *Ethik, Recht und Politik bei Spinoza,* eds. M. Senn and M. Walther (Zurich: Schultheiss, 2001).

16. Hobbes, *Leviathan,* 126.

17. Joseph Butler, *The Works,* ed. W. E. Gladstone (Oxford: Clarendon, 1897), 80.

18. Ibid., 80.

19. Ibid., 82.

20. See Smith's review of Rousseau in his Letter to the *Edinburgh Review* (1756), in *Essays on Philosophical Subjects,* 242–254. Also, see: Force, *Self-Interest,* 14–24; Spencer J. Pack, "The Rousseau Smith Connection: Towards Understanding Professor West's Splenetic Smith," *History of Economic Ideas* 8, no. 2 (2000): 35–62; Eric Schliesser, "Adam Smith's Benevolent and Self-Interested Conception of Philosophy," in *New Voices on Adam Smith*, eds. Leonidas Montes and Eric Schliesser (New York: Routledge, 2006), 328–354.

21. Both Leonidas Montes and Gloria Vivenza demonstrate that Smith's version of Stoicism was a construction in which he selected the elements most congenial to him and omitted others. See Leonidas Montes, "Adam Smith as an Eclectic Stoic," *The Adam Smith Review* 4 (2008): 30–56; Gloria Vivenza, *Adam Smith and the Classics: The Classical Heritage in Adam Smith's Thought* (Oxford: Oxford University Press, 2002).

22. Smith omitted "whining" from this passage after the first edition of *The Theory of Moral Sentiments*, although he allowed it to stand in a later, very similar, passage in which he denounces the "whining tone of some modern systems" (p. 283) of moral philosophy. The editors in a note connect this latter passage to Smith's description of Hume in his last days as "dying very fast, but with great chearfulness and good humour and with more real resignation to the necessary course of things, than any Whining Christian ever dyed with pretended resignation to the will of God." Letter 163 (August 14, 1776) to Alexander Wedderburn

23. Alec Macfie, in "The Invisible Hand of Jupiter," *Journal of the History of Ideas* 32, no. 4 (1971): 595–599, argues that the meaning of the invisible hand in Smith's work changes significantly. In the "History of Astronomy" the invisible hand of Jupiter functioned as a principle used to explain irregular events in nature that the ignorance of an earlier superstitious age did not permit it to comprehend. In both *The Theory of Moral*

Sentiments and *The Wealth of Nations*, however, the invisible hand expresses both the regularity and justice of the market, and, in Macfie's view, Smith's Christianity. Irrespective of whether Smith considered himself or can be considered a Christian, the persistence of the invisible hand raises interesting questions about the provenance of Smith's conception of the market.

24. John Locke, *Two Treatises of Government* (New York: New American Library, 1960). Of the "several nations of the Americans," Locke has this to say: "a king of a large and fruitful territory there, feeds, lodges and is clad worse than a day-labourer in England" (25–26).

25. Mandeville, *Fable of the Bees*: "the very poor / Lived better than the rich before" (line 26).

26. On the textual history of the impartial spectator, see D. D. Raphael, "The Impartial Spectator," in *Essays on Adam Smith,* eds. Andrew S. Skinner and Thomas Wilson (Oxford: Clarendon, 1975), 83–99.

27. Smith apparently overlooked Hutcheson's earlier criticism of the use philosophers made of the accounts of the savages of America:

> A late ingenious Author has justly observed the absurdity of the monstrous taste which has possessed both the readers and writers of travels. . . . They are sparing enough in accounts of the natural affections, the families, associations, friendships, clans of the Indians; and as transiently do they mention their abhorrence of treachery among themselves, their proneness to mutual aid, and to the defense of their several states; their contempt of death in defense of their country, or upon points of honor. "These are but common stories.—No need to travel to the Indies for what we see in Europe every day." The entertainment therefore in these ingenious studies consists chiefly in exciting horror, and making men stare. The ordinary employment of the bulk of the Indians in support of their wives and offspring, or relations, has nothing of the prodigious. But a human sacrifice, a feast upon enemies' carcasses, can raise an horror and admiration of the wondrous barbarity of Indians, in nations no strangers to the massacres at Paris, the Irish rebellion, or the journals of the Inquisition. These they behold with religious veneration; but the Indian sacrifices, flowing from a like perversion of humanity by superstition, raise the highest abhorrence and amazement. (205–206)

Francis Hutcheson, "An Inquiry into the Original of Our Ideas of Beauty and Virtue," in *Two Treatises* (London: J. and J. Knapton, [1726] 1729), http://files.libertyfund.org/files/2462/Hutcheson_1458_EBk_v7.0.pdf (accessed March 31, 2014).

28. This eloquent and persuasive account of the Stoic attitude toward voluntary death is succeeded somewhat later in the text by a far more muted consideration of the same topic, which, if not exactly compatible with Christian doctrine, is at least less offensive to it. There Smith argues that suicide is less a crime than a kind of pathology that renders its victim an object of pity rather than disapprobation. The fact remains the earlier portrayal of Stoic "courage" is delivered with far greater force and conviction.

29. See Foucault's very interesting account of Smith and the concept of *homo oeconomicus* in the context of the emergence of biopower in which the retreat of the state

from the market is seen as a form of governmentality: Michel Foucault, *Naissance de la biopolitique: Cours au Collège de France, 1978–1979* (Paris: Gallimard, 2004).

30. Albert O. Hirschman, *The Passions and the Interests: Political Arguments for Capitalism before Its Triumph* (Princeton, NJ: Princeton University Press, 1977).

31. Alexander Pope, *An Essay on Man*, Epistle II, line 6.

32. Nicolas Malebranche, "De la recherche de la vérité," in *Oeuvres* (2 tomes) (Paris: Gallimard, 1979), I: 269.

33. Ibid.

34. G. W. F. Hegel, *The Phenomenology of Spirit*, trans. A. V. Miller (Oxford: Oxford University Press, 1977), 121.

35. G. W. F. Hegel, *Lectures on the History of Philosophy* (3 vols.) (New Jersey: Humanities Press, 1974), II: 235.

36. One of the most valuable discussions of Spinoza and Stoicism is in Alexandre Matheron, "Le moment stoïcien de l'*Éthique* de Spinoza," in *Le stoïcisme aux XVIe et XVIIe siècles*, ed. Pierre-François Moreau (Paris: Albin Michel, 1999).

37. See Pierre Macherey's discussion of affects and passions in *Introduction à "l'Éthique" de Spinoza: La troisième partie: La vie affective* (Paris: P.U.F., 1995).

38. If we can never truly know what another feels, from what position or perspective is it possible to judge whether or not there exists a correspondence between individuals' sentiments? It appears here as elsewhere that Smith presupposes a kind of transcendental subject without which many of his assertions would be impossible.

39. For Malebranche, the "air of the face of an impassioned man penetrates those who see it and naturally imprints in them a passion similar to that which agitates him" ("Recherche de la vérité," II: 1.1). In the same way, the "contagious communication" of powerful imaginations constituted one of the great sources of error and heresy: "The disorders of the imagination are extremely contagious, and they slip into [*se glissent*] and spread within most minds with great facility." Impassioned authors communicate their passions to us and by means of their force "persuade us without our knowing why, nor even of precisely what we have been persuaded" ("Recherche de la vérité," II: 3.2). At the same time, imitation "is necessary to civil society" in that it is the means by which the authority of parents over children, sovereign over subjects, master over servants is realized. Descartes discusses the imitation carried out by animals (who for him are machines without will) in the Letter to the Marquess of Newcastle (November 23, 1646) in *Philosophical Letters* (Minneapolis: University of Minnesota Press, 1970), 205–208.

40. William Blake, "The Human Abstract," in *Songs of Experience*, ll: lines 1–4.

41. François, Duc de La Rochefoucauld, *Maximes*, 583.

42. Pierre Macherey, *Hegel ou Spinoza* (Paris: Maspero, 1979), 216.

43. In the *Ethics*, Spinoza cites the example of Seneca (one of the very few proper names to appear in the work) as someone "coerced by another," namely, "a tyrant who forced him to open his veins" (IV, 20, schol.).

44. See Alexandre Matheron, "Indignation et le conatus de l'état spinoziste," in *Spinoza: Puissance et ontology*, eds. Myriam Revault D'Allones et Hadi Rizk (Paris: Kimé, 1994), 153–165.

45. The magnitude of Israel's *Radical Enlightenment* is itself a testimony to the extent to which Spinoza, despite his importance, remained, and to a certain extent continues to remain, invisible—an invisibility that cannot be understood as a simple lapse in the rigor of intellectual historians.

46. Caning and flogging (or "scourging") both appear later in *The Theory of Moral Sentiments* (p. 60).

47. See Warren Montag, *Bodies, Masses, Power: Spinoza and His Contemporaries* (London: Verso, 1999), chap. 3.

48. Hobbes, *Leviathan,* chap. 17.

Chapter 3

1. Henry Fielding, *The True Patriot: and the History of Our Own Times, No. 18* [March 4, 1746], in *The Criticism of Henry Fielding,* ed. Ioan Williams (New York: Routledge, 1970), 31.

2. Adam Smith, *An Inquiry into the Nature and Causes of the Wealth of Nations,* eds. R. H. Campbell, A. S. Skinner, and W. B. Todd (Indianapolis: Liberty Fund, 1981), 42.

3. For a further discussion of the role of reading in *Tom Jones,* see Homer Obed Brown, *Institutions of the English Novel: From Defoe to Scott* (Philadelphia: University of Pennsylvania Press, 1998), chap. 5.

4. David Hume, *The History of England* (6 vols.) (Indianapolis: Liberty Fund, 1983), VI: 47.

5. For more on the relationship between Jacobite unrest and the Manchester unemployed, see Bruce Lenman, *The Jacobite Risings in Britain, 1689–1746* (London: Methuen, 1980), 11.

6. Adam Smith, *Lectures on Jurisprudence,* eds. R. L. Meek, D. D. Raphael, and P. G. Stein (Indianapolis: Liberty Fund, 1982), manuscript B: 541.

7. For more on General Wade, see J. D. Mackie, *A History of Scotland,* eds. Bruce Lenman and Geoffrey Parker (New York: Penguin, 1984). Also see Leith Davis, *Acts of Union: Scotland and the Literary Negotiation of the British Nation: 1707–1830* (Stanford: Stanford University Press, 1998), 46.

8. Nicholas Rogers, "Riot and Popular Jacobitism in Early Hanoverian England," in *Ideology and Conspiracy: Aspects of Jacobitism, 1689–1759,* ed. Eveline Cruickshanks (Edinburgh: John Donald, 1982), 70–88.

9. On the statistics of Jacobite popularity, see Murray Pittock, *Jacobitism* (London: St. Martin's, 1998), 33. Data on riot in the Midlands can be found in Nicholas Rogers, *Crowds, Culture, and Politics in Georgian Britain* (Oxford: Clarendon, 1998), 53.

10. Rogers here uses a different model of power than the strictly oppositional one he finds in George Rudé's work, for example, in *The Crowd in History: A Study of Popular Disturbances in France and England, 1730–1848* (New York: Wiley, 1964). See *Crowds, Culture, and Politics,* 6–7.

11. Cairns Craig uses the term "intra-national" in *Intending Scotland: Explorations in Scottish Culture Since the Enlightenment* (Edinburgh: Edinburgh University Press, 2009), 52.

12. Colin Kidd, *Union and Unionisms: Political Thought in Scotland, 1500–2000* (Cambridge, UK: Cambridge University Press, 2008), 82.

13. Defoe's poem is cited in David Daiches, *Scotland and the Union* (London: J. Murray, 1977), 138.

14. Ibid.

15. Davis, *Acts of Union,* 1.

16. On Highland fluidity, see Geoffrey Plank, *Rebellion and Savagery: The Jacobite Rising of 1745 and the British Empire* (Philadelphia: University of Pennsylvania Press, 2005), 10.

17. Leith Davis, "Scottish Literature and 'Engl. Lit.,'" *Studies in Scottish Literature* 38, no. 1 (2012): 20–27; see p. 24. On the Scottish colonial adventure at the Isthmus of Panama, see John Prebble, *The Darien Disaster: A Scots Colony in the New World, 1698–1700* (New York: Holt, Rinehart and Winston, 1969).

18. Pittock, *Jacobitism,* 16.

19. Robert Ferguson, *The History of All Mobs, Tumults, and Insurrections in Great Britain from William the Conqueror to the Present Time . . . Rioters* (London: J. Moore, 1714–1715), 1–2.

20. Pittock, *Jacobitism,* 2. On the relationship between Jacobite unrest and enclosures, see Paul Kleber Monod, *Jacobitism and the English People, 1688–1788* (Cambridge, UK: Cambridge University Press, 1989), 63.

21. Pittock, *Jacobitism,* 79.

22. Ibid., 59–60.

23. Ibid., 64.

24. Murray Pittock, "Treacherous Objects: Toward a Theory of Jacobite Material Culture," *Journal for Eighteenth-Century Studies* 34, no. 1 (March 2011): 39. On the idea of networks in eighteenth-century Scotland, see Steve Murdoch, *Network North: Scottish Kin, Commercial and Covert Associations in Northern Europe, 1603–1746* (Boston: Brill, 2006).

25. Pittock, "Treacherous Objects," 46.

26. Ibid., 45.

27. See E. P. Thompson, *Whigs and Hunters: The Origins of the Black Act* (New York: Pantheon, 1975).

28. Monod, *Jacobitism and the English People,* 248.

29. Quoted in E. P. Thompson, "Patrician Society, Plebeian Culture," *Journal of Social History* 7, no. 4 (Summer 1974): 382–405; at 383.

30. The return of unemployed and unemployable soldiers due to rapid demobilization after 1745 caused its own problems with the so-called mob. See Nicholas Rogers, *Mayhem: Post-War Crime and Violence in Britain, 1748–53* (New Haven, CT: Yale University Press, 2012).

31. P. W. J. Riley, *Union of England and Scotland: A Study in Anglo-Scottish Politics of the Eighteenth Century* (Manchester: Manchester University Press, 1978), 284.

32. Daiches, *Scotland and the Union,* 148.

33. Riley, *Union of England and Scotland,* 221.

34. Pittock, *Jacobitism,* 65.

35. Mansfield is quoted in George C. Caffentzis, "On the Scottish Origin of 'Civilization,'" in *Enduring Western Civilization: The Construction of the Concept of Western Civilization and Its "Others,"* ed. Silvia Federici (Westport, CT: Praeger, 1995), 13–36; at 26. For an additional account of Mansfield, see Peter Linebaugh, *The London Hanged: Crime and Civil Society in the Eighteenth Century* (Cambridge, UK: Cambridge University Press, 1993).

36. See Plank, *Rebellion and Savagery,* 6.

37. Colin Kidd also notes the promotion of Church music in SSPCK schools, which brings up interesting questions in terms of Smith's insistence that music did not require interpretation and so was among the safest of the arts for popular consumption. See Colin Kidd, *British Identities Before Nationalism: Ethnicity and Nationhood in the Atlantic World, 1600–1800* (Cambridge, UK: Cambridge University Press, 1999), 138.

38. Plank, *Rebellion and Savagery,* 110.

39. Pittock, *Jacobitism,* 79. In a vein similar to the reintegration of Jacobite issues into English history, Devoney Looser calls for closer attention to women's writing for "exploring new generic and historiographical ground." See her book, *British Women Writers and the Writing of History, 1670–1820* (Baltimore: Johns Hopkins University Press, 2000), 10.

40. Plank, *Rebellion and Savagery,* 69.

41. Cruickshanks, *Ideology and Conspiracy,* 3.

42. Pittock, "Treacherous Objects," 49.

43. Cruickshanks, *Ideology and Conspiracy,* 4.

44. Pittock, "Treacherous Objects," 44.

45. See Jürgen Habermas, *The Structural Transformation of the Public Sphere: An Inquiry into a Category of Bourgeois Society* (Cambridge, MA: MIT Press, 1991), chap. 7.

46. Pittock, "Treacherous Objects," 46.

47. David Hume, *An Abstract of . . . A Treatise of Human Nature,* in *A Treatise of Human Nature,* eds. David Fate Norton and Mary J. Norton(Oxford: Oxford University Press, 2009), 403–420; at 409.

48. David Hume, *An Enquiry Concerning Human Understanding,* ed. Peter Millican (Oxford: Oxford University Press, 2008), 22.

49. David Hume, *A Treatise of Human Nature,* ed. Ernest C. Mossner (New York: Penguin, 1985), 195.

50. David Hume, "Whether the British Government Inclines More to Absolute Monarchy, or to a Republic," in *Essays Moral, Political, Literary,* ed. Eugene F. Miller (Indianapolis: Liberty Fund, 1985), 51.

51. On the "march of the vulgar," see David Hume, *A Dissertation on the Passions; The Natural History of Religion,* ed. Tom L. Beauchamp (Oxford: Oxford University Press, 2007), 57.

52. Benedict Anderson, *Imagined Communities: Reflections on the Origins and Spread of Nationalism* (London: Verso, 2006).

53. Habermas, *Structural Transformation,* 43.

54. Anderson, *Imagined Communities,* 27.

55. For more on the importance of forgetting to the national imaginary, and for an excellent response to Anderson in general, see Jonathan Culler, "Anderson and the Novel," *Diacritics* 29, no. 4 (1999): 20–39. For a reworking of Anderson's theses in a more global context, see Rita Barnard, "Fictions of the Global," *Novel: A Forum on Fiction* 42, no. 2 (2009): 207–215.

56. For a more detailed account of civilian deaths at Culloden, with a focus on the brutality of Cumberland and his troops, see W. A. Speck, *The Butcher: The Duke of Cumberland and the Suppression of the '45* (London: Blackwell, 1981). It should be noted that Lord Chesterfield wanted a naval blockade to starve the Highlanders. See Lenman, *Jacobite Risings*; and Plank, *Rebellion and Savagery*, 70.

57. Further statistics on Jacobite readers are provided in Monod, *Jacobitism and the English People*, 30.

58. For more specific details on the transportation of criminal Jacobites, see Mackie, *History of Scotland*, 279; and Plank, *Rebellion and Savagery*, 18. The deportation of Jacobite prisoners after the Battle of Preston in 1715 was used to compensate for white labor shortages in Maryland, Virginia, South Carolina, Jamaica, Barbados, Antigua, and St. Kitts (though some were pardoned to become indentured laborers at home). Most of those transported were Highlanders. For a further account of Jacobite transportation, see Plank, *Rebellion and Savagery*, 18.

59. On Jacobite pardons, of which there were greater numbers in the "Fifteen" than the "Forty-Five," see Leo Gooch, *The Desperate Faction? The Jacobites of North-East England, 1688–1745* (Hull, UK: University of Hull Press, 1995). On the last Jacobite hanging in 1753, see Lenman, *Jacobite Risings*, 70.

60. Fielding, *The Covent Garden Journal* 3 (January 11, 1752): 66–69, in Williams, *Criticism of Henry Fielding*.

61. Ibid., 67.

62. Ibid., 70.

63. See Clifford Siskin, *The Work of Writing: Literature and Social Change in Britain, 1700–1830* (Baltimore: Johns Hopkins University Press, 1999).

64. Fielding, cited in Williams, *Criticism of Henry Fielding*, 98.

65. Dipesh Chakrabarty, *Provincializing Europe: Postcolonial Thought and Historical Difference* (Princeton, NJ: Princeton University Press, 2000), 243.

66. Cited in Lenman, *Jacobite Risings*, 17.

67. Fielding, cited in Williams, *Criticism of Henry Fielding*, 70.

68. Fielding, *True Patriot*, 31.

69. Ibid., 32.

70. Ibid., 23.

71. Ibid.

72. On the relationship between Smith's and Hume's theories of jurisprudence and the traditions of Roman and natural law, see Knud Haakonssen, *The Science of a Legislator: The Natural Jurisprudence of David Hume and Adam Smith* (Cambridge, UK: Cambridge University Press, 1981); and Duncan Forbes, *Hume's Philosophical Politics* (Cambridge, UK: Cambridge University Press, 1975).

73. Anonymous, *The Arraignment of Co-Ordinate-Power; Wherein All Arbitrary Proceedings Are laid open to all Honest Abhorrers and Addressers: With a Touch at the London-Petition And Charter, 1683*, in *The Struggle for Sovereignty: Seventeenth-Century English Political Tracts* (vol. 2), ed. Joyce Lee Malcolm (Indianapolis: Liberty Fund, 1999).

74. See George Rudé, *Wilkes and Liberty: A Social Study of 1763 to 1774* (London: Clarendon, 1962).

75. Samuel Johnson, "The False Alarm," in *Political Writings*, ed. Donald J. Greene, (Indianapolis: Liberty Fund, 2000), 313–345; at 335.

76. See Rosemary Goring, ed., *Scotland: The Autobiography: 2,000 Years of Scottish History by Those Who Saw It Happen* (New York: Penguin, 2009), 104.

77. For further details on the Scottish tobacco trade, see T. M. Devine, *The Scottish Nation: A History 1700–2000* (New York: Viking, 1999). On economic disparity in Scotland's port cities, see Iain McLean, *Adam Smith, Radical Egalitarian: An Interpretation for the Twenty-First Century* (Edinburgh: Edinburgh University Press, 2006), 3.

78. Johnson, quoted in Greene's *Political Writings*, 300.

79. Ibid., 395.

80. Ibid., 393.

81. For more on "rabbling," see Neil Davidson, "Pop Insurgency During the Glorious Revolution in Scotland," *Scottish Labour History* 39 (2004): 14–31.

82. Thompson, "Patrician Society," 395–396.

83. Adam Smith, "'Early Draft' of Part of *The Wealth of Nations*," in *Lectures on Jurisprudence*, eds. R. L. Meek, D. D. Raphael, and P. G. Stein (Indianapolis: Liberty Fund, 1982), manuscript B: 562–586; at 572.

84. Henry Fielding, "An Enquiry into the Causes of the Late Increase of Robbers," in *The Works of Henry Fielding, Esq . . . ,*" (London: 1806), 333–467; at 345.

85. Johnson, quoted in Greene's *Political Writings*, 338–339.

86. *The Riot Act* (approved short title) of 1714 (1 Geo.1 St.2 c.5).

87. Defoe cited in Goring, *Scotland: An Autobiography*, 110.

88. See Michel Foucault, *"Society Must be Defended": Lectures at the Collège de France, 1975–1976* (New York: Picador, 2003).

89. Jesse Molesworth, *Chance and the Eighteenth-Century Novel: Realism, Probability, Magic* (Cambridge, UK: Cambridge University Press, 2010), 56. See also, F. N. David, *Games, Gods and Gambling* (New York: Hafner Publishing, 1962).

90. On land enclosures and the growth of wage labor in the eighteenth century, see A. L. Morton, *A People's History of England* (New York: Random House, 1938), 327.

91. See John Brewer and J. H. Plumb, *The Birth of Consumer Society: The Commercialization of Eighteenth-Century England* (London: Europa, 1982), 24.

92. Ian Hacking, *The Emergence of Probability: A Philosophical Study of Early Ideas about Probability, Induction, and Statistical Inference* (Cambridge, UK: Cambridge University Press, 1975). See also, Barbara Shapiro's *Probability and Certainty in Seventeenth-Century England* (Princeton, NJ: Princeton University Press, 1983).

93. This is not to undermine James Chandler's comparison, for example, between Pascal and the codes of expectation enforced by sentimental fiction. See Chandler's

"Moving Accidents: The Emergence of Sentimental Probability," in *The Age of Cultural Revolutions: Britain and France, 1750–1820*, eds. Colin Jones and Dror Wahrman (Berkeley: University of California Press, 2002), 137–170. On Bernoulli in the eighteenth century, see Lorraine Daston, *Classical Probability in the Enlightenment* (Princeton, NJ: Princeton University Press, 1995), chap. 2. We use the word "contrived" in this passage regarding the use of accident after Michael Witmore's reading of Baconian induction, the notion that "contrivance and [experiential] knowledge go hand in hand." See Witmore, *Culture of Accidents: Unexpected Knowledges in Early Modern England* (Stanford: Stanford University Press, 2001), 9–10. Ross Hamilton further distinguishes between the importance of accident in Bacon and Locke and earlier mathematical modes of problem solving in *Accident: A Philosophical and Literary History* (Chicago: University of Chicago Press, 2007), 117ff. Jonathan Cohen argues that David Hume, one of Bacon's admirers, was the first of the eighteenth-century philosophers to recognize that "there is an important kind of probability which does not fit into the framework afforded by the calculus of chance." This is evidence, according to Cohen, that "Hume's skeptical arguments are aimed against the possibility of obtaining knowledge by enumerative induction" (p. 225). See Cohen's essay, "Some Historical Remarks on the Baconian Conception of Probability," *Journal of the History of Ideas* 41, no. 2 (April–June 1980): 219–231.

94. Nicholas Rogers, *Whigs and Cities: Popular Politics in the Age of Walpole and Pitt* (Oxford: Oxford University Press, 1989), 354.

95. Daniel Defoe, *Captain Tom's Remembrance to His Old Friends the MOBB of London* . . . (London: 1711), http://quod.lib.umich.edu/e/ecco/004777928.0001.000/1:1?rgn=div1;view=fulltext (accessed April 8, 2014).

96. Monod, *Jacobitism and the English People*, 197.

97. John B. Bender and Michael Marrinan, eds., *Regimes of Description: In the Archive of the Eighteenth Century* (Stanford: Stanford University Press, 2010), 15.

98. J. C. D. Clark, *Revolution and Rebellion: State and Society in England in the Seventeenth and Eighteenth Centuries* (Cambridge, UK: Cambridge University Press, 1986), 1.

99. Ibid., 100.

100. Ibid., 56.

101. Rogers, "Riot and Popular Jacobitism," 83.

102. Penny Fielding, *Scotland and the Fictions of Geography: North Britain, 1760–1830* (Cambridge, UK: University Press, 2008), 12.

103. William Robertson, *The History of Scotland* (2 vols.) (London: Pickering, 1825), 351.

104. Kidd, *Subverting Scotland's Past: Scottish Whig Historians and the Creation of an Anglo-British Identity, 1689–c. 1830* (Cambridge, UK: Cambridge University Press, 1986), 115.

105. István Hont, "The Language of Sociability and Commerce," in *The Languages of Political Theory in Early Modern Europe*, ed. Anthony Pagden (Cambridge, UK: Cambridge University Press: 1987), 276.

106. John Locke, *An Essay Concerning Human Understanding*, ed. Peter H. Nidditch (Oxford: Oxford University Press, 1975), 184.

107. Henry Home, Lord Kames, *Elements of Criticism*, ed. Peter Jones (Indianapolis: Liberty Fund, 2005), 121, 220.

108. William Robertson, *The History of America* (London: Strahan, 1788), 821.

109. Dugald Stewart, "Account of the Life and Writings of Adam Smith, LL.D.," in *Adam Smith, Essays on Philosophical Subjects*, eds. W. P. D. Wightman, J. C. Bryce, and I. S. Ross (Indianapolis: Liberty Fund, [1793] 1982), 293. We are not suggesting that all historical thought in the eighteenth century was founded in the commitment to historical progress. Progressive history gained new strength and influence from the 1730s to the 1780s, but it also ebbed and flowed with different levels of hope for, and fear about, popular contention throughout the period. For a more focused account of different brands of "conjectural history," see David Spadafora, *The Idea of Progress in Eighteenth-Century Britain* (New Haven, CT: Yale University Press, 1990), 9ff.

110. Hugh Blair, "On Fictitious History," in *Lectures on Rhetoric and Belles Lettres* (New York: Carvill, [1783] 1829), 417.

111. Christina Lupton, *Knowing Books: The Consciousness of Mediation in Eighteenth-Century Britain* (Philadelphia: University of Pennsylvania Press, 2012).

112. J. Paul Hunter, *Before Novels: The Cultural Context of Eighteenth-Century English Fiction* (New York: Norton, 1990), 5.

113. For further discussion of the quantitative turn in literary studies, see *The Contemporary Novel: Imagining the Twenty-First Century*, special issue of *Novel: A Forum on Fiction* 45, no. 2 (Summer 2012).

114. William Beatty Warner, *Licensing Entertainment: The Elevation of Novel Reading in Britain, 1684–1750* (Berkeley: University of California Press, 1998), xiii.

115. Deidre Lynch and William Beatty Warner, eds., *Cultural Institutions of the Novel* (Durham, NC: Duke University Press, 1996), 2.

116. Clifford Siskin, "Epilogue: The Rise of Novelism," in *Cultural Institutions of the Novel*, 423–440.

117. Franco Moretti, "Conjectures on World Literature," *New Left Review* 1 (January–February 2000): 54–68; at 54. For a relatively early critique of quantitative modes of literary analysis and its connection to conjectural modes of thought, see Douglas Lane Patey, *Probability and Literary Form: Philosophic Theory and Literary Practice in the Augustan Age* (Cambridge, UK: Cambridge University Press, 1984). More recently, see John Richetti, "Formalism and Eighteenth-Century English Fiction," *Eighteenth-Century Fiction* 24, no. 2 (Winter 2011–12): 158–160; and David A. Brewer, "Counting, Resonance, and Form: A Speculative Manifesto (with Notes)," in the same issue of *Eighteenth-Century Fiction*, 162–170.

118. James Beattie, "On Fable and Romance," in *Novel Definitions: An Anthology of Commentary on the Novel, 1688–1815*, ed. Cheryl L. Nixon (Peterborough, Ontario: Broadview, 2009), 350.

119. Nancy Armstrong, *How Novels Think: The Limits of Individualism from 1719–1900* (New York: Columbia University Press, 2005).

120. John Bender, *Ends of Enlightenment* (Stanford: Stanford University Press, 2012), 23. On the relation to Lockean notions of probability and its relation to eighteenth-cen-

374   NOTES TO CHAPTER 3

tury literature, see Kenneth MacLean, *John Locke and English Literature of the Eighteenth Century* (New Haven, CT: Yale University Press, 1936), 2–3.

121. Bender, *Ends of Enlightenment*, 23.

122. Ian Watt, *The Rise of the Novel: Studies in Defoe, Richardson, and Fielding* (Berkeley: University of California Press, 1957).

123. Brown, *Institutions of the English Novel*, xii. Before Brown, see Margaret Anne Doody, *The True Story of the Novel* (Newark: Rutgers University Press, 1996).

124. Moretti, "Conjectures on World Literature," 54.

125. Michael McKeon, *The Origins of the English Novel, 1600–1740* (Baltimore: Johns Hopkins University Press, 1987), 56–64. On Fielding and probability, see Matthew Wickman, "Of Probability, Romance, and the Spatial Dimensions of Eighteenth-Century Narrative," *Eighteenth-Century Fiction* 15, no. 1 (October 2002): 59–80.

126. Francis Hutcheson, *An Essay on the Nature and Conduct of the Passions and Affections, with Illustrations on the Moral Sense*, ed. Aaron Garrett (Indianapolis: Liberty Fund, [1728] 2002), 55.

127. George Turnbull, *Observations Upon Liberal Education, in All Its Branches*, ed. Terrance O. Moore (Indianapolis: Liberty Fund, 2003), 383.

128. Samuel Johnson, *The Rambler* 4 (March 31, 1750), in Nixon, *Novel Definitons*, 146–152; at 149.

129. Ibid.

130. Ibid.

131. See James Raven, *The Business of Books: Booksellers and the English Book Trade 1450–1850* (New Haven: Yale University Press, 2007).

132. Statistics for the numbers and editions of *Tom Jones* can be found in Martin C. Battestin's "Introduction" to *The History of Tom Jones, a Foundling*, ed. Fredson Bowers (Middletown, CT: Wesleyan University Press, 1975), xxi.

133. Adam Smith, *The Theory of Moral Sentiments*, eds. D. D. Raphael and A. L. Macfie (Indianapolis: Liberty Fund, 1984).

134. Adam Smith, *Lectures on Rhetoric and Belles Lettres*, ed. J. C. Bryce (Indianapolis: Liberty Fund, 1985), 71.

135. David Hume, "Of Simplicity and Refinement in Writing," in *Essays Moral, Political, Literary*, ed. Eugene F. Miller (Indianapolis: Liberty Fund, 1985), 191–196; at 193.

136. Hume, *Natural History of Religion*, 40.

137. David Hume, "The Rise and Progress of the Arts and Sciences," in *Essays Moral, Political, Literary*, 111–137; at 118.

138. David Hume, *The History of England* (6 vols.) (Indianapolis: Liberty Fund, 1983), I: 5.

139. On the novel's ability to mitigate its own newness, see Scarlet Bowen, *The Politics of Custom in Eighteenth-Century British Fiction* (New York: Palgrave Macmillan, 2010), 1–44; at 174.

140. On the sentimental novel and consumer desire, see Markman Ellis, *The Politics of Sensibility: Race, Gender, and Commerce in the Sentimental Novel* (Cambridge, UK: Cambridge University Press, 1996). On the novel as commerce, see John Brewer, *The*

Pleasures of the Imagination: English Culture in the Eighteenth Century (New York: Farrar Straus & Giroux, 1997); and George Justice, *The Manufacturers of Literature: Writing and the Literary Marketplace in Eighteenth-Century England* (Newark: University of Delaware Press, 2002), 154–157.

141. Ann Blair and Peter Stallybrass, "Mediating Information, 1450–1800," in *This Is Enlightenment*, eds. Clifford Siskin and William Warner (Chicago: University of Chicago Press, 2010), 139–163; at 139.

142. James Lackington, *Memoirs of the First Forty-Five Years of James Lackington . . .* (London: 1792), 350.

143. Anna Laetitia Barbauld, "Preface," in *On the Origin and Progress of Novel Writing* (London: F. C. & J. Rivington, 1810), 36, 23.

144. Adam Ferguson, *An Essay on the History of Civil Society*, ed. Fania Oz-Salzberger (Cambridge, UK: Cambridge University Press, 1999), 76–77.

145. David Hume, "Of the Protestant Succession," in *Essays Moral, Political, Literary*, 502–511; at 503.

146. Anthony Jarrells, *Britain's Bloodless Revolutions: 1688 and the Romantic Reform of Literature* (London: Palgrave Macmillan, 2005).

147. See Ruth Perry, *Novel Relations: The Transformation of Kinship in English Literature and Culture, 1748–1818* (Cambridge, UK: Cambridge University Press, 2006).

148. John Dwyer, *Virtuous Discourse: Sensibility and Community in Late Eighteenth-Century Scotland* (Edinburgh: John Donald, 2003), see especially chap. 6, "The Novel as Moral Preceptor," 141ff.

149. Henry Abelove has attempted to historicize heterosexuality as concurrent with the time of the novel. See Abelove's "Some Speculations on the History of Sexual Intercourse During the Long Eighteenth Century in England," *Genders* 6 (November 1989): 125–130.

150. David Hume, "Of Essay Writing," in *Essays Moral, Political, Literary*, 533–537; at 535.

151. Ian Duncan, *Scott's Shadow : The Novel in Romantic Edinburgh* (Princeton, NJ: Princeton University Press, 2007), 17.

152. David Hume, "Of the Original Contract," *Essays Moral, Political, Literary*, 465–487; at 469.

153. Colin Kidd, "The Ideological Significance of Robertson's *History of Scotland*," in *William Robertson and the Expansion of Empire*, ed. Stewart J. Brown (Cambridge, UK: Cambridge University Press, 1997), 122–144; at 122.

154. Ibid., 123.

155. Murray Pittock, *Poetry and Jacobite Politics in Eighteenth-Century Britain and Ireland* (Cambridge, UK: Cambridge University Press: 1994), 10.

156. Ibid., 2.

157. Ibid., 232.

158. Murray Pittock, *The Myth of the Jacobite Clans* (Edinburgh: University of Edinburgh Press, 1995), 7.

159. Christopher Berry, *Social Theory of the Scottish Enlightenment* (Edinburgh: Edinburgh University Press, 1997), 61.

160. "Introduction," in *Robertson and Expansion of Empire*, 1–6; at 3 and 5.

161. See Karen O'Brien, "Robertson's Place in the Development of Eighteenth-Century History," in *Robertson and Expansion of Empire*, 74–91. David McInerney shows how Robertson's description of "Asiatic despotism" is commensurate with his dread of insurrection. See McInerney, "Monarchy, Despotism, and Althusser's 'Linguistic Trick': William Robertson and the Literary Reproduction of Montesquieu's Concept of 'Fundamental Law,'" in *Althusser and Law*, ed. Laurent de Sutter (London: Routledge, 2013), 49–66.

162. Brown, *Robertson and Expansion of Empire*, 11.

163. Ibid., 32.

164. Ibid., 25.

165. Henry Home, Lord Kames, *Essays upon Several Subjects Concerning British Antiquities* (Edinburgh: A. Kincaid, 1747), 150.

166. Henry Home, Lord Kames, *Sketches on the History of Man* (3 vols.), ed. James A. Harris (Indianapolis: Liberty Fund, 2007), III: 724.

167. On the importance of Enlightenment notions of probability for commerce, see Mary Poovey, *A History of the Modern Fact: Problems of Knowledge in the Sciences of Wealth and Society* (Chicago: University of Chicago Press, 1998); and Lorraine Daston, *Classical Probability in the Enlightenment* (Princeton, NJ: Princeton University Press, 1987).

168. For the significance of Scotland as England's "barbarian frontier," see J. G. A. Pocock, *Barbarism and Religion: Narratives of Civil Government* (5 vols.) (Cambridge, UK: Cambridge University Press, 2000), II: 262.

169. On the eighteenth-century appearance of the term "civilization," see *Inventing Human Science: Eighteenth-Century Domains*, eds. Christopher Fox, Roy Porter, and Robert Wolker (Berkeley: University of California Press, 1999), 20.

170. On the role of geography and the resistance to historical progress, see again Penny Fielding, *Scotland and the Fictions*.

171. The classical origins of conjectural history with Tacitus are traceable in this connection to the savage stage and war. See Andrew S. Skinner, *A System of Social Science: Papers Relating to Adam Smith* (Oxford: Oxford University Press, 1979), 14. Further on the Greco-Roman origins of conjectural history, see Pocock, *Barbarism and Religion*, vol. IV.

172. On the Highlands and military enlistment, see Juliet Shields, "From Family Roots to the Routes of Empire: National Tales and the Domestication of the Highlands," *English Literary History* 72, no. 4 (2005): 919–940. On the relationship between the clearances and its impact on the modernization of the Highland economy, see Eric Richards, *The Highland Clearances: People, Landlords, and Rural Turmoil* (Edinburgh: Birlinn, 2012), 3–12. On the Highland's military service on behalf of the British empire, see Andrew Mackillop, *The People's Clearance: Highland Emigration to British North America, 1770–1815* (Edinburgh: Edinburgh University Press, 1982); and *"More Fruitful than the Soil": Army, Empire, and the Scottish Highlands, 1715–1815* (East Linton, Scotland: Tuckwell Press, 2001). Robert Clyde documents further critical accounts of Highland soldier

activity in Clyde, *From Rebel to Hero: The Image of the Highlander, 1745–1830* (East Linton, Scotland: Tuckwell Press, 1995), 1–17.

173. On the celebration of Ossian-like virtues in Highland recruits to the British army, see Shields, "From Family Roots," 925–927.

174. The Gaelic scholar Charles O'Connor attempted to debunk Ossian's authenticity in 1766. He expanded on criticisms in a new book in 1775 called *Dissertation on the Origin and Antiquities of the Ancient Scots of Ireland and Britain*. This book is cited in Thomas M. Curley, *Samuel Johnson, the Ossian Fraud, and the Celtic Revival in Great Britain and Ireland* (Cambridge, UK: Cambridge University Press, 2009), 151. For more on O'Connor, see pp. 123–156 in Curley's book; for more on Johnson, see the last two chapters of Curley's book. See also, Howard D. Weinbrot, *Britannia's Issue: The Rise of British Literature from Dryden to Ossian* (Cambridge, UK: Cambridge University Press, 1994).

175. Henry Fielding, *Tom Jones* (Oxford: Oxford World Classics, 1998), 336.

176. Ibid., 336.

177. David Hume, "Of Passive Obedience," in *Essays Moral, Political, Literary*, 488–492; at 490 and 492.

178. Ibid., 471.

179. Ibid., 470.

180. Hume, "Of the Protestant Succession," in *Essays Moral, Political, Literary*, 507.

181. Ibid.

182. See Spadafora, *Idea of Progress*.

183. Rogers, *Whigs and Cities*, 383.

184. J. G. A. Pocock, *The Machiavellian Moment: Florentine Political Thought and the Atlantic Republican Tradition* (Princeton, NJ: Princeton University Press, 1975), viii.

185. For a more developed account of Ferguson's critique of Enlightenment belief in historical progress, see Iain McDaniel, *Adam Ferguson in the Scottish Enlightenment: The Roman Past and Europe's Future* (Cambridge, MA: Harvard University Press, 2013).

186. Thomas Hobbes, *On the Citizen*, eds. Richard Tuck and Michael Silverthorne (Cambridge, UK: Cambridge University Press, 2003), 76.

187. Homer, *The Iliad,* trans. Richard Lattimore (Chicago: University of Chicago Press, 1961), 489.

Chapter 4

1. Roger Wells, *Wretched Faces: Famine in Wartime England 1793–1801* (New York: St. Martin's, 1988). Wells points out the systematic avoidance of the term "famine" and of any mention of increased mortality when describing food shortages in eighteenth-century England in modern historical accounts, especially those motivated by a belief in inevitable progress embodied in the unrestricted market. For a detailed examination of parish records showing the severity of the crisis of 1766, see Dale Edward Williams, "Were 'Hunger' Rioters Really Hungry? Some Demographic Evidence," *Past & Present* 71, no. 1 (May 1976): 70–75.

2. E. P. Thompson, "The Moral Economy of the English Crowd," *Past & Present* 50 (February 1971), 76–136.

3. G. W. F. Hegel, *The Phenomenology of Spirit*, trans. A. V. Miller (Oxford: Oxford University Press, 1977), 13.

4. Ibid., 213.

5. See the commentary of Michel Foucault, *Naissance de la Biopolitique: Cours aux Collège de France, 1978–1979* (Paris: Gallimard, 2004), 282–90.

6. See Craig Smith, *Adam Smith's Political Philosophy: The Invisible Hand and Spontaneous Order* (London: Routledge, 2006).

7. Giorgio Agamben, *The Kingdom and the Glory: For a Theological Genealogy of Economy and Government* (Stanford: Stanford University Press, 2011). Also, Lisa Hill, "The Hidden Theology of Adam Smith," *European Journal of the History of Economic Thought* 8, no. 1 (2001): 1–21; Paul Oslington, "Providence, Divine Action and Adam Smith's Invisible Hand," in *Adam Smith as Theologian*, ed. Paul Oslington (New York: Routledge, 2011), 61–76; Brendan Long, "Adam Smith's Theodicy," in *Adam Smith as Theologian*, 98–105.

8. Jacob Viner, *The Role of Providence in Social Order: Jayne Lectures for 1966* (Philadelphia: American Philosophical Society, 1972), 81. Also Paul Oslington, "Jacob Viner on Adam Smith: The Development and Reception of a Theological Reading," *European Journal of the History of Economic Thought* 19, no. 2 (2012): 287–301.

9. Viner, *Role of Providence*, 79.

10. Ibid., 81–82.

11. Léon Walras, *Éléments d'économie politique pure ou théorie de la richesse social* (Paris: Pichon, 1874).

12. Odo Marquard, *In Defense of the Accidental: Philosophical Studies*, trans. Robert M. Wallace (Oxford: Oxford University Press, 1991).

13. François Quesnay, *Tableau économique*, eds. Marguerita Kuczynski and Ronald L. Meek (London: Macmillan, 1972), 12.

14. Above all, Gerhard Richter, *Der Gebrauch des Wortes Oikonomia im Neuen Testament* (Berlin: Walter de Gruyter, 2005).

15. There are exceptions. See Kurt Singer, "Oikonomia: An Inquiry into the Beginnings of Economic Thought and Language," *Kyklos* 11, no. 1 (February 1958): 29–57. On Adam Smith specifically, see Richard Kleer, "The Role of Teleology in Adam Smith's *Wealth of Nations*," *History of Economics Review* 31 (Winter 2000): 14–29; Lisa Hill, "The Hidden Theology of Adam Smith," *European Journal of the History of Economic Thought* 8, no. 1 (2001): 1–29; R. Klay and J. Lunn, "The Relationship of God's Providence to Market Economics and Economic Theory," *Journal of Markets and Morality* 6, no. 2 (2003): 541–564; François Dermange, *Le Dieu du marché: Éthique, économie et théologie dans l'oeuvre d'Adam Smith* (Paris: Broché, 2003); Christian Marouby, *Economie de la nature: Essai sur Adam Smith et l'anthropologie de la croissance* (Paris: Seuil, 2004).

16. Hans Blumenberg, *The Legitimacy of the Modern Age* (2nd ed.), trans. Robert M. Wallace (Cambridge, MA: MIT Press, 1983).

17. Louis Althusser and Étienne Balibar, *Reading Capital*, trans. Ben Brewster (London: Verso, 1969), 17.

18. Jacques Derrida, *Of Grammatology*, trans. Gayatri Chakravorty Spivak (Baltimore: Johns Hopkins University Press, 1976).

19. Jacob Viner, "Possessive Individualism as Original Sin," *Canadian Journal of Economics and Political Science* 29, no. 4 (November 1963): 548–559.

20. Blumenberg, *Legitimacy*, 55.

21. Ibid.

22. Ibid.

23. Ibid., 37.

24. Ibid., 39.

25. Ibid., 70. Augustine, *De doctrina Christiana* II, 39–40, 60.

26. Spencer J. Pack, "Adam Smith's Economic Vision and the Invisible Hand," *History of Economic Ideas* 4, no. 1–2 (1996): 253–265.

27. Giorgio Agamben, *Il regno e la Gloria* (Roma: Neri Pozza, 2007), 287–304.

28. Nicolas Malebranche, *Treatise on Nature and Grace*, trans. Patrick Riley (Oxford: Clarendon Press, 1992).

29. François Fénelon, *Réfutation du système du Père Malebranche, Oeuvres de Fénelon* (vol. II) (Paris: Lefevre, 1835).

30. Jacques-Bénigne Bossuet, *Discours sur l'histoire universelle* (Paris: Institut National de la Langue Française, [1681] 2006), 268.

31. Ibid.

32. Ibid., 209–210.

33. Ibid., 268.

34. Ibid., 269.

35. In his Course on "Problems in the History of Philosophy" in the year 1955–56, Althusser devoted a session to Bossuet as among the most interesting and influential theoreticians of history in the seventeenth century. He credited him with the introduction into the philosophy of history of two new concepts: (a) the ruse of reason and Le Verstellung (perversion of action), and (b) being the human consequence of (a).

36. G. W. Leibniz, *Theodicy*, trans. E. M. Huggard (La Salle, IL: Open Court, [1710] 1985), 395.

37. G. W. Leibniz, *A Refutation Recently Discovered of Spinoza by Leibniz*, trans. Octavius Freire Owen (Edinburgh: Thomas Constable and Co., 1855), 150.

38. G. W Leibniz, "A Vindication of God's Justice Reconciled with His Perfections and All His Actions," in *Monadology and Other Philosophical Essays*, trans. Paul Schrecker and Anne Martin Schrecker (Indianapolis: Bobbs-Merrill, 1965), 122.

39. Ibid., 120.

40. Bernard Mandeville, "The Grumbling Hive: Or, Knaves Turned Honest," in *The Fable of the Bees* (2 vols.), ed. F. B. Kaye (Indianapolis: Liberty Fund, 1988), I: 4.

41. Ibid., 24.

42. Ibid.

43. G. W. F. Hegel, *Lectures on the History of Philosophy* (3 vols.), trans. E. S. Haldane (London: Kegan Paul, 1892), II: 249.

44. Ibid.

380 NOTES TO CHAPTER 4

45. Ibid., III: 348.

46. Michel Foucault, *The History of Sexuality: An Introduction,* trans. Robert Hurley (New York: Pantheon, 1978).

47. Ibid., 138 (translation modified).

48. Achille Mbembe, "Necropolitics," *Public Culture* 15, no. 1 (Winter 2003): 11–40.

49. See James R. Otteson, *Adam Smith's Marketplace of Life* (Cambridge, UK: Cambridge University Press, 2002).

50. On the prevalence of thieves and pickpockets over murderers and the importance of property in the application of the death penalty in Smith's time, see Peter Linebaugh, *The London Hanged: Crime and Civil Society in the Eighteenth Century* (Cambridge, UK: Cambridge University Press, 1992).

51. See, especially, Marouby, *Economie de la nature,* 232–234.

52. Ian Ross, "The Physiocrats and Adam Smith," *Journal for Eighteenth-Century Studies* 7, no. 2 (September 1984): 177–189; István Hont and Michael Ignatieff, "Needs and Justice in the *Wealth of Nations*: An Introductory Essay," in *Wealth and Virtue: The Shaping of Political Economy in the Scottish Enlightenment,* eds. István Hont and Michael Ignatieff (Cambridge, UK: Cambridge University Press, 1983), 1–44; David McNally, *Political Economy and the Rise of Capitalism: A Reinterpretation* (Berkeley: University of California Press, 1990). For a general discussion of French debates about the grain market, see Steven L. Kaplan, *Bread, Politics and Political Economy in the Reign of Louis XV* (2nd ed.) (London: Anthem, 2012).

53. Claude-Jacques Herbert, *Essai sur la police générale des grains* (Paris: A. Berlin, 1755), x. All translations from the French from this point on are our own.

54. Ibid.

55. Ibid., 176.

56. Ibid., 30–31.

57. Ibid., 63–76.

58. Louis Paul Abeille, *Principes sur la liberté du commerce des grains* (Amsterdam: 1768), 1. Emphasis in original.

59. Ibid., 3.

60. Ibid., 5. Emphasis in original.

61. Ibid., 12.

62. Ibid.

63. Ibid., 13.

64. Ibid., 16.

65. Ibid., 108.

66. Ibid., 113.

67. Michel Foucault, *"Security, Territory, Population": Lectures at the Collège de France, 1977–1978,* trans. Graham Burchell (London: Palgrave Macmillan, 2007), 42.

68. See Kaplan, *Bread,* 590–614; McNally, *Political Economy,* 130–132; Gilbert Faccarello, "Galiani, Necker, and Turgot: A Debate on Economic Reform and Policy in 18th Century France," in *Studies in the History of French Political Economy, from Bodin to Walras,* ed. Gilbert Faccarello (London: Routledge, 1998), 120–185.

69. Turgot, "Lettre à Abbé Morellet," 17 janvier 1770.

70. Joachim Henry le Mercier de la Rivière, *L'intérêt general de l'État et la liberté de la commerce des blés* (Amsterdam: Desaint, 1770), 10.

71. Ibid., 11.

72. Ibid., 25.

73. Ibid., 17.

74. Ibid., 29.

75. Pierre Joseph André Roubaud, *Récréations économiques* (Paris: Lacombe, 1770).

76. Ibid.

77. Ibid., 396.

78. Ibid., 397.

79. Ibid., 70.

80. Ibid., 89.

81. Ibid., 371

82. Ibid., 398–399.

83. Ibid., 39.

84. Roberto Esposito, *Communitas: The Origin and Destiny of Community*, trans. Timothy Campbell (Stanford: Stanford University Press, 2010), 6.

85. Walter J. Shelton, "The Role of Local Authorities in the Provincial Hunger Riots of 1766," *Albion: A Quarterly Journal Concerned with British Studies* 5, no. 1 (Spring 1973): 50–66.

86. Thompson, "Moral Economy."

87. Anne-Robert-Jacques Turgot, "Lettre aux Officiers de Police des villes de sa Généralité où il y a des Marchés de Grains," 15 février 1765, *Oeuvres de Turgot* (Paris: Guillamin, 1844), I: 660–672.

88. Ibid., 670.

89. Ibid.

90. E. P. Thompson, *Customs in Common* (New York: New Press, 1993), 278–279.

91. As a number of commentators have correctly argued for the last twenty years, Smith is neither Milton Friedman nor Hayek; he clearly believed that government had an important role to play in commercial societies and did not suffer from the state phobia of twentieth-century neoliberals: See, for example, Emma Rothschild, *Economic Sentiments: Adam Smith, Condorcet, and the Enlightenment* (Cambridge, MA: Harvard University Press, 2002); Spencer J. Pack, "Murray Rothbard's Adam Smith," *Quarterly Journal of Austrian Economics* 1, no. 1 (1998): 73–79; Spencer J. Pack, *Aristotle, Adam Smith, and Karl Marx: On Some Fundamental Issues in 21st Century Political Economy* (Cheltenham, UK: Edward Elgar, 2010), 88–108. Thompson's point here is that Smith's position on the grain market in particular, however, was unambiguous: There was no cause of "famine" than government "attempting . . . to remedy the inconveniencies of a dearth." And unlike, say, the market in pins, the grain market was intimately and directly connected to the question of life and subsistence.

92. Kenneth Pomeranz, "Political Economy and Ecology on the Eve of Industrialization: Europe, China, and the Global Conjuncture," *American Historical Review* 107, no. 2 (April 2002): 425–446.

93. Jean-Baptiste Du Halde, *Description géographique, historique, chronologique, politique et physique de l'empire de la Chine et de la Tartarie chinoise* (Paris: 1735).

94. Cormac Ó Gráda, *The Great Irish Famine* (Cambridge, UK: Cambridge University Press, 1989), 12–13.

95. Ibid.

96. Cited in William Lecky, *A History of Ireland in Eighteenth Century* (2 vols.) (London: Longmans, 1913), I: 187.

97. Ibid.

98. John Eastburn Boswell, "*Expositio* and *Oblatio*: The Abandonment of Children and the Ancient and Medieval Family," in *Medieval Families: Perspectives on Marriage, Household, and Children*, ed. Carol Neel (Toronto: University of Toronto Press, 2004), 234–272.

99. Lucretius, *De rerum natura*, II: 251–259.

100. For a discussion of the French famines, see Cormac Ó Gráda, "Markets and Famine in Pre-Industrial Europe," *Journal of Interdisciplinary History* 36, no. 2 (Autumn 2005): 143–146.

101. Amartya Sen, *Poverty and Famine: An Essay on Entitlement and Deprivation* (Oxford: Oxford University Press, 1981).

102. Thompson, "Moral Economy," 89.

103. Turgot letter to Hume, March 25, 1767, in Anne-Robert-Jacques Turgot, *Reflections on the Formation and Distribution of Riches by Turgot*, trans. W. J. Ashley (New York: Macmillan, 1898), 109–110.

104. Williams, "Were 'Hunger' Rioters Really Hungry?"

105. Turgot letter to Hume, March 25, 1767, in *Reflections*, 109.

106. Charles Smith, *Three Tracts on the Corn-Trade and Corn-Laws* (2nd ed.) (London: J. Brotherton, 1766).

107. Frederic Morton Eden, *The State of the Poor; or an History of the Labouring Classes in England from the Conquest to the Present Period* (3 vols.) (London: J. Davis, 1797), III: 709–711.

108. Anton Menger, *The Right to the Whole Produce of Labour*, trans. M. E. Tanner (London: Macmillan, 1899), 4.

109. In the preface to the second German edition of *Socialism*, dated January 1932, von Mises wrote:

We stand on the brink of a precipice which threatens to engulf our civilization. Whether civilized humanity will perish forever or whether catastrophe will be averted at the eleventh hour and the only possible way of salvation retraced—by which we mean the rebuilding of a society based on the unreserved recognition of private property in the means of production—is a question which concerns the generation destined to act in the coming decades.

Ludwig von Mises, *Socialism: An Economic and Sociological Analysis* (2nd ed.) (Indianapolis: Liberty Fund, [1932] 1981).

110. See Henry Calvert Simons's 1934 response to calls for state intervention to address the economic crisis, *A Positive Program for Laissez Faire: Some Proposals for a Lib-*

eral Economic Policy (Chicago: University of Chicago Press, 1949), 41. In this he lacked the Austrians' faith in the boundless self-correcting capacities of the market.

111. Foucault, *Naissance de la biopolitique*, 191–220.

112. A decade after Austrian social democracy was crushed by pro-Nazi governmental and paramilitary forces, Hayek felt the need to denounce its capacity for mass mobilization as incipient totalitarianism; see Hayek, *The Road to Serfdom* (Chicago: University of Chicago Press, 1944), 125–126.

113. Von Mises, *Socialism*, 63–64.

114. Ludwig von Mises, *Human Action: A Treatise on Economics* (Indianapolis: Liberty Fund, [1949] 1996).

115. Friedrich A. Hayek, *The Constitution of Liberty* (Chicago: University of Chicago Press, 1960).

116. Hayek, *Road to Serfdom*, 219.

117. Eugen Bohm-Bawerk, *Karl Marx and the Close of His System* (New York: A. M. Kelly, [1896] 1966).

118. Carl Menger, *Principles of Economics* (New York: Free Press, [1871] 1950).

119. A. Menger, *Whole Produce*, 4.

120. Ibid., 11.

121. Ibid., 39.

122. Ibid., 9–10.

123. Ibid., 10.

124. Ibid., 15.

125. V. I. Lenin, "Theses and Report on Bourgeois Democracy and the Dictatorship of the Proletariat," *Theses, Resolutions and Manifestos of the First Four Congresses of the Third International*, trans. Alix Holt and Barbara Holland (London: Ink Links, 1980), 7–20.

126. Nothing shows the triumph of necro-economics like the recent comments by Christine Lagarde, managing director of the International Monetary Fund, who responded to a question concerning Greek children's diminishing access to basic medicines by arguing that things could be much worse: They ought to look at the children of Niger, for example. She neglected to mention that the IMF had forbidden the government of Niger to distribute free food during the famine of 2005 and had encouraged them to sell off their emergency food stores to pay their nation's debt. Nick Dearden, "Greece Can Do Without the 'Sympathy' the IMF has Shown Niger," *The Guardian*, May 29, 2012, http://www.theguardian.com/commentisfree/2012/may/29/greece-sympathy-imf-niger (accessed April 16, 2014).

127. Jacob Grimm and Wilhelm Grimm, *Deutches Wörterbuch* (32 vols.) (Leipzig: Verlag von S. Hirzel, 1854–1961), 26: 407.

128. Hayek, *Road to Serfdom*, 199–200.

129. In response to a question about democracy in Latin America in an interview in a Chilean newspaper, Hayek remarked, "Personally I prefer a liberal dictator to a democratic government lacking liberalism," *El Mercurio*, Santiago de Chile, April 12, 1981.

130. See the commentary of William E. Scheuerman, *Carl Schmitt: The End of Law* (New York: Rowman & Littlefield, 1999), 209–224.

INDEX

Physiocrats, 268–69, 279, 290, 299–301, 306, 311
Pinochet, Augusto, 339
Pitt, William, the Younger, 48
Pittock, Murray, 156–58, 160, 161, 165, 179, 181–82, 211–12, 227
Pity, 110, 113–14, 117, 136
Plank, Geoffrey, 17, 19
Plato, 58
Pleasure: aesthetic, 30–32; of converting ignorance to knowledge, 28; in deriving unity from particularity, 60; diverse sources of, 235–36; in mental classification, 58; in systemic order, 128–29
Plebian agency, 176
Pocock, J. G. A., 36, 217, 228–29
Poetry, 206
Poker Club, 16, 50, 79, 219–20
Political oeconomy, 258
Politics, parallels of criticism with, 94–95
Poor Laws, 306, 309
Poovey, Mary, 63
Pope, Alexander, 12, 35, 130, 194, 254
Popular contention, 7–9, 11, 13, 148–234; over Act of Union, 19–20; diverse character of, 150–55, 160–61; historiography and, 148; Jacobitism and, 25, 148–64; literature and, 39; meaning of, 23; novels and, 148, 195, 206; problem of, 25; Smith and, 21. See also Multitude, the
Popular Party, 213
Porteous Riots (1736), 159, 200
Positivism, 336
Poverty, 25; attitudes of those in, 120; attitudes toward, 56, 118–21; beneficial aspects of, 128; Hanoverian succession and, 173; relative character of, 127–28, 291, 326, 334, 383n126; and the right to subsistence, 264–88; scholarly silence on subject of, 10; state role and responsibilities concerning, 4, 266–88, 292–93, 303–4, 310–42
Presbyterians, 102–3, 157
Press, freedom of, 166
Price controls, 270–73
Printed material, 71–104; and the constitution of literature as a discipline,

33–34; dangers of, 193; Hume on, 166–67; increase in, in early modern period, 37, 73–74, 80–81, 85–88; legal case affecting, 85–89; proliferation of, 166
Probability, 191, 196–201, 203–4, 216
Prodigality, 235–36
Progress, historical, 149, 184–85, 192–93, 373n109. See also Stadial history
Property: corporeality and, 87–89; God and, 228; neoliberal prioritization of, 329, 333, 337; one's person as, 273–74, 291–92; right to, 280–82; state's securing of, 225; violence stemming from equality of, 221–22
Providence, 3; chance and, 254–55; Christianity and, 249–51; early modern controversies over, 251–60; failures of, 295–96; Hegel on, 260–61; invisible hand likened to, 259–60; neoliberalism and, 314; in Smith's thought, 237–38; in social-economic relations, 241–45, 259. See also Theodicy
Public sphere, 50, 152, 157, 161, 168–69, 172–73, 208
Pufendorf, Samuel, 184
Punishment and torture, 111, 123
Puritanism, 166–67, 175, 183, 231

Quesnay, François, 244, 250–51

Rabbling, 175, 176
Ramsay, Allan, 16
Rapin, René, 33
Rational choice theory, 122
Raven, James, 201
Reading, 10, 74
Realism, 197
Reality: aspects of, 64; equality and, 46; perspectival character of, 42–43; unknowability of, 50, 56–57, 62, 64, 82
Reciprocity, 47
Regenting, 362n119
Reid, Thomas, 19, 35, 98, 356n37
Religion, and economic thought, 242–58. See also Theodicy
Renan, Ernest, 168
Resentment, 117